THE HUMANIST TEMPER

— THE HUMANIST TEMPER —

The Life and Work
of
Elton Mayo

Richard C.S. Trahair

With a Foreword by

Abraham Zaleznik

Transaction Books
New Brunswick (U.S.A.) and London (U.K.)

306
M 473t

Library of Congress Catalog Number: 83-24116
ISBN: 0-88738-006-9 (cloth)
Printed in the United States of America

Library of Congress Cataloging in Publication Data
Trahair, R. C. S.
    The humanist temper.

    Bibliography: p.
    Includes index.
    1. Mayo, Elton, 1880-1949. 2. Industrial sociologists—United States—
Bibliography.   3. Industrial sociology—United States.   I. Title.
HD6957.U6T73 1984   306′.36′0924 [B]   83-24116
ISBN 0-88738-006-9

Contents

Foreword: The Promise of Elton Mayo

Abraham Zaleznik

George Elton Mayo pioneered in the field of industrial human relations and for that work deserves a place in business history. I seriously doubt, however, that Mayo would have secured this position were it not for the labor and dedication of his countryman and biographer Richard C.S. Trahair.

Understanding Elton Mayo, the man and his ideas, requires more than a reading of his few books or studying the results of the Western Electric researches. Almost everyone takes for granted today that the success of an enterprise requires careful attention to human factors. No one believes that Frederick Taylor and scientific management provide the key to industrial management. Almost everyone accepts the idea that management is more than applied economics and that decision making is much more than the mathematics of probability or applied game theory. All schools of business and public administration appoint social scientists to their faculties, and courses in organizational behavior are routinely accepted in the curricula. Yet in Mayo's time, management was hardly viewed as a profession, and the idea of considering human relations in factories and offices was astonishing. From the perspective of the 1890s, what Mayo urged in broad outline has become part of the orthodoxy of modern management. Despite this diffuse acceptance of Elton Mayo's ideas, few students know who he is, and even the most mature managers probably spend little time reflecting on his work.

In writing the biography of Elton Mayo, Richard Trahair sought to discover the facts about this man and his work and to report them faithfully and accurately. It was never his intention to make a hero of Mayo, nor to apologize for his foibles and limitations. The foibles and limitations were in abundance, and to his great credit, the author does not spare his subject by glossing over facts that lead to questions about the nature of this bold figure in industrial history, the content of his psychology of the workplace, and the manner of the cure he sought to impose on the sickness of an acquisitive society. Richard Trahair had to face and report the fact that Mayo was not averse to overpresenting his formal qualifications or that he eagerly sought acceptance from medical practitioners and psychiatrists. It was remarkable how easily he gained the confidence of respected physicians who invited him into their clinics and referred patients to him for psychiatric treatment. Among respected management specialists such as Colonel Urwick, Mayo was known as "doctor," and referred to as a psychiatrist specializing in the treatment of mental disorders. Mayo did attend medical school in Australia and England, but he dropped out of the course of study for reasons that are not clear but that suggest the anxieties of a young man who felt overwhelmed when faced with making commitments or accepting conventional roles. Despite the fact that he left medical school, he appeared drawn to the practice of psychiatry such as it was in his time, and indeed, the record seems clear that Mayo had an extraordinary capacity to touch people who were in distress and for whom a healer was a godsend.

I did not know Elton Mayo personally. When I accepted my first appointment as a research assistant at the Harvard Business School in February 1947, Elton Mayo was preparing to retire the following June. I first became aware of this strange figure of a man when the head teller of the Cambridge Trust Company, a local bank, pointed him out to me and said in a voice mixed with awe and amusement: "There goes Elton Mayo." Years later, a colleague described how Mayo, with uncanny acuity, recognized his distress over the illness of his infant child. Mayo asked the kinds of questions and made the kinds of comments that were reassuring if only on the level of showing human concern for another's commonplace anxieties. Many people thought that he had magical powers as an interviewer. Putting the question of magic aside, Mayo's rules of interviewing still deserve attention from researchers who think they can advance knowledge by studying people in the places where they live and work or, as we often say at the Harvard Business School, "in the field." To listen and not to talk does not come naturally to most of us; we can obtain huge dividends by reflecting on Mayo's simple advice for conducting studies in the field.

From the perspective of psychoanalytic knowledge, Mayo's talents were not so uncanny as they appeared to his students or to the industrial managers who accepted his guidance in the conduct of research into the conditions of productivity and morale in the factory. Nevertheless it took extraordinary talents and nerve to venture into factories with a method based on a theory derived from psychiatry. Imagine what it must have been like in the 1920s and 1930s to conduct research in factories into the human aspects of productivity and morale. From the textile mills in Philadelphia to the Hawthorne Works in Cicero, Illinois, this slim, gangly figure, with his long cigarette holder, held court on the problems of reveries and their interference with a worker's ability to concentrate and perform his tasks.

Mayo's cure for these unsettling reveries was to establish contact with the worker and give him a feeling of no longer being alone. Mayo believed that the isolation of the workplace produced the symptoms of distress such as boredom, fatigue, and the sense of hoplessness that often accompany isolation—what the sociologist Emile Durkheim called "anomie." Mayo believed there was a variety of ways to interfere with the morbid process that he ascribed to reverie—ranging from taking a worker's blood pressure and getting him to talk about what was on his mind, to establishing rhythms of work and rest, with the periods of rest including an opportunity for workers to talk to each other. In advance of Carl Rogers, Mayo practiced nondirective interviewing, primarily designed to establish human contact among otherwise isolated individuals.

As I have indicated, Mayo's practice was not magical or uncanny. He utilized the power of transference to affect the people he saw. Lest the accusation be made that he used transference only with members of the working class, who could easily be seduced into a dependency relationship, the following pages clearly show that managers were also susceptible to the powers of transference, and placed extraordinary trust in this odd figure who spoke like an Englishman and carried a handkerchief in his sleeve.

After reading Elton Mayo's work—a lean legacy considering the many years he spent in universities—I doubt that Mayo understood that he was using transference to reform industrial practice and human relations. Mayo, professing to a strong aversion to Freud, confessed in a letter that he was no longer a Freudian. Indeed, he may never have been one. Because of his limited understanding of transference, Mayo may have been caught up in it emotionally as much as the subjects who sat quietly as he took their blood pressure and only gradually began to give voice to their inner thoughts and feelings.

The systematic study of transference, whether in the clinic or the factory, creates an awareness of the varying kinds of emotions that bind people to one another. It also produces a healthy antidote to the tendency to manipulate people by gaining some access to, and even control over, their emotions. However, Mayo was anything but a cautious man. Either the power of the tools he was using was outside of his awareness, or he believed that greater dangers came from the psychological isolation of the factory than from the fallouts of the kind of seduction he practiced.

There was still another side to Mayo's simplistic view of psychopathology and the remedies he proposed and practiced in its amelioration. Mayo's strategy was to seek complex fact and apply simple theory. This strategy may explain his attraction to the neurologist Pierre Janet who, as intellectual history demonstrates, was a minor figure in the pantheon of the psychopathologists of the nineteenth and twentieth centuries. Janet proposed that the symptoms of hysteria resulted from the hypnogogic states that certain individuals were predisposed to as a result of unspecified organic factors. Mayo took Janet's theories of the hypnogogic state and the effects of suggestibility and applied them to the industrial scene. He believed that instead of organic factors predisposing the individual to hypnogogic reverie it could occur as an effect of the social isolation of the workplace and the repetitive quality of the work itself. Strangely enough, Mayo seldom specified, or for that matter investigated systematically, the content of a reverie to seek its meaning and identify what was noxious in its substance. Instead, Mayo looked for its social causation—in particular the absence of interpersonal ties under conditions of repetitive work activity. Mayo's prescriptions for these human problems of an industrial civilization followed from his theory, but the key point in his strategy was to keep the theory simple. What we shall have to consider later in this essay is the consequences of this strategy on investigators who followed him and on the practitioners who tried to apply his remedies. As we shall see, one of the dilemmas of applying a transference cure to any illness, is that the healing effects usually last only so long as the transference figure is around to keep the seduction alive and the promise a continuing source of hope. Mayo, like many transference figures before and after him, did not have the power to maintain the effects of his personality on the people who came under his influence.

Mayo's formula of simple theory and complex fact enabled him to communicate a message that provided the industrialist with fresh ideas with which to confront the popular program of scientific management that then dominated the theory and practice of industrial management. In providing these fresh ideas, Mayo found powerful allies in the Rockefeller Foundation and in the dean of the Harvard Business School, Wallace Brett Donham, the physiologist Lawrence J. Henderson, and the philosopher Alfred North Whitehead. Mayo's other allies included his friend Bronislaw Malinowski, the gifted anthropologist, and child psychologist Jean Piaget, whom Mayo knew mainly from his writing. These latter figures provided Mayo with support from the social sciences for his methodology of field work and for his strategy of simple theory and complex fact.

Wallace Brett Donham was the second dean of the Harvard Business School. A lawyer and banker, Donham's legal education and experience in practical affairs underpinned his strong support of the faculty of the Business School in their use of the case method of instruction. Mayo's experiences in the clinic and his advocacy of field studies matched Donham's enthusiasm for the case method. But Donham's agenda went well beyond fostering a teaching approach which already had the enthusiastic support of his faculty. At the time, business administration lacked depth largely because it was tied to theories of economics and to arts of practice that were narrowly drawn and intellectually uninteresting. Business education was scorned by the intellectual community, and this tended to put the Business School faculty on the defensive or—what may have been worse—

to adopt the aggressive posture of the antiintellectual. Much of what appeared to be cultishness to others was a reflection of the difficult atmosphere in which faculty at the Harvard Business School worked through the 1950s. I had to learn, for example, how to be adroit in dealing with Cambridge cocktail party conversation in which silly ladies with high voices reflected the community's disdain for what we were doing "across the river" by shrieking: "Oh, you're at the busy school! What in the world do you do over there?" In the face of such derision, many of us turned inward and developed a great cohesion, but at the cost of intellectual isolation.

Donham had his own way of dealing with this disdain while simultaneously fostering business education and the growth of the people leading this development. With an astute sense of how to kill more than two birds with one stone, Donham attracted his own followers, and they were men of high intellectual standing at Harvard and in the wider academic world. For example, Donham bought the Herbert Somerton Foxwell collection of early economic literature. With the financial support of Claude W. Kress, the merchant, he organized the Kress rare book collection at Harvard Business School's Baker library and, indeed, built Baker Library itself—the greatest institution of its kind. Both are anomalies at a school committed to the case method of instruction. Building the library was part of Donham's plan to gain academic standing for business education at Harvard. By bringing Elton Mayo to the faculty of the Harvard Business School from the University of Pennsylvania, Donham at once drew the support of the Rockefeller Foundation, attracted Professor Lawrence J. Henderson to the school, and gained the sympathetic wisdom of the great philosopher Alfred North Whitehead, thus helping to build an intellectual foundation for business education. By hiring Mayo, Donham gave substance to his conviction that nothing was of greater importance to business education and the job of business leaders than to understand human relations.

Scholars will argue for many moons over the quality of Donham's vision and, in particular, Mayo's contribution to building the substance of the human relations approach. But while carrying on the debate, we should remember the context and the times before we conclude that Mayo was both too simplistic and too sparse in his approach.

Mayo's theory of reverie and work was in place before he came to the Harvard Business School. He did not originate the Western Electric Researches, but guided a program underway and offered crucial suggestions and interpretations. The work he published while he was at Harvard contained observations and theories, but its aim was mainly to persuade practitioners in, and teachers of, business administration to change their ideas about work and management. Mayo proposed little research after the Western Electric studies. He encouraged the publication of the results of these investigations but did not choose to participate as author. Instead he left the writing to Fritz J. Roethlisberger and William Dickson. His influence always seemed to be indirect, and it involved few initiatives on his part.

The studies in the Harvard Fatigue Laboratory, in which Mayo collaborated with L.J. Henderson, produced almost no empirical findings and conclusions. Mayo's interest in this work was probably half-hearted. He espoused the importance of pedestrian research and detailed observation, but he could not resist the "big picture"—a bombshell which would excite people but not necessarily foster critical observation and judgment. Typical of such statements was the following: *"If our social skills had advanced step by step with our technical skills, there would not have been another European War."*[1] This statement typifies Mayo's seductive style. It obviously cannot withstand careful scrutiny or a critical reading of history. It is an astonishing oversimplification, but what a grandiosely seductive statement! It excited managers and gave them, perhaps for the first time, a vision for their everyday practice. If one of the jobs in building a profession is to help construct an ego ideal for its members, Mayo's style moved Donham's enterprise a long way forward.

Mayo himself taught only sparingly, a matter that did not endear him to his colleagues at the Harvard Business School who were excellent and dedicated teachers. He gave only occasional lectures, and as a result had limited impact on the generation of students at the school during his tenure there. It is interesting to reflect on why teaching did not appeal to Mayo considering its potential for such a powerful personality. I believe Mayo experienced enormous empathy only for those people who needed to be patients, the troubled souls in search of a healer. The students of the Harvard Business School, then and now, were not looking for therapy. In a curious way, Mayo could use his empathy in a one-to-one situation and also in communicating with an impersonal audience such as that addressed by an author. His language was seductive and was aimed at affecting the emotions of his readers. But he wrote so infrequently as to suggest that an unseen audience did not command nearly as much of his energies as the single individual in distress. All the people close to Mayo were, in one form or another, his patients. He could help them in their personal and professional lives without asking them to declare themselves either as patients or people in need of help. While healing them, Mayo gave them work and a method. Invariably, the method consisted of having them conduct interviews in clinics or factories through which they too could break loose from their reveries, attend to someone other than themselves, and through a reflective process, gain insight into them. This training program was so devoid of structure as to confuse Mayo's colleagues, but many people benefited from his therapeutic work and were grateful to him. They showed, however, varying states of confusion about their seductive healer.

Fritz Jules Roethlisberger was, by far, Mayo's most famous student.

Roethlisberger, along with William Dickson of the Western Electric Company, wrote the story of the Hawthorne studies in the book that was to become a classic in the literature of management and the social sciences. The book made Roethlisberger famous and established a debt to Elton Mayo that was difficult for him to repay. Largely on the strength of *Management and the Worker,* Roethlisberger became a full professor at the Harvard Business School. More than that, he found his healer in Elton Mayo. In his memoir entitled *The Elusive Phenomena,* Roethlisberger tells his story of Mayo and the work he himself accomplished after Mayo's retirement. Roethlisberger effectively completed Mayo's program by introducing human relations into the curriculum of the Harvard Business School. This work substantially ended Mayo's isolation from the school, although he was not around to enjoy the fact. Roethlisberger also preserved Mayo as a legend, a fact that reflected Roethlisberger's struggle with his transference toward Mayo.

I was a student of Fritz Roethlisberger soon after the end of World War II. In retrospect, it seems that Roethlisberger perpetuated the legend of Elton Mayo in order to support his own style. The residual guilt Roethlisberger felt in trying to be like his mentor while repaying the debt he owed him, made Roethlisberger's world even more confusing. Roethlisberger was misled by his perception of Mayo as a researcher, and in his own seductiveness he was more like Mayo than he could admit. Like others in academic life who become associated with a famous work, Roethlisberger could not escape from the shadow of the Western Electric studies and the so-called Hawthorne effect, and become free to plan and carry out an independent research program. Teaching became his forte and in this he made a lasting contribution to moving Mayo's ideas into the classroom. Roethlisberger could not settle for that formidable accomplishment. Instead he tried to live up to his own image of Elton Mayo as a researcher. The reader can decide for himself the stuff of which this legend was made, but I know that Roethlisberger's need for this legend only added to the confusion he felt.

The content of the legend of Elton Mayo, as celebrated by Fritz Roethlisberger and others, is of some interest. The outstanding legend came out of period twelve in the Relay Assembly Test Room study. The formal findings appear in *Management and the Worker* and in countless dissertations in universities all over the world, but the legend is something else.

The main idea in back of the Relay Assembly Test Room experiments at the Hawthorne Works of the Western Electric Company was to observe the effects on worker productivity of variations in the conditions of work. As the conditions were changed (e.g. introducing rest periods or shortening hours), productivity increased. This seemed a logical consequence of the changes, and, very intelligently, the investigators restored the original conditions of work as a control on their observations. From the logic of the experiments, the investigators expected output to go down. Instead it increased, just as it had with the introduction of each variation in working conditions. This gave rise to the interpretation called the "Hawthorne effect"—that people will respond positively, despite the logic of the situation, if they feel good and have a strong attachment to the authority figures involved. The Hawthorne effect is transference. It is also the phenomenon that in medicine is called the "placebo effect." A patient complaining of symptoms may not have anything physically wrong with him, but as a means of reassuring him, the doctor will prescribe a placebo (some harmless substance) which in fact makes the patient feel better. Medical practitioners have long been aware of the placebo effect, but they also view it with extreme caution. Many a diagnosis will be overlooked if the physician concludes too quickly that a patient's complaints are grounded in his psyche or result from psychological stress.

The placebo is also used in clinical trials in medicine. Experimenters administer a neutral substance to a control group to measure the effects of a new medication which has been given to the experimental group. To make certain that the effects of the doctor-patient relationship (or transference) cannot contaminate the results, clinical trials are "double blind"—neither patient nor doctor knows whether the substance administered is medicine or a placebo. The psychology underlying the placebo effect, as with the Hawthorne effect, is the transfer of emotions previously attached to a parent or authority figure. The parental figure to whom these unconscious feelings are attached has considerable influence over the person who experiences the transference. If it is a doctor, the ministering of a neutral substance will ameliorate symptoms as though some genuine medication were at work. Transference of the positive kind can be likened to falling in love. As in any love relationship, elements of power exist and can be used for good or evil.

The legend of the Hawthorne effect is that Mayo had a blinding flash of creative insight and designed period twelve of the experimental study to demonstrate its validity. This legend led to an idealization of the creative moment at the Harvard Business School and set back research at that institution at least one generation. As young researchers, we felt defeated if the creative flash or the eclaircissement did not occur. It usually did not. Alas, the reality of research is that at best we are toilers in the vineyard. We must toil daily or nothing will come of the work. If one is blessed by some creative inspiration, more power to him. But this is not the stuff of which science is made. Rather than let go of the myth and face reality, we had our little tricks of denial, one of which we called "writing the last chapter."

In the interest of being insightful, creative, and above all, relevant, we would attempt a grand last chapter to say what the research meant for managers. Somehow we believed that to appeal to managers, we had to be eloquent, moving, and capable of drawing the big picture. If this entailed a leap of fancy, an extrapolation light years beyond our data, so be it. Everyone understood this was the last chapter with no holds barred. There were some very strange last chapters written at the Harvard Business School. Fritz Roethlisberger tried to be an expert at the last chapter and this nearly killed him. He took his longing for the grand last chapter into the classroom where the seduction worked for a while, but it caught up with him there too, and he finally ran out of space. The idea of the last chapter was the legacy of Elton Mayo and the legend of his creativity. I hope that Richard Trahair's biography of Elton Mayo will destroy the legend once and for all. If it does, we will all be better off for the work that lies ahead and in return will afford to Elton Mayo the honor that is his due.

I tried my hand at the last chapter in my youth at the Harvard Business School. But I was luckier than most in having the chance to work with the gifted sociologist George C. Homans. He had a great deal to do with my achieving some clarity about the nature of investigation in industry and the problems of observation, evidence, and inference. This awakening occurred for me when we conducted the research that resulted in publication of *The Motivation, Productivity, and Satisfaction of Workers: A Prediction Study,* which I coauthored with C. Roland Christensen, Fritz J. Roethlisberger, and George C. Homans. Not long after publication of this book in 1958, I began formal training in psychoanalysis. George Homans published *Social Behavior: Its Elementary Forms* as a follow-up to the widely acclaimed *The Human Group.* In *Social Behavior* Homans showed how a theory of explanation differs from a conceptual scheme. The theory he used to construct an explanatory structure is a direct derivative of behavioral psychology and the work of B.F. Skinner. While I turned my energies to a vastly different psychology in becoming a student of Sigmund Freud's psychoanalysis, I still admired Homans's masterful use of theory. One of the uses I made of George Homans's work was to put to bed the legend of the last chapter and Elton Mayo's creativity. As Homans often liked to say, "science is done by the damndest methods," but one of them, I am sure, is not in the longing for the last chapter. To be intelligent ought to be good enough. To be grandiose is the road to disaster.

Fortunately, George Homans has written his intellectual memoir, which Transaction Books is publishing simultaneously with the Mayo biography. Together, these two volumes provide important accounts of the development of industrial studies. Professor Homans represents sociology and the social psychology of the primary group. As he indicates in his intellectual autobiography, Homans studied under Elton Mayo as well as Lawrence J. Henderson while he was a member of the Society of Fellows at Harvard University. It was during these formative years that Homans developed the conviction, which he maintained as a sociologist, that field studies are essential to the understanding of groups, organizations, and the nature of work in an industrialized society. Whereas Roethlisberger extended Mayo's ideas by teaching managers and fledgling academics, Homans concentrated on the uses of field observation to construct explanatory theory. Professor Homans continued the work he had begun as a student of Mayo and Henderson in the Department of Social Relations at Harvard and later in its Department of Sociology where he also served as chairman. The American Sociological Association recognized Professor Homans's important contributions by electing him president of the association.

Perhaps because of his interest in the science of the group and the organization, Homans remained aloof from the effects of transference and was able to maintain a perspective on Mayo that was not available to Roethlisberger and others who continued their work at the Harvard Business School. Homans admired Mayo and learned much from him, but he was never persuaded by the potential for healing that was at the core of Mayo's interests. Above all, Homans hated the last chapter.

Observing Roethlisberger and Homans over the course of "The Prediction Study" during the mid-1950s, I had the sense that each served as alter ego for the other and probably reflected two sides of Elton Mayo's personality. Roethlisberger was the healer and Homans the scientist. One was tender-minded and the other tough-minded, one the twice-born and the other the once-born personality. But there were more than two sides to Mayo. He was also an entrepreneur, a side alien to both Roethlisberger and Homans.

Mayo promoted the study of human relations in industry and, like many entrepreneurs, he had a bit of the juvenile deliquent in him. He never conformed to the expectations of the Harvard Business School. Nearly all the faculty adopted the work habits of business and scorned the leisurely pace of the academy. It was nine to five with a half day on Saturday and plenty of overtime besides. Summer holidays, while ostensibly belonging to the individual, were seldom taken except for a brief few weeks, and only rarely a solid month. Everyone, with the exception of Mayo, showed up at the office early in the morning. Mayo arrived at midmorning, worked a few hours conducting interviews with his assistants, in which he mixed therapy and work (for him the two were the same). He would then repair to St. Clair's restaurant in Harvard Square where he would take lunch and sherry late in the afternoon. Whether Mayo enjoyed this routine as much as he did flouting the culture of the Harvard Business School is an open question.

Apart from a few students and L.J. Henderson, Mayo had only distant relations with his colleagues on the faculty. He did maintain a close relationship with Dean Donham, who protected Mayo during his years on the faculty. There are some indications that Mayo tried Donham's patience, much as delinquent adolescents cause concern to their parents and other authority figures. Mayo would not write except at his own pace, and he certainly taught sparingly. What he did with his time was a matter of conjecture. Perhaps the simple answer is that Mayo was fundamentally a lazy man who managed to dodge the pressures of the Protestant work ethic.

Mayo wrote about the "conviction of sin" and its effects on people. He was also interested in obsessive thinking. The conviction of sin and obsessive thinking were part of Mayo's theory of reverie, following the psychology of Pierre Janet. I suspect that Mayo learned about the conviction of sin and obsessive thinking from his own inner experience. For some, the solution to the ravages of guilt is to plunge into activity, to work hard and hope for some salvation as a result. At a minimum, working hard allays the anxiety that surrounds the conviction of sin. The so-called Sunday neurosis attests to the important part activity plays in avoiding guilt. But Mayo clearly did not take advantage of the opportunity that hard work provides to escape an unpleasant inner world. Perhaps this avoidance of activity as a defense provides a clue to the mind and personality of Elton Mayo.

Whatever the contents of his fantasies, Mayo appeared to be drawn to them. This likelihood becomes greater when one recognizes that Mayo had few close relationships. He spent much time apart from his wife and daughters and would not allow his students to get too close to him. He enjoyed creating an aura of ambiguity about him, including unsolved mysteries about his experiences in childhood and youth. In whatever way he sought identity, Mayo avoided the comfort one can enjoy from belonging to a profession, gaining accreditation, and benefiting from the esteem others accord in accomplishing fine work within a field. While his desire for privacy—bordering on secrecy—makes it difficult to know the man, some general observations, perhaps speculations, can be made.

For most obsessive personalities, the contents of their ruminations disguise the lines along which their conflict flows. Above all, they use their elaboration of thinking to repress feelings. In the most extreme forms, obsessives keep themselves so preoccupied with their thoughts that they can be rendered helpless when it comes time to act. But despite the fact that thinking hides feeling, the contents of obsessive ideas are not without meaning, acting very much like a dream with its uses of symbols to yield and disguise meaning. An illness for most, obsessive thinking may also provide a pathway for original work on the part of talented people. While psychology has provided limited understanding of talent, it may be true that once a talented obsessive overcomes the terror connected with his inner thoughts, he may begin to use them in the service of his work. But the definition of that work will not necessarily follow conventional pathways.

I strongly suspect that Elton Mayo became thoroughly acquainted with his reveries, tried to accept them, and then began to use them in constructing a new role (healer in the industrial world) he practiced at the Harvard Business School and in his researches in the factory. Mayo tried to make this role an intrinsic part of supervisory practices, and it was this idea that caught Roethlisberger's interest and led him to train people in nondirective counseling. The idea of listening with the empathy of the healer began to infiltrate the courses at the Harvard Business School, particularly in the human relations offerings. The idea soon became applicable to the group dynamics of the classroom and fueled the imagination of many faculty members and students from the end of World War II to the beginning of the 1960s when it began to collapse of its own weight.

In this connection, scholars will be interested in comparing Elton Mayo with Kurt Lewin. Each pioneered in social reform, but utilizing different theories and approaches to their respective work. Kurt Lewin was a German psychologist who emigrated to the United States to escape the Nazis. He originated the group dynamics movement, which also found its way into industrial studies and practice. The one idea that unifies Mayo and Lewin is the principle of removing noxious elements from the workplace to afford people an escape from the tyranny of stress that arises in the face of mounting rage and the sense of helplessness people experience when they begin to lose control. The key idea that caught Mayo's attention, along with most other participants in the human relations movement of the postwar era, was to change the practices of authority figures to incorporate the efficacy of healing that is sometimes possible in a relationship.

But the remedies of the human relations practitioners encountered another model that aimed at dealing with the same problems, but in vastly different ways. The American labor movement viewed Mayo's work in a hostile light. The object of the labor movement was to secure countervailing power so that management and the worker could meet as equals over the bargaining table and thereby assert the independence and sense of control necessary for the economic and psychological well-being of working people. The intellectual leaders of the labor movement saw in the work of the human relations practitioners a means of blocking workers' political motives with the consequence (whether intended or not) of increasing the dependency of workers on management. The American solution of countervailing power, and the resolution of conflict through political activity, may explain why the human relations movement as a practical application of a psychological theory of work failed to take hold. But the present dilemmas of America's competitive situation suggest that a further evolution has to occur if our industrial society is to be healthy. The laws of economics and the marketplace are impersonal, often cruel, but nevertheless real. If the only form of discourse between management and labor is in the confrontations of power, we might have to endure a period of economic decline such as we have not experienced since the Great Depression.

Mayo lacked economic sophistication and an understanding of institutions and the problems of power. Others at the Harvard Business School were not afflicted with the same blind spots which are common to healers. The former dean of the Harvard Business School, George Pierce Baker, expressed the vision this way: the profession of management needs a new synthesis of economic, political, and psychological ideas to fuel an ego ideal of the executive capable of acting with competence, courage, and humanitarian impulses.

The Harvard Business School is celebrating its seventy-fifth anniversary, and the appearance of Richard Trahair's biography of Elton Mayo is in commemoration of this event. The current dean, John H. McArthur, and the director of the Division of Research, Professor E. Raymond Corey, made it possible for this book to be published in order to encourage reflection and debate about the nature of man, his role in institutions, and the challenges facing business education in the years ahead. The community of the Harvard Business School owes Richard Trahair a great debt for writing the biography of George Elton Mayo.

Note

1. George Elton Mayo, *The Social Problems of an Industrial Civilization* (Boston: Harvard University, Graduate School of Business Administration, Division of Research, 1945), p. 23.

Preface

This biography answers many questions scholars in the social sciences have been asking about Elton Mayo. He is known for having established the scientific study of what today is called "organizational behavior" when he gave close attention to the human, social, and political problems of industrial civilization while he was professor of industrial research at the Harvard Business School from 1926 to 1947. But little is known about Mayo's background, and puzzling questions emerge from scrutiny of brief biographical sketches and obituaries.

How did an unknown philosopher from Queensland, Australia, become a major contributor to the study of human relations in American industry? Why did he put so much emphasis on medical science? Was he a medical practitioner, and, if so, how did he become the most notable academic associated with the famous Hawthorne studies of the Western Electric Company? What qualifications did he have to make him accepted at the Harvard Business School? Why did he concentrate on the study of fatigue and cooperation at work? Was he working for management? If so, why was he so interested in the welfare of workers? How did he become interested in such topics as shell-shocked soldiers, Jung, labor agitators, industrial morale, the League of Nations, Pierre Janet, economic depression, anomie, psychoanalysis, child rearing, sex, and sin? The catalogue of questions is endless. This biography grew from such questions as these, and was written so as to answer them in an orderly way by tracing the personal and intellectual origins of Mayo's remarkable influence in industrial sociology and social psychology.

Mayo attracts the attention of a biographer for other reasons. He is the only Australian to have made a contribution to the social and behavioral sciences before the end of the Second World War. His work has been praised and condemned for almost fifty years. Many references to his work in popular textbooks on industrial sociology and organizations are in error and inconsistent, and use Mayo's ideas to illustrate almost every argument, viewpoint, or principle that can be advanced about people at work. To some people Mayo's ideas on the impact of rapid industrialization of work are in support of Western capitalism and should therefore be condemned; others say Mayo's ideas are those of a dangerous psychiatrist; and still others maintain he has made the best recommendations ever for the de-

15

mocratization of industry and the improvement of the quality of working life. Over the past ten years the work of Mayo and his associates has been the subject of vigorous debate at every conceivable level of discussion by scholars in the United States, Britain, Europe, and Australia. This biography sets down Mayo's ideas and traces their origins in his personal life so that the dust may settle around the debate and allow the man and his work to be seen clearly.

The first chapter establishes Mayo's medical background and how tragedy in the family contributed to his ambivalent orientation to medical science; the conflict between his parents in their approach to the role of peers in a child's social development; the agreement between his parents on the role of ambition and high purpose in a career; the experience of economic depression, its social ills, and the bankruptcy of modern ideologies that offer political solutions to human and social problems. The second chapter relates Mayo's adolescence directly to his adult thinking. When young he learned the value of participation in decision making, optimism in the face of adversity, harmony in conflicted social relations, and the proper place of work in a well-balanced life. But he turned away from conventional attitudes to professions, especially medicine and religion, and, in a state of youthful melancholy, looked for adventure in Europe. There he learned something of the inhumanity that flowed from the rapid industrialization of work, the degradation that work imposed on most who had to do it to live, and the difference between real adventures and those in the mind.

Chapter 3 answers questions about Mayo's business experience in South Australia, how he became an able and respected philosopher, and what values that he acquired from his family were congruent with his development as a mature university student, e. g., science applied to human problems; order, unity, and variety in nature; the lack of administrative skills among politicians; and politicians' overemphasis on material development at the expense of understanding social ills. Where did he go to become an academic? And how did his interest turn from academic philosophy to medical psychology? What part did his emotional life play in the change? How did the change contribute to his outstanding skill as a public speaker and lecturer?

At the University of Queensland Mayo rediscovered his adolescent melancholy, treated it with overwork, and searched for some principles of relaxation that would help him master fatigue. A rebellious spirit re-emerged and he began to attack many conventions imposed on him by those whom he did not respect. He turned his attention from the way men deliberately used their minds to the impulsive forces of mental life that were being discussed as "the new psychology": Jung, Freud, and Janet. He fell in love, married, and raised two daughters. He became a settled and respected academic.

In the reorganization of his university after the Great War, Mayo was promoted to professor and, with assistance from one of his students, turned away from abstract theories of mind to the treatment of the minds affected by war neurosis, hysteria, and obsessional disorder. A chance meeting with the anthropologist Malinowski started a long friendship and extended Mayo's intellectual horizons into primitive thinking.

Chapter 6 answers the question: How did Mayo use psychological ideas to understand political issues? From consultations with the Queensland government, observations on an election campaign, panic in a crowd, and rowdiness at union meetings, Mayo set down a theory of political psychology that recommended for the success of modern democracy—the central issue for him raised by the Great War—that state controls must be curbed in times of peace and that cooperative relations among society's main groups must replace competition. His first book, *Democracy and Freedom,* was written to promote worker education programs, and to outline the core of his beliefs in the human social and political issues that had been caused by the too rapid industrialization of work.

Mayo was a social activist who sought to make his society more civilized and humane. Chapter 7 describes how he diagnosed its maladies, his clinical insight, and the way he taught university students, businessmen, professionals, and workers the unfortunate consequences of the way work had been organized and the way children had been reared.

In middle age Mayo faced crises in his personal life and career, and tried to leave Queensland for those parts of Australia where his ideas would be more widely accepted and his work would attract more respect. Chapters 8 and 9 tell why he left Australia and was offered the fortunate opportunity to pursue research on his ideas while on sabbatical leave. With strong financial support from the Rockefeller Foundation and Philadelphia's businessmen, deep sympathy for his psychological and sociological explanations of industrial conflict in the United States, and great respect from psychiatrists for his clinical skills, Mayo made a niche for his work, resigned his Queensland position, and quickly established himself as a leading psychologist. With a remarkable capacity to integrate ideas from diverse disciplines, he persuaded associates to fund more of the research he thought would be valuable. Chapter 10 describes his techniques of investigation, his early research, his relations with Pierre Janet, the popularization of his research in industry, and the important social connections he made among industrialists, psychologists, and social scientists.

How did he attract the interest of Harvard University, and what work did he do at the Harvard Business School to justify the enormous grant he and Lawrence J. Henderson received from the Rockefeller Foundation? Chapter 12's answers show how Mayo's early failures to interest New England industrialists led him to consider undertaking sociological work in Colorado and administrative problems in the movie industry.

Mayo's most noted contribution to industrial sociology and psychology began when the Western Electric Company asked him to make physiological studies of a few employees. Chapters 14, 15, and 16 detail what Mayo did in Chicago and New York to clarify, promote, protect, and extend the research being done at the Hawthorne Works; the role of the business community in making such research public; and the publicity and sadistic criticism to which the studies at Hawthorne were exposed.

Mayo published *The Human Problems of an Industrial Civilization* when his career was at its peak. At that time his wife and daughters went to live in England, and he remained at Harvard. He himself did no research for ten years but instead concentrated on helping his associates on problems of collaboration and the value of clinical observations for understanding political solutions to the economic depression.

The deaths of two colleagues and the demands of the Second World War took away much of Mayo's personal influence and initiated the final stages of his work in the United States. He undertook two large research studies and used them to illustrate theses he had been refining for twenty-five years. Before retiring he published *The Social Problems of an Industrial Civilization,* a book that was favorably received.

Mayo wanted to carry forward in England his work on educating administrators to a scientific understanding of industrial problems and the humane, democratic treatment of subordinates. Sudden illness prevented this, and the task was taken over by his elder daughter who for ten years had followed his ideas and practices. The final chapter evaluates Mayo's character by reconstructing the image he left with the people who remembered him, and by drawing on the main personal themes in his early development.

The biography is a simple narrative—work, family, ideas, and sentiments—and is interrupted only by short summaries of Mayo's published and unpublished writings and speeches. This is done to show that his experiences and feelings at the time were closely tied to ideas he was developing. Much of Mayo's thought is not readily available because he preferred talking to publishing; what did appear in print is repetitive and fails to include accounts of research he did for private reasons.

The narrative assumes that important shaping experiences occur early in life, and for this reason gives as full an account of Mayo's young years as the evidence allows. The reader will see that Mayo continuously interpreted his own conflicted life and character with considerable insight. He wanted to live an energetic adventure but without heavy effort; to uphold scientific, humane, and democratic values yet enjoy the recognition that he needed; to influence men of affairs without suffering the obsessional melancholy that follows their rejection of one's ideas. He believed he was the product of an orderly society that put great store on civilized and respectable living yet spent a lifetime in actively combating its vulgarities. And in his work he had his family's support, affection, disappointments, and problems, albeit on an irregular basis.

Acknowledgments

Basic research for the biography was done with the Mayo papers in the Baker Library, Harvard Business School, in 1975 and 1981-82. Laurence J. Kipp and Mary V. Chatfield allowed me unrestricted access to the papers, and Robert Lovett, Florence Bartoshesky, and Marjorie Kierstead gave sound advice on their use. At the Rockefeller Archives Center, J. William Hess and staff showed me papers on Mayo's research. Michael Ryan helped me see correspondence on Mayo's work in the Special Collection at the University of Chicago's Joseph Regenstein Library. Also I acknowledge help from P. Allen, at the British Library, and considerable guidance from David Muspratt, Working Men's College, London.

In South Australia I had access to the Mayo papers at the State Library, Adelaide, and with the help of J. H. Love was permitted to see private papers of people whom Mayo knew well. I am grateful to the registrars and their staff at the Universities of Adelaide, Melbourne, and Queensland for helping me to find documents related to Mayo's academic activities in Australia. The staff of the La Trobe University Library helped collect copies of Mayo's published work.

In January 1974 I was shown a collection of private correspondence between Elton Mayo and his wife and daughters, which Patricia and Ruth Elton Mayo allowed me to use to add to my knowledge of their father's life. I acknowledge a great debt to them. These letters are on microfilm in the Baker Library and their use remains restricted. Also I acknowledge the help of Oliver Mayo, who kindly allowed me to see the private diaries of the late Herbert Mayo, Elton's younger brother. These books are also restricted.

Research for this biography began in January 1974 in Luxembourg, where Patricia Elton Mayo showed me her father's letters, and at the Harvard Business School, where the late Fritz J. Roethlisberger and George F.F. Lombard gave me valuable information and advice on how to undertake the study.

In 1975 and 1981-82 I had considerable help from George Lombard; he found information on Mayo, directed me to people who had been closely associated with him, and was always willing to answer fully any of my questions. He has read what I have written, and his criticism of my conclusions about Mayo were friendly and his corrections were extremely helpful. Without this close and cooperative working relationship the biography would not have been as accurate and comprehensive as it is. I am in great debt to him for making possible this research. And in Australia Julie Marshall assisted me splendidly by searching for information on Mayo as well as by offering sharp, cogent criticism of the work as it was being written.

The study was funded by the Ford Foundation in 1975, and for several years before and after by La Trobe University in Melbourne. I am grateful for the generosity of both institutions. The Australian Research Grants Commission gave funds to finish the study in 1981. The Division of Research at the Harvard Business School and the Baker Library provided office space needed for the work and access to the privileges of the Harvard University community.

As well as with persons named above, I was fortunate to have conversations with the following people who knew Mayo well, or could give vivid accounts of the time they spent with him. *Australia:* Lady Hilda Axon, E.M. Jones, Mrs. S. A. Kyle, Katherine E. McGregor, Dr. and Mrs. T.H.R. Matthewson, A.E. Pearse, F.W. Paterson, Eric Partridge, Lyndall Urwick. *United States:* Arlie V. Bock, Joseph C. Bailey, Eliot D. Chapple, Hilda Carter-Fletcher, Don A. Chipman, John H. Findley, W. R. Hockenberry, George Homans, A. G. Holmes, Frances R. and W. K. Jordan, Harold D. Lasswell, Osgood S. Lovekin, Edmund P. Learned, Henry A. Murray, Ruth Norton, David Riesman, E.C. Tessman, Andrew Towl, Mildred Warner. *England:* Lord Monsell.

The following people provided me with information and advice that was helpful in finding evidence on Mayo and the conditions under which he lived. *Australia and New Zealand:* David Anderson, Leo Behm, Alfred W. Clark, H. Alan Cubbon, W.G.K. Duncan, Frank Davidson, G. J. Hart, J.W. Hayward, Margaret B. Horan, A. H. Jackson, D.A. Kearney, D.C. McDonald, D.W. McIlwain, George M. Mayo, Lady Gwen Mayo, Mrs. Eric Mayo, J. S. Miller, Sir Mark L. Mitchell, Ray B. Malloy, Charles McConnel, Elizabeth Morrison, Margaret O'Keefe, Andrew D. Osborne, Joan Paton, Hollis W. Peter, C. Robertson, S.A. Raynor, S. Routh, G. S. Reid, C. Streton, L.G. Stubbings, Elizabeth R. Simpson, H.E.W. Smith, John A. Salmond, Joanna Thomson, G.E. Thompson, Claudio Veliz, L.P. Weber, Betty Wigg, J.L. Weir. *Britain:* Y.D. Barrett, Dustan Curtis, Fiona M. Picken, Neil Robertson, John H. Smith, Marion White, Dorothy Wardle. *Canada and the United States:* Bruce J. Biddle, Chauncey Belknap, Byron Barnes, Mariam Chamberlain, Francis J. Dallett, Henri F. Ellenberger, William Gormbley, Max Hall, Pearson Hunt, Everett C. Hughes, J. William Hess, Hilda Holton, George E. Johnson, Solon T. Kimball, Fred Keefe, Jack Kaufmann, J. Lorsch, Paul J. Lawrence, Charles M. McArthur, Richard Rosenbloom, Michael T. Ryan, Fred A. Stint, Jeff Sonnenfeld,

Helen Q. Schroyer, Renato Tagiuri, Richard E. Walton, Harriet E. White-head, Abraham Zaleznik.

Colleagues who have seen sections of the manuscript and made valuable comments include Julie Marshall and Alfred Clark. I am grateful to Max Hall for editorial criticism and help, especially in the early stages of writing the biography.

Typing and deciphering a frequently illegible script was undertaken cheerfully by Norma Cann and Julie Stayner, in the School of Social Science, La Trobe University, Australia. The final draft was typed by Robyn Ripper in Australia and Vy Crowe in Boston.

I am grateful to my family and close friends who provided the support that I am sure biographers need and look forward to but may never fully understand or set down for readers to examine.

Abbreviations and Sources

The following symbols refer to sources.

1. In the Manuscript Division, Baker Library, Graduate School of Business Administration, Harvard University:

AA929.41	Industrial and Physiological Research Memoranda.
AFFD1	Administration. Faculty (Former) Deceased, Mayo, Elton, file 1.
AFFD2	Administration. Faculty (Former) Deceased, Mayo, Elton, file 2.
ARIP	Administration. Research: Industrial and Physiological, 1927-1940.
BLA	Baker Library Archives.
FJR	Roethlisberger Papers.
Mf 1-186	Microfiche of Western Electric Company records.
MM	Mayo Manuscript, drawer and file number.

2. Harvard University Press.

HUP	Two files, Elton Mayo—Some Notes on the Psychology of Pierre Janet.

3. Rockefeller Archive Center, New York.

RF	Folders in: 1. United States, Boxes 342,343, Series 200 2. L.R.S.M., Series 3, Boxes 35, 75, 76.

4. State Library of South Australia, Adelaide, South Australia.

SAA	Mayo family archives.

5. Mayo letters in the possession of Patricia Elton Mayo (Mrs. Dunstan Curtis).

   Mayo's elder daughter, Patricia Elton Mayo, was called "Patricia," "Toni," "Patty," and "Poppet." Her sister was known as "Ruth" and "Gael Elton Mayo." To avoid confusion, in the text the elder daughter is called "Patricia"; the younger, "Ruth." In the notes the elder daughter is "Toni" and the younger is "Gael" because that is the name they used.

6. Interviews.

A diary was kept of conversations with people who knew Mayo. They are indicated by "conversation with" followed by the person's name and the date.

7. Letters.

Many of Mayo's students and young associates wrote to the author. The letters are indicated by, for example, "Hargraves to Trahair" and the date.

8. Sir Herbert Mayo's Notebooks.

These books are in the possession of Dr. Oliver Mayo, Adelaide. Each item in the books is numbered.

1

Mayo Family in Adelaide, 1880-1893

The moon was full on a summer night in the mid-1890s when the head of one of South Australia's respected families led his two elder sons into the spacious back garden of their family home. He carried a double-barreled, muzzle-loading fowling piece. The boys were shown how to put gun to shoulder and fire. Each lad took careful aim and fired one shot. But, like their father who had been taken through the same ritual years before, the boys missed their target. It was the moon.[1]

The younger son did not forget this ritual of paternal protection and high hope. He pleased his family by studying well at school and university, becoming a prominent lawyer and judge, and being knighted. But Sir Herbert Mayo upon retirement quickly sold all his law books and devoted the rest of his life to the only activity that had deeply interested him, astronomy.[2]

The elder son disappointed his family. They had hoped he would become a doctor, like his grandfather, but after desultory studies he took to psychology, was made a professor, went to the United States, and became a prominent social scientist.

George Elton Mayo was born on December 26, 1880, in Adelaide, the capital city of the colony of South Australia. He died on September 1, 1949, at Guilford in Surrey, England. Elton was reared in Adelaide, attended St. Peter's College and the University of Adelaide, and at thirty-eight became the first professor of philosophy at the University of Queensland. In July 1922 he sailed across the Pacific to San Francisco on his way to spend sabbatical leave in England. He had arranged to lecture at the University of California, take a train to the East Coast, and sail to England. The arrangements fell through, and he spent the rest of his academic life in the United States helping to establish the study of human and social problems of people at work. He never returned home.

Elton was born into a respected family in a society that was based on families and that put great store in respectability.[3] The family lived in a home beside Nibley House, which had been built for Elton's grandfather, Dr. George Mayo. As surgeon aboard the *Asia* in 1839, Dr. Mayo had come from England to the new colony of South Australia. He married Maria Gandy, once the housekeeper of Colonel William Light, who had planned the city of Adelaide. Maria bore three girls and one boy, George Gibbes Mayo, born in 1845. She died of tuberculosis in 1847. In 1851 Dr. Mayo visited American relatives and went to the Great Exhibition in London. While in England he was elected a Fellow of the Royal College of Surgeons, attended his father's deathbed, and, before returning home, married again. His second wife suffered a decline in mental health and lived in seclusion. For thirty years, "Old Doctor Mayo" as he came to be called, was the leading surgeon in the colony, prominent in the administration of its medical institutions, a lieutenant colonel in the Adelaide Regiment, and an active support to Trinity Church.

Doctor Mayo was primarily a surgeon but maintained the warmth, sympathy, and conscientiousness of the family doctor. He was keen on exercise, enjoyed walking and bicycling, and was one of the last doctors in Adelaide to ride on horseback to see his patients. With age he became gruff and blunt, a little eccentric, and developed a retiring manner, a dislike for notoriety, and a rooted objection to being photographed. Upon his death in 1894 the family inherited money, property, and a prominent position in Adelaide society.

George Gibbes Mayo, Elton's father, did not achieve the same prominence as Doctor Mayo. After Maria died, George and his sisters were reared by servants and friends until 1853, when Dr. Mayo returned from England. George Gibbes Mayo's childhood was not happy but his adolescence included an amusing potpourri of lost opportunities, curious rewards and boyish adventures, and his stories about them would entertain his own children. At his first school George had been so underfed that he stole food. He was caught, and was enrolled in St. Peter's College. He ran away, the police tracked him down, and the college authorities made him a prefect. After his schooling he chose to work on a sheep station rather than study at Oxford University; later he went prospecting for coal in a region of West Australia that afterward was one of the country's richest gold fields. He spent his twenty-first birthday in 1866 as a member of an expedition to find suitable grazing land in northern Australia. The expedition failed in its purpose but introduced George to sharks, alligators, floods, and starvation. The following year George studied engineering under the physicist Lord Kelvin at the University of Glasgow. He spent a year as an apprentice to a shipbuilder on the Clyde, later toured the Continent, and in 1873 returned to Adelaide to live with his father and work as an engineer on the expanding railways. From 1889 until retirement in 1914 he was a real estate agent.[4]

In September 1877 George Gibbes Mayo married Henrietta May Donaldson, daughter of a schoolmaster. They lived in a house on Adelaide's West Terrace. Hetty, as she became known, bore seven children: Helen in 1878, Elton in 1880, Olive in 1883, Herbert in 1885, William Godfrey in 1887 (he lived only three weeks), Mary Penelope in 1889, and John Christian in 1891.

Elton lived with his family until 1900. During his youth the colony of South Australia underwent economic, political, and social changes that affected him and from which he drew many illustrations for use in his later work.

The colony depended on rural industry—wool, wheat, copper—but, during Elton's childhood, the rural population was drifting to Adelaide. By 1900, 45 percent of the colony's population lived there. People moved to the city because it offered employment, prospects for advancement, shorter working hours, a brighter life, a haven for widows, and the welfare and medical services needed by the aged. Also, because education beyond primary level was not available in the country, boys were sent to Adelaide for their secondary education. When the statistics on the migration became known, the press, public officials, and touring speakers tried to reverse the movement by persuading people in the country to make their style of life more attractive, and to improve farming methods by adopting scientific techniques.[5] Hetty traveled often to speak to members and friends of the Mother's Union.[6] So in his youth, Elton was exposed to the problems of urbanization as well as the arguments in support of using science to help solve them.

During Elton's early life the colony underwent an economic depression with only slight and temporary recoveries. Rents rose, wages dropped, the labor market swelled with immigrants from the neighboring colony of Victoria, and sweated labor was common. The respectability of colonial life was threatened by the growth of billiards saloons, betting clubs, "two-up" schools, and the appearance of pimps and brothels. Responses to the depression, destitution, and social evils varied, and were often misguided. For example, unions tried to distribute the burden of poverty by demanding that all members work the same number of hours; this simply increased the distress of breadwinners with many dependents. Education, a valued pathway to a respected position in Adelaide society, which was prized strongly in the Mayo household, was found to be no guarantee of a job. Charity inspired relief movements; socialists and anarchists spread their propaganda; and unions tried to teach tolerance, Christianity, and fair-mindedness to all members. But there was not enough charity to go around. Teaching self-help through revolutionary ideology and worker education failed because most of the victims of poverty were uncomprehending and inarticulate people who believed that poverty was self-inflicted; that it originated with alcohol, indolence, and incapacity; and that individuals, alone, had the duty to raise their own living standards. A political solution was needed.

South Australia's politics became democratized as Elton was entering adolescence. In his boyhood, colonial gentlemen had constituted many short-lived governments, all headed by a member of the Adelaide Club—the Mayos' club. Before the depression these men had remained in power for many reasons: they had always upheld the progressive liberal policies of the colony's founders; they had overcome most of the problems involving the ownership of land; they had not been aloof, nor had they maintained a superior attitude to the less-respected colonists; they had been visibly active at the hub of the colony's political and economic affairs. Nevertheless the consequences of the depression were so great that in 1893 the last government to be formed by a member of the Adelaide Club was replaced by that of the radical Charles Kingston. For six years Adelaide was astonished by Kingston's demands for higher taxes, his attacks on the legal and medical professions, his demagogic blasts at the interests and privileges of former politicians, and his personal power in the cabinet. Elton saw himself as a colonial gentleman, and believed that self-understanding could be gained through broad education. He came to loathe the demagogues and crowd pleasers who, with subtle propaganda and ill-will, destroyed opportunities for every man to learn and come to terms with the real problems of the day. Political and economic changes in South Australia laid a solid foundation for Elton's approach to the political problems of industrial civilization.

Enlightened attitudes toward the distress of Adelaide's poor followed the changes in Adelaide's political life. At first the government gave food to the starving; later, land was made available for cultivation during periods of unemployment. In the liberal tradition, crime was fought by establishing a criminological society, and then by teaching that environment rather than inherent evil was the main cause of crime. Courts were established for children, prisons were modified, and institutions were introduced for prostitutes and inebriates.

Women's rights raised a political issue for Elton. In 1880 the University of Adelaide had accepted women; in 1894 Catherine Spence helped South Australia's women win the right to vote. But the Mayo family was not united on the issue. During Spence's campaign, in a letter to the daily paper, signed "Suffragette," Elton pointed to the few opportunities for women in a man's world. He listed the inequities, then asked, "If men are allowed to mix bathe, why not women?" When his father saw the letter he exploded: "Fancy giving the vote to such silly women. If this is how the majority of them think, then they should not be given the vote."[7]

Women were expected to marry; five children was the norm. But because more women than men lived in Adelaide, women were accepted in laundries, offices, and shops. Prevailing opinion turned women from attempting to join the professions. A few women fought that attitude and completed medical degrees. Elton's sister Helen was one; she became a successful specialist in child care.[8]

Social status in Adelaide was determined by success in both rural and urban industries. Merchants and professional men invested in grazing land, pastoralists took seats on the boards of banks and insurance companies, and wool brokers and shippers capitalized mining ventures. Social status and influence were reinforced by the interlocking of family and business. Two strata were at the top of Adelaide society: the first included pastoralists, then lawyers, and merchants; the second included land agents, brewers, flour millers, and doctors. Status was dictated by wealth—providing it was not acquired in shopkeeping—and, to a lesser extent, by education and profession. The gentlemen of Adelaide built substantial mansions in the city; they enjoyed such refinements as ventilation, bathrooms, potted ferns and flowers, fashionable bric-a-brac, and a piano. To avoid the city's hot summer, they drove their families to their country homes, or to cottages of friends, or guest houses by the sea. Although Elton's family had a substantial mansion in Adelaide, it did not have a country home; so, in terms of wealth, residence, and occupation, the Mayo family was of the second level in Adelaide society.

The cultural life of Adelaide developed during Elton's youth. Good taste and intellectual achievement, which the Mayos enjoyed, were everywhere congratulated and celebrated. People from the governor's associates down to bank clerks and schoolboys attended local and imported productions of Shakespeare, musicals, and opera. The literary associations of prominent local churches organized lectures, recitations, concerts, and intellectual discussions on social issues. A club life developed for deerstalking, yachting, polo, and archery. The Mayo family and friends patronized, administered, and subscribed to the public library, university, botanic gardens, zoo, geographical society, and charities. Lighter popular pursuits were tea and tennis parties and "conversaziones," Adelaide's precursors to cocktail parties. Elton drank tea, played tennis well, and enjoyed—and would lecture on—the art of conversation.

South Australians were proud and jealous of their public image. Adelaide was known as the "Queen City of the South," a garden city that boasted astounding refinements and encouraged its inhabitants to imagine they lived in the Philadelphia of Australia. But they still called England "home." Elton's career as an industrial social psychologist was to begin in Philadelphia; throughout his life he would idealize England; he retired and died there in 1949.

George Gibbes Mayo and Hetty Mayo raised a close and affectionate family but on some points they differed. Few professional families lived in the west end of Adelaide, so in the neighborhood were no playmates of appropriate background. The Mayo children felt isolated, and had to ask their mother to invite companions from other parts of town. Hetty was troubled by this, but George could see no disadvantages. His sister Helen believed that residential isolation had put severe limitations on the children's social development; Elton would emphasize the same point in his study of child psychology many years later.

The Mayo children were both seen and heard; to this extent their family life was far from the authoritarian image of the mid-Victorian period. George, who had been lonely as a boy, objected strongly to leaving the children with servants. Hetty did not want the children to hear everything parents said, and preferred that the little ones be shielded from the burdens of adult talk. She had a strong influence on Elton's emotional life. She did not comfort him as a close, warm, and touching mother but was a cool, distant, strong person to imitate. But she was an ambiguous figure, and therefore Elton would never know whether or not he had pleased her. She frowned upon his assertiveness, thought him "cock-sure" and overconfident, and did not congratulate him for his initiative. At the same time she held high aspirations for him; when he achieved a degree of success, she expected him to do better. This relationship prepared Elton for an adulthood dominated by swings of mood from excitable, aggressive thrusting to melancholic withdrawal, a conviction of sin, and obsessive reveries about his shortcomings. George was more capable than Hetty of sacrificing himself to the children, and for encouraging their initiative.[9]

George and Hetty were united on the value of education. George had had his adventures, then his training at Glasgow. Hetty was not an educated woman, but she was intelligent and particularly keen to educate, and be educated. Much to the children's amusement, George would tell how he had furthered Hetty's education during their courtship by teaching her the principle of the lever. He said she had responded readily. Hetty was ambitious for her children and believed that education was the way to self-improvement. Well-educated people could be identified by fluent and accurate speech, so Hetty encouraged her children to speak well and pronounce words properly and set them an example by lecturing in public. At the dinner table the children were encouraged to read aloud and give their opinions on intellectual matters. Elton's lecturing talent and skill in conversation can be partly attributed to his training at home.

Elton's education began in an unregulated and leisurely fashion. Early in 1889 a governess, Miss Kekwick, came to give the children lessons in a small schoolroom at the bottom of the garden, well away from the house. They learned to sing English, Scottish, and Irish songs at the piano. Helen, Elton, and Olive did some work, but, because the schoolroom was out of earshot of the house, the younger children often made noise and trouble for Miss Kekwick. Herbert—the future Sir Herbert—was mainly to blame, so when he was about six, the family decided that he should be banished to a school. When confronted with his grandson, Dr. Mayo next door would offer the family faint hope by saying, "Of all my grandchildren I see myself in Herbert," and then add, "I was a dreadful humbug, too." Each day George walked Herbert half a mile to a strict Lutheran school. Private tuition continued for the others until Helen began at the Grote Street Advanced School for Girls and Elton went to Queen's School. Herbert joined him for one year in 1894, before both attended St. Peter's College.

George, in his real estate business, had an office at home that gave onto Franklin Street, but most of the time he attended to the domestic tasks that Hetty did not care for. He seemed motherly, wise, gentle, and capable of bridging the gap between the different lives of youth and middle age. He encouraged the children's independent growth.[10] For example, to combat the alarming hazards of increased traffic in Adelaide, he taught them a poem with a play on words in its tail:

> *The rule of the road is a paradox quite*
> *Both in riding and driving along,*
> *If you keep to the left you are sure to be right,*
> *If you keep to the right you are wrong.*[11]

If the children were ill, Dr. Mayo attended them; if they felt poorly, George administered that foul-tasting, mid-Victorian cure-all castor oil. The tasteless variety was not available in those days, so the potion was mixed with warm milk or taken neat. Castor oil was used freely to open bowels, to relieve nausea, and even to lubricate engines, weatherproof boots, and treat the ills of cats, dogs, fowls, and ponies.[12] In Elton, castor oil helped banish melancholy moods: "As is usual with me (after castor oil) I woke up this morning in highest spirits."

In summer George took the children camping, or to stay at a holiday home, or a boarding house on the coast. On the camping trips the children were allowed to bring along their friends and share George's wisdom in organizing expeditions and identifying rocks, plants, and animals. If possible, they gathered mushrooms; and once Helen bagged a swan on the wing for the family's collection of native fauna.[13]

A September holiday in 1896 was the prelude to a tragedy. Olive, then thirteen, gentle and like a mother to the boys, was sent with Herbert to stay for ten days at a guest house by the sea. They came home when she complained of pain and tenderness in the center of her stomach, developed a slight fever, and began to vomit. Doctor Mayo had died in December 1894, so it was another doctor who diagnosed a bowel disorder. Olive was of course given castor oil. Subsequent treatment eased her pain but did not improve her health, for she had appendicitis and the castor oil had made it worse. Although surgery for appendicitis was available, it was not commonly performed. Olive died on November 19, and for years after on Sunday afternoons Hetty put flowers on her daughter's grave.[14]

Elton often told his children of how his father once was almost robbed. In his office George kept a large safe. One night burglars started to bore a hole in the safe, were disturbed, and dashed away. On discovering the intrusion, George deposited valuable papers with his bank, placed in the safe papers of no value to anyone but himself, and installed a crude obvious alarm. The burglars tried again to bore a hole in the safe, but again they were disturbed and took off. This amused the family because, had the burglars turned the handle, the unlocked safe would have opened. The burglars made a third unsuccessful attempt but this time left sufficient traces for a tracker to find them and the loot they had amassed. The gang called the Dyke brothers served a term in prison.[15]

Even though George Mayo was gentle, humble, unambitious, and devoted to his family, he did have enemies. His enemies used one of the most powerful weapons that mid-Victorian life could offer to degrade the head of a respectable family: gossip. During his lifetime George received poison-pen letters that alleged, directly or by imputation, that he was the illegitimate son of Colonel Light. Such libelous letters troubled him deeply, for he, his sisters, and Doctor Mayo had held Maria Mayo in the highest esteem and regarded her as a woman of great virtue.[16]

George had had no definite career, but he did shape the careers of his children. No doubt Hetty had her say, and so did the children. Helen decided to be a doctor, and her parents were delighted for her to try, although prevailing attitudes were opposed to women's entering medicine. It was considered to be mannish, and most brothers in those times did not relish a bluestocking for a sister; not so the Mayo boys. Helen went on to an outstanding career.

John followed Helen into medicine and, continuing his youthful interests in engineering and electricity, contributed to developments in radio-therapy and radiography. Penelope stayed at home and looked after Hetty until her death in November 1930. Penelope completed an honors course in philosophy, an M.A., and, using family documents, published *The Life and Letters of Colonel Light.* Herbert had always wanted to be an astronomer, and would have settled for engineering, but George advised him that there was no future in it.[17] So Herbert drifted into law, became an eminent judge, and was knighted.

Elton was pushed into medicine.

Notes

1. Sir Herbert Mayo's Notebooks 320, held by the Mayo family in Adelaide.
2. Conversation with Lady Mayo, Sir Herbert's widow, 25 May 1974.
3. Douglas Pike, *The Paradise of Dissent* (Melbourne: Melbourne University Press, 1957), ch. 20. The following account of life in South Australia is taken from John Hirst, *Adelaide and the Country: 1870-1917* (Melbourne: Melbourne University Press, 1973), and C. Chinner, "Earthly Paradise: A Social History of Adelaide in the Early 1890's," honors thesis in history, University of Adelaide, Adelaide, South Australia, 1960. Information about the Mayo family comes from the Mayo papers in the South Australian Archives, especially Helen Mayo's "Biographical Notes on Elton Mayo," and A. A. Lendon's essay "Old Doctor Mayo"; C. H. Mayo, *A Genealogical Account of the Mayo and Elton Families of Welts and Herefordshire and Some Other Adjoining Counties, Together with Numerous Biographical Sketches,* 2d ed. (London: Privately printed, Chiswick Press, Whiltingham, 1908); Sir Herbert Mayo's Notebooks.

4. George Gibbes Mayo did not qualify as a civil engineer, as his family thought. He received a Proficiency Certificate in Engineering Science. In her biographical notes on Elton, Helen Mayo wrote that her father's lecturers thought him an able student. *South Australian Directory, 1883-1915* (Adelaide: Sands & McDougall, n.d.).
5. Hirst, *Adelaide and the Country,* p. 5.
6. *Adelaide Advertiser,* 6 November 1930, p. 10; conversation with Dr. Margaret B. Horan, 11 July 1974.
7. Margaret B. Horan, "A Goodly Heritage: An Appreciation of the Life and Work of the Late Dr. Helen Mayo," *Medical Journal of Australia,* 20 February 1971, pp. 419-24.
8. Ibid.
9. Elton to Dorothea, 1 April 1916; 24 April 1919; Hetty to Herbert, 28 September 1914, SAA; Hetty to Elton, 17 April 1928, MM 1.007; Helen Mayo to Roethlisberger, 20 August 1960, FJR.
10. Conversation with Dr. Horan, 11 July 1974.
11. Sir Herbert Mayo's Notebooks 553.
12. Ibid., 912; Elton to Dorothea, 6 April 1920.
13. Horan, "A Goodly Heritage."
14. Sir Herbert Mayo's Notebooks 1315.
15. Ibid., 336, 1108.
16. Ibid., 199, 1318.
17. Conversation with Lady Mayo, 25 May 1974.

2

Early Failures, 1893-1904

In 1893, at the age of twelve, Elton was sent to Queen's School in North Adelaide to introduce discipline to his education. At home Elton had shown that he was intelligent and could master anything that interested him. He had devoured the novels of Scott and Dickens, and finished Gibbon's *Decline and Fall of the Roman Empire.* He had learned to recite poetry, grave and gay, to discuss history, and to describe birds, and, by his father, had been introduced to geology, botany, and physics. But Elton was impervious to what he did not like, as Hetty found when she had tried to teach him the multiplication tables.[1]

Queen's School was new and enjoyed no reputation except that its headmaster, Mr. Linden, had been the senior master at St. Peter's College, one of Adelaide's long-established private colleges for boys. However, during Elton's first year, his school earned a high assessment from the school's examiner, who reported that the boys wrote and spelled well, their arithmetic and German were excellent, algebra was progressing, and French would improve.[2]

Elton was on good terms with his teachers, but believed that his school work "had travelled very little as compared with other people."[3] This pessimism stayed with him through his schooldays; in an effort to enhance his self-esteem he studied hard. The results were excellent; he won prizes for Latin, French, chemistry, mathematics, and Greek, and at Speech Day, Chief Justice Sir Samuel Waye presiding, Elton was chosen to recite a humorous poem.[4]

From 1896 to 1898 Elton studied at St. Peter's College, a private school for Christian gentlemen, founded by Doctor Mayo and his contemporaries and attended by Elton's father.[5] Elton was unhappy at St. Peter's. After the first year his scholastic interests faded, and he gave up team games and athletic interests because he was not able to remain on good terms with the teachers who were in charge of classroom and sporting activities.[6] One schoolfellow recalls that Elton was an intellectual snob, obtuse, pedantic, and comic, whose only memorable contribution to school life was climbing the spiked gate at the school's entrance.[7] Such odd behavior at school earned Elton the nickname "Bill," after Billy Elton, a well-known traveling comedian.[8] Years later Elton wrote to his wife: "In school I used to have

35

rotten times, and I learned that if you wait things pass. In my teens I used to think it a blessed thing that one could sleep and forget."[9]

Elton was happier at home than at school. His parents maintained a democratic atmosphere, and, although they encouraged the children to do well at whatever they chose, heavy effort was thought by their father to be more comical than virtuous.[10] At school control was strict and authoritarian, and working hard—or the appearance thereof—was considered the best answer to charges of adolescent laziness and daydreaming. Because the school aimed to produce Christian gentlemen, religion was used to spread moral virtues and curb unholy activities among the boys.[11] Religion was put to such use at home only when Elton's Aunt Jane descended on the family and unwittingly entertained the children with her forceful caricature of Victorian morality.[12] At the slightest sound from Aunt Jane, Elton would amuse the family with his favorite cry, "Aunt Jane! Aunt Jane! My God! What a noise!" The Mayo children were taken to church more often for the spiritual experience and the opportunity to develop a sense of faith than to be impressed by eloquent convictions of sin.[13]

At home Elton's reading and intelligent conversation were encouraged, and his occasional moods of depression and withdrawal were attributed to his sensitiveness. At school depression and withdrawal were seen as symptoms of intellectual snobbery. Outdoor sports were encouraged at Adelaide's private schools, and most boys could get onto some team or other. Elton had pale and sensitive skin that burned quickly in the dry wind and hot sun, so he had to stay indoors or cover his skin completely, which partly explains why he did not appear in team games at school. Instead he took up independent sports like swimming, tennis, and golf, which allowed him to wear the clothes he liked and decide when he would play.

The Mayo children formed a circle of their own. Professional families did not live nearby so the neighborhood offered no suitable playmates. And school afforded Elton few friends. Together the children played charades, rode horses and bicycles, and camped out. Elton was called "Stilts," Penelope was "Puddles," and Herbert was "Tubb." Helen and Olive had no nicknames. Sometimes a friend was admitted to the circle and saw how rich and varied was family life with the Mayos. Elton's father tried hard to teach the children to live together in peace and amity, and to be willing to give and take in their relations with one another. "Our background was amazingly different from most of them," wrote Helen Mayo, "we were lucky—and that alone is enough to show how important an excellent home life is."[14]

Elton was not always well behaved. In some of his boyish pranks and tilts at authority he was joined by Herbert. For ten years they slept upstairs in the same bedroom with shuttered windows that overlooked their grandfather's backyard. The boys had been given a six-foot blowpipe from

Borneo. Green olives fitted it admirably, and the olives carried straight for sixty yards. Hidden by shutters, Elton and Herbert blasted away mercilessly at grandfather's chicken shed. The gardener would wake at the sound of the olives raining onto the iron roof, search about, scratch his head, and walk away, much to the boys' delight.[15] On a summer holiday during the Boer War, Elton and Herbert were encouraged one night to set fire to a thirty-ton stack of longwood on the beach. It was in readiness to celebrate the end of the war. People rode for miles to see the great blaze, and the boys were amused to hear them ask, "Has peace been declared?"[16] Elton also delighted in visiting a certain pier to annoy the old men fishing from it by outcasting them and catching more fish than they did.[17]

Elton's academic work was good but not outstanding. From the boys in Form VI at St. Peter's he was chosen for the College's Westminster scholarship in classical studies, but his performance was mediocre. In November 1897 he took the Senior Public Examination for entry to the University of Adelaide. Six boys from St. Peter's College performed with credit, and were awarded high passes. Elton passed at a low level in English, French, pure mathematics, and chemistry. In November 1898 he repeated the examination, but his performance was no better.

Elton was eligible to enter the university to study arts or law but not medicine because he had not taken Latin. This regulation was known to Elton and his family because his sister Helen had begun her studies in medicine. Elton had decided not to follow her. However, with a heavy push from his parents he changed his mind, and in March 1899 passed yet another examination in English, French, pure mathematics, and, this time, Latin.[18]

In July 1899, with seven other young men, Elton became a student of medicine at the University of Adelaide.[19] Facilities there were miserable. The library was small, cold, and damp. Students sat on a hard bench in a dark lecture theater. They had to take down every word uttered in formal lectures because textbooks were scarce, and few abstracts and journals were available. Many of the students envied their peers whose parents had had enough money to send them "home" to England where they could study at Oxford or Cambridge.[20]

The medical course lasted five years, and students were expected to attend at least three-fourths of the lectures given during the two sessions, from March to August and from September to December. Examinations were held in the second session. In the first year lectures were in anatomy, biology, physiology, chemistry, botany, and physics; there was practical work in the first three subjects so the students had to learn the elements of the subjects and demonstrate skill in dissection and in the preparation of specimens for close study. Elton worked well, and received a second-class pass, to share top place with two others.[21]

Elton's second year was directed more to specific topics for medical students. In anatomy he learned about the nervous system, sense organs, parts of the lung and the brain, and how to dissect the elbow and the knee. He studied physiology, organic chemistry, *Materia Medica,* and learned some elementary therapeutics.[22] The students were hard pressed to complete their work before the numerous examinations at the year's end. To help in their studies, medical students founded a society that encouraged members to write papers and promoted fellowship. In the first part of the year they met once each month, and at the end of the year celebrated their success with a dinner.[23]

Comfortable facilities for students were not available at the university, so the Adelaide University Union was established, and Elton joined its committee. He helped the union to promote social life amongst the members of the university, to receive and discuss academic papers, and to hold debates on approved subjects. The union acquired a handsome, commodious room, furnished it with tables, magazines, and newspapers, and invited members to enjoy smoking, reading, and club life.[24]

In his second year, then, Elton had a secure place in the general life of the university and the exclusive community of medical students. At the end of 1900 he lost all this when he failed the examination. A recent history of the university records: "In the days of our grandfathers a student who failed his chosen profession's entrance qualifications was in dire straits. As in the noble game of cricket, he was either 'in' or 'out.'"[25] Elton was out.

Elton's failure changed his career and life. Why he failed is not securely known. His sister Helen said he lost interest in medicine, found amusing companions, got into debt, and did insufficient work; his brother Herbert mentioned a certain woman and heavy losses at the race track. Also, Elton was unsuited to the way medicine was taught. Under Hetty he had rebelled against learning the multiplication tables; it seems likely he rebelled against requirements of the university's medical staff "to memorize and be able to regurgitate an enormous amount of anatomical detail and clinical facts and figures."[26] Further, a sharp difference existed between his parents in their attitude to work. Hetty and George had agreed that their children should be pushed toward not only a professional vocation but a broad range of human affairs, but they had disagreed on how this was to be done. Hetty had learned that success followed from persistent and concentrated attention to the task at hand; George had learned to be more skeptical, and was convinced, in his whimsical way, "that heavy effort was excellent comedy."[27] At nineteen years Elton had not reconciled the two approaches; instead he chose George's way, found amusement inside the university and out, broadened his experience of human affairs, but failed to hold his place among the most hard-pressed and examination-ridden university students.[28]

Hetty and George were deeply disappointed. Elton was ashamed of himself and suffered a great loss of self-esteem. He never forgot the feeling that he had let down his family. "I think I told you about my phantasy," he wrote to his daughter in 1938, "that I should like to meet my father and grandfather in the happy hunting grounds (on terms of complete equality) and to compare and discuss experiences with them."[29] He was sorry that Hetty had not lived to see his success in the United States.[30]

At the time of his failure the family decided that Elton's companions had led him astray—he could not bear to confess to being uninterested in medicine—so, to rid him of their influence, he was sent to the University of Edinburgh to continue his studies.

Little is known about his activities in Scotland. In June 1901 he represented students of the University of Adelaide at the Ninth Jubilee of the University of Glasgow.[31] Elton told of arriving so late at one important dinner that no seat was available; he sent his card to the chairman, who found a seat beside a former governor of South Australia.[32] In September Elton matriculated at the University of Edinburgh,[33] but he did not study medicine for long. In Adelaide, Elton's parents held to the belief that he had still not freed himself from the wrong sort of companions, so George decided to send him to the small medical school at St. George's Hospital, London.[34] At the end of April 1903 Elton had enrolled to take the conjoint-examinations of the Royal College of Physicians and the Royal College of Surgeons, which would lead to diplomas equivalent to bachelor's degrees in medicine and surgery in Australia.[35]

Elton lived at Colonel Charles Mayo's home, "Folkdene,"in Grove Park, London. A boyhood friend, Dr. John Cleland, visited him in September 1903 and found him apparently studying assiduously.[36] In truth Elton was not absorbed in medical studies; he was in a dilemma. On one hand he shrank from disappointing his father, and on the other, no matter how hard he tried, he could not make himself like medicine. Earlier this conflict had prevented him from writing home, but now he wanted to be rid of study. In December 1903 he dropped medicine for the third time.

George accepted the decision and suggested that Elton find a vocation for himself, offering a small allowance to support him during the search. Elton found a position with the Ashanti Mining Company, miners of gold in Obuassi, West Africa,[37] where life was unhealthy for Europeans and proved dangerous and disappointing for Elton. Many white men suffered and died from blackwater fever; and most of those who survived the hazards of the first six months were shipped back to England with diseases that took a lifetime to throw off. Elton was determined to make good in West Africa. He had failed to follow the respectable profession of medicine, so there was little to lose by taking up an adventure, as his grandfather and father had done before him. Years later he told his children that he went to West Africa looking for diamonds, and "to see what it was like." The decision had been taken to escape failure, and to become sure of what he should do with his life.[38] But the adventure was another failure.

Elton worked at the company's headquarters, applied himself diligently, and even rose early each morning.[39] When his health failed, the medical officer decided to send him back to England in late March 1904. He brought back with himself a nightmare: dengue fever.[40]

Later Elton drafted a short story based on his experience, in which West Africa is a place of "stern reality" where "death sudden and unaccountable" awaits the white man. The bed-ridden main character fears death and is being deafened by "the roar of the stampers grinding out more gold for millionaires." The doctor assures him that he has only a touch of fever. The patient laughs wildly: "It's touch and go then Doctor; and I'm going this time. . . . Can't you put me right? Damn it! Where's your skill and science?" The doctor replies grimly: "Science? All science has so far achieved is to confirm our certainty of annihilation."[41] Years afterward Elton reported that, following the death of a white man, his West African valet "disappears for at least a week until such time as the magic which has slain his master may have dispersed."[42] As Elton's interests in psychology and anthropology developed, he called on his West African experience to illustrate similarities between the primitive mind of natives, the mental processes in childhood, the thoughts of neurotic adults, and the superstitions and irrationalities in everyday life.

Two reasons were circulated to explain Elton's unexpected return to Colonel Mayo's home: an abcess in the ear, and appendicitis.[43] By the first week of April he had regained his health sufficiently to accompany his two female cousins'to Tilbury to meet the S.S. *Arcadia,* which had brought his sister Helen to London. She had completed her undergraduate work in medicine at the University of Adelaide, and planned to continue her studies in tropical medicine before spending a year in India. Cleland was there to welcome her too. For about a month Elton and Helen lived at Grove Park, and Cleland visited them weekends. With the Mayo girls and their friends the three Australians lunched, played tennis and croquet, rode bicycles, and enjoyed the city's sights. They talked about their families at home, their childhood, and the future. It was clear that Elton had not measured up to the standards of his own homeland; he had no qualifications, no clear future, and no income.

Elton decided to write. The papers he read reported much news about Australia and the British Commonwealth. The *Westminster Budget* published an article on how the Children's Court worked in South Australia; the *Pall Mall Gazette* reported on the cricket successes of Trumper and Rhodes, the gold rushes in Queensland, the impact of British imperial strategies on the Australian navy, winemaking in South Australia, Canada's need of immigrants, the success of Chinese labor in the mines of Australia's Northern Territory, the training of women for medicine. And Elton knew of Alan Burgoyne's success; at the age of twenty-three Burgoyne had written for *Harper's, World Wide,* and *Pall Mall Magazine,* and had received thirty pounds for accounts of his adventures in Siam and New Guinea. It seemed reasonable that Elton could be a journalist as well. He was twenty-three, too.

Late in April, Cleland helped Helen find comfortable rooms in Gower Street, close to the School of Tropical Medicine. Through the University Women's Club she made friends, some of whom took tea with her in her rooms. Edith Hooper, an intelligent philosophy graduate from Philadelphia, became a close friend, and she impressed Elton when once he came to tea. He himself had no close friends, and now that Helen was gone from Grove Park, he was unhappy.

Elton was unhappy for many reasons. He depended on his father for money. This forced him to be less extravagant than in the past, but he still could not acquire the prudent habits needed to prevent his expenditure from exceeding his income. At the same time he had little energy and no inclination for work. And because he had no job or position in view, he believed that he could not easily borrow money, even from those who thought highly of him. At Grove Park his attitude was perverse and uncooperative; he became a nuisance because he stayed up until 2 A.M. and never rose before 11 A.M., he refused to be corrected by the mistress of the house, and if anyone tried to advise him or manage his affairs, he became quite savage. He idled about the house, wrote a little, spent his money, and then thought of writing a little more. The growing difficulties at Grove Park, combined with the curious working habits Elton was cultivating, led him to find some digs at 49 Great Ormond Street, a short walk from Helen's room.

In the evenings he often visited her and they would sit in the little garden, Elton puffing on a cigarette, Helen reading aloud her letters from home. Together they planned the future, daydreamed, and recalled their fortunate upbringing—how it afforded them a "mental hinterland" of varied interests and wide knowledge that, they assured each other, would lead to a deeper understanding of life's problems.

In these confidential conversations Helen gave her brother close attention, assured him of sympathetic support, and kept back her own disappointment at his poor university record. She listened to him because she loved him, and his thoughts interested her. She decided not to argue with him nor to give him advice because "it would destroy any influence I now have."[44] By listening, she encouraged him to talk and say many things about himself and the family that would otherwise have been difficult to say. She knew that it was not only a chronic shortage of cash that bothered Elton but also a sustained loss of self-esteem exacerbated by the absence of close friends with whom to share his youthful plans. She believed he carried a deep but suppressed affection for his parents, and refused to write home because he had wanted to maintain the view that they deliberately failed to understand him. Helen helped Elton to appreciate the complexity of their disappointment and to see that it was he who had failed them and then turned away from them in search of a challenge on which to deploy his talents. In time, she brought her brother back to the opinion that he was lucky to have had the parents he did. Their talks seem to have had many of the features of clinical relationships that Elton discussed years later.

Elton worked for a short period as a proofreader in a firm that published the Bible. People chuckled when he told the story that because he had been so familiar with the work he had had to read every line, closely, from right to left.[45] Also, Elton wrote for the newspapers.

Elton had an early piece in the *Pall Mall Gazette* on a political crisis in Australia.[46] He had left South Australia at about the time the colonies federated and the commonwealth was proclaimed. In April 1904, after the breakdown of a political coalition, the Australian Labour Party (ALP) had sufficient support to form a federal government. Elton drew the attention of the English to the "grave significance," the "danger to the Constitution," and the "great anxiety" in Australia following the ALP success. He accused the party of placing great financial burdens on the new nation and failing to foster settlement outside the cities. To illustrate his case, he pointed to the old age pensions, village settlements, and the immigration bill. ALP policy benefited only one class. The leaders were incompetent; their scheme for a "white Australia" and their socialist ideology would limit immigration of colored laborers and thereby raise wages artificially; their special land tax would give the state full control of all property, and their plan to introduce state-controlled industries would "crush private commercial enterprise." Elton here argued a point that he would repeat in his political writings and in his views on education. "Ignorant men may be led by their intellectual superiors: the insufficiently educated, particularly when a large majority has entire control of affairs, are obstinately self-opinionated, and, as such, are a distinct menace to the social well-being of the community."[47]

Elton attacked socialism, not because he objected to the ideology but because in Australia "labour politicians and stump or pot-house orators" approached socialism wrongly, emphasized selfishness and class jealousy, and, by playing on the mob's ignorance, planned to drag down "advanced individuals . . . to the level of the common herd." He scorned the idea that the redistribution of wealth would stabilize; to him it was basically unfair, and, if done quickly, would lead to anarchy and civil war. He wrote that "the idle and extravagant must necessarily sink, those naturally industrious and thrifty cannot but rise," and advocated social improvement by education not legislation. The blame that he first attributed to the ALP politicians he directed also to the lethargic "colonial upper classes" who, he warned, would shortly be the victims of a "rude awakening." Elton's politics were clear enough. He loathed socialism because it flourished on mob ignorance, and preferred "a high ethical Socialism" that developed from "the voluntary sacrifice of certain advantages by a more cultured class in order to raise the moral and intellectual level of their less enlightened brethren."

Nine years later, on the eve of his marriage, Elton was rummaging through his papers when he found a copy of his analysis of Australia's political crisis of 1904. He considered sending it to his fiancée, for its style was interesting, but he was so horrified by its impertinence and lack of honesty that he burned it instead.[48]

Elton's article caught the eye of an Australian in London at this time. Signing himself "P.N.R.", he wrote a reply that appeared five days later in the same place on the front page.[49] First, the village settlements and old age pension schemes were state not commonwealth schemes; the former was introduced by a conservative not a socialist government, and the latter was supported by both parties and not a divisive issue. Second, no attempts had been made to limit the immigration of "desirable persons," and most parliamentarians—not simply Labourites—had supported the "White Continent" policy and agreed on the definition of "desirable." "P.N.R." further asserted that it was common knowledge that the desert interior was not suitable for economic development, and, because most arable land along the coasts was controlled by a few wealthy individuals, young agriculturalists had been forced to seek work in the cities, thus raising urban unemployment levels. A progressive tax was the most appropriate way to redistribute land, and ease the economic distress; it would not become a single tax as Elton had predicted. "P.N.R." refused to discuss Elton's views on socialism, but countered those on the origins of economic troubles in Australia by declaring that they had been caused by the bank crashes of 1893 and not recent ALP practices.

Ten days after "P.N.R.'s" rejoinder, W.H. Irvine, the conservative former premier of Victoria who had earned great praise at home for saving his state from a railworker strike, disembarked at Tilbury. Replying to reporters' questions on Australia's political crisis, he too contradicted Elton by asserting that all Australians, including Labourites, wanted increased immigration. Then he comforted British investors with assurances that the ALP had bound its irresponsible elements hand and foot, and that the party's socialist legislation could never endanger commercial growth because the states, not the commonwealth, secured investors' property.[50]

The delight of seeing his writing published gave way to melancholic preoccupations when Elton learned that Helen planned to visit Hetty's family and friends in Edinburgh. Shortly before her holiday Elton went to see her. He looked pale, complained that bedbugs kept him awake, and told of how the rejection of manuscripts was discouraging him. She listened without comment to unhappy accounts of his inability to write, failures at journalism, loneliness, and homesickness aroused by the occasional visitor from Adelaide. "We all have to work these things out for ourselves" she wrote to her parents; she was not tempted to take her brother in hand, except to recommend he begin some outdoor exercise and take a tonic.[51]

Elton's insensitivity toward his English cousins had so alienated them that he was regarded as a permanent irritant. He was not welcome except by special invitation. Only Cherie, his cousin, had any time for him. When her marriage was announced in September, Elton, Helen, and John Cleland were invited, but with the marriage Elton lost the most sympathetic of his Grove Park cousins, the one who had done all she could do "to gain his confidence and prevent friction."[52]

Twenty years later when Elton was alone in the United States he remembered the London summer of 1904. He had talked with no one, and had eaten alone. All the small things that fill up life had disappeared. He had learned how much he needed the company of others, and doubted that he would ever be able to make friends.[53] Elton's melancholia drove him to walk about the streets, a pitiful wraith, obsessed with a deep and genuine sense of his own worthlessness. This emotional circle of loneliness, self-denigration, loss of personal contact, and further loneliness seemed an impossible one to break. He was "idle and extravagant" and "must necessarily sink." Then one day his eye was caught by a three-story house at 46 Great Ormond Street. Fifteen-inch black lettering on a bold white strip above the windows of each story told the pedestrian he was passing the Working Men's College. Elton stopped. One notice said that on September 27 evening classes for beginners would commence; above the front door another notice pleaded urgently for £15,000 to expand the college. He went in. The ring of loneliness was broken; Elton had taken his first step into education of people at work.

Although the Working Men's College would play only a brief part in Elton's development, the ideas on which it was established were congruent with his later beliefs on the proper attitude toward work. In 1854, under the leadership of F.D. Maurice, a prominent theologian and academic, the college had been founded to provide working men with organized human studies in a self-governing and self-supporting institution with standards comparable to a university college. Christian fellowship set the tone for human relations in the college; liberal rather than technical studies were encouraged; education technique was centered on the limited experience and interests of mature adult workers rather than the privileged background of clever young men. Although the teachers had university experience, and came from among middle-class professionals, they were chosen for their sympathy toward the working class, their Christian sense of duty, their humility and good-will, and their preference for cultivating human understanding through cooperative learning rather than for handing down knowledge through expert instruction. Freedom and order were the prominent values; working men were to be unshackled from their forced ignorance and shown the right order of their social and political world. The college gave "an answering response in the social conditions of the times; in the indignity and frustration which the conditions of the new industrial society forced upon workers, denying them their status as full members of society."[54]

The college flourished until 1872. After a short crisis it was reorganized, and from 1884-1902, under the influence of a prominent businessman, George Tansley, emphasis on Christian socialism and social reform gave over somewhat to the establishment of a stable educational system. In 1902 changes in British education led to fresh plans for the college. Since 1896 the college had been trying to raise money for expansion. Next door the Children's Hospital had a similar scheme; it received a handsome grant and offered to purchase the college. So plans were drawn up for a new building in Crowndale Road. Elton joined the college at this time. Further changes were in the air. The control of London schools was being transferred from a central agency to local authorities, and England's education system was beginning a rapid expansion that would continue until the Great War. Voluntary education associations were growing; in particular, the Worker's Education Association (WEA) spread throughout England and the colonies to fill gaps in adult education that other movements had overlooked. In Australia ten years later, Elton would embrace such WEA activities.

Between September 9 and December 17, 1904, Elton was on the staff of the Working Men's College. Because a shortage of teachers had affected many London schools, Elton's application to conduct an advanced course in English grammar was welcomed. The class met on Thursday evenings from 8 to 10; Elton was not paid. What Elton taught ranged far from grammar and kept his pupils' interest. Also, he attracted them with his charming and considerate manner. They admired his brilliant style of argument, and his extraordinary memory. It was an audience that gave Elton the chance to see how rapidly he could develop his remarkable capacity to use facts and that gave him much respect.[55]

In time Elton's attempts at journalism gave over to playing chess and reading in the library at the college. Also he began to enter the college's social life. In Australia the Labour government had lost power, and Elton entertained the Debating Society with his argument "This house welcomes the recent downfall of the Labour Ministry in Australia," which carried by a vote of ten to five. This was a notable success in view of the ethos of social reform that was upheld in the college. Late in October Elton attended the jubilee dinner in the company of the founder's son, C. Edmund Maurice, A.V. Dicey, and G.M. Trevelyan.[56] At a smokers' concert where prizes for athletics were being distributed Elton offered the company a musical item, and shortly before Christmas the Old Student's Club had him to supper. Of Elton the college journal wrote: "It is remarkable to what extent he entered into the College life during the six months. . . . He carries many friendships and pleasant memories . . . with him." Seventeen years later Elton wrote to

Dorothea: "As a youngster I walked into the Working Men's College and was immediately taken into the confidence of the workers themselves."[57]

News of Elton's desultory activities had reached the family in Adelaide, and George wrote suggesting to Helen that she and Elton take a holiday on the Continent. The first week of October was free, so they bought tickets on the Belgian railways and took Cook's hotel coupons, "the cheapest and nicest way of doing it."[58] The tour was a brief tour of churches, castles, and museums, all hastily summarized on picture postcards. One museum—the Wiertz Museum—was to become of particular significance to Elton.

Antoine Wiertz (1806-1865) had bequeathed to the citizens of Brussels a permanent exhibition of the sculptures and paintings in his home. "To make the transfiguration of Raphael and then die" had been the aim of the young Wiertz;[59] as he matured, he was possessed by humanitarian ideals, which he expressed by drawing attention to war, threats to family life, capital punishment, and social injustice. His technique was to shock the observer with realistic imagery. The exhibition is dominated by enormous gruesome paintings. With few exceptions they depict beautifully formed men and women being decapitated, impaled, dismembered, and otherwise subjected to mysterious rituals or physical and mental torment: Satan and Christ watch a man blowing off his head with a pistol; a woman, wild with hunger and unable to pay her taxes, is chopping up her child and cooking it in a pot; a mother with no place to leave her infant during the day is snatching its charred body from the stove; children play war games beside a great cannon; orphans pine over the coffin of their parents recently killed by the collapse of their house; women flee with their children from rapacious, drunken soldiers.

Helen and Elton marveled at the "instinct with insane genius. He was mad for a time before his death."[60] They were drawn, particularly to: *Une Scene de l'enfer,* in which a proud Napoleon is called to account for his butchery by his victim's families, who thrust at him the bloody limbs of their dead; *Inhumation precipitee* depicts horror in the face of a man peering from under his coffin lid, marked "Mort du cholera—certifie par nous Docteuss Sans doutes"; a triptych, *Pensees et visions d'une tete coupee,* shows the suffering that a person was believed to endure for three minutes after decapitation. Many paintings depict Jesus and Satan; in all of them, Elton and his sister agreed, the face of Satan or Lucifer had greater strength and beauty than that of Christ. "Elton was immensely interested and very anxious to buy a book of the pictures," wrote Helen, "but I personally would not care to have such morbid things with me, and we did not get any."[61]

During his life Elton developed no personal interest in painting even though Wiertz's work did intrigue him. Wiertz upheld many values that were important to Elton and were characteristic of romantics of his day. For example, in Wiertz's enormous *Le dernier canon,* the message is to end war, slaughter, and artificial boundaries between human beings: "Progress breaks the cannon, Genius sets it alight, and the civilized activities of Science, Art and Work spread peace and kindness throughout the world." Wiertz painted to capture the attention of important authorities, to shame them with vivid, realistic images of their uncivilized accomplishments, and to show the "light of kindness, of reason, of fraternity."[62] Sympathy for Wiertz's feelings are present in Elton's later orientation to authority figures, human experience at work, relations between people in organized life, and the passing of traditional community life with the growth of industrialization. Whenever the opportunity arose, Elton visited the Wiertz Museum.[63]

Heidelberg was of particular interest to Elton and Helen because George had often told them of the happy time he had spent there thirty years before, but when they arrived Elton was unwell. In London he had taken to eating lightly all through the day and had developed a habit of having tea and cakes rather than a proper midday meal. Malnourished, he tired from extra exertion, like night travel, and in Heidelberg showed symptoms of malaria, so he rested for two nights.[64]

After the holiday Helen enlisted John Cleland to help Elton improve his health. Helen shortly noted a recovery in his "mental tone." His morbid obsessive daydreams, which she attributed to West Africa, were being replaced by a growing interest in the Working Men's College, an increasing group of friends, and high hopes for his writing.[65] But toward the end of October Elton was complaining of tiredness, inability to work, and eye strain, and at the same time his future was becoming unclear. He had had no more articles accepted. Helen was planning to study midwifery in Dublin then go to India for a year. The family in Adelaide seemed sympathetic toward him, so he planned to rejoin them. Yet, he had almost landed an important secretarial post, which showed London offered opportunities not readily available in Adelaide. Finally, Elton decided to return home and try his hand at various things.[66]

In mid-December Elton changed his mind, and decided, once more, to escape misery by following an adventure. Five good reasons presented themselves. First, Elton and his father appear to have had a misunderstanding about who should have paid for the vacation in Europe. Second, Helen was in Dublin and not available to help clarify the problem. Third, classes had ended at the Working Men's College. Fourth, a lonely Christmas stared at him. And fifth, Christmas day would be followed by his birthday; Elton loathed his birthday because all his life it had been treated as the fag-end of the holiday celebrations.[67] It was the day to run away from. Elton decided to try Canada.[68]

Canada? Early in 1904, the Honorable James A. Smart, Canada's deputy minister of the interior, had visited London to encourage farmers and laborers to migrate to Canada. He had predicted that by 1914 Canada could feed all England, and that its industrial expansion would rival that of the

United States.[69] In December 1904, Canada looked like a better adventure-land than had West Africa in December 1903. Elton wrote to Helen asking for passage money, but she could no longer maintain her neutral attitude. She felt she had to take him in hand. "It seemed . . . too silly to go to an unknown country without money or influence when there was his own home waiting for him."[70] He accepted her advice, and she advanced him money for his fare and expenses. On January 19, 1905, he departed from Liverpool for Adelaide aboard the S.S. *Persic*. He sent Helen a postcard, "Ave atque vale," and left a message, "So long," on the mantelpiece in the common room at the Working Men's College.[71]

Notes

1. Helen Mayo, "Biographical Notes on Elton Mayo," SAA.
2. R. J. Nicholas, "Private and Denominational Secondary Schools of South Australia," thesis in education, University of Melbourne. Parkville, Victoria, Australia, 1951.
3. Elton to Herbert, 16 November 1937, SAA.
4. In the personal libraries of Patricia and Gael Elton Mayo; Helen Mayo, "Biographical Notes on Elton Mayo."
5. Reports differ as to when Elton was at St. Peter's; school records show he attended 1896-98. Evans to Trahair, 22 May 1974.
6. Helen Mayo, "Biographical Notes on Elton Mayo."
7. Hargraves to Trahair, 24 May 1974.
8. Sir Herbert Mayo's Notebooks 1073, 1293.
9. Elton to Dorothea, 22 October 1922.
10. Elton to Toni, 19 April 1935.
11. Sir Herbert Mayo's Notebooks 134.
12. Ibid., 876.
13. Elton to Dorothea, 18 November 1922.
14. Sir Herbert Mayo's Notebooks 930, 1048, 1293. Helen to Elton, 3 February 1945, MM 1.007.
15. Sir Herbert Mayo's Notebooks 504, 506, 573.
16. Ibid., 83.
17. Mayo to Roethlisberger, 20 August 1940, FJR.
18. University of Adelaide, *Calendar,* 1898, 1899, 1900; Elton to Toni, 19 April 1935.
19. Medical Student Register, University of Adelaide.
20. W. G. K. Duncan and R. A. Leonard, *The University of Adelaide, 1874-1974* (Adelaide: Rigby, 1974), ch. 6.
21. University of Adelaide, *Calendar,* 1900.
22. Ibid.
23. Ibid., 1901.
24. Ibid.
25. Duncan and Leonard, *University of Adelaide,* p. 59.
26. Ibid.
27. Elton to Toni, 19 April 1935.
28. Duncan and Leonard, *University of Adelaide,* p. 59.
29. Elton to Toni, 7 January 1938.
30. Elton to Toni, 19 April 1935.

31. McKenna to Muspratt, 10 September 1975, Library correspondence, University of Glasgow.
32. Helen Mayo, "Biographical Notes on Elton Mayo."
33. White to Trahair, 25 September 1974.
34. Helen Mayo, "Biographical Notes on Elton Mayo."
35. Mackay to Trahair, 17 July 1974.
36. John Cleland's Diary, SAA.
37. Helen Mayo, "Biographical Notes on Elton Mayo"; Helen Mayo to Meecham, 8 July 1959, SAA; John Cleland's Diary.
38. Conversation with Gael Mayo, 12 February 1975.
39. Helen Mayo to her parents, 11 November 1904, SAA.
40. Helen Mayo to her parents, 14 October 1904, SAA; conversation with George Homans, January 1974.
41. Mayo's Notebook, pp. 98-99, BLA.
42. Elton Mayo, "The Irrational Factor in Society," *Journal of Personnel Research* 1 (1923):419-26.
43. John Cleland's Diary.
44. Helen Mayo to her parents, 28 April 1904, SAA.
45. Conversation with Ruth Norton, 4 March 1975.
46. Elton Mayo, "The Australian Crisis," *Pall Mall Gazette,* 12 May 1904, pp. 1-2.
47. Ibid.
48. Elton to Dorothea, 13 March 1913.
49. Elton Mayo "The Irrational Factor in Society."
50. Op. cit., 27 May 1904, P. 9.
51. Helen Mayo, in "Biographical Notes on Elton Mayo," indicates that other articles were accepted and that for each one Elton received one guinea. Copies of the articles have not been found in the papers to which she referred.
52. Helen Mayo to her parents, 28 April 1904, SAA.
53. Ibid.
54. Elton to Dorothea, 20 September, 7, 25 October 1922.
55. Harrison, J.F.C., *A History of the Working Men's College, 1854-1954.* (London: Routledge & Kegan Paul, 1954), p. 25.
56. Helen Mayo to her parents, 24 November 1904, SAA.
57. Mayo to Donham, MM.3.036.
58. *Working Men's College Journal* 8 (1904): 396, 434, 447, 453; IX (1905): 2, 19, 32, 71.
59. Helen Mayo to her parents, 6 October 1904, SAA.
60. Potvin, J. *Antony Wiertz,* English ed., trans. by the author (Brussels, 1913), p. 115.
61. Helen Mayo to her parents, 6 October 1904, SAA.
62. Ibid.
63. Potvin, *Anthony Wiertz,* p. 122.
64. Conversations with Patricia Elton Mayo, January 1974.
65. Helen Mayo to her parents, 6 October 1904, SAA.
66. Helen Mayo to her parents, 14 October 1904, SAA.
67. Helen Mayo to her parents, 10 November 1904, SAA.
68. Conversations with Patricia Elton Mayo, September 1975.
69. Helen Mayo, "Biographical Notes on Elton Mayo."
70. *Pall Mall Gazette,* 78, 27 January 1904, p. 12.
71. Helen Mayo, "Biographical Notes on Elton Mayo."
72. Helen Mayo, "Biographical Notes on Elton Mayo"; *Working Men's College Journal* 9 (1905): 32.

3

Education and Career, 1905-1911

It was February when Elton reached South Australia. With Helen in India and Herbert studying law in Melbourne, only Penelope, sixteen, and John, fourteen, were still at home. They delighted in getting reacquainted with their errant brother, who told stories of adventures abroad and gave practical advice on school work.

Hetty and George established close and happy relations with Elton, and, within a few weeks of his arrival, acquired for him a partnership with George W. Jacobs in the printing firm J.H. Sherrington and Co., Bickford Buildings in Leight Street, Adelaide. Experience at the Working Men's College had helped him to manage some administrative difficulties, but he never adapted fully to conventional office hours and other routines. He stuck to it until 1910.[1]

Elton's welcome home did not extend much beyond the family. He recalled, "When I came back to Australia from England . . . everyone [was] pointing the finger of scorn or else disregarding me." He was ostracized for two good reasons: first, he had twice failed medicine, and this was not easily forgotten by those who knew him; second, he had gone into business, which had a social status well beneath the profession of his grandfather and sister. Worse, he had become an enigma. On one hand, his lower social standing was incongruous with his family's respectable connections; on the other, he had a capable mind and was remarkably skilled in associating with different people, something that Helen had recognized and admired. Further, he was a showman; in 1905, he played a waiter in an impromptu performance at a guest house at Port Elliot and, with no script, kept his audience fully entertained.[2] In short, Elton's intelligence and charm were acknowledged, but his social standing partially denied him the status that his family once enjoyed.

Although Elton was sometimes depressed by being cut and was rankled by his associates, he managed himself constructively by turning to his notebooks.[3] He composed flippant dialogue and witty verses about his feelings, casting himself as the "Ostracized Agnostic," a poor fellow at times in love with the "Dainty Patricia," a young woman of high degree.

We learn that between the Ostracized Agnostic and Dainty Patricia lies a wide gulf. The Ostracized Agnostic is properly a Bohemian, in whose society women of good taste have "subjugated the conventional delusions" and taken to drinking champagne and placing their feet on the nearest mantelpiece. Of course the Dainty Patricia would never behave so, because she imagines the Ostracized Agnostic would quit the room in disgust. She prefers to keep her illusions, her taste for Russian tea, and her detestation of "humbug—even in bishops." To this nonsense he replies:

> To be in the world, fortuitously as it were . . . is a far happier condition than to be of it socially. To be content with ephemeral pleasure is, no doubt, a crime; but it is more easily justifiable than to exist for the single purpose of snubbing one's next door neighbour. I am no hedonist, not even in the altruistic sense. (And regarding humbug in a bishop) . . . I detest wings that creak audibly in an archangel. Nothing annoys me more intensely than the complete self satisfaction of those 'society leaders' who, after merely making themselves unpleasant in their life, are assured by their respective padres of front seats in eternal bliss.

In a love poem to the Dainty Patricia, our Ostracized Agnostic again attacks bogus social distinctions. Poor fellow wants to send her a note but suffers "from affright of High Society." Why? His own social rank is too low, but "tho' ne'er a Socialist" he is determined:

> *I'll overcome, so help me Fate,*
> *The difference in our stations;*
> *I have indeed no aspirates,*
> *But lofty aspirations.*

Sometimes Elton used his intellect aggressively in response to real or imagined hypocrisy in those who scorned or disregarded him. At one social gathering he asked people for their opinions on a new book, "Perdition." Some approved it, others condemned it. No such title had been recently published. Although the revenge was no doubt sweet enough, it was civilized, because, like the entries in his notebook, it was secret, and hurt no one. And Elton convinced Herbert, who had known of the ruse, that it was not a childish prank but rather the establishment of a new moral: don't be misled into talking about books![4]

By 1906 Elton shared with George Jacobs a directorship in their printing, lithographing, bookbinding, stationery, and rubber-stamp-making firm. In 1907 Jacobs withdrew and he was joined by Horace G. Mumme and E. Sherring. But business was not Elton's calling, and he turned instead to academic studies under the influence of Professor William Mitchell.

Mitchell, a Scot born in 1861, had been a lecturer in moral philosophy at the Universities of Edinburgh and London and, at thirty-three, had accepted the Hughes Chair of Philosophy at the University of Adelaide, where eventually he achieved the standing of a philosopher-king. His unassailable authority was based on an impressive physical stature, a quiet forceful assurance, true intellect, and a deep sense of morality. At Adelaide he studied and taught mental and moral philosophy, zoology, anatomy, psychology, political science, logic, theory and practice of education, and English language and literature. He was titled "Professor of English Language and Literature and Mental and Moral Philosophy," and joked that he occupied not so much a chair as a sofa. Mitchell was a genuine nineteenth-century liberal, and respected conservative and reactionary colleagues alike. By 1934 he was a tremendous influence in the university, and for his contribution he was knighted. He died at 101.[5]

Mitchell's *Structure and Growth of the Mind,* published in 1907, was to play an important part in Elton's intellectual growth. The book comprises lectures on the body-mind problem, the field of academic psychology, and how to explain and analyze human experience. Mitchell also considers psychological explanations of social relations in discussions on imitation, fellow-feeling, and aesthetics; outlines how intelligence develops through the complex refinement and raising of sensory and perceptual experience; and looks at the place of scientific explanation in psychology.

Elton admired Mitchell, studied under him, and became a close friend. Mitchell spoke of Elton with pride. How they became known to each other is not clear. In 1896 and 1897 Helen Mayo had been an arts student under Mitchell; no doubt he learned of her prize-winning record in medical studies, as well as Elton's failures. Probably the Mayo and Mitchell families knew each other. In 1906 Mitchell had been abroad. In 1907 when the acquaintanceship was renewed, after Mitchell's trip, Mitchell and Elton discussed the dissatisfactions of business life. Mitchell could answer Elton's questions, so, Elton tells us, he decided to begin an undergraduate degree in philosophy.[6]

In his first year Elton took economics, logic, and psychology, attending Mitchell's lectures, in the late afternoon, four days each week. Economics was a two-year course based on Gide's *Principles of Political Economy,* Syke's *Banking and Commerce,* and Cunningham and McArthur's *Outline of English Industrial History.* For private reading Elton was encouraged to tackle Marshall's *Economics of Industry,* and Mill's *Principles of Political Economy.* In a class of sixteen students, Elton and two others shared a high pass. Logic was a one-year course. Elton used *Elementary Lessons in Logic* by Jevons, and by himself studied Bosanquet's *Essentials of Logic.* Again he did well. In psychology his performance was outstanding; his medical knowledge helped because the course centered on elements of physiological psychology, following the texts of Huxley and McDougall. The psychological components of the course were drawn from Stout's *Manual of Psychology* and, of course, Mitchell's own book. In a class of twenty-five Elton shared, with Eirene M. Williams, the Roby Fletcher Prize, an award named after the university's former vice-chancellor and given for the best matriculated or graduate student in psychology.[7]

Elton had educational interests outside class. Again we see the influence of Mitchell, who inaugurated and presided over the Adelaide University Arts Association. This attracted Elton's interest because Mitchell encouraged discussion and debate on topics that students liked, and promoted the university's social life by drawing together groups of mature students and professors.[8]

Elton kept in touch with the Working Men's College in London, whose officers held him in high regard for his work there in 1904. Sir Charles Lucas, a vice-principal of the college in Elton's day, visited Australia in 1909; at that time he was assistant under secretary of state for the colonies, and had come at the suggestion of Alfred Deakin, the prime minister. In Adelaide Sir Charles stayed at Government House as the guest of the governor, Sir Day Bosanquet. Elton was sent for. Sir Charles relayed a request from the college that Elton return to handle meetings of workingmen. Elton chose to continue his studies in philosophy.[9] Penelope joined Elton in studies at the university.

Using Seth's *Ethical Principles* and Sedgwick's *History of Ethics*, Elton was introduced to ethical hedonism and the contributions of Bentham, Mill, Kant, and Nietzsche, together with criticisms of utilitarian doctrines and Spencer's application of the theory of evolution to society. The course considered egoism versus altruism. Hobbes on social structure; rationalism; the work of Butler, Clarke, and Locke; the commonsense writers like Reid and Douglas Stewart; and Kant's ideas on pure reason, law, God's existence, freedom, inevitability, and good-will. Elton combined his ideas on psychology and ethics when he considered the scientific status of studies in ethics, concluding that "the facts for ethics (i. e. what we ought to know) are found in psychology." And in his study of the state—an important mediator of what we ought to know and do—Elton was drawn to the notion that the ideal (i.e., highly ethical) society in any community "is that in which individuals can lead their fullest life."[10]

In philosophy Mitchell's lectures drew on Schwengler's *History of Philosophy* and Royce's *World of the Individual.* Particular emphasis in the history of epistemology was placed on ideas of Locke, Berkeley, Hume, and Kant, ideas that subsequently helped Elton with his distinction between academic and medical psychology. Close attention was given to Ward's work and the first hundred pages of T.H. Green's *Prolegomena to Ethics.*[11] In addition to the British philosophers, Mitchell introduced Elton to the early philosophers, for which he acquired some competence in Greek. In both ethics and philosophy, Elton passed examinations at the highest level.

In 1909 Elton completed a first-year course in French. No lectures were available. In two examinations students were expected to translate into and from the French, and to show that they understood the growth of the language and were familiar with set texts by Racine, Michelet, Barine, and Anatole France. Elton performed well.[12] French was important for his later work on Pierre Janet's theories and research in psychopathology.

A mature undergraduate, Elton proved that he had the perseverence and intelligence required for a scholar's career. At the same time he developed an interest in less academic matters. He became an active member of the Pickwick Club,[13] which gave him a chance to display his talent at public speaking, and to learn more about topics from art to immortality and from romantic poetry to fanatical socialism.

Late in February 1909 Elton addressed the Pickwick Club. In "The Criticism of Art," with special reference to fiction, he made two points regarding unity in a work of art: first, each part of the work must have a place in the whole scheme; second, unity must not be achieved at the expense of variety. Thus, unity is not governed by simplicity but by well integrated complexity. This principle can be found in Elton's later work on human personality and his recommendations for the study of social life. To illustrate his principle Elton applied his ideas to historical studies and religious discussions on higher criticism of the New Testament, calling for support from Percy Gardner and Edersheim. Shaw's *Major Barbara,* one of Elton's favorites, was examined in the same way. He asked whether or not Shaw is caught between the roles of artist and reformer, thereby weakening the play's dramatic quality. Elton argued that although a work of art can be judged best by its degree of internal consistency, this should not preclude its having moral elements with external referents. *Major Barbara* meets the aesthetic criteria of a work of art because it does not call upon external elements or raise questions of its purpose at its most dramatic points, i. e., when Barbara, her notions of the universe shattered, leaves the army, and, again, when she returns to work. For this reason Elton asserted the play has high aesthetic unity, dramatic quality, and diversity.

In July the Pickwick Club was entertained by Elton's "Personal Immortality." He began with the kind of quip that would become a regular feature of his talks: "Personal Immortality . . . this is not a religious paper [so it] need not offend any. . . ." He took up one of his favorite openings, the apparent conflict between scientific and religious opinions, and argued that although they differ they complement one another because both are founded on faith in the unity of the universe. Science asks questions about the unity; religion concerns itself with a mystical orientation toward all things unknown. Only in particular cases does conflict emerge between religious and scientific positions. Having put any conflict behind him, Elton asked whether the scientific position and personal immortality are incompatible. Quickly Elton set aside mystical issues, pantheism, and the Upanishads, to take up immortality in terms of the brain's functions, sensory experience, perceptual understanding, and objective versus subjective knowledge. He concluded that no substantial proof exists in the persistence or otherwise of life after death. From death he turned to life processes, and asserted that to persist, rather than to be immortal, one must have added to subjective knowledge and to the practice of relating the self to "the other self," i.e., to the understanding of people and relations between them. This talk is worth noting fully because it shows Elton, a promising academic, trying to apply himself to human and social problems of everyday life.

Political life interested him too. In a debate before Mitchell's Arts Association, Elton led, in the affirmative: "That in practical politics principle is of less importance than expediency." His notes are a valuable introduction to the political problems he saw in industrial civilization. He began by stating that just as ideals of truth and perfection do not help us judge a particular case, so fanatical political principles and causes prevent us from hearing criticism and, thus, from learning by experience. Although a cause may be important to a person, the person must regard it principally as a working hypothesis and an opportunity to ask not only "What ought I to do?" but also "What can I do?" As a rule, he argued, reformers fail to see this point, and are carried too far. These ideas came from Elton's studies in ethics, and to illustrate them he discussed fanatics in the French Revolution who were overcommitted to their cause, and misfits in West Africa who were devoted to consuming whiskey. In West Africa many people died; missionaries, who went to save souls from whiskey, also died; only the government resident had the answer: "I drink as little as possible, but, at night, I take something to overcome the utter lassitude of the tropics." So devotion to a cause is important, but not to the exclusion of all other causes. At that time Elton's case rested on a plea for common sense.

A month later Pickwick members listened to "Fanaticism and Indifference," in which Elton further elaborated his political views. Fanaticism and indifference (or apathy) indicate decadence in national politics. Facing Elton were the fanatics of socialism in the Australian Labour Party, and the mass of Australians, who were far from convinced that this political arm of the nation's trade union movement was the best answer to the nation's development. Elton argued that common sense says political action is best determined by political principles in relation to the facts of a particular case. Political principles include systematic knowledge (theory) and plans for the future (ideals); decadence emerges when people fail to systematize their political facts and deny the reality of the facts in favor of fanatic ideals, or when they accept their political fate with indifference. Elton asserted that the scientific orientation that had been successfully applied to problems of commerce ought to be tried for social and political problems as well. "Our very party system of government is founded on the idea of opposing fanaticisms," and this is dangerous. Why? Fanatics are obsessed with principles and dogma, and have a blankly defiant attitude to the universe; they miss the important difference between a theory and an ideal, draw a line across the path of progress, and remain indifferent to any contradiction. Using an issue within the Australian economy—free trade versus protection—Elton recommended that, although we should be devoted to a cause, we must welcome criticism and recognize other causes.

"Criteria for Social Progress" was Elton's honors thesis prepared under the supervision of Mitchell. No copy is available, but some points in it can be reconstructed from Elton's notes. In the modern world progress is possible through following scientific principles and methodology, and having faith in the existence of lawfulness and order. If our intellectual system of laws simply strives to achieve perfect unity, this is no argument for its actuality. Social progress requires both devotion to some moral beliefs as well as skill in the scientific study of what ought to be done and what can be done. Utopian and revolutionary conceptions of progress are fallacious. From considering the vexed question of how individuals are related to the state, two points emerge. First, assume that an individual develops in a society; second, society makes the individual's development possible through its members' collaborating in an effort to realize an ideal or absolute unity. Individuals differ in the value of their collaborative effort. An individual's contribution matters only if it makes a difference of value— concrete and complex—to the unity of society. So social progress consists of the increments to the unity of a society, which are made possible through the competence of those people who have learned to understand, scientifically, the society that encourages their development.

With this general thesis in mind, Elton tackles the problems of socialism, particularly as they were presented by the rise of the Australian Labour Party with support from trade unions. In 1904, Elton's views on ALP socialism had appeared in the *Pall Mall Gazette;* in 1909 he had a more sophisticated, less hostile argument. He declared that socialism could be justified if it achieved "a difference of value in social unity" and if it was based on skilled investigation, observation, and application of facts, combined with an open mind regarding contradictory attitudes. Socialism could not be justified if its aims were achieved through extreme action. From Elton's observations, one important basis on which socialism could be justified was "skill in administration," which he believed was an intellectual skill. Of course, if this skill was all that was needed, then socialism would develop best through aristocrats of intellect, and government by aristocrats of intellect might be preferable to government by aristocrats of wealth. But he thought more was required than skill in administration; a moral stance was necessary because the intellect alone would produce merely abstract thought systems for socialism. Such abstract theory reveals only inconsistencies in itself and in its conception of a society; it is inadequate to deal with the facts of reality, the problems raised by social change. Because society is concrete and changes in it carry consequences, it should be reconstituted with great care and in a definite direction according to acceptable ideals. What ideals are available?

Elton thought that both capitalism and the current labor movements overemphasized material efficiency. Democratic socialism seemed promising, but its philosophy was largely unwritten; its study was "so imperatively needed that the future of civilization may be considered to depend on its developments." To Elton it seemed that social progress was being so poorly directed that even a genuine social philosophy might be carried to a dangerous excess. Blind experimentation could ensue without the benefit or restraint of systematic, scientific criticism of its results. In theory, democratic government could answer this point.

But, as a theory of government, democracy was to be questioned. When democracy is combined with utilitarian interests "in which the greatest good accrues to the greatest number, hopelessly abstract arguments arise as to what is good, and how it can be equated with number." Elton recognized that democratic principles established the importance to the state of each community member, but on balance, "democracy is founded on a vicious attempt to equate good with numbers." And because, in practice, democracy fails to discriminate social ills from their remedy, inequalities and injustices arise, and these make current institutions of society inadequate.

Elton argued that skill is needed to understand complexity in social problems. Democracy prefers easy solutions instead; witness the Australian politicians, incompetent leaders, who stumble "blindly from one bad solution to another learning through a maximum of suffering." Elton preferred socialism to a foolishly led democratic government, but suggested a critical comparison of capitalism and socialism. He recognized good elements in socialism, but disliked the principle of imposing a fixed system of ideas on a community, and mounting socialist institutions before having made a systematic study of social problems and appropriate solutions. So Elton concluded that the development of a society depends on its individuals rather than the erection of institutions. But how could one determine who were the right people, the noble volunteers skilled and able enough to appreciate ethical rather than materialistic socialism? Elton believed the answer might be found in psychology and eugenics; these he much preferred to extreme political doctrine.

Elton had a practical as well as an ideological approach to social problems. His sister Helen, who had returned from India, shared this view, and could see the merits of his arguments. She was working to have the South Australian government change the Childrens' Act in respect to the age at which foster children could come under the responsibility of the Education Department. Elton helped her draft a letter to the press in which seven years of age was argued forcefully. The letter was discussed in Parliament, and her recommendation became law.[14]

From early childhood, through adolescence, and well into maturity, Elton was interested in the art of conversation. At the dinner table the Mayo parents had encouraged good conversation among the children; in Brisbane, and later at the Harvard Business School, Elton developed a mature skill in conversation. At the University of Adelaide he began to discuss conversation as an art. He held that long ago there had been only drawing room chatter. Dinner guests preferred horseplay, idle vaporizing, vulgar repartee, foul jokes, or tales of self-aggrandizement. To Elton, wit was central to good conversation, and he argued that although "middle-class humour . . . may be trite and obvious, . . . it has improved" on what passed for the mainstay of early conversation.[15] Twenty years later Elton would underplay the role of wit, and stress the unique contributions an individual could make to a conversation.

In the spring of 1909 Elton wrote a poem for a competition among members of the Pickwick Club.[16] "Addressed to Incog(nito)" and intended to be "serious if possible," it was about a "Fair idyll of my dreams—far away." This is the only evidence that illuminates a family story that Elton admired a beautiful wealthy young woman in vice-regal circles in Sydney. He was advised against proposing marriage because of the wide gap between their social positions.[17] Echoes of "Dainty Patricia." Probably he would have ignored the advice had he been ready to marry, because a similar objection would be raised to his engagement some years hence. The poem showed that Elton had a romantic image of love and a serious interest in an ideal woman; later, he would combine them with a religious conviction in the decision to marry.

In 1910 Elton continued studies in French and philosophy. The French course was difficult, for again no lectures were available, and this time students were expected to answer all examination questions in French. He achieved a low pass.[18] In the honors course in philosophy under Mitchell's supervision, Elton read Kant and completed a thesis, "The Criteria of Social Progress."

Elton and Mitchell were coming closer. Elton joined the committee of Mitchell's Arts Association.[19] In September he relinquished his business partnership.[20] During the year he learned to shed the role of a respectful student who addressed his teacher as "Sir" and to adopt, uneasily, a collegial relation with "Mitchell."[21] In November, Mitchell recommended Elton's thesis for the David Murray Scholarship, a prize for meritorious scholarship. In April 1911, at a special congregation, Elton was awarded an Honours Degree, Bachelor of Arts in Philosophy.[22]

Meanwhile the Senate of the newly established University of Queensland had invited applications for a foundation lectureship in logic, psychology, and ethics. Elton applied, and within a fortnight, Mitchell sent a note saying: "Mr. Mayo . . . was my best student . . . during the fifteen years I have held this chair." Drawing attention to Elton's "facility and clearness," Mitchell asserted that he "would be an excellent teacher and would do much to promote philosophical studies outside the University as well as in it."[23]

Elton Mayo took up his first academic position in Brisbane, Queensland, in April 1911.

Notes

1. Helen Mayo, "Biographical Notes on Elton Mayo," SAA; *South Australian Directory, 1905-1912* (Adelaide, Sands & McDougall).
2. Helen Mayo, "Biographical Notes on Elton Mayo."
3. Elton Mayo's large notebooks, pp. 90-91, BLA. Dates are not certain; all quotations are taken from these pages.
4. Sir Herbert Mayo's Notebooks 579.
5. W.G.K. Duncan and R. A. Leonard, *The University of Adelaide, 1874-1974* (Adelaide: Rigby, 1974), pp. 19-20, 77-81.
6. William Kyle, "Elton Mayo," ANZAAS Conference, 29 May 1951, SAA.
7. University of Adelaide, *Calendar,* 1908; Student Records, Registrar's Office, University of Adelaide.
8. Helen Mayo, "Biolographical Notes on Elton Mayo"; University of Adelaide, *Calendar,* 1909.
9. *Working Men's College Journal* 10 (October 1907):181; ibid., 11 (October 1909):224; J.F.C. Harrison, *A History of Working Men's College, 1854-1954* (London: Routledge & Kegan Paul, 1954), p. 153; Elton to Dorothea, 2 November 1921; Sir Charles Lucas, *Notes on a Visit to Australia, New Zealand, and Fiji, in 1909* (London: H.M.S.O., 1910).
10. Elton Mayo's small notebooks, No. 2, GA 54.4, BLA.
11. Ibid.
12. University of Adelaide, *Calendar,* 1909.
13. The origins and aims of the Pickwick Club are uncertain. What follows is a reconstruction of lecture notes from Elton Mayo's small notebooks, particularly Nos. 6, 13, 14, GA 54.4, BLA. All quotations are from these notes.
14. Margaret B. Horan, "A Goodly Heritage: An Appreciation of the Life and Work of the Late Dr. Helen Mayo," *Medical Journal of Australia,* 20 February 1971, pp. 419-24.
15. Elton Mayo's small notebooks, No. 6, GA 54.4, BLA.
16. Ibid.
17. Conversations with Lady Mayo and Mrs. Wigg, May 1974, and Patricia Elton Mayo, November 1975.
18. Student Records, Registrar's Office, University of Adelaide.
19. University of Adelaide, *Calendar,* 1911.
20. Sir Herbert Mayo's Notebooks 819.
21. Mayo to James, 23 July 1945, MM 1.049.
22. Sir Herbert Mayo's Notebooks, 819, 833, 925.
23. Mitchell to University of Queensland, 13 March 1911, SAA.

4

Early Years in Queensland, 1911-1913

The University of Queensland occupied Queensland's Government House beside the botanical gardens of the state capital, Brisbane. Mayo lived at Montpelier, a three-story private hotel in Brisbane's Wickham Terrace, a twenty-minute walk from the university.[1] Queensland residents who had traveled believed Montpelier to be the best hotel in eastern Australia, better than Sydney's Wentworth and The Windsor in Melbourne. Its refined atmosphere was maintained by two gentle theosophists, Mrs. John Forsyth and Miss Marcella Clark. Afternoon tea was served by waiters in brown linen uniforms, and at dinner the guests wore formal attire and intelligent conversation was the rule. Montpelier was Mayo's home during his early years in Brisbane.

Mayo thought that his experience in London had taught him to cope without the family, but he felt a sense of loss for more than a year.[2] When Herbert decided to marry that May, Mayo recalled their happy boyhood—excursions, blasting grandfather's ducks—but this brought with it the painful realization of his own shortcomings. He knew that his world centered on the Mayo family, and that his greatest pleasure was to serve its interests before his own.[3] Since 1905 the family had given him security, direction, and self-esteem, but the great distance between Adelaide and Brisbane cut the flow of affection he needed to overcome emptiness and doubt.

Work was Mayo's antidote for loneliness. He was an early appointment to the Faculty of Arts, which directed the teaching of the classics, modern languages and literature, mathematics, and, in his charge, moral and mental philosophy.[4] Because of his publishing experience he was chosen to edit the *Official Report of the Inaugural Ceremony of the University of Queensland.*[5] He was appointed to the Board of Examiners, which controlled entry to the new university and to junior posts in government agencies. Mayo examined the candidates' English papers for competence in language, grammar, composition, and knowledge of Shakespeare, and nineteenth-century poets and novelists.[6]

Early in 1912 a young economist, E.O.G. Shann, who shared Mayo's study, accepted a professorship in West Australia, and teaching economics became Mayo's responsibility, together with logic, ethics, metaphysics, and psychology.[7] Also, he had plans to develop a new course in education, so a lectureship was advertised. No suitable candidate was found, but the position was kept open and his work load remained heavy.[8]

Mayo's courses covered a wide range. In systematic economics he considered problems in defining the market, in changing money supply, applying Gresham's Law, and the connection between wealth, credit, and the banker's role; he lectured on Malthus's theory of population, protective tariffs, and the economic effect of Wages Boards in Australia. His two courses in logic examined the validity of deduction, scientific classification, the truth of syllogisms, causality, Mill's methods, and the psychology of using hypotheses. In his two courses on psychology, Mayo lectured on associationism, Locke, Hume, and the meaning of sensation, reality, belief, will, perception, explanation through experience, the Weber-Fechner Law, Kant, Mitchell on thinking, Bosanquet on consciousness, McDougall and James on emotion, Sherrington's experiments, and the place of psychology in epistemological studies. In ethics and metaphysics, he introduced students to the ideas of Socrates, Aristotle, Spinoza, Rousseau, and Descartes, and their critics Royce, Seth, and Bosanquet; topics included hedonism, idealism, empiricism, sophistry, institutions, habits, emotions.[9]

In March 1913 an assistant lecturer was found for Mayo, but John F. Adams then refused the position because the annual salary was only £300 for five years, and outside employment was forbidden. Mayo had to shelve again plans for a course in education, and begin another search for an assistant. The salary was raised £50 to attract more applicants; meanwhile a law graduate, Mr. K. ffoulkes Swanwick accepted the post of temporary lecturer.[10]

Mayo was interested in adult education outside the university. In April 1913 the university learned that Albert Mansbridge, secretary of the Worker's Educational Association (WEA) in Britain, was visiting Australia. Through its affiliation with the Working Men's College Mayo had become familiar with the association and was keen to have Mansbridge visit Brisbane and explain its aims to the University Senate. Within the university this proposal was resisted; the Board of Faculties thought the WEA was suited only to large population centers like Sydney and Melbourne, so the university could hardly benefit from Mansbridge's visit to Brisbane. But Mayo had his way. After the visit of Mansbridge in August, the University Senate received an application for tutorial assistance in economics and economic history, and Mayo undertook the tutorial duties for that year.[11]

Mayo accepted more tasks. Inside the university he became a member of the Faculty of Science as well as Arts, and outside he agreed to examine candidates at the Military College.[12] Mayo enjoyed participating in the student life and addressing groups outside the university. In 1912 he delivered "Criticism" and the "Inadequacy of Pragmatism" before the Student Christian Union; at the Australian Church Congress in Brisbane he lectured on the philosophical attitude to religion.[13] To enlighten new students at the university, and to answer its outside critics, Mayo published a brief paper rejecting the commonsense goals—vocational training, practical knowledge, democratic attitudes—and arguing that a university should develop in people the capacity for independent thought and investigation rather than simply instruct them in the rules and methods of well-established specialties.[14]

Australia's dentists were at that time trying to gain professional status, and one deplorable practice that stood in their way was the advertising of painless extractions. Invited to speak to Queensland's Odontological Society on professional ethics, Mayo began by saying that whenever "he had opened his mouth . . . before a member of the dental profession, he had immediately had a gag put in it."[15] Much laughter indicated that he had their attention, and he launched into the reasons that tradesmen advertise and that professionals do not. Their assured income meant that the community's welfare benefited from their practicing a special skill. He encouraged the audience to continue to raise the requirements for entry to the profession, to pursue research, and to organize themselves for their own and the community's welfare. Loud applause and praise followed, and hopes were kindled that the university would establish a school of dentistry.

Through strenuous work, public speaking, and publications, Mayo was advancing his academic career. Spurring his ambition were his earlier luckless ventures and his disappointed family. He loathed himself for failure, and, in an effort to banish it turned his hostility toward the medical profession. In published papers and debates Mayo remarked on the language, origins, professional status, community service, and intellect of doctors. He implied that only an uncritical mind would be satisfied to explain the cause of death with the term "syncope," a pathologist's word for heart failure.[16] He belittled doctors when he used them to show how a simple calling that had once apprenticed its young had become complex by using universities for the purpose of professionalization.[17] He accused doctors of operating a beneficent monopoly and making it difficult to be admitted to their ranks.[18] At the University Union, Mayo joined the affirmative side in a debate: "That the services of the Medical Profession be Nationalised." When the debate was over and before the motion was put, Dr. Hirschfeld of the University Senate and Sir David Hardie spoke against the motion. Mayo replied so well that the president of the union suggested that a vote not be taken on the motion;[19] no doubt the result would have embarrassed the respected spokesmen of medicine. A year later, Mayo's contempt for muddled thinking among the profession appeared in his evaluation of Mercier's *A New Logic*: "Perhaps this is why Dr. Mercier, founding his notions of reasoning on the practice of medicine, is so little able to understand the significance and utility of logic."[20] With few exceptions, Mayo's hostility toward doctors was restrained, intellectualized, and placed in a context of wit and good humor.

Among students Mayo's reputation was enhanced in 1912 when he gave much energy to the production of Sheridan's *St. Patrick's Day* by the dramatic society. He and E.O.G. Shann coached the actors, but the press reviewed their efforts so unkindly that Mayo wrote his own account: the audience had been pleased; some players had performed difficult characters with success; giggling and forgetting lines had been caused by nervousness; and the rehearsal had been better than the final public performance.[21]

A year later Mayo helped with the production of T.W. Robertson's *School,* a frothy comedy first produced in London in 1869. It was an excellent choice for young amateurs because it is set in a women's college and demands little of the actors. The plot is based on the Cinderella fairy tale and includes lost identity, romantic love, misconstrued motives, elopement, and reunited love. Again Mayo wrote the criticism, a witty catalogue of excuses and reasons for a theatrical disaster. Nevertheless, one actor portrayed villainy so well that in the audience three clergymen had hooted, and, Mayo quipped: "Not everyone can make an archdeacon hoot."[22] Both of Mayo's critiques are encouraging and constructive.

Religion had a central place in Mayo's work, his personal life, and his view of society. In "The Philosophical Attitude to Religion," he remarked that philosophy makes easy questions difficult. Why? Because philosophy aims for truth, not by using vague labels to explain it away but through constructive, impartial criticism. Mayo illustrated the philosophical approach by outlining weaknesses in Laplace's mechanical theory of the universe and in Tyndall's attack on the efficacy of prayer. He concluded that only psychology, history, and sociology—certainly not the physical sciences—can help us understand human values and society. Religion is the vital means for teaching values of civilized life to each generation; religious values and customs are based on precedent, not on rationality, and, for this reason, seem inconsistent and unclear at times. The church must be conservative and careful about attacks on religious doctrine, especially those from scientists whose own doctrines are no less inconsistent than the dogma of Christ. Religious doctrines are valuable working hypotheses created from the facts of experience; one such important fact is that "warmth and intimacy of a personal affection is necessary for the highest form of religious emotion, and through it necessary also to the continued well being and progress of society."[23]

Before the Student Christian Union Mayo emphasized the stabilizing effect of religious institutions, and their support in helping young people learn the customs and practices of community life. He also advocated continuous reform—not revolution—of religious practices to improve community life. Religion could aid individuals by helping them to cope with their problems. This is particularly so when sins are forgiven and cares plucked out, when personal isolation is banished, and a sense of community and fellow-feeling encouraged. Mayo believed that religious con-

version could change a self-seeker into an altruistic citizen, thereby bene-
fitting society. But, when taken to extremes, religious services can produce
saints and mystics; saints never escape the conviction of sin, and mystics
always embrace impractical activities. Thus, the shortcoming of religious
practice is that, although it can show people a better way, it cannot make
them desire it. "When man has developed to the extent of finding his
deepest or truest or most complex emotion in personal affection, then his
religious emotion—as the highest of all—demands an object for which he
can feel personal affection."[24] Late in 1912, the desire in Elton Mayo found
its object in Dorothea McConnel.

Dorothea McConnel came from one of Queensland's most respected
and prominent families. Her grandfather, David Cannon McConnel
(1818-1885) of Manchester, had studied natural science at Edinburgh University, and in 1840 sailed to New South Wales. A private income enabled
him to travel with pioneers to various pastoral districts, there to select and
stock land. In 1840 he acquired land on the Brisbane River at Cressbrook,
becoming the first settler between the coast and the Darling range. He
imported purebred shorthorns and established a prize-winning herd. In
1848 he married Mary McLeod in Edinburgh, brought her to Brisbane,
and built for her "Bulimba," the first stone house in the town. On his 220-
acre farm he experimented with the cultivation of many varieties of grains,
and milked fifty head of purebred cows. He helped found Brisbane's Presbyterian Church, was one of the first local directors of the great Bank of
New South Wales. Research in the natural sciences fascinated him, and he
sent ornithological and geological specimens, meteoric stones, and shells to
the Manchester museum. On the last of many visits to England, he died
suddenly after an operation, and his valuable collection of land and sea-
shells went to the Brisbane museum.

In 1850 a son, James Henry McConnel had been born. Like the other
seven children, James was raised at Cressbrook. He was educated at Edinburgh Academy and Cambridge. In 1869 he took over the management of
Cressbrook. He pioneered the consignment of frozen meat to London, and
promoted the development of Queensland's railways. In 1876 he married
Mary Elizabeth Kent of Queensland, and on August 30, 1877, the first of
six daughters, Dorothea, was born.[25]

Dorothea was raised at Cressbrook. She was an energetic child who
pursued her interests with a sense of adventure. She learned to ride well
and would mount wild horses bareback. To many people she seemed dash-
ing and graceful. In her adolescence she gave the appearance of a natural
aristocrat: beautiful, sensitive, loyal, and always considerate. But family life
was not always happy.

Mary McConnel bore seven children in eleven years, so Dorothea had
little opportunity in her early life to develop a close affectionate bond with
her mother. Many family chores fell to Dorothea, and often she had to play

hostess for her father. When she was twelve, while her parents were away, Dorothea had the terrifying task of organizing life at the homestead during so great a flood that carcasses of cattle floated into the house.

Dorothea was educated at home and later at local schools. When she was seventeen, her mother bore the first of two more children, and, consequently, Dorothea's duties at home expanded. Mary McConnel scolded and dominated her easygoing husband, maintained a rigidly straitlaced attitude toward her children's development, and encouraged her daughters to believe that their duty was to the home and the ways of the church. She seemed convinced that a high-spirited and attractive young woman like Dorothea could easily fall into sin unless tight constraints were placed on her life. Mary punished her, maltreated her with puritanical vigor, heaped duties on her, and, more than once, insisted that she was ugly and plain. Mary McConnel was a victim of her own sincere conviction of sin, a conviction that Mayo would regard later as a hallmark of the McConnel girls' upbringing.

Heavy responsibilities at home, a wretched relationship with her mother, a distant and ineffectual but respected father, and incessant demands from a growing band of sisters and brothers affected the development of Dorothea's social character. Under these conditions she could become highly strung and sometimes neurotic, and her high intelligence and fluency would emerge as intellectual snobbery. She dreamed of escaping her enforced round of duties and fleeing to Europe to the civilized life and unconventional people she idealized.[26]

The McConnels often visited relatives in England and Scotland, and at the turn of the century Dorothea was given her first chance to travel. Between 1900 and 1912, she frequently visited Europe, and, at least once, crossed the United States.[27] By 1909 her French was fluent enough that she completed a postgraduate degree in art history at the Sorbonne, with a thesis on landscape art. She learned sufficient German and Russian to be an interpreter and guide for relatives and friends. In 1912 Dorothea returned home, a mature, civilized woman who had enjoyed the company of admirers in Europe, but who had been induced to believe that she ought to accept her mother's dictum to become a teacher in Queensland.[28]

In November, Dorothea's sister Barbara invited two bachelors from the university to call at Cressbrook. No doubt they had been drawn to Barbara's attention when she had stayed, as the McConnels usually did, at Montpelier. Professor John Michie, the young classicist, and his friend Elton Mayo arrived by carriage. At his first sight of Dorothea, Mayo was moved: "I said to myself—'Well you have been an ass.'" He fell in love.[29] Her hair shone like gold; she was a woman of ideal and incredible beauty. "All my wise resolutions not to think of marriage until the future was achieved and certain, all my doubts as to the possible congruency of marriage and work—these considerations that had ruled my whole life with a rod of iron went by the board and were as though they had never been." But his heart fell when he saw a sapphire ring on her finger. He asked himself: "Was she already engaged?"[30] It turned out that she was not. Within three weeks they were engaged.

Why had Mayo not married before he met Dorothea McConnel? Two conventional replies appear in his letters to her: first, he had resolved not to think of marriage until he had an established career; second, he had always found women were "mentally ineffective and distinctly amusing—even though I loved all the dear creatures."[31] One night these reasons gave way when he was talking with a forty-three-year-old, wealthy, lonely, and world-weary bachelor friend who was trying to persuade himself to propose marriage to a nice woman for whom he felt no real enthusiasm. The poor fellow was being led to marriage simply to have some interest in life. In Adelaide Mayo had been tempted to this path but found always that he could not continue for fear of having to live forevermore with someone who would not understand his work, his ideas, his eagerness for self-development, or who would regard him as a freak.[32] Dorothea was quite different. At their first conversation Mayo spoke about his plans so strongly that her eyes filled with tears; he saw her concern for his work, and what it would mean for other people.[33] After snatching a few hasty, insufficient meetings together, they decided to marry as soon as possible.[34]

Impediments to the marriage took one major form: Mayo could not support Dorothea as the McConnels had done. For this reason, a close friend advised him to postpone the event. But they had agreed that poverty would help them to become free.[35] Yet Montpelier would be expensive. Was he being selfish in taking Dorothea from her environment, and forcing the McConnels and their friends to see her having to economize? He could hardly afford even to have people to stay with them after their marriage.[36] But he believed poverty was the price when people bid for both a career and happiness.[37] Even so, toward the end of March 1913, Mayo was still asking himself how he could have had the temerity to propose marriage on the income of a university lecturer. He considered going into business, but since businessmen did not value thinking, and thinking was what he did best, it seemed to be an unreal alternative. Writing fiction might pay. This was another obsession that, like his constant worry about being short of money, would command his attention whenever he felt lonely, tired, and indecisive.[38]

Doubt about his self-worth, indecisiveness, and feelings of loneliness were Mayo's symptoms of melancholy. If he was tired as well, he would treat the disorder by isolating himself and using an oriental technique for maintaining silence; if he was not tired, he would "musate," a relaxing form of meditation he had learned from reading the work of Charles S. Peirce, the American philosopher. Years later he would recognize his symptoms of melancholy in Pierre Janet's theory of psychopathological obsession.

He described his method of coping with melancholy in a letter to Dorothea: "For when I get that far it is better either to work, or retire to realms that are not of this world. And in these excursions you always come with me, now. . . ."[39] In those realms Dorothea became Mayo's ideal woman; she was his gracious queen, mature, straightforward, charitable, and gifted. In her he found all the heroines of fiction, all comedy and tragedy, all the music of the world. She was his universe.

Mayo wrote to Dorothea about a strange incident that had occurred on his fourteenth birthday. He was on holidays with some school fellows at Port Elliott. They were looking into a shop window when an old woman stopped and asked him for his name. He had felt embarrassed, but was courteous enough to answer her. She wrote down his name, and said, "I shall expect to hear of you in twenty years." Mayo believed she must have foreseen his long sleep, and that Dorothea had been chosen to be "the one woman in the world who could, and did, rouse me from my slumbers."[40]

Before Dorothea met Mayo, he had seen himself as gentle, pessimistic ascetic, self-contained and self-determining.[41] After their first meeting he felt reborn, revitalized, a new man cast in a condition of sustained gladness. He believed she had taught him more about himself than anyone before her, and he wanted to continue his development with her help.[42] In return he offered her his mature understanding of theories, people, the everyday world, spiritual values, freedom, aesthetic experience, and art, and his sympathetic ear for fearless discussion.[43]

Dorothea had doubts too. She could remember reading that on entering marriage individuals should keep part of themselves in reserve. This was a variation on the proverb "Familiarity breeds contempt," and played on normal childlike fears of trust and intimacy between adults. Mayo saw no wisdom in deliberately making a mystery out of oneself; people who did were not cultivating a "secret orchard" but trying to hide a barren mental hinterland.[44] Dorothea had been led to think that keeping something in reserve could help prevent a marriage from becoming stale. Mayo's answer was that only an average marriage—a "species of civil contract" blessed by the church, and fit only for the unthinking—required its partners to follow the convention of keeping something in reserve. He would rather cut his throat than enter an average marriage; his marriage would be a special relationship between intelligent people who worked together with vigor, communicated without fear, and were free to discuss and doubt each other's ideas. "The idea that either of us under these conditions (if we honestly work on) could exhaust the interest of the other is psychologically absurd and profoundly silly."[45]

Psychological criteria were applied to Dorothea's second doubt. She was in love, and, feeling uncertain of herself, she wrote asking him never to let her go. Her plea went deep, and Mayo replied with "the truest letter I have ever written." Dim race-memories came to him; he was a cave-dweller, an ugly troglodyte with a somber face, gazing across a dangerous world, and behind him in the cave Dorothea was sleeping. Time passed, and in a matriarchal clan, ruled by her, he helped with future plans and institutions. Later still he deserted her and became a priest. Five thousand years passed, during which she suffered and became uncertain of herself. Now they are to be united, and will be so for the next thousand years. Together they will go where the big battalions are, and, with a clearer vision than that which clouds today's so-called democracies, they will take charge again, guide and direct in rational ways the force that life has entrusted to them.[46]

Mayo believed that race-memories helped to explain human development. They included early original sensations and instinctive activities, and gave the foundation for higher and more complex stages of personal growth. He felt that philosophers were well equipped to understand this because they had a broad view of life, and could clearly, serenely, and without prejudice or interference from material values, see the divine spark, the vision, the way to beauty, humor, and the proper conditions of civilized life. He tried not to overestimate his own ability, but instead to argue for those who he believed knew where civilized man ought to go. And Mayo wanted Dorothea to join him on the journey through the great universal order that was life.

A vision of life was important to Mayo. He did not want to be immersed in practical detail as were businessmen in sordid commerce. He did not want to lose a vision of life and thereby lose his soul, become afraid, and fall prey to doubts and melancholy. Religion had helped him, but he rejected intellectualized religion because it lost God and combined a materialistic, suburban, and banal existence with the futile and agonizing wait for a new religion. Instead, he developed a vision of high human attainment and drew personal comfort from a psychological understanding of religious experience. He wanted Dorothea to share this understanding with him.

Because Mayo was in love, he believed that he and Dorothea made a unique couple to whom normal conventions could never apply. He did not care two straws for what people said and thought. He and Dorothea were among the few who had vision, and who had the work of the world to do. They did not have to conform to things that "a mere idle 'toshing' Bohemian could never understand."[47]

So the predictable doubts that arose from Elton's decision to marry were immersed in solitary musation, and, there, transformed into romantic, absolute certainties about Dorothea, his career, and the golden years to come. The usual warm congratulations flowed in after the announcement of the forthcoming marriage, but so did a few predictable disencouragements. One jealous friend suggested Mayo and his bride were entering a financial and social disaster. Another exclaimed, "But you don't know her!"[48] John Michie, Mayo's bachelor-friend, who was the handsome, shy,

idol of young ladies in the classics lectures, expressed a charming ambivalence. He said the worst of it was that he would have to change his
views on marriage, but to show deference to the institution, as well as a
warm regard for Mayo, he offered his rooms for a party at which selected
university staff might pay their respects to Dorothea and take tea with her
attractive sisters.[49] On April 18 the marriage was celebrated by the archbishop of Brisbane, the honeymoon was spent on the sands of Coolangatta,
and the Elton Mayos returned to live at Montpelier.

Within three years Mayo had founded an academic career, married a
beautiful and intelligent daughter from one of Queensland's prominent
families, and developed a good following outside the university. Gone were
the grounds for scorn from his Adelaide critics; Mayo had become respectable. In October 1913, he wrote to the factor of the Otago Presbyterian
Church Board of Property, Dunedin, New Zealand, and requested application forms for the chair of mental and moral philosophy.[50]

Testimonials in support of Mayo's application came from seven men.[51]
First, Mitchell testified that since 1911 Mayo had "proved his capacity as a
teacher and public lecturer," and that if he got the chair he could specialize
more than was possible in the University of Queensland. Second, the Most
Reverend St. Clair Donaldson, archbishop of Brisbane, declared Mayo to
be a "man of exceptional power—a man of the world," an inspiring, attractive, impressive teacher. Third, the governor of Queensland, Sir William
Macgregor, added that Mayo had given loyal service to the university and
had earned the esteem of his colleagues. Fourth, Michie told how Mayo
had built the Philosophy Department, given loyal support to other valuable
academic endeavors, and gained the confidence of students; also, Michie
valued his alertness, independence, decisiveness, capacity for command,
ability to hold an audience without popularizing, and his sane outlook.
Fifth, Professor Bertram Steele praised Mayo's gift of lucid exposition,
charm, high character, and ideas. Sixth, Lewis Radford, once a Cambridge
fellow and now warden of St. Paul's College at the University of Sydney,
stated that Mayo's thinking was clear, his language careful, and his presentations simple and fluent. The under secretary for public instruction was
fully supportive, too. In spite of the testimonials and a sumptuously
printed application, Mayo was overshadowed by Francis W. Dunlop.[52]
Nonetheless. Mayo began 1914 as a success; his salary was raised to £440,
he had an assistant,[53] and he knew that his colleagues and people in high
places respected him.

Notes

1. Elton to Dorothea, 16 March 1921.
2. Elton to Dorothea, January 1923.
3. Elton to Herbert, 11 May 1911.

4. Minutes, Faculty of Arts, University of Queensland, 20 April, 22 November 1911.
5. Mayo papers, SAA.
6. Minutes, Senate, University of Queensland, 13 September 1911; University of Queensland, *Manual of Public Examinations, 1910-1912,* pp. 20, 42, 131, 145.
7. Minutes, Faculty of Arts, 20 September 1912; Minutes, Senate, 16 October 1912; Minutes, Board of Faculties, 31 October 1912; Minutes, Senate, Schedule 11, 11 September 1912, University of Queensland.
8. Minutes, Faculty of Arts, 26 April 1912; "Seventh Report of the Education Committee," 12 October 1912; Minutes, Board of Faculties, 25 November 1912, University of Queensland.
9. University of Queensland, *Calendar,* 1914, pp. 304-10.
10. Minutes, Senate, University of Queensland, 14 May, 11 June, 9 July 1913.
11. Minutes, Senate, University of Queensland, 9 April, 14 May, 20 August 1913; University of Queensland, *Calendar,* 1922.
12. Minutes, Board of Faculties, University of Queensland, 29 July 1913.
13. Elton Mayo, "The Philosophical Attitude to Religion," *Official Report of the Australian Church Congress* 8 (1913):69-74.
14. Elton Mayo, "The University and the State," *University of Queensland Magazine* 1 (May 1913): 148-49.
15. Elton Mayo, "Professional Ethics," *Australian Journal of Dentistry,* September 30, 1913, pp. 264-67.
16. Mayo, "Philosophical Attitude to Religion," p. 69.
17. Mayo, "University and the State," p. 148.
18. Mayo, "Professional Ethics," p. 266.
19. *University of Queensland Magazine* 1 (August 1913): 184. A month later Mayo was elected chairman of the University Union after another interesting debate. Ibid., 2 (October 1913): 19.
20. Elton Mayo,"The Limits of Logical Validity," *Mind* 24 (1915): 70-74.
21. *University of Queensland Magazine* 1 (August 1912): 107; ibid., 1 (October 1912): 139-40.
22. Ibid., 2 (October 1913): 9; Elton to Dorothea, 2 April 1913.
23. Mayo, "Philosophical Attitude to Religion."
24. Elton Mayo, "The Function of Religious Services," special lecture to the Presbyterian Men's Society, Brisbane, SAA. No final draft is available; this paragraph is based on notes about the topic in Mayo's notebook, No. 7, GA 54.4, BLA. The date is uncertain; probably 1912.
25. E.W.J. McConnel, *James McConnel of Carsiggan, his Forebears and Descendants* (privately printed, 1931); Mary McConnel, *Queensland Reminiscences and Memories of Days Long Gone By* (privately printed, n.d.); Mary M. Banks, *Memories of Pioneer Days in Queensland* (London: Heath. Cranton, 1930?).
26. Conversations with Gael Elton Mayo, 12 February, 7 August 1975; and Patricia Elton Mayo, 6 February 1975.
27. Elton to Dorothea, 27 September 1922.
28. See note 26 above.
29. Elton to Dorothea, 12 March 1913.
30. Ibid.
31. Ibid.
32. Elton to Dorothea, 27 March 1913.
33. Elton to Dorothea, 3 April 1913.
34. Elton to Dorothea, 12 March 1913.
35. Elton to Dorothea, 7 March 1913.
36. Elton to Dorothea, 13, 28 March 1913.

37. Elton to Dorothea, 13 March 1913
38. Elton to Dorothea, 26 March, 2 April 1913.
39. Elton to Dorothea, 13 March 1913.
40. Elton to Dorothea, 28, 29 March 1913.
41. Elton to Dorothea 12, 13 March 1913.
42. Elton to Dorothea, 24, 28, 29 March 1913.
43. Elton to Dorothea, 7, 12, 13 March 1913.
44. Elton to Dorothea, 29 March 1913.
45. Elton to Dorothea, 2 April 1913.
46. Elton to Dorothea, 16, 27 March 1913.
47. Elton to Dorothea, February, 13 March 1913.
48. Elton to Dorothea, 24 March 1913.
49. Ibid.
50. McDonald to Trahair, 2 October 1974.
51. Mayo papers, SAA. The paragraph is based on letters and testimonials in Elton Mayo's application.
52. McDonald to Trahair, 2 October 1974.
53. Minutes, Senate, University of Queensland, 12 November 1913.

5

Career, Family, and Friends, 1914-1919

From 1914 to 1918 Mayo was lecturer in charge of the Department of Philosophy in the Faculty of Arts. He taught psychology, ethics, metaphysics, and, until March 1916, systematic economics.[1] Percy A. Seymour, an Oxford graduate, was appointed assistant lecturer early in 1914; he taught education and logic, and assisted Mayo in teaching the honors course in philosophy.[2] Seymour's first year was not entirely happy; in September he talked with Mayo about resigning,[3] but the war froze such plans. In early 1918 the University of Western Australia offered him a full lectureship.[4]

Early in 1918 Mayo, too, was dissatisfied with his career. University ideals did not enthuse him as once they had, and he was beginning to believe that he had made no progress in the academic community. He thought of turning to law,[5] a fantasy that gave Mayo hope whenever academic life went stale but had insufficient substance to initiate a change of career.

Mayo and Seymour were not the only lecturers to feel discontented. The question of salaries and status had been raised a year earlier in a proposal put before the University Senate to reorganize the entire university. From Mayo's viewpoint the greatest change would have been the establishment of an associate professorship and a lecturership in the Department of Philosophy and Education. The Senate approved the scheme pending an increase in government funds, which did not come about. A deputation from the staff was received by the Senate, but all it could do was to regard the deputation with sympathy.[6] By the summer of 1918 Mayo had become uninterested in the cause.

When he returned from vacation, his colleagues again put to him the question of salaries and status. In his role as senior among the lecturing staff, Mayo induced them to send a letter to the University Senate asking that it regard as urgent the question of salaries. He also persuaded his friend Michie to demand that the Senate ask the Queensland government to raise the university's endowment from fifteen to twenty thousand pounds to extend the scope of the arts faculty and raise the salaries of lecturers. The time was right because the government was to face the electorate in March. Mayo planned to have a deputation of workingmen re-

73

quest the government to support plans to extend teaching to include sociological studies.[7] In the light of these moves, Seymour decided to stay
rather than accept the offer from Western Australia.

While planning possible developments for the university after the election, Mayo hoped "most fervently that this may be the last year at Brisbane."[8] He believed that he was not achieving success commensurate with
his maturity. And when he heard of Seymour's decision, and the rumor that
a friend in Sydney had declined a professorship in Adelaide, Mayo wished
that someone would offer him something. "Even Sydney [University], I
think, would make me young again."[9]

The University of Queensland responded quickly to the demands of its
staff. The Select Committee in University Organization and Expansion was
established, made inquiries, and at the end of 1918 recommended that four
new chairs be established and the professor's salaries be raised.[10] Mayo was
promoted to professor of philosophy, and Seymour was made a full lecturer. Seymour was satisfied with his increased status and salary, and
pleased with Mayo's advancement because the Philosophy Department had
been given the only new chair in the Arts Faculty, which meant that in
university councils the department had proved itself over the Department
of History and Modern Languages, and would be represented in the newly
established Professorial Board.[11] Seymour's satisfaction with the university
would not last long.

When Mayo had come to the university it was understood that academic
staff would work toward raising intellectual standards throughout Queensland and not simply limit their teaching to Brisbane. Early in 1913 the
Senate had formed a committee to administer the policy; correspondence
studies were developed and lecturers visited inland towns. War curtailed
this work until 1919, when education in the common problems of a changing world became widely discussed. The university appointed a committee
to sponsor lectures in a central hall in Brisbane, and with the cooperation
of the Chamber of Commerce a series of addresses were given to businessmen. Further, it was announced that any university course might be attended by the public for a prescribed fee; special intramural courses were
offered, as well as courses in inland towns. From the beginning of his career
at the university Mayo supported these activities as an administrator and
public lecturer.[12]

Mayo was also at the center of efforts to educate people who were not
eligible to enter the university and who had not enjoyed the advantages of
an advanced education. In 1913 he had undertaken to serve in tutorial
classes for the new branch of the Workers' Educational Association (WEA)
in Brisbane, and was joined by his colleagues. Interest in the program grew,
and by early 1916 more lecturing staff were needed. The University Senate
formed a joint committee of four university staff and four WEA members
to organize the classes. Mayo was always a member of the committees that

promoted education among members of the WEA, and often held classes himself.[13]

Mayo's psychology students had to appreciate Locke's contribution to the history of psychological theory and some of the errors in his work; to distinguish among sensation, memory, understanding, learning, instinct, attention, and apperception, to show some grasp of James's "self"; to relate the appeal of art to race-memory; and to be familiar with the connection between mental processes and the physiology of the nervous system. In their second year, students of psychology were acquainted with James's "stream of consciousness" as a theory of mental activity, and Mayo's criticism of that theory from his doctrine of the "total situation." Personal identity, dreams, original thinking, and the process of the education were discussed as well as the status of psychology as a science.[14]

Students of ethics concentrated on the meaning of nature, consciousness, the effect of intellect on morality, psychology and the theory of mind, idealism, self-denial and temperance, hedonism, natural and normative science, social evolution, free-will, utilitarianism, and justice.[15] Metaphysics dealt with how recent developments in psychological theory affected idealistic philosophy; problems in sensationism, and the doctrine of the self; and causation, knowledge, and reality.[16]

Between 1914 and 1915 Mayo taught psychology in two parts. In the first, students were directed to Mitchell's work on the mind, Huxley's *Elementary Physiology,* and Meyers's *Experimental Psychology.* In the second part, Mitchell's work was supplemented with McDougall's *Physiological Psychology.* In his courses on ethics and metaphysics Mayo used the texts by Green, Sidgwick, Bosanquet, Dewey, and Tufts. In later years he also used Stout's *Manual of Psychology.* Mayo's psychology courses changed little until 1918, when he became interested in teaching how irrational and extralogical factors affected thinking. In 1920 students in the second part of his psychology course were referred to Jung's *Analytic Psychology;* and in 1921 Elton began to use Tansley's psychoanalytic text, *The New Psychology.*[17]

Until 1916 Elton was also responsible for teaching systematic economics; he used Marshall's *Economics of Industry,* Hobson's *The Industrial System,* Barker's *Cash and Credit,* and Sykes's *Banking and Currency.* Students were expected to understand how the law of supply and demand determined prices; to discuss the relation between rent and price for retail services, manufactured and agricultural products; to outline differences between nominal and real capital, gross and net interest; to know how currency in banking theory regulated note issues; to grasp the impact of changes in gold supply; to evaluate the effect of monopolies; to study changes in working conditions; to discuss single-tax theories and the doctrines of Marx, Rousseau, and Ricardo.[18]

In the morning students in the Faculty of Arts attended hourly lectures between nine and one; afternoons were free; and evening lectures began at seven and finished at ten. In 1914 and 1915 Mayo's teaching load was heavy, but after 1916 it eased. On a Monday morning, he lectured on psychology for two hours and a further hour at night; on Tuesday morning he met his ethics class for an hour; Wednesday evening he taught more psychology for an hour; Thursday he began and finished the day with classes in systematic economics as well as two evening classes in psychology from seven to nine; Friday morning he taught two more hours of psychology. Between 1916 and 1918 he had two lectures on Monday, one on Tuesdays, three on Wednesdays, and one on Thursdays and Fridays. In 1919, after the University had been reorganized, Mayo no longer taught logic in the Faculty of Science—a task he had undertaken years before—and his teaching load dropped to one lecture each day except Friday.

Mayo was a memorable lecturer. Before lectures began twenty to thirty students in black gowns gathered outside the classroom. On the hour they entered the room; young gentlemen stood aside for young women, who took seats in the first row. Before them was a wooden table on a raised dais in front of the blackboard. When Mayo entered, chattering ceased. Mayo was above average height, athletic, clean shaven, and lightly tanned beneath his freckles. His auburn hair was balding at the forehead, and he was always impeccably dressed. The prime feature of his appearance was his footwear; in those days most lecturers wore boots, but Mayo wore shoes. Most lecturers either stood to address the students or delivered a lecture sitting behind a table, but Mayo began his lectures sitting cross-legged on the front edge of the table, then paced back and forth across the room. The students quickly chose Mayo's socks to distinguish him from other lecturers, and, because his socks were never the same color from one day to the next, the young women in the front row would make sport of guessing the color before his arrival. In time, his socks became items of such humorous conversation and satire around the university that in the 1917 student production of "Twelfth Night" a line was altered to incorporate "a flame-coloured Mayo sock."[19]

Mayo kept a close eye on students because he wanted to be sure they understood him. Once at the start of a lecture to first-year psychology students he enunciated an abstract point, and then saw a man scratch his head in puzzlement. So Mayo thought he should make the abstract point more clear. He suddenly found a new idea, and lectured extemporaneously for the remaining fifty minutes on that point, drawing illustrations from recent experiences as well as his texts.[20]

No one was bored in Mayo's lectures. No one played the fool. Students listened attentively until he asked for questions.[21] He spoke effortlessly, rarely used notes. His voice was quiet. He neither orated nor declaimed, and was always eloquent and often witty. He had some of the qualities of an enthusiastic visionary, preferring to weave an outline on a favorite subject and put it in broad perspective rather than doggedly plow through a textbook. He would give his own view, illustrate it with amusing stories and case studies, and then put questions to the students. At times he would warn that they would be examined on a topic he had no time to cover in lectures. Mayo's teaching style contrasted with that of his assistant Seymour, who stuck to the textbook and repeated his points as if to fix them permanently in the students' minds.

Mayo was not close to his students, and only a few spoke with him outside class. He was not rude, overbearing, or sarcastic; students found him uncommunicative, intellectually able, and with a general knowledge well above the average. To some people he seemed arrogant, especially to those who spoke on topics he knew well, and with which they had had only a passing familiarity. Although he was impatient with foolishness, he did seem kind and gracious to young people who approached him. So most students respected him from a distance, but felt they were beneath his serious attention. A few students who enrolled for final honors in philosophy took tutorials with Mayo, and came to know him better than did most undergraduates.

Mayo's manner was once taken for hostility by two students. He called them before Michie to answer a charge of systematic collusion in missing lectures. Mayo's attendance records showed each had cut a lecture but on different dates. He charged that they had arranged to copy each other's notes and thus avoid the lecture. In fact, one student had had military duties, and the other had simply forgotten to come. After Mayo's intense cross-questioning the latter student blurted out something he had learned from Mayo: "You know, Mr. Mayo, we cannot forget systematically." Michie smiled, but played the unflappable arbitrator. He accepted Mayo's evidence but said it did not show the students had colluded systematically.

From the student viewpoint, Mayo's effectiveness as a teacher was limited in three important ways. First, philosophy and psychology were well above the heads of most students. Second, Mayo did not follow a text closely, so students felt compelled to take down verbatim all that he was saying, which was impossible because he spoke quickly. In reaction, one student published a poem, in rhyming couplets and with the same meter as "How They Brought the Good News from Ghent to Aix," "How We Took Down the Words of Prof. Mayo B.A." In the poem all students but one drop with writer's cramp to the classroom floor. The next day in class Mayo said he deliberately paced his delivery so that students could take down only his important points.[22]

Third, students were anxious about their examination grades. In 1914 an anonymous contributor to the university magazine reported that in a dream he had accepted an invitation to visit Mayo's home where he met Ward, the philosopher, who stood at one end of the hearth and glared at the student while he tried to read a prayer. In the dream Ward represented the study of philosophy; the hearth was the world, the flesh, and the devil, all of which separated the student from his studies; and the prayer symbolized the only means by which the student could hope to satisfy his examiner, Mayo. Examination anxiety was to remain with his students, but over the years the form of its expression changed with the subject matter of his lectures. As soon as Mayo learned of the early work in psychoanalysis, he introduced it to his psychology students. A student's poem records Mayo's loquacious praise of Freud and Jung and is signed "Exam Neurotic."[23]

> *Exams draw on; we're feeling cloyed,*
> *Our joy is not so unalloyed;*
> *We feel as if our knell has rung,*
> *For we must cram on Freud and Jung.*
> *What wonder then we feel annoyed,*
> *Loquacious Prof.*

Examinations were important to students, and Mayo's attitude about examinations was clear. He maintained that when he had to fail a student he did not care a straw for what others thought. He knew the university would back his decision, and felt a strong duty to the Queensland of tomorrow and nothing for what he called "the hydra-headed mob that thinks it is Queensland now."[24] But individual decisions were never easy. For example, students thirty to forty years old took his psychology course, and some would perform badly; he would pass them because he saw no virtue in setting back people's careers if their approach to the subject was disciplined and performance in other subjects was improving. Also, Mayo believed psychologists were born, not made; some students could never master psychology, for they lacked speculative capacities; and other students with ordinary practical minds always found the subject matter too abstract. In short, Mayo evaluated his students in a context broader than the one in which he taught. And when he had made a decision, he held to it because he felt his position in the university was secure and that he should keep its future in his sight.

Mayo was active in academic life outside class. The university appointed him to examine essays submitted for the Archibald Prize, a reward for scholarship in commerce; from 1914 to 1916, when Mayo was examiner, the set topics included general problems of civilization and specific taxation issues in Queensland.[25] In 1915 the university asked Mayo to give an official welcome to new students, which he did with his customary wit and logic: "The fresher, being young, is miserable, but not being very young, is not very miserable."[26] Students elected Mayo president of the University Union; at the Essay Club he joined discussion of a paper on intellectual authority and individual judgment; he read the lesson at the annual service of the Student's Christian Union; he coached the Dramatic Society in productions of *Lady Windemere's Fan* and *Twelfth Night*.[27] Dorothea joined Mayo in this work. She was elected president of the Women Students Club, and she helped stage an entertainment, which, like the production of *Twelfth Night,* raised funds for the University Red Cross Society.[28]

In July 1914, Mayo and Dorothea rented a house, Bulwurradah, in the Brisbane suburb Kangaroo Point. Dorothea, who was obsessed by cleanliness and neatness, had the general services of cheerful Mrs. Reid, who had affectionate regard for Dorothea and was most anxious to work for her. Mrs. Reid had a maid, Nellie, to help with the housework, and a gardener was available. Mayo was happy at Bulwurradah, but Dorothea never seemed to enjoy a house once she had arranged it to meet her needs. In August 1918 they returned to rooms at Montpelier, where they lived until the end of 1921.

In September 1915 the Mayos' first child, Patricia Elton—Patty—was born in Sydney. Dorothea took her to Tasmania that summer to avoid the tropical heat in Brisbane. Mayo was ambivalent about his new role; on the one hand he was overjoyed at becoming a father, on the other he was less certain of his world. He liked to give advice on infant care but had difficulty in imagining the atmosphere that would surround him at Bulwurradah when Dorothea brought Patty home. "I cannot 'see' the part that the dearest daughter will play," he wrote to Dorothea. But he could see the humorous side of his fatherhood. One day in Brisbane he laughed aloud outside a movie house, where beneath an outrageous cardboard figure of a mother holding a child was the inscription: "Poor unfortunate infant—cursed from the beginning with a likeness to her father." Also Patty's birth affected Mayo's standing with his associates. He was gratified to learn that he and Dorothea had "'come up' immensely in the eyes of many since Patty arrived . . . the verdict has been 'human after all.'"[29]

As Patty grew, Mayo turned to psychology to help him define his task as her father. In March 1918 he learned from Jung's *Collected Papers on Analytic Psychology* that the influence of the father dominated the personality development of most children and adolescents to their detriment. Reflecting on his own upbringing, Mayo concluded that George must have been most unusual, for unlike the type of father that Jung described, he had had an enduring capacity for sacrificing himself to his children and for encouraging initiative in them. Mayo believed George's approach was "the chief 'cause' of his children's interest in things academic."[30] So Mayo decided he too would try not to be dogmatic, autocratic, or narrow-minded; instead, he would encourage Patty to approach life as an adventure and never "try to insist upon Patty believing anything."[31]

Mayo had no relatives of his own in Brisbane but the McConnels were often close at hand. They lived at Cressbrook on the family's cattle station about ninety miles away; on visits to the city they stayed at Montpelier.

When Mayo and Dorothea were married in 1913, Dorothea's parents were living, as were two brothers and five sisters. In 1914 Dorothea's father, James McConnel died, and Edgar, the elder son, took charge of Cressbrook. He had been born in 1881, and lived there as a grazier and breeder of stud cattle. He had a diploma from an agricultural college, became an associate of the Surveyor's Institute in London, and, during the First World War served as a major in the Australian Light Horse. In 1909 he had married Phyllis, daughter of Thomas Murray-Prior. Edgar and Mayo were on good terms, but Phyllis held the view that he was a "packet of crackers."[32] She gave up this attitude when Patty was born. Dorothea's brother Kenneth, born in 1882, was a captain in the Second Australian Infantry in Europe during the war; eventually he became an architect. Mayo had little contact with him.

Most of Dorothea's sisters became important figures in Mayo's life at different times. Elspeth, born in 1882, had trained as a teacher, in 1916 married Bevis Geral White, and lived in Queensland; Barbara, born in 1884, lived at Cressbrook until she died in 1921; Katherine, born in 1886, studied at the University of Cambridge and later qualified as a school teacher in Sydney; Ursula, born in 1888, studied at the University of Queensland, became an anthropologist, and worked with Radcliffe-Brown and Edward Sapir; the youngest girl, Judith, born in 1894, lived at Cressbrook until she married Aubrey W. Biggs in 1920.[33]

Ursula developed a close relation with Mayo and Dorothea, and accompanied Dorothea to Tasmania after Patty's birth. Ursula was twenty-seven and had started studies in philosophy under Mayo. Like Dorothea, Ursula was attractive, intelligent, and enjoyed talking. As an undergraduate she argued earnestly with Mayo, and often he would turn the weaknesses of her argument to his own amusing purposes. She resented his playfulness and effortless domination of her arguments, and, for a short time their friendship cooled. Often he lent her books he had recently read; she would speak on any topic with him, and discuss even her most personal feminine discomforts. He liked her frankness and confidence but found that she always made heavy going of her studies. She progressed "up the slopes of Parnassus, shins . . . bruised and bleeding . . . it is her way never to save herself but, having sensed the difficulty, to sail straight at it."[34]

In March 1918 Ursula finished her final examination in philosophy, which Mayo invigilated. He observed her tension and anxiety, and was concerned for her health. He believed she needed his personal encouragement so that she would give her best effort, but hesitated because she was fearful of speaking with him until the ordeal had ended.[35] Afterward she was fit again, and seemed to rejoice in the lightening effect that follows examinations. Mayo recalled the quiet ebbing of tension after his studies and there were echoes of old failures. He remembered how Dorothea had helped him, and he envied Ursula, thinking, "It must be beautiful to have enough resources to wander off looking for adventure after a bout of work."[36] When he talked with Ursula about her career he carefully avoided making suggestions because he felt his influence on her had been sufficient. They discussed the possibility of a master's degree in economics at the University of Sydney or Melbourne, but no decision was taken. Later Ursula raised the topic again, and Mayo was secretly delighted when she suggested studying political philosophy and social psychology at the University of Queensland.[37]

What is known of Mayo's marriage can be learned from letters he wrote when they were apart. For their wedding Dorothea had given him a writing board with the carved initials "EM." She expected him to write to her every day they were apart. All his married life he went to great trouble to meet that expectation; he calculated the intervals between letters to ensure she received some kind of message daily. And she did the same. In his letters he acknowledges her moral and financial support, and that she had made a brave sacrifice in marrying him.[38] Their first separation was during the summer vacation of 1915-16, when Dorothea took baby Patricia to Tasmania. To Mayo their time apart was a divorce; he missed her deeply, wanted her near him, his love for her intensified, and he felt "afflicted with fears and tremors—so dependent am I—and cannot understand how I can be cross with the dearest woman."[39] She was still his "lady of dreams" who made marriage a delight, a rebirth, a finding of himself. To banish thoughts of her, he worked, but she and Patty remained "background to my work, dearest wife, dearest daughter, so much my mental hinterland in these days of absence."[40] His ardor provoked her to write about their love. They agreed that the sex relation was not even interesting unless it was set in broad context of affection; in that context she appeared to him a gracious, kind, "royal head—so courageously parting the wide world."[41]

Mayo's idealization of Dorothea was tempered by good advice to protect and guide her through real and imagined problems. He never ceased to worry about whether or not she had enough money to spend. And when she was afflicted by periodic skin eruptions Mayo would send an urgent telegram of sympathy and arrange for the vaccine she needed.[42] He counseled her on keeping her intellect alert: "Read books not newspapers."[43] In the summer of 1917-18, when she was in Sydney seeking advice about her second pregnancy, Elton was insistant she "not do too much, avoid rushing around, get the taxi driver to drive slowly, see Dr. Rennie on how to achieve your hopes, and mine, for a son or daughter." He wanted her to be comfortable, "no risks please, no sense in rushing 'til you're ill, rest, in six months you'll be in Sydney again."[44] But the second child did not live, and it was not until April 1921 that Dorothea bore their second daughter, Gael.

Letters between Dorothea and Mayo examine difficult social questions and show something of their intellectual life together. Once Dorothea wrote asking for his views on the morality of sex relations outside marriage and whether polygamy should be condoned to overcome the shortage of men that would necessarily follow the end of the Great War. He held that morality was not necessarily endangered provided sex relations were systematic and not promiscuous, but that the family, as he knew it, would lose ground if the "wild promiscuity which we politely ignore" were to continue. Because men would be too few after the war he assumed a lapse from rigid sex standards would follow, as had been so in Sparta. But "promiscuity is definitely anti-social and disintegrative in its tendencies." From studying Aristotle's writings on Sparta, Mayo concluded that "directly systematic sex relations are relaxed, promiscuity sets in, and promiscuity notoriously does not make for increased population." Men should be allowed to procreate, providing they stand by their women during gestation, and support their women and children during infancy, youth, and later; the state cannot maintain a system of sexual relations and an infancy system if odd women all over the land produce inexplicable children. "As a result," he wrote, "sex anarchy follows and social disintegration" as serious as any revolution. If anything were to be done about the shortage of men then "it will have to be done carefully by people of intelligence and means, *and it will have to be concealed:* the State cannot recognise as a lawful union any but marriages which fulfil the prescribed conditions of monogamy" (italics Mayo's).[45]

Mayo's letters to Dorothea reveal the organization of his emotional life and his image of himself. When first in Brisbane he had been lonely because he was without family or close friends; and he had worked hard to help himself through recurrent periods of sadness. During his short engagement to Dorothea he had endured separation from her by working through the doubts surrounding their decision to marry, by applying his mind to imaginative schemes, and by idealizing her and their future life. A more comprehensive pattern presents itself in letters to her between 1915 and 1918. When he was alone Mayo's mood would swing to depression and his self-esteem would fall. "I am very much like a cheap jewel torn from its setting. As part of a beautiful scheme possessing some meaning, but as solitary as a thing of neither beauty nor moment."[46] Her absence was like losing a limb or half his life's work, and her gentle criticism was needed to keep him on course.[47]

He employed several means to overcome his sadness and lack of self-worth. One lonely Christmas eve many years after, he recalled that "years ago as I walked to the University in Brisbane I used to sit down in the small park below Montpelier, where we lived, on many a morning when I felt chunks of gloom or 'fatigue' rolling about—and chase or rather trace its source—often some silly thing like a personal reflection on my capacities or prospects or appearance. Usually I could pick up the silly thing that had provoked all the gloom—and so laugh and get rid of it."[48]

Belittling the apparent cause of gloom and laughing it away were not the only means Mayo used. Occasionally the mood would be transformed into an aggressive censoriousness toward others, and attach itself to an especially tiresome colleague, a driveling companion at dinner, or a Jew, because of a residual schoolboy prejudice. Then would come a stab of compassion, an attack of moral anxiety, a childish fear of retribution. On a long hot train journey to Brisbane he felt "utterly wearied by the essential commonness of my fellow passengers . . . a contrast to the ship passengers—I decided I had been too censorious of late, and set myself to like them. And behold, this morning even the Jew who is the other occupant of my compartment stood revealed as a decent enough citizen."[49] A few days later at the university this mood prevailed again, and Mayo recorded, "I have not been altogether pleased with some of my actions. At Faculty meeting, for instance, I pitched into poor Priestly—and so passed Friday with transgressions, but hope to do better."[50]

To manage his dislike for himself, Mayo often needed another target, and over the years Henry James Priestly, professor of mathematics, filled the position well. Mayo never failed to find him irritating in matters of organization and self-centered, a fussy old hen and first-class bore who spent his energy making everything become distressingly important.[51] (He also played tennis badly.) But to complete Mayo's emotional life he needed a good friend. Friendship was vital to Mayo; when explaining William James's idea of "me," and how friends contribute to one's personality, Mayo asserted that "to lose one is like (and actually is) cutting off a great piece of oneself."[52] John Michie, played this role for Mayo, and needed Mayo for a friend too. When they had been bachelors together, Michie was helped over his shyness of women by the assurance of Mayo's company; in preparing lectures Michie would consult with Mayo; and in 1918 when the university was being reorganized, Mayo wrote, "Michie and I have fallen back into the old relationship—I think that Priestly's notorious inadequacies to certain questions drives him back on me."[53]

Mayo's most rewarding friendship was with Bronislaw Malinowski, the anthropologist, whom he met in July 1914. Malinowski, a student of mathematics and physics who had turned to anthropological work on the Australian aboriginal family, came to Australia to speak to the British Association for the Advancement of Science, and then go on to Papua to work among the Mailu.[54] His approach to anthropology was to study the actual behavior and experience of exotic tribes rather than imitate his contemporaries and theorize imaginatively on social evolution and universal history. Malinowski's address considered a fundamental problem in religious sociology: the importance of the distinction between the sacred and the profane among primitives. Scholars were divided on the issue, but Malinowski believed that the available evidence showed that among primitives who valued religion highly, the distinction was sharp; among those who did not, the distinction was unclear. He held that evidence, not polemics, properly determined knowledge in religious sociology; the more ample the evidence the more reliable the knowledge.

Mayo and Malinowski became friends shortly after they first met. They had a common interest in the scientific approach to social research, shared the belief that human behavior and experience were best understood in the context to which they belonged, and emphasized the importance of both psychological and social facts in studies of mankind. Their friendship grew for other reasons, too. Because of the conflict in Europe many people were suspicious of Malinowski's interest in studying life in the German colony of Papua, but Mayo and Dorothea offered sympathy and hospitality whenever he was in Brisbane. In March 1916 Mayo attended to Malinowski's luggage problems; in October the next year the Mayos looked after him, discussed the university's problems, Mayo's political theories, and planned to take holidays together; when Malinowski left for his field research they were there to wish him well.[55] Malinowski was immensely pleased by their charm and hospitality; and his friendship was sealed with a warm letter expressing a high opinion of Mayo's work.

> The real scientific mind is absolutely in touch with life—and whatever is done, created, and impressed upon humanity by such a one is of direct practical value, though it may have to be cashed only after many detours. During my wanderings in English-speaking countries I had the privilege of meeting such a mind only once—at a backwater university in sub-tropical Australia.[56]

Mayo was heartened by these comments, which came at a time when he felt particularly low. He wrote, "No Englishman would have the decency to say such things . . . no Britisher would come to such a conclusion. . . . I don't suppose anyone else will ever speak of me like that."

At the end of 1918 Mayo went to Melbourne to work and to stay with Malinowski.[57] At first Mayo had welcomed the opportunity, but he later found it to be a powerful test of friendship. Malinowski used the visit to repay Mayo's hospitality in Brisbane; he bought Mayo cigarettes and food, served him breakfast in bed, and even took him to the opera. In the face of such heavy efforts at reparation Mayo could do very little. The problem was that Malinowski lived in "slavonic squalor" in Grey Street, East Melbourne where he housed Mayo in a box-like room with a rickety old bed and coarse bedclothes. Mayo ameliorated the squalor with frequent bathing, and once caught his friend in a weak moment and bought him a decent meal at the Hotel Australia.

Mayo found work with Malinowski was rewarding but exhausting. All day in Malinowski's room at Melbourne's public library they worked together on problems in psychology and sociology until Mayo was ready to drop. "It is the doing of two kinds of work, psychological and social, is the killing element in a visit of this kind." The routine was broken only when

Malinowski went to spend time with Elsie Masson, his fiancée, or when the two men visited friends at the University of Melbourne. At night in the Grey Street rooms they would continue their work. After three days Mayo proposed courteously and firmly to return to Brisbane to help Dorothea prepare for holidays. Malinowski would have none of this. He insisted that while they were in a working vein, it would be better for Mayo to stay and get all the benefit he could. The escape was delayed by five days.

Mayo and Malinowski did not meet again until 1926 in the United States, when the warmth of their friendship seemed as genuine to Mayo as it had been at their first meeting. In 1928 he was doubly grateful for that friendship when it helped smooth the way for entry to British intellectual circles.

Notes

1. Elton to Dorothea, 16 March 1916; University of Queensland, *Calendar*, 1915, p. 310; ibid., 1916, p. 58.
2. Minutes, Board of Faculties, University of Queensland, 20 September 1920.
3. Bronislaw Malinowski, *A Diary in the Strict Sense of the Term: 1914-15, and 1917-18* (London: Routledge & Kegan Paul, 1967), p. 4.
4. Elton to Dorothea, 3 March 1918.
5. Elton to Dorothea, 7 March 1918.
6. Minutes, Senate, University of Queensland, 15 June, 12 October 1917.
7. Elton to Dorothea, 11 March 1918.
8. Ibid.
9. Elton to Dorothea, 3, 17 March 1918.
10. Minutes, Senate, University of Queensland, 13 December 1918, 14 March 1919.
11. Elton to Dorothea, 21 March 1919.
12. *The University of Queensland, 1910-1922: A History* (Brisbane: University of Queensland, 1923).
13. University of Queensland, *Calendar*, 1922, pp. 279-85; Minutes, Education Committee, University of Queensland, 3 November 1914, and Minutes, Senate, University of Queensland, 20 April 1917.
14. Elton to Dorothea, 11 January 1923; University of Queensland, *Calendar*, 1914, pp. 313-14; ibid., 1915, pp. 60-62.
15. University of Queensland, *Calendar*, 1914, p. 315; ibid., 1915, p. 63.
16. Ibid., 1914, p. 315; ibid., 1915, p. 316.
17. Ibid., 1917, pp. 56-57, 129-32; ibid., 1918, pp. 62-65, 130-33; ibid., 1920, p. 111; ibid., 1921, p. 112.
18. Ibid., 1915, p. 310; ibid., 1916, p. 58.
19. *Queensland University Magazine* 6, no. 2 (1921):334; conversation with Miss E. K. McGregor, 22 August 1974; Jones to Trahair, 7 October 1974; Kyle to Trahair, 20 September 1974.
20. Elton to Dorothea, 2 April 1913.
21. Sources for Mayo's behavior in class are: Kyle to Trahair, 20 September 1974; Pearse to Trahair, 5 November 1974; Partridge to Trahair, 26 September 1974; Jones to Trahair, 7 October 1974; conversations with Lady Axon, 21 August 1974, and Miss K. E. McGregor, 22 August 1974.
22. *Queensland University Magazine*, 20 October 1920, pp. 38-39; Jones to Trahair, 7 October 1974.

23. *Galmahra* (formerly *Queensland University Magazine)* 1, no. 3 (1921):45, 46. In this issue appears another verse on Mayo's lectures:

> *Old Mayo's a psycho-analyst, enraptured by Jung and Freud;*
> *If you tell him you're a Sensationist, he's certain to feel annoyed.*
> *For he feels convinced that Locke and Hume are very much out of date,*
> *And the lower levels of consciousness he loves to investigate.*

24. Elton to Dorothea, 13 March 1913.
25. Minutes, Faculty of Arts, University of Queensland, 19 August 1914, and Minutes, Senate, University of Queensland, 14 August 1915; University of Queensland, *Calendar,* 1915.
26. *Queensland University Magazine* 4, no. 1 (1915):18.
27. Ibid.,2, no. 2 (1914):48, 49, 54; ibid., 3, no. 3 (1915):77.
28. Ibid., 2, no. 4 (1914):106; ibid., 3, no. 2 (1915):47-48; ibid., 4, no. 3 (1917):14, 50.
29. Elton to Dorothea, 18 November 1915; 13, 14, 21, 24, 30 March, 2-5 April 1916; 6, 7, 15, 18 March 1918; 18 March 1921; conversation with Patricia Elton Mayo, January 1974.
30. Elton to Dorothea, 5 March 1918.
31. Elton to Dorothea, 16 March 1918.
32. Elton to Dorothea, 5 April 1916.
33. E.W.J. McConnel, *James McConnel of Carsiggan, his Forebears and Descendants* (privately printed, 1931).
34. Elton to Dorothea, 5 April 1916.
35. Elton to Dorothea, 4-6 March 1918.
36. Elton to Dorothea, 10 March 1918.
37. Elton to Dorothea, 11 March 1918.
38. Elton to Dorothea, 2 April 1916.
39. Elton to Dorothea, 24 March 1916.
40. Elton to Dorothea, 25 March, 5 April 1916.
41. Elton to Dorothea, 4 April 1916.
42. Elton to Dorothea, 16, 21 March, 3 April 1916.
43. Elton to Dorothea, 30 March 1916.
44. Elton to Dorothea, 4-7, 11 March 1918.
45. Elton to Dorothea, 14, 15 March 1918.
46. Elton to Dorothea, 14 November 1915.
47. Elton to Dorothea, 23 March 1916.
48. Elton to Toni, 24 December 1937.
49. Elton to Dorothea, 10 March 1916.
50. Elton to Dorothea, 21 March 1916.
51. Elton to Dorothea, 3, 5, 6, 16 March 1918.
52. Elton to Dorothea, 24 March 1916.
53. Elton to Dorothea, 4, 11, 15, 16 March 1918.
54. British Association for the Advancement of Science, *Report of Eighty-Fourth Meeting* (London, 1915); J. A. Barnes, Introduction to *The Family Among the Australian Aborigines,* by B. Malinowski (New York: Schocken, 1962; originally published 1913).
55. Elton to Dorothea, 13, 16, 21 March 1916; Malinowski, *Family Among the Australian Aborigines,* pp. 4, 108, 111.
56. Elton to Dorothea, 7 March 1918.
57. Elton to Dorothea, December 1918.

6

War, Politics, and the New Psychology, 1914-1919

The Great War gave Mayo opportunities to extend his influence among colleagues in Queensland, but when he tried he was frustrated on every point. His ideas were too radical for conservative men, and too elitist and compromising for those who wanted great changes in the social and political order; his recommendations were misjudged by businessmen and socialists alike, political commentators were divided on his policies, and politicians would not follow his advice. To Mayo politics seemed irrational, so he turned to the new theories of psychology for an explanation of social and political problems, and wrote a small book on them before taking up the neurotic problems of men who were returning from the war.

Conflict in Europe led Australian and British intellectuals to examine relations between Great Britain and its colonies. Among the British spokesmen was Lionel Curtis, who had helped create the Union of South Africa after the Boer War and who had founded *Round Table,* a liberal magazine that published discussions of Britain's imperial problems. Before war was declared in 1914 Curtis had visited Australia, New Zealand, and Canada to establish Round Table groups and extend discussion of relations among members of the British Empire.[1] Mayo attended a small meeting in Brisbane at which Curtis revealed the purpose of the Round Table organization. It aimed for a theory of the state based on a liberal view of the British Empire; and individuals' duties, opportunities, and challenges were to be pursued within guidelines of British imperial policy. At the time *Round Table* subscribed to a policy of devolution and the notion that the British Empire was best understood as a single political unit whose members should act as one in world affairs. It argued that imperial matters should be managed by a representative imperial council; and although dominions should manage their domestic affairs, ultimately Britain would be responsible for their citizens. Those who opposed Round Table groups condemned their policy as statism and deplored the view that the British Empire should be an omnipotent political unit shaping the moral personality of its citizens. Mayo believed the state was the individual's servant not an overbearing master, and placed himself among Curtis's opponents by pointing out that Round Table policy was "exceedingly silly and utterly irrelevant to the facts in Australia at the time." Mayo's politics were too radical for his peers; he was censured, and from then on "was very nearly prevented from having anything in the nature of an effective say in the affairs of my own country."[2]

In university affairs Mayo always enjoyed an effective say, and was put on the university's War Committee when it was founded in 1915. Students lampooned Mayo's first contribution, calling it an obscure, irrelevant, abstract argument, and they presented Mayo's associates as buffoons.[3] But later his help was invaluable. He edited early publications of the War Committee,[4] while many of his colleagues toured country towns lecturing on how people might direct their efforts toward Queensland's contribution to ending the war. Mayo could not tour—Percy Seymour went in his place—because Dorothea was about to have their first child.

The War Committee's first document was a call to service in the militia, to manufacture munitions, and to maintain necessary industries.[5] It was distributed in July 1915 at a meeting where leading citizens heard the new governor of Queensland, Sir Hamilton John Goold-Adams, ask for support.

The second document concerned organization for the production of war munitions. To ensure efficiency, it recommends that a census be taken of all labor and machinery to establish the resources available for production; that the English system of contracting production be avoided because it leads to profiteering; that profits be limited to 8 percent on capital; and that unions relax their regulations so as to allow for more shift-work, the employment of nonunionists, and unskilled workers on machines. The third pamphlet outlined the state's normal and real losses in wartime, and ways to limit them. Under normal competitive market conditions, which are subject to the laws of supply and demand, the cost of war would double or treble, and few people would reap great benefits. So "the production of munitions by means of contract with private firms is a wrong method for providing for" wartime needs. The proper action would be for the commonwealth government to control munitions factories; it would prevent competitive demand for labor and materials from swelling the costs of production, and offset industrial dislocations that might occur.[6]

Mayo's active work on the committee ended in November 1915. At one meeting the members had spent time criticizing Queensland's Labour government and carping at Mayo's radical ideas. "I lashed out at them—told them they seemed to be politicians first and patriots afterwards." Overwork had contributed to Mayo's outburst. Athough the meeting moved a vote of thanks for his efforts and he apologized for not behaving well, later he wrote to its senior members—including the archbishop of Brisbane—saying that he would retire.[7]

To provide "authoritative and impartial guidance" at a time of "political stress" and "widespread political changes engendered by the war" Mayo believed Australia needed a journal that published impartial, reasoned political and theological discussions. Earlier attempts at such a journal had failed for lack of subscribers. But at the University of Melbourne, a neurologist, Professor Berry, had given the matter thought and suggested that in each state an editorial committee be established. Mayo offered to help in Queensland. He wanted an "Australian Review" similar to the *Hibbert Journal*. Most subscribers would come from two groups. "In the Queensland club I have often heard reputed staunch supporters of the so-called liberal cause, pastoralists, express views of the most astounding [political heresy and] heterodoxy," Mayo wrote to Berry, and assured him these people would subscribe to a review "that welcomed honest expression of opinion." Also, "the rank and file of the Australian Labour Party will read with avidity any definitely Australian publication which endeavours to take account of their political difficulties and disabilities."[8] Mayo's enthusiasm went unrewarded, for the journal did not come into being.

Mayo's efforts appeared with a lighter touch in April 1916. A friend in Adelaide, Mrs. Anna Booth, who had admired his understanding of human experience and benefited from his psychological advice on children's problems, asked him to join her in a contribution to the *Lady Galway Belgium Book*. The book was sponsored by the Red Cross and the Belgian Relief Fund, and compiled by Lady Marie Galway, wife of South Australia's governor. Short stories, poems, scenes from Belgium, paintings and articles on diverse subjects appear in the book. Anna Booth and Mayo offered a short story or playlet of four scenes.[9] The story is set in a hotel at a fashionable resort, where a young, overworked barrister, Peter Fawcett, is resting at his physician's instructions. Fawcett is warned that a guest, Mrs. Addison, is a siren. Within two weeks she inveigles Fawcett into kissing her, but to her surprise he refuses to abandon himself utterly to her influence. In three days he changes his mind and suggests they elope. She is astonished; he is insistent; she declines; he laughs uproariously. She is puzzled, so he tells her the truth about herself: she is incapable of loving men, and all she really wants is to collect them. The plot is slight, and probably held more significance for Anna and Mayo than for any reader. The occupations of the characters and their names allude to Anna's Adelaide acquaintances. The risqué and brittle dialogue suggests Bernard Shaw, whose *Major Barbara* Anna and Mayo had enjoyed immensely.[10]

Mayo's view of the political problems of citizens in wartime appears in "Socialism and War," a talk he gave to Socialists at the Trades Hall.[11] As did the pamphlets he edited, the address attacked wartime profiteering and undemocratic government. First, he denigrated profiteers and outlined Marx's theory of surplus value. Marx's criticism of profits "may be wrongly based if considered from the point of view of scientific economics, but is nonetheless probably true"; and modern economic writers assume wrongly that entrepreneurs profit legitimately as a result of superior intelligence. Mayo said Marx "knew perfectly well that large profits, more often than not, were not due to superior but inferior brains [and] to the absence of human qualities and a veritable obsession of selfish interest, [so] caution is the only factor that operates to restrain [the entrepreneur's] cupidity." In wartime, community needs become urgent, and unscrupulous capitalists can easily profit from real or feared shortages, e.g., the cheese and flour merchants cited in the June 1915 issue of *Round Table*. Socialists and "every honest citizen" had the duty to prevent "predatory raids of this kind on the community." Second, Mayo asserted, the war's end would pattern world politics. To him the war was a struggle between democracy and military autocracy, and, therefore, the possibility of anything but a victory for England and her allies was alarming. Finally he asked: "Where do Socialists stand on this point?" When Mayo returned from his summer vacation of 1915-16, colleagues told him that he was popular at the Trades Hall because his audience had decided that he was a Socialist and "a true friend of the cause."[12]

Mayo was both amused and annoyed by reaction at the Trades Hall. He had no objection to publicity for good work done; he enjoyed public speaking and the discussions that followed his addresses. But he abominated political publicity, and loathed party politics. He could not support socialism, because it was based on the Marxist view of class war, which he believed aimed to destroy social order not build it. He objected equally to capitalism because it harbored greedy and dull-witted businessmen. However roundly he criticized each political camp, Mayo saw his duty in helping both sides to understand and accept their shortcomings, and to address themselves, together, to a better industrial organization for the community.

Business interests were cool to Mayo's approach on ways industries should plan their organization,[13] but the Queensland government was interested. In May 1915, for the first time, the Labour Party won the Queensland state election. Edward G. Theodore became state treasurer and acting premier during the premier's absence. When Labour came to power, Theodore was given ministerial responsibility for industrial matters.[14]

In Mayo's opinion the Queensland cabinet knew neither where nor how to begin work on problems of industrial organization in wartime. His pamphlet for the university War Committee had outlined how industrialists should forgo immediate interests and unions should curb their controls on work, and how both should cooperate for the community's benefit. Now he was keen to develop these ideas in a scheme that the government might use to administer industries during the war. He sent a short account of his views to the government, and Theodore invited Mayo for a discussion of them.

Mayo's ideas came directly from his reading of Barker's *Political*

Thought in England from Herbert Spencer to Today.[15] The final chapter draws apart four strands of socialism: Marxism, Fabianism, syndicalism, and guild socialism. Mayo's attention was caught by the discussion of syndicalism, a French school of political thought advocating more social and economic autonomy for professions and occupations, and, at the same time a severe curb on the power of the state. The chapter also briefly reviews Graham Wallas's *The Great Society,* an evaluation of social psychology and its promise to diagnose, forecast, and offer control over human behavior, especially the evils of modern democrary, e.g., politicians who hypnotize electors, and classes of voters who pressure governments for whom they work. It argues that syndicalism, by emphasizing cooperative relations within professions and occupations and limits to state power, could correct these evils. Mayo wrote to Dorothea that his upcoming discussion with Theodore would include two propositions; "The day of Socialism is over and the day of Syndicalism arrived," and "Will, not force, is the basis of the State." The latter proposition was drawn from Barker's second chapter, which summarizes the ideas of T.H. Green, the liberal idealist and author of *The Principles of Political Obligation.* In time Mayo would cast syndicalism aside, but Green's maxim would remain central to Mayo's political beliefs for the rest of his career.[16]

Because Theodore's Labour ministry was committed to socialism, Mayo believed his own views would not be readily adopted, so he worked assiduously to prepare a strong and persuasive case. On the night before the meeting with Theodore, Mayo reviewed his scheme carefully and rehearsed his arguments, but his vision of a syndicalist organization for industry was clouded by personal doubts. To convince the socialist government was "a tough job, since my councils of moderation might be twisted into criticisms of Government measures."[17] And he was ambivalent about the government's adoption of his scheme. He thought that it may promote politicians' careers, but that his own reputation could be easily smashed if his conservative friends were to hear of his influence. He asked Dorothea to say nothing of the meeting. Further, he expected his fatigue from ceaseless work on the scheme would combine with his fear that Theodore would dismiss the scheme, and doubt would give way, as it so often had, to feelings of worthlessness and depression. But he was wrong.

The interview with Theodore was far from disappointing. Mayo was treated courteously, given an excellent cigar, and afforded ample time. "It was a new experience for me to be listened to by [an Acting] Premier . . . able fellow whatever his other qualities or defects."[18] Theodore's copious notes showed Mayo that he was having some influence on the politician's thinking.

Although Theodore accepted some of Mayo's ideas, he was told his scheme was foreign to the declared policy of the Labour Party, and possibly was dangerous to it. Mayo knew he had not clarified the political safeguards that the scheme would need. Theodore acknowledged Mayo's reasoned criticisms for a failed syndicalist scheme in France. But central to all schemes was the problem of raising money for the reorganization of industry, and Theodore wanted to exclude the capitalists entirely. Mayo, knowing money would be difficult to raise, wanted the capitalists included within a limited form of syndicalism. Theodore believed money could be raised in England, but Mayo reasoned that the war militated against such a loan. Finally, Theodore's attention was caught by Mayo's critical comments on modern democracy and the behavior of politicians. He outlined his own views for Mayo to consider, and closed by saying he would be pleased to review the discussion.

Mayo saw Theodore's government could not accept his scheme without great changes to Labour Party policy, so he asked if he might publish his views as his own. Theodore assented, asking that he be sent anything that appeared in print. A title had already come to mind: "Democracy and Government." It would appear in 1919 as *Democracy and Freedom,* the first in a series of Workers' Educational Association pamphlets.

The question of conscripted or voluntary service for the war divided Australians in the 1916 referendum: 1,087,557 voted for conscription; 1,160,033 against. Shortly after the referendum Mayo published a letter, "National Organization: The Referendum and After,"[19] a social psychological explanation of the referendum results and an exhortation to reconsider Australia's military and economic future. Mayo assumed the meaning of conscription varies with the culture in which it is found. In Germany conscription was undemocratically forced upon the blindly obedient populace in the one form of military service and in the interests of militarism. In Australia conscription could take different forms and should rest on the people's enthusiastic desire for efficient national organization.

Mayo analyzed the intentions of the Australian electorate, and, contrary to the views of most political commentators, argued that the voters did not take what they thought was the safest course but were motivated by insecurity and self-interest. They lacked confidence in the political leaders because they had offered no carefully considered scheme of industrial and military organization but had merely debated the issue of "compulsion." Mayo thought both sides had misled the voters. In democracies compulsion was not relevant, and "will (human desires), not force (compulsion) is the basis of the State." He argued that the desire to undertake duty comes from within; compulsion imposed from without has relatively little effect on doing one's duty. In this light, conscription was nothing more than a procedure for organizing human desires to act in the general interest. Australian voters preferred the current military and industrial system of 1916 because, Mayo argued, they feared militarism and industrial conscription, and they distrusted politicians who would have had to unite liberal with syndicalist policies if conscription was adopted. Mayo stated that Australians, because of inadequate leadership, were ignorant of the real-world problems raised by the Great War. The European civilization that existed before August 1914 would never return; economic and industrial changes had occurred more rapidly than Australians had realized; war had ended economic competition and brought in the new era of national organization. Australians must learn this, Mayo wrote, because Australia's fate was tied to that of Europe in a war for democracy.

Mayo was passing through Sydney early in 1918 when the government's plan for the repatriation of soldiers attracted his attention. Mayo attacked it because it smacked of charity, failed to consider adequately the economic situation to which the soldiers were returning. He denounced proposals to establish secondary industries (e.g., piano making) that made no use of Australia's natural resources, and advocated extending primary industries and their markets (e.g., pig farms). Mayo predicted that unless his advice was followed Australia would become bankrupt. His advice was not taken and he was roundly criticized, but the general principle that repatriation of soldiers should occur in a well-understood and properly managed context guided recommendations of the Subcommittee on Rehabilitation that Mayo chaired thirty years later for the National Research Council in Washington.[20]

During 1917 Mayo became interested in the application of social and psychological ideas to Australian politics. The University Senate appointed him to the John Thomson Lectureship, and he gave two public lectures on "Psychology and Politics."[21] They constitute his earliest and most systematic statement on the political problems of an industrial society, and show clearly how influenced he was by social psychology and Green's ideal conception of the state.

For Mayo, society comprised individuals organized in occupations. Each occupation had its social function. Individuals' political attitudes and behaviors are created not by the party to which they belong, but by their race-tradition or inherited characteristics, and by occupation. Of the two, occupation is the stronger. For a society to be stable and healthy, individuals must see clearly and accurately the functional relation between their and other occupations in society.

Mayo asserted that in Australian industry these ideal conditions are not present. Australian industry originated with the economic expansion of nineteenth-century Europe. During this expansion social chaos was wrought by an economic creed that advocated competition, survival of the fittest, and no political interference in industry. In the twentieth century, much distress was alleviated as capitalism and industrialism grew, but these attitudes did not promote social stability, unity, or health. Because of the inhumane working conditions of the last century, most workers, understandably, supported Marxism, and viewed industry as the scene of class war. Because of the ruthless competition in nineteenth-century commerce, most employers, understandably, adopted the view that workers were items in the cost of production, and not responsible citizens serving a social function. Notwithstanding the restrictions on competition, the employers' attitude remained. As long as workers did not understand the complex economics of industry, and employers did not see the social function of work, industrial strife would persist and social unity would not be achieved.

In Australia false political cures for economic ills predominated, Mayo stated. Craft unionism turned to political unionism, based on Marxism and class war. And although the Australian Labour Party's goal—One Big Union of Workers—was necessary to achieve humane work conditions, the social consequences had been unfortunate. Industrial grievances flared into political issues, and every industrial function lost sight of its social purpose; the New South Wales Railways strike of 1917 was a case in point. The Labour and Liberal Parties showed no mutual understanding, logic, or reason; instead, traditional selfish sentiment shaped their attitudes. The Liberal Party's capitalism assumed that superior skill entitled one to the sole right of ownership and control in industry; Labour's industrialism discounted all skill and upheld democratic control of industry without the knowledge to manage its problems.

The state, Mayo argued, and its politicians should be passive and critical of society's activities, and offer only moral criticism. Instead, through the Commonwealth Arbitration Court, the state legalized social disintegration of industry. Arbitration is sound when it encourages reasoned discussion of common problems, but in Australia the Arbitration Court assumed that no mutual interest could exist between the two parties, and intruded itself between them to uphold the public interest. It encouraged workers to think only of "logs of claims" and to ignore work's technical problems; it provided a tedious incomprehensible list of work regulations that prohibited cooperation and social progress, and killed initiative, leadership, and the individual's sense of citizenship.

In Mayo's opinion trusts and unions held some hope for social unity, because they reduced the host of petty competitors and curbed ideas of class war. In such monopolies a consciousness of social function could grow because large social organizations required their members to take a broad view of the world, forgo political ideologies, and emphasize cooperation rather than hatred. Mayo's opinion was shared by few; most people suspected both unions and trusts of inspiring class interests and conflict rather than industry harmony.

Finally Mayo criticized Australia's universities for emphasizing professional training in law and medicine and giving too little attention to economics and arts, which properly study social and industrial problems. Also he argued that if Australia were to achieve a stable, unified, civilized society, more reliance must be put on the scientific study of conditions that promote social unity and less on the irrationalities of politicians.

The two lectures were well attended, and were accurately and favorably reported in the *Brisbane Courier*, but were followed by such a disappointing lack of concern among Mayo's associates that he did not draft his lecture notes for publication as a pamphlet by the university. "One does need the stimulus of interest aroused somewhere. . . . For many years I have had to go without much," he wrote to Dorothea.[22] Interest in Mayo's ideas came from distant and friendly colleagues, close family, and local unionists. Meredith Atkinson, director of tutorial classes at the University of Sydney and president of the Workers' Educational Association in Australia wanted a chapter from Mayo for a new book. Dorothea's mother so approved the lectures that she wanted to distribute copies when they were printed.[23] A heartening letter from Malinowski, a personal note from another faraway friend, and a warmly received speech to a small group of the National Council of Women combined to raise Mayo's enthusiasm for the task. Too, he won another great success at the Trades Hall. He had been asked to speak on industry and education, and when he arrived hundreds were waiting to hear him. To Mayo it seemed the Workers' Educational Association had come into its own in Queensland. The audience followed the description of his scheme for arts and studies in social sciences attentively, and a loud cheer followed his final claim that "the office of education is to break down the shackles of custom, convention and social environment, and set man free to think."[24] Mayo revised the lecture, called it "Australia's Political Consciousness," and sent a copy to Atkinson early in March 1918.[25]

In March 1918 the first term of Queensland's Labour government ended, and the main issue of the elections was the efficacy of Labour's socialist schemes. Inflation had been high and the government had spent freely on its state-controlled enterprises, e.g., cattle stations, butcher shops, insurance, and banking. Other Australian states had tried similar schemes without success, so Labour's opponents, the Queensland Nationalist Party, predicted financial disaster if Labour were returned to office. The election campaign and its curious aftermath gave a special thrust to Mayo's application of psychoanalytic psychology to political problems, and to ideas that would become the basis of his early work in the United States.

Labour won the election by an unexpected majority of two to one. At first Mayo took only a minor interest in the result because his wife's uncle had been a Nationalist candidate. In Mayo's opinion the Nationalists deserved to be beaten because they had campaigned badly, dwelt on the defects in the personality of Labour's leader, put up poor candidates, and delivered no constructive criticism of Labour's state-run enterprises.[26] But later he turned to the irrationalities of politicians and voters and the psychology of the election.

Early in March 1918 Mayo was reading the analytical psychology of Jung, and began to apply it to problems of his own fatherhood and to the

neuroses of various friends.²⁷ The application called for the use of association tests to identify unconscious patterns of emotion or "complexes."
Jung assumed complexes were important unconscious determinants of
observable behavior and could be brought into awareness by uttering mental associations to certain words. In fact, Mayo believed that he had independently discovered the association method for himself when reading a
story about Sherlock Holmes. And he became even more excited by Jung's
work when he read that Jung had applied the association method to discover the culprit in a case of theft at a hospital.²⁸

On the day after Labour's success, "I began to make notes about
the election," Mayo wrote to Dorothea, "and it has worked out as a new
chapter for [my book] 'Democracy and freedom.'" He assumed the
campaigners had made the electorate psychasthenic or neurasthenic, and
concluded, "The Nationalists lost because in the endeavour to be logical
they took no account of 'phobias' (anxiety neuroses) motivated from the
'unconscious.'" Mayo believed this idea was congruent with, and could lead
to the improvement of, the theories of the French crowd psychologist Le
Bon, and might be a sound basis for a study of "elector psychasthenia and
twilight-thinking."²⁹

Two days later a crowd of depositors made a run on the Queensland
Government Savings Bank because rumors had spread that the government would appropriate the depositors' funds. Both the state premier and
the leader of the Nationalist Party deprecated the rumor, excessive with-
drawals were declared unnecessary, the Commonwealth Bank offered support to the bank under siege, and, at the end of the week, the bank scare
was over. This panic impressed Mayo greatly, showing him that obsessions,
fears, and confused ideas like those that had been aroused during the
campaign were similar to the emotional distress of neurotics and to the
thought patterns of children. And authoritarian fathers' attempts to control thoughts and feelings of their children resembled the Queensland politicians' manipulation of the voters' notions. During that year Mayo set
down these thoughts for his *Democracy and Freedom,* which would be the
first in a series of authoritative texts on the social conditions of life in the
British countries of the South Seas, published by the Workers' Educational
Association of Australia, and edited by Mayo's colleague Meredith
Atkinson.³⁰

Democracy and Freedom is short and is Mayo's only full statement on
the political problems of industrial civilization. The first chapter shows
how modern democracy failed to engender social growth and individual
autonomy, and the second outlines Mayo's ideal of democratic government. The third chapter criticizes the inadequate leadership in modern
democracies, and the fourth condemns state regulation of industrial conflict. The final chapter summarizes Mayo's thesis by arguing that in a civilized society the social will is expressed in law, equity, marriage, contracts,
public opinion, trades, professions, and other moral institutions.

Chapters 2 and 3 include Mayo's ideas on psychology and politics for democratic government. Modern democracies in Britain, the United States, and Australia do not base policies on sane logical discussion, nor do they employ properly trained people to execute the policies. Instead of logical discussion, politicians use fear and hatred to win office. Le Bon stated that terrifying images have strong immediate effects on crowds; and Ostrogorski, the Russian constitutional democrat, showed that party politics has introduced to modern popular government collective mediocrity based on confused judgment. Further, because political organization of parties is being preferred to systematic political education, and political brokers are replacing statesmen, party victory is sought at the expense of society's good, and thus democracy is degraded.

Modern psychologists help us understand one problem in modern democracy. Freud and Jung show that unconscious irrational fears in neurasthenics and hysterics can be studied systematically, and that these fears can arise in, and disrupt, the controlled conscious thinking of normal people. Jung found reaction time increased with the sensitiveness of certain ideas and feelings. In political meetings, skilled speakers appeal to, and stimulate, unconscious emotional fears of the audience, attach them to social and industrial problems, and then profess the cure. The politician tests ideas on an audience, sees what emotional reactions can be aroused, and then develops a topic by intensifying people's emotions and directing them to a purpose. During the 1918 Queensland campaign candidates had talked about recruitment, conscription, relatives in combat, unemployment, cost of living, and social class differences. Mayo illustrated his ideas with a story about the rumor that the reelected Socialist government would appropriate savings of the middle-class and the subsequent run on the local bank.

Continuing political education and enlightened leadership are needed for effective democracy. But, in Australia, political organizations exploited sectional distrust and irrational fears rather than promoting political education, and politicians manipulated mob prejudice instead of eloquently inspiring ideals of social progress. Could the problem be solved? French social theorists had stated that crowds respond largely to unconscious irrational thoughts, so a community's action is determined not by especially able people but by these unconscious elements of the collective mind. Thus, the social theorists concluded that as a group specialists are no more able than imbeciles to make rational decisions. Mayo asserted that this pessimistic and unwarranted conclusion has been disproved by modern psychologists. Freud and Jung show that normal rational thought and understanding are achieved repeatedly through the use of reason.

In a hastily drafted review for the *Melbourne Herald* Herbert Heaton, lecturer in economics and director of tutorial classes at the University of Adelaide, introduced *Democracy and Freedom* with a bitter lament about the failure of Australia's universities to provide for the scientific study of social psychology, politics, and economics.[31] He outlined Mayo's application of psychology to politics, but feared that because the "excellent little book" did not fully develop its main ideas, many unsophisticated readers might not understand Mayo's thesis. Heaton sent Mayo a copy of the review, apologized for its shortcomings, and, praised him for his discussion of guild socialism and state regulation of industry. "It's a pity you made the book so short though; doubly-distilled political writing is not easy to understand by those not trained to philosophical or psychological language, and I fancy you will 'catch it' from some labor reviewers for having used technical terms without having explained them."[32] Mayo thought the review reflected Heaton's breezy, cheerful personality, and he was much amused by the notion that he would have difficulty in surviving unsophisticated criticism.[33]

Brisbane's *Daily Mail* stormed at Mayo for writing in an ivory tower and providing a typically obscure, abstruse, verbose, literary, unconvincing, and inadequate contribution to Australian political thought. Le Bon, Freud, and Jung were denigrated; sociology and social psychology were dubbed "learned nonsense." After recounting the thesis on the role of the state, the reviewer asserted that Mayo had deceived himself and misconceived democratic politics, and was nothing but a "kind of (philosophic) anarchist . . . who does not want to be bothered by Governments."[34] Brisbane's *Daily Standard* was more favorably inclined, and regarded the work as "thought-provoking" but "not satisfying."[35] The reviewer recommended the book as a "helpful criticism" of democracy, but warned that although Mayo ridiculed, regretted, and condemned both state socialism and capitalism, he did not offer a firm alternative to either. "Very friendly, very sane," thought Mayo.[36]

"Mr. Mayo hits right and left" wrote Professor William Mitchell, Mayo's mentor and friend, in Adelaide's *Advertiser.*[37] Mitchell thought Mayo qualified as an "advanced" labor leader for his progressive views but he would not be accepted because, Mitchell believed, the majority of Australian workmen feared private masters and would always prefer the safe alternative of state regulation of industry. "This is why Democracy must be saved from itself," wrote Mitchell. "The best service that Mr. Mayo's book may do is keep that single fact to the front." Also in Adelaide, the *Australian Christian Commonwealth*[38] praised the book as "one of those best of all books to read," vigorous, original, clear, and stimulating. The *Sydney Morning Herald* held the same view; the book was "distinctly original . . . interesting . . . thought-provoking."[39] And the Melbourne *Argus,*[40] although condemning the work because it was not constructive, stated, "If Mr. Mayo, and his [W.E.A.] colleagues . . . can only induce workers to think seriously and honestly upon politics and economics, they will do a magnificent service, no matter what their own views may be."

Late in 1919 Mayo restated the main ideas of *Democracy and Freedom* in a short essay on industrial autonomy among workers. In postwar industrial reconstruction, he wrote, competition among individuals must give way to social cooperation, and company directors must take on community responsibilities in any plan to increase worker's participation in industry. Autonomy in industry comes through self-control, not voting and representation; and only those people who know the methods and conditions of work, market factors, modern economics, and the history of social organization are competent to share in industry. This knowledge would remove the intellectual fetters of the working class and help it achieve industrial autonomy.[41]

Thirty years later a conference was held on human relations in administration at the Graduate School of Business Administration, Harvard University. Mayo had been prominent on the faculty for twenty-one years and the conference was held in recognition of that service upon his retirement. His two lectures, "The Modernization of a Primitive Community" and "Changes and its Social Consequences," were published as *The Political Problem of Industrial Civilization,*[42] a book that calls for comparison with *Democracy and Freedom.*

The books have many points in common. Society is assumed to be a cooperative system of groups; relations among them are based on personal understanding, tradition, customs, and the will to work together. "Will, not force is the basis of the State"; centralist organization directed with compulsion is suited only to crises and emergencies, not peacetime work. The Queensland politicians who manipulated crowd sentiment are replaced by ignorant men, Hitler and Mussolini, who thrust heroic patterns of domination on modern democracies rather than use civilized ways of administration. Civilized administration requires enlightened leadership from educated administrators whose technical skills are supplemented by social skills; they are able to engender cooperative relations among people at work, and to ameliorate the hostility that flows from competition in the pursuit of self-interest. Marxist solutions to industrial problems are inadequate.

The theses are similar but the styles are different. In both writings Freud is mentioned, but in the later work psychoanalytic ideas are absent; instead, strong weight is given to the assumption that the psychological need for security and happiness is best satisfied by group membership and continuous association with others. As a young man Mayo had known how depressed a solitary person could become, and how important it had been for him to have the company of others. "The solitary who works alone is always a very unhappy man," he said in his final lecture.[43]

Mayo's understanding of this experience was deepened when, in 1919, his attention was drawn away from the political problems of Australia's postwar reconstruction, to the psychological problems of soldiers who suffered from war neurosis.

Notes

1. Curtis to Shepardson, 25 December 1948, in J. J. Conway, "The Round Table: A Study of Liberal Imperialism," Ph.D. dissertation, Harvard University, 1951.
2. Mayo to Keppel, 25 August 1941, MM 1.052.
3. *Queensland University Magazine,* August 1915, pp. 45-46.
4. Mayo papers, SAA.
5. University War Committee, *The University War Committee* (Brisbane: McGregor, 1915), p. 1. Mayo papers, SAA.
6. University War Committee, *Industrial Organization and the Cost of War* (Brisbane: McGregor, 1915), p. 2.
7. Elton to Dorothea, 18 November 1918.
8. Notes for a letter, Mayo to Professor Berry, n.d., probably 1916. Mayo's Notebooks, No. 7, GA 54.5, BLA.
9. Anna F. Booth and G. Elton Mayo, *Ring Down the Curtain,* in *Lady Galway Belgium Book,* comp. Marie C. Galway (Adelaide: Hussey & Gillingham, 1916).
10. Booth to Mayo, 23 July 1946, MM 1.022.
11. Elton Mayo, "Socialism and the War," MM 2.055.
12. Elton to Dorothea, 16, 24 March 1916.
13. Elton to Dorothea, 24 March 1916.
14. I. Young, *Theodore, His Life and Times* (Sydney: Alfa, 1971).
15. Elton to Dorothea, 1 April 1916.
16. Elton Mayo, *The Political Problem of Industrial Civilization* (Boston: Harvard University, Graduate School of Business Administration, Graduate School of Business, 1947).
17. Elton to Dorothea, 30 March, 2 April 1916.
18. Elton to Dorothea, 3 April 1916.
19. The letter is undated; probably October 1916. Mayo papers, SAA.
20. *Sydney Morning Herald,* 1 March 1918, p. 1; ibid., 8 March 1918, p. 8; Subcommittee on Rehabilitation of the Committee on Work and Industry, *Rehabilitation: Man and the Job,* Reprint and Circular Series, 121 (Washington, D.C.: National Research Council, March 1945).
21. Minutes, Senate, University of Queensland, 15 June 1917.
22. *Brisbane Courier,* 29 September 1917, p. 7; ibid., 6 October 1917, p. 4; Elton to Dorothea, 15 March 1918.
23. Elton to Dorothea, 14 March 1918.
24. Elton to Dorothea, 8, 11 March 1918.
25. Elton Mayo, "The Australian Political Consciousness," in *Australia, Economic and Political Studies,* ed. Meredith Atkinson (Melbourne, 1920), pp. 127-44.
26. Elton to Dorothea, 17 March 1918.
27. Elton to Dorothea, 3 March 1918.
28. Elton to Dorothea, 5 March 1918.
29. Elton to Dorothea, 17 March 1918.
30. Elton Mayo, *Democracy and Freedom: An Essay in Social Logic* (Melbourne: Macmillan, 1919).
31. *Herald* (Melbourne), 6 February 1919, MM. 1.060.
32. Herbert Heaton to Mayo, 14 February 1919, MM. 1.060.
33. Elton to Dorothea, 21 March 1919.
34. *Daily Mail* (Brisbane), 15 February 1919, MM. 1.060.
35. *Daily Standard* (Brisbane), 27 February 1919, MM. 1.060.
36. Elton to Dorothea, 23 March 1919.
37. *Advertiser* (Adelaide), 18 February 1919.

38. *Australian Christian Commonwealth* (Adelaide), 6 June 1919, M. 1.060.
39. *Sydney Morning Herald,* 8 March 1919.
40. *Argus* (Melbourne), 9 May 1919, M. 1.060.
41. Elton Mayo, "Industrial Autonomy," *Queensland University Magazine* 6, no. 8 (1919):5.
42. Mayo, *Political Problem of Industrial Civilization.*
43. Ibid.

7
Professor, Clinician, and Lecturer, 1919-1921

After the Great War Mayo's reputation grew as a successful academic, clinical psychologist, and public speaker. When the university was re-organized he was promoted to professor, and his psychology lectures attracted a young doctor who needed help with neurotic patients, especially shell-shocked soldiers. As he saw them Mayo developed the unique clinical skills that enabled him to treat cases that had baffled other clinicians, and to help his wife's three sisters with their emotional problems. Mayo applied his clinical experience and the new psychology he was reading (Janet, Freud, Adler, Jung) to problems in religion, politics, education, industrial relations, and child development, and he gave many public lectures on these topics.

Early in March 1919 Mayo left Dorothea with Patty and Ursula at Bowral, an inland holiday resort in New South Wales, and traveled home to Brisbane for the beginning of the academic year. On the way he stopped in Sydney to lunch and dine with academic colleagues, and, at the Australia Club, took the opportunity to discuss his ideas on social reform and the new psychology with the aging Sir Edmund Barton, Australia's first prime minister. Later Mayo packed his luggage carefully for a week's detention at Wallangara Camp, a quarantine station on Queensland's border for all northbound travelers who had been exposed to the frightening influenza epidemic in Australia's southern states.

At Wallangara Camp the showers and lavatories were so primitive and the camp grounds so dirty that he advised Dorothea to bring Patty home by ship or through a camp on Queensland's coast. What irritated him more was that his carefully packed luggage had been misplaced so he was without clean linen or adequate changes of clothing. But Mayo enjoyed the opportunity to talk seriously with working men on current issues in economics, sociology, religion, and psychology, and he was particularly pleased to discuss "French investigations of the superior and inferior psyche" with the camp doctor. The doctor called Mayo "Sir," and in doing so "amused [his] unconscious considerably."[1] But the most memorable day came when he received a telegram congratulating him on being promoted to the chair of philosophy at the University of Queensland. Mayo had hoped for changes in the organization of the university and had expected promotion for himself, but he was surprised by the swiftness and courage of the Senate's decisions.[2]

For two weeks after the telegram arrived Mayo's thoughts were occupied with real and imagined consequences of his promotion. Never far from them was the comforting image of Dorothea. On first hearing the news he wrote to congratulate her on becoming "Madame la Professeur," indicated what the salary would be, but asked her to mention the news only to friends and relatives, and especially not to tell certain medical specialists whom she was consulting on Patty's behalf because they might raise their fees when they learned of his new financial status. At the same time Mayo did not feel absolutely sure the telegram was true. Word spread through the camp and Mayo was pleased to accept congratulations, until one of his university colleagues, suffering from an acute attack of envy, insulted Mayo and roundly condemned the Queensland government for wasting its money by adding to the university's professorial staff.

When he returned to the university Mayo was gratified to learn of his new salary—£550 annually rising by £50 per annum to £800—and felt the initial change in status odd and uncomfortable, a feeling that was exacerbated by the irritating sycophants who insisted on "Professor Mayoing" him at every turn. But mild flattery from his assistant Percy Seymour, who was delighting in his own promotion to lecturer and that of philosophy to membership on the new Professorial Board at the expense of other departments, and increased deference from people outside university made Mayo pleased with himself. Then quickly he denied himself this pleasure, and countered the feeling of increased self-worth with an imagined "return along the road, eight years, to the solitary devil, an acknowledged failure, travelling, gloomily enough northwards to Queensland," and with the memory of an excellent mother and father who had been disappointed by their son's desultory achievements as a student, laborer, journalist, and printer. Yet he knew that he was a success, and reminded himself that as the university's first professor of philosophy he had the intellect and talent to match his peers on the Professorial Board. He resolved the conflict between expanding self-esteem and the anguish of old failures by sharing the feeling of achievement with Dorothea—"the prettiest woman in Queensland"— and by turning to his new work in medical psychology.[3]

Mayo found in his evening class for psychology students a Dr. Thomas R.H. Matthewson, whom he had met at a friend's home. Matthewson, a year younger than Mayo, had been born in Queensland, been educated in Brisbane, and had studied medicine at Edinburgh. He had impressed his teachers as an intelligent, painstaking, and first-class student. From 1910 to 1912 he had held medical and surgical posts at three hospitals in Edinburgh and Glasgow and then had returned to practice privately in Brisbane.

When he first met Mayo he was physician at the Sick Children's Hospital, and was specializing in functional and nervous diseases. In 1917 he reported on an epidemic of polio encephalitis in Brisbane and later published papers on the treatment of gastroenteritis among children and on a case of Hodgkin's disease. He had joined Mayo's class to learn more of the new psychology and of psychic factors in disease. When classes finished Matthewson would drive Mayo home to Montpelier and discuss cases he had seen. Mayo sent Matthewson a patient, and it was not long before they began clinical work together.[4]

Their first patient was a thirty-five-year-old man who, since the age of seventeen, had suffered from sexual anxieties, insomnia, and irrational fear of crowds. In an effort to treat himself he had read Freud, Brill, and Jung, understood them a little, and subsequently sought psychoanalytic treatment. To activate memories of early emotional life, Mayo talked with the man about his childhood activities, feelings, and ideas associated with them. Hoping that "my ancestors' flair for diagnosis has descended on me," Mayo began the analysis on the assumption that, first, the neuroses had started well before the age of seventeen, and, second, that the patient's assertions were the result of gradual mental development rather than a recent event or experience. Mayo administered Jung's association test, and noted that the word that occasioned the shortest reaction time was inconsistent with the patient's belief that the neurotic symptoms had first appeared at seventeen. After the test Mayo explained "free associations" and encouraged the patient to express his ideas freely by saying whatever came to mind. Then, as a stimulus to free associations, Mayo shot in the inconsistent word; immediately the patient related a long coherent story of events during his eighth year. "Matthewson was thunderstruck," and so was Mayo at the success of their first session. From what the patient had said, it seemed to Mayo that he and Matthewson were the first in Australia to use psychoanalysis as a therapeutic.[5]

Their second patient was a twenty-four-year-old, good-looking man from a decent family. His sister, who brought him to see Matthewson, said the family was distressed by the effect of the war on him. He was tense and nervous, suffered from headaches, blinked constantly as he looked at people, and started violently at the slightest sound. The patient told Mayo that at nineteen he had gone to war. While a sergeant major in the Medical Corps at Gallipoli, he was wounded and endured shell-shock. He was treated in Egypt and discharged as cured, but, because he was repulsed by the sight of blood and battlefield injuries, he was transferred to the Artillery and sent to France. Ten months later he was again wounded. The ship on which he was being sent to England was torpedoed and sank, but he was rescued. Subsequently he was put into the Flying Corps, but crashed on his first flight. While recovering he enrolled in Officers' School, and as a lieutenant returned to France, where he was soon promoted to captain. In battle outside Amiens, he saw four fellow officers and eight soldiers die and all his artillery destroyed. He struggled back to camp only to be sent back with more men and equipment. Within five minutes German airplanes dropped one hundred bombs on them and all his men were killed. He was brought in unconscious; when he came to he was unable to hear, speak, or see.

The man's symptoms formed a classic case of war neurosis and his experience with medical treatment had left him "sick of doctors," so Matthewson concluded there was little he himself could do. He called urgently for Mayo, who believed that the man would not be amenable to any treatment until he had developed some confidence in his doctor. Mayo administered Jung's association test, followed it with free associations, and discovered that the patient had been engaged to marry for almost three years before he had gone to war and that while he was away his fiancée had thrown him over for another man. To be told this fact meant to Mayo that he had taken an important step in winning the man's confidence. When he said he wanted to return for another session, Mayo believed successful treatment could begin.[6]

This patient was important because he gave Mayo another illustration for his university lectures and strengthened his belief that ideas in the classroom could be used successfully outside it. Also, the second case enhanced Matthewson's growing esteem for Mayo.

Mayo's third patient was more difficult to treat but led him to a dazzling analysis. No amount of questioning by Matthewson could uncover the cause of an eighteen-year-old girl's emotional distress. He asked for Mayo's help. The association test yielded nothing, so Mayo asked for a dream; she could recall only one and it was six months old. "At the time of the Armistice I dreamed that the Kaiser was walking about on the verandah talking to someone about poison pins. He came close to me, I screamed and woke up."

Because Mayo could get the girl to give no associations to "Kaiser" he tried "poison pins." She remembered a book about German spies who used poison pins, but recalled nothing more, so Mayo tried "pins" alone. "Dressmakers use them instead of tacking," she said, and remembered a story about a jealous dressmaker who threatened to stick pins into a certain customer who had shown an interest in the dressmaker's husband. Mayo asked the young patient for more. "Last year," she said, "my sister pricked her finger with a pin and poisoned it." Mayo wanted her to continue. "When my sister tries on dresses she sticks pins into me." Mayo asked, "What is your sister?" The girl replied, "A dressmaker." Mayo asked, "Is she jealous of you?" The girl answered, "Yes," and then the full account of the jealous spiteful sister was poured out.

Mayo was not satisfied that the dream itself had been fully analyzed because nothing of sexual significance had been revealed to the girl. Probably association to "Kaiser" would have eventually produced repressed sexual material, but as Mayo wrote to his wife, "I tried to get at it—but what can one do with a girl of eighteen—anyway we had found the neurosis."[7]

To have another case of his own to cite in lectures was valuable in itself, but it was particularly gratifying to Mayo to see his friend, the dour classicist John Michie, intrigued by the story.

The fourth case illustrates a new development in Mayo's clinical technique. Matthewson put the patient, a chauffeur stricken with anxiety neurosis, into a private hospital. The man could not sleep, and often when angered he would faint. He was too tense to respond to psychoanalysis, or complete an association test, so Mayo suggested that Matthewson try hypnosis. Matthewson was not confident enough to use hypnosis, so Mayo decided that he would try. First he explained "anxiety neurosis" to the chauffeur—when a slight emotion appears in the front of the mind the mental hinterland falls into a furious mental turmoil—and said that psychological analysis can show that mental turmoil is a response to an earlier shocking experience. Mayo had the patient sit comfortably, watch the skylight, and count "all the sheep in Australia." He said: "Your eyes will feel heavy and close, and you will sleep." The man's eyes closed, his breathing deepened, and he went to sleep. "Lift your right hand." He obeyed. Two minutes later he woke. Thereafter when the patient's agitation occurred, Mayo instructed he was to sleep for one minute and the agitation would disappear. Mayo rid the patient of a headache, and, through hypnosis, helped him recall the name of a book, and finally managed to administer an association test.

The session itself had lasted ninety minutes, but afterward Mayo spent forty-five minutes in conversation with the man, explaining that if he composed himself and relaxed properly then he could increase his control over the turmoil in his mental hinterland. A moment before their meeting ended Mayo suddenly said, "Sleep." The patient's eyes closed, he lay back quietly, relaxed, then shook himself, smiled, and said, "That was funny, wasn't it? I suppose you call that mesmerism."[8]

The assumption that proper relaxation engenders control over mental processes would guide Mayo three years hence in his industrial research on fatigue, boredom, mental disorder, and political activism in one of Philadelphia's spinning mills.

By 1920 Matthewson's medical practice had expanded so much that he turned away patients, especially in psychological work and curbed his early interest in children's diseases.[9] Much of the change was due to Mayo's help and advice. He assisted Matthewson with difficult psychoneurotics, and arranged for him to be a resident medical officer in New South Wales at Russell Lea, the Red Cross hospital for shell-shocked veterans.[10] For Matthewson's first psychological paper, "The Psychic Factor in Medical Practice," Mayo suggested dropping the question of the sexual etiology of psychoneurosis, concentrating on fear as a complication in disease, and illustrating the thesis with six of their clinical cases. The paper showed clearly the influence of Mayo's expressions and ideas, and was received as an "excellent epitome of modern thought in psycho-analysis."[11]

Matthewson's success was a source of vicarious gratification to Mayo. Because he was not a medical doctor he could not enjoy the recognition that he often felt their work in medical psychology deserved. He was pleased to see Matthewson's psychological practice grow and was grateful for such a keen and active associate, but he sometimes envied Matthewson's financial gains.[12]

The clinical work became too strenuous for Mayo, so in 1921, at Dorothea's suggestion, Matthewson stopped asking Mayo to take on the more difficult cases.[13] Occasionally they would see a patient together, and if Matthewson was out of town Mayo would care for a distressed individual, but in the last year of their association, their regular meetings were given over to discussion of psychic research and religious problems.[14]

Although the association between Mayo and Matthewson was close and had effectively changed their respective careers, their individual techniques of psychotherapy diverged. Matthewson was gentle, sympathetic, often playful, and largely submissive to the patient's fantasies; he was not openly aggressive, and emphasized rest as a central therapeutic. Although Mayo thought that he, too, was sympathetic with patients, he believed that he should eradicate irrational fear by dominating them forcefully and directing them tactfully in how to recover and enjoy mature and responsible relations with others. The case of Miss G. illustrates how different were the two techniques.

Matthewson was to be absent from Brisbane for a fortnight, and he suggested to Miss G. that, if need be, she could consult Mayo. Mayo wrote to Dorothea:

> The need accordingly appeared at once. She was to have seen me on Thursday but on Sunday she became 'miserable', poor thing, and rang up, so I agreed to see her this afternoon. I refused to enter into the game which she and Matthewson have devised of 'letting misery in', and 'putting him out' again. I talked to her for an hour and pointed out the game led nowhere—was in fact taking her back to her former position (she admitted this). I discussed the meaning of repression again, told her how she was refraining from talking to people or finding an interest in living simply in order to play a childish game with 'Misery.' I asked her if she played cards and she said that her father (dead 30 years ago) didn't like to. I rubbed this in—infantile. At the end of the interview she said she was miserable, but I didn't tone down my advice at all. I urged her to talk to people and listen to them—very unpalatable advice. I may have to see her—but I am going to make sure that she gets the right counsel—however miserable it makes her. I am inclined to think sometimes that Matthewson sometimes gives way too much to his patients' fantasies. She was really talking quite intelligently at the end of the interview—though miserable ... she cannot possibly get better while the 'scuffle' game with

'Misery' persists—it gets between her and all human relations. (Nine days later). I had a long interview with Miss G. . . . I grudged the afternoon to the poor old thing but she was very miserable—and Matthewson returns on Saturday. She is much more sensible—quite sees that she hasn't been backing up as she might and is prepared to try new methods. I finished by getting her to relax and doze on the front verandah while all the world came in and out.[15]

Although most of Brisbane's medical establishment was skeptical of Matthewson's methods and had little respect for Mayo's ideas, Matthewson was sent difficult cases. And though Mayo had decided not to treat any more patients, he felt obliged for their sakes to offer a second opinion when asked. Among Mayo's patients were youngsters, women with inexplicable pains, insomniacs, melancholics, and people with hysterical fits and tics; among his methods were muscular relaxation, mental distraction, hypnosis, and, as the case of Miss G, shows, persuasion.[16]

In an amusing way his work attracted the attention of visiting house guests at Montpelier. One such guest was the wife of the leading player in a touring Gilbert and Sullivan company. After dinner one evening she suggested Mayo show his skill, asking him in the lounge room to give her an association test for all the guests to see. He obliged and, to her surprise, found two complexes at once![17]

Mayo's psychological studies were enriched by a sad and frightening illness that Patty had contracted in 1918, when she was about two and a half. She began vomiting and became feverish, the surface of her left thigh reddened and became tender, and muscular spasms gave her acute pain. Medical specialists diagnosed osteomyelitis, an infection carried by the blood from one part of the body to the shafts of the bone where the blood supply is poor. Many children had died from the disease as it spread through their bodies. Patty grew weak and the pain increased. She was put to bed, her leg was immobilized in a splint, and she was to keep as still as she could. For eighteen months she was under these restrictions, until early in 1920 when the infection was contained, her temperature returned to normal, and she could run without pain.[18] Mayo was distressed by the need to restrain Patty so severely; during her slow convalescence he carried her gently on his shoulders, and helped her to restore the wasted leg muscles with regular swimming.

Patty's response to being kept in bed showed Mayo that a child's mental life was like that of a neurotic adult or a savage insofar as all three often fail to distinguish real from imagined events. Patty had no regular companions, so, as her nurse suggested, she invented two brothers, Ernest and Fred. During the endless loneliness they were her playmates, and helped her personality to grow by expressing her wishes and fears, sharing her difficulties, and personifying her interests and desires. She was frightened of wars and violence, so the brothers made excellent soldiers; because she could not move, they were endowed with great agility and enduring strength; and to fulfill her frustrated wishes to destroy the bonds upon her and at the same time be obedient, she made Ernest all evil and Fred all good. Mayo noted: "It is the infant's method of self-analysis and self-exploitation."[19]

Absence of companionship had played a part in the lives of Mayo's siblings and in his own adolescence and young adulthood; now he saw its impact on his own child. The experience contributed to his explanation of the personality disorders among compulsive neurotics that he gave in a public lecture, "Psychology and Religion," in September 1921:

> The child, like the adult, requires two spheres of social interest—the home and the wider social group outside the home. When either of these interests is lacking, the result is certain to be harmful. The identity in respect of the personal history of compulsion neurotics is often surprising—no school life before the age of twelve, solitary childhood, much association with adults. . . . The child who, during infancy has not associated with other children beyond the four walls of the home, and learned to hold his own with them, is unequal to the task of associating with them on terms of equality in adolescence and maturity. . . .[20]

In examination of psychoneurotics Mayo was often concerned with the role that religion had played in their lives. One case was the son of a prominent businessman who was deeply religious, highly agitated, and unable to manage his anxiety. Mayo had Matthewson put the man in Brisbane's Pyremont Hospital to rest and to read quietly. The treatment had some beneficial but insufficient results, for the young man found lying still to be difficult. Mayo explained that to lie still would be hard at first, and that it was his job as a patient to concentrate on this task, await simple rises in his emotions, and then "to sit on them." The patient had problems recognizing the kinds of emotions he was supposed to inhibit, and in his unsuccessful efforts to cooperate, began to play off Matthewson against Mayo. He acknowledged Matthewson's sympathy and decency but said he preferred Mayo's therapy because it directed him exactly what to do. Mayo thought this an ungrateful act and sought to reestablish both himself and Matthewson in the treatment. In light of the patient's religious convictions, Mayo invited him to discuss what was meant by the everlasting mercy of God. In time the patient understood that God's mercy was, in reality, an attribute of the individual's experience, i. e., his serenity of mind. He became much quieter, was very grateful for the help of both men, and in less than a month was much improved.[21]

In his patients Mayo found that the punitive features of religious dogma and practice gave rise to irrational fears, which he referred to as "conviction of sin,"[22] following Starbuck's idea. Three important patients whose lives had been shaped by this conviction were his sisters-in-law, Katherine, Ursula, and Barbara.

Katherine, at thirty-four, was still living with Mrs. McConnel, and in Mayo's view was doing nothing but expending mental energy and emotion. She was neurasthenic, and overtired, and had difficulty sleeping. She approached Mayo about her insomnia, attributing it to blood poisoning, which she suspected had been caused by a cut on her finger. Mayo examined the small clean cut, explained why there was no blood poisoning, and suggested she see Matthewson. Matthewson gave her an association test and coached her in how to rest. He regarded her condition as serious, and believed its origin lay somewhere in her infancy or youth but was uncertain as to the appropriate treatment. Mayo, who was familiar with the results of Mrs. McConnel's strict child-rearing practices, suggested to Katherine that she ask Matthewson if she could be admitted to Pyremont Hospital for two weeks under the Weir-Mitchell regimen. Matthewson agreed and, although Katherine went willingly, she felt ashamed of herself for letting down the family by being unable to manage her own life. Mayo helped her by cutting off all contact with her family, and asking Mrs. McConnel to suppress all letters to her. He stopped Katherine from reading, writing, and sewing, and persuaded Matthewson to keep her in a torpid state, free of visitors. She began to sleep well, dream, and otherwise yield up her troubles one by one. The aim of the treatment was to induce a humble and quiescent state into which distressing emotions could enter and then be consciously suppressed. Afterward Katherine's life became a little easier to bear, but she and her sisters remained under the mother's influence, and were a group of aloof, unenterprising women who waited for but rarely initiated social contact. Thus they perpetrated conditions that helped convince them of their own unworthiness and enjoyed few opportunities to enhance their self-esteem through easy association with others. To help Katherine escape from the family Mayo tried to get her some charity work with the church; meanwhile, she kept seeing Matthewson.[23]

Ursula, at thirty-two, was in Melbourne, where she had recently declined an offer to become a housemistress at a girls college. Shortly after her decision she complained of "flaming nerves." Mayo thought her symptoms were serious, and suggested to Dorothea, who was in Melbourne for the summer, that she ask Ursula if upon her return to Brisbane she would like to help him teach psychology. He thought she could administer Jung's association test to thirty or forty students, and follow this with Freud's free association test. She could also help demonstrate psychological cases and phenomena after Mayo's public lectures. Results of her work might even be prepared for publication in some American journals. After a year she could return to Melbourne equipped with considerable knowledge and some valuable skills, and continue her studies. Although Mayo wanted to help her, he did not want to take on her psychological problems. "If she gets nerves, I'll bully her into Pyremont." He preferred to see her in a job without pay rather than go under the Weir-Mitchell regimen.[24]

Within a week Ursula arrived at Montpelier and agreed to be Mayo's unpaid research assistant and psychological demonstrator. He gave her Jung's association test, and found a few easily recognizable and manageable complexes. She was keen to work with Mayo because he gave her a sense of purpose, and she promised that she would curb her readiness to suppose everyone who spoke to her was insulting her.

With Ursula he began a practice that would later become an essential part of his work with students. He took her to Pyremont Hospital to see a woman who was having fits. While he tried to persuade the patient that her fits were unnecessary, Ursula sat still and watched silently. "I am teaching her to suppress all her ideas and to observe the patient only," Mayo wrote to Dorothea.

Two days later he was discussing plans for his psychology class when conversation turned to an analysis of Ursula. She was amenable to the process, open-minded, and, Mayo thought, courageous. He saw that when the lacunae in her knowledge were filled, she would overcome her neurotic behavior, and easily develop a normal attitude to other people. From her point of view the work with him, his lectures, and the psychoanalysis combined to keep her out of an asylum for the insane.[25]

Barbara, the eldest of his three unmarried sisters-in-law, was Mayo's most difficult patient.[26] Early in 1921 she suffered a nervous breakdown, felt a loss of control over herself and her destiny, and could not sleep because her chest muscles and throat convulsed with a spasmodic tic. She had more social poise than the other two sisters. She had traveled through Europe, Russia, and the United States, and enjoyed a reputation as an opera singer, but her emotional life was little more than a string of tragic love affairs. In consequence she believed wrongly that she was immensely egotistical, and had developed the habit of becoming rattled, i.e., psych-asthenically confused, whenever two or more people spoke to her.

Mayo talked with Barbara for two days. His first task was to master an emotional problem aroused by the remarkable likeness between Barbara and Dorothea, and his longing for Dorothea, who was in Sydney with their newborn daughter Ruth. He had seen Dorothea beset by irrational fears, and he had been able to help her overcome them. Now he saw the same fears in Barbara, and his heart ached for the presence of Dorothea to help him separate his erotic interest in Barbara from the equally powerful need to be a detached and expert clinician.

Mayo attributed Barbara's anxiety primarily to Mrs. McConnel's strong distaste for and strong attraction toward sex. Barbara firmly resisted any suggestion that she should seek psychological help, had no intention of being hospitalized and preferred to manage her difficulties herself with, perhaps, a little help from Mayo. She said this in the lounge at Montpelier, and the opportunity arose to bring Matthewson into the conversation; Mayo and Matthewson talked freely of their cases, how well they were going, and this had its effect on the resistant Barbara. Later Mayo explained the meaning of "nervous break-down" and told her about the content of his lectures, and she accepted from him one of Herbart's books. She began to talk about herself, her fear of the future, and the horrifying idea that never again would she be able to control her voice because of the involuntary contractions of the throat and chest muscles. Mayo learned that at the age of three years her hands had been tied to the sides of her cot to stop her from tearing off her nightclothes in the hot weather, and at the same time she had been severely punished for not going to sleep. This was one origin of the neurotic muscular contractions and insomnia, but Mayo believed that her fear of never again being able to sing brought on the contractions, was related to her unhappy love affairs, and could be attributed primarily to Mrs. McConnel's attitudes toward sex. But how? It seemed that her symptoms constituted an ingenious rationalization to keep her from the emotional distress that had emerged from her wish to be a singer and also to enjoy gratifying sexual experiences.

Elton promised Dorothea that he would treat Barbara, and pledged to himself that she would be his last case. She agreed to cooperate. After the two days of talking and analysis Elton administered an association test; he diagnosed a compulsion neurosis with a strongly repressed conviction of sin. She found religion horrible, especially as it was practiced on Sundays at Cressbrook, imagined God was an avenger, felt ambivalent toward her family, harbored sadistic impulses and was driven by a strong sexual curiosity. As well as infantile traumas, she recalled another vision or dream she had had while under an anesthetic at nineteen: a taunting devil, a vicious God, and Ursula weeping tears of blood over Barbara's wickedness. She also recalled a love affair in London that had been spoiled by a sudden conviction that she was being sinful. Such thoughts as these brought on the tic of which Mayo would manage to rid her.

Barbara was deeply shaken, and understood that satisfactory treatment could be done only if she were in hospital. Pleased that he had overcome her resistance to treatment, Mayo with Matthewson's help arranged for Barbara to have a quiet room in a new hospital. Mayo believed he had not been given sufficient respect by the nursing staff at Pyremont Hospital, so at the new hospital the staff were instructed by Matthewson that Mayo was not to be disturbed. Barbara saw Mayo twice a day. When he was absent she concentrated on her feelings about the conviction of sin, and many bitter experiences came back to her. Fears of incest appeared in her dreams about life in England, which Mayo attributed to Mrs. McConnel and her banning of sex from the girl's youth. Barbara was staggered by this revelation. As more unhappy material emerged her misery deepened, and she saw that she must stay longer in hospital to work on the problems when Mayo was not with her. In time she could so control her approach to the therapy that she began to see, for example, that her broadmindedness on sexual matters concealed ignorance and confusion rather than displayed sophisticated understanding, and that a complete reconstruction of her emotional life was needed if she were to master fully her insomnia and spasmodic convulsions.

Mayo was determined to treat her successfully. Although he knew that other therapists would not follow him, he was convinced that his "down with all the barriers method" was appropriate. She was his most important patient because she had enough confidence to weather the therapeutic storm he initiated, the intelligence to reflect sensibly on what of herself was being revealed, the willingness to accept his directions, and the good sense to see how firmly he believed in her capacity for self-analysis. And because she shared these attributes with Dorothea, Mayo found Barbara's case one of the most difficult to treat.[27]

In September 1921 Barbara was so much better that Mrs. McConnel noted the change as "extraordinary." Later that year Barbara decided to undergo an operation from which she knew she would probably not recover. She asked Mayo to await a communication from her after death. He agreed, and waited in vain; but then he did not really imagine that contact with the after life was as easy as Barbara had expected.[28]

At the time Mayo was developing his skill and practical understanding of clinical psychology his attention was arrested by the general and growing disposition in the community to attack the university. The attack was joined by utilitarians who wanted to use the university for training professionals, and labor supporters who thought the university should educate more of the underprivileged citizens. On another front a sharp battle developed between the university and extremists in the Workers' Educational Association over control of workers' education. The latter conflict drew Meredith Atkinson from Melbourne to conciliate. Mayo was involved in the solutions to both problems.[29]

To resolve the problem of general attacks on the university and its relation to the community, the Public Lecture Committee was established in April 1919, and Mayo offered the services of his department to give "extension lectures designed primarily to arrest the attention of the general public."[30] The second problem required a clear, full statement of the relation between the WEA and the university. The Senate announced that in Queensland the WEA was a self-governing body and independent of the university. Its aim was to federate working-class organizations and to educate men and women through public lectures and tutorial classes. In this latter aim the WEA and the university were to be associated, neither having a say in the other's affairs. The tutorial classes were to be limited to thirty members, whose task was to undertake three years intensive study in history, economics, biology, literature, and other disciplines. The Joint Committee for Tutorial Classes was established and guidelines for it were laid down by the University Senate and the WEA. Mayo volunteered to take a class in psychology and offered ten lectures without fee.[31]

When he began teaching in 1919 Mayo had been impressed by a political skirmish among returned soldiers. On March 24 *The Daily Standard,* a labor newspaper with the largest circulation in Brisbane, published an editorial recommending that the ban on flying the red Russian flag be abolished. That evening a crowd of former soldiers rioted in protest against the Russian Association in South Brisbane. Next day *The Daily Standard* condemned the riot, and that evening the offices of the newspaper were stoned by another crowd of former soldiers who howled, cheered, and, after listening to patriotic speechmakers, burst into "God Save the King." *Democracy and Freedom* had pointed up the psychological origins and dangers of mob action, and now Mayo noted that "it is extraordinary how much soldier fury that straggling Russian red flag procession has aroused."[32] The person allegedly responsible for rousing political turmoil by raising a red flag was charged, and his case had been well publicized when Mayo gave two lectures for the Public Lecture Committee.

The lectures were given in Brisbane's Albert Hall. At the first the chairman was Minister for Public Instruction John Huxham; at the second, Archbishop Donaldson.[33] The lectures were Mayo's first public lectures on psychopathological aspects of personality and social processes.

The first lecture, "The Emotional Factor in Society," asserts that all forces leading to either civilized or anarchical activity originate in the human mind. The conscious part of the mind helps individuals alone and in groups to adapt natural instincts to environmental demands and so meet their needs. Civilization is the product of this adaptive action. Children enter the world with instinctive desires and capacities for survival. To survive and gratify the desires they must learn to understand their chaotic instincts and the pressures of the environment, and, with intelligence, blend the two into a purposive organic whole. But understanding oneself is difficult because at the back of one's mind is the race consciousness that criticizes and intervenes in one's personal growth toward organic unity. The race consciousness does not insist upon only instinctive gratifications; it demands personal growth and the achievement of individuality. Men are society's civilizing agents, not only from choice but also from nature, and men's lives are emotional struggles to achieve individuality through the integration of inherited or racial attributes with demands of the physical and social environment. Emotions indicate the adequacy of the relation among the three elements: race consciousness, developing self, and environment. A neurasthenic person—eccentric, self-centered, and unreasonable—suffers emotionally from an inadequate relation among the three elements, and in an extreme situation race consciousness may rise, smash the developing individuality, and cause its disintegration into uncoordinated primary impulses.

Because current theories of human nature ignore the person's natural urge to be an individual and ignore the impact of race consciousness, the present social system does not meet today's demands. For example, the leaders of the industrial system ignore the human elements in work, use outdated abstractions, and impose work systems that upset the adequate relation between the working individual and race consciousness, and consequently provoke destructive impulses. Also, the utilitarians who dominate the education system impose too many unnecessary examinations, which requires that school be like a prison and that the student's broad outlook be narrowed to a prelude to merely professional interests. Current educational practice excludes learning about human nature, whereas it should make education a prelude to adventure, allowing persons to think for themselves and pursue interests free of custom and convention.[34]

The second lecture, "At the Back of the White Man's Mind," includes ideas that Mayo would use often in later years. The title reveals two ideas that he frequently used in discussions with students, i. e., the false dichotomy and the "twisteroo," as his student Fritz Roethlisberger would call it.[35] The title is taken from Donald Crawford's *Thinking Black,* an account of a missionary's life in Central Africa between 1890 and 1912; Mayo's approach to the mind and Crawford's lifelong observations show a remarkable parallel.[36]

Conventional opinion held that the mind of a White was different in kind from that of a Black, that logical syllogisms and foresight were the unique features of the White's civilized mind, and that old customs, natural phenomena, and superstitions dominated "black thinking." Crawford gives many examples of customs that govern "black thinking": Nkole, a custom whereby a harmless third party is kidnapped and held as surety against a crime committed by someone unknown in the belief that the unknown person will someday retaliate by claiming damages for illegal seizure; a young innocent girl is beaten for a crime committed by her twin sister because both were born twins, lived as twins, and must therefore suffer as twins. But when Crawford describes the process of "black thinking," he reveals that although the customs that govern it appear uncivilized the processes themselves are no different from, and sometimes superior to, "white thinking." He says the rationalizations in "black thinking" show neither stupidity nor deficiency of intelligence, and often function at a high level of abstraction. Furthermore, in the ease of superacute senses, the Black's mind is the more sophisticated of the two. Most White's consider superacute sense as a sense *in addition to* the five senses and call it the "sixth sense." In "black thinking" the sixth sense is the *coalescence* of the five senses into a fresh pattern of thought that incorporates real knowledge. With evidence of five senses the Black would debate or argue a case syllogistically, but with the real knowledge derived from the sixth sense— wisdom—there is no room for debate or argument because syllogisms do not apply to deep thought of unconscious origin.[37]

Mayo argues that processes in the back of the White's mind, the mental hinterland, determine conscious thinking and behavior and, consequently, conventional opinion promotes a false dichotomy when it holds that the minds of Blacks and Whites differ in kind. In this way he expands the point he made in the first lecture: the individual's race consciousness—the passive critic of personal development—lies ready in the mental hinterland to intervene actively when occasion demands.

The lecture assumes, contrary to current texts on psychology, that thought and consciousness are not equivalent, that the personal self, does not incorporate the consciousness, and that the self can be analyzed. Many examples and authorities show thought and consciousness are not the same, e.g., when we sleep we are conscious of events around us, and we experience several intermediate stages of consciousness between sleep and waking (William James, Sigmund Freud, Auguste Forel, Charles Peirce, Paul Bjerre, Otto Wetterstrand).

That there are different levels of consciousness is the starting point for Mayo's theory of the self. The first level of attention or consciousness includes the personal self of which we are immediately aware, and the idea that when we think we are thinking about something and can easily name it. The second level of consciousness comprises our memories of forgotten events, outlined in Freud's dream theory, and evident when a feverish person becomes delirious, or in the works of a poet like Coleridge. To emphasize the difference between the two levels of the psyche Mayo contrasted the early British philosophers of psychology with modern psychologists by saying: "The sensationist psychologists of the nineteenth century studied memory while the modern psychologist studies forgetting."

Modern psychologists, Jean-Martin Charcot, Pierre Janet, and Alfred Binet are concerned with dissociation of the mind or split consciousness. Janet discovered that apparently anesthetic areas of the body were controlled by a split-off portion of consciousness, concluded that in the body are areas of lessened attention, and illustrated the conclusion with a patient who would not heed shouting but had a secondary self that could hear whispering. The two dissociated areas are complementary; thus we have the "dual personality." This abnormal condition involves a definite loss of intelligence and mental power. It is like the second level of consciousness in a normal person because that also involves some monotony and routine control of automatic actions like habits and forgotten events preserved in one's memory. That the distortion between the first and second levels of consciousness is valid for normal as well as dissociated personalities has been shown in experiments by Binet and in clinical casework with Janet's method of distraction.

The third level of consciousness is illustrated with cases from work by Richard von Krafft-Ebing, Janet, Binet, Charles Fere, and Joseph Delboeuf. The continued control of this level of consciousness is so difficult to demonstrate that the best illustrations appear in the hypnoid state or when the primary self is disintegrated. This third level of consciousness is Jung's impersonal consciousness; it comprises the inherited control of instincts and reflexes and is called by Mayo "race consciousness."

When the demands made of life by the "race consciousness" are inconsistent with the mode of living that a civilized individual has adopted, the lower two levels of consciousness conflict, and the person may suffer from nervous disorders. To support the psychological etiology of neuroses, Mayo cites Freud, Jung, and Alfred Adler, and adds that Arthur F. Hurst, author of *Medical Diseases of the War* (1917), found that in his experience all neuroses had psychological origins. This indicates that healthy individual development must be guided by a social purpose that suppresses some natural capacities of the race consciousness and sublimates others.

Human conflicts are difficult to manage because they begin beneath the level of personal consciousness. The essential part of curing human conflict is through abreactions—release of the emotion along new lines—and purposive reeducation. Amnesia in wartime and shell shock are good examples.

Failure to reduce inner conflict and to achieve an integrated personal self (individuality) causes physical ill health, personal unhappiness, and social disintegration. So in the struggle and search for individuality the person must take account equally of inherited factors and difficulties presented by the environment. He will find himself "out there in the world, in society, in the universe; [and] the spirit of the universe is in man—if he can find it."[38]

During 1920 Mayo continued using his clinical experience to illustrate lectures and extend his theory of the mind, and also to get support for his ideas on education, and how everyday life could be more humane, enjoyable, adventurous, and effective if people understood themselves better. To this end he considered opening his Psychology I lectures to the public, and offering a series of twelve lectures to people far from Brisbane.[39]

One such lecture was "Fear," given first at the inland town of Toowoomba, where the organizer of the event was so pleased that he began a movement to establish a course of such lectures for the community.[40] Mayo repeated the lecture in Brisbane two months later.[41]

The lecture distinguishes normal from abnormal development, arguing that in the normal person the capacities for thought, feeling, emotion, and action are equally and harmoniously developed. Normality is achieved when the individual has learned to understand and control both environment and racial consciousness. "Life is a struggle for individuality and control—a struggle in which the individual is compelled to take account equally of forces in the environment and of inherited factors in himself." Fear interrupts normal living. Some fears are directly tied to the environment, e.g., ferocious animals, which we either fight or flee from; other fears are subjective and persist as uneasy elements in our consciousness. The latter fears may be attached to illnesses, anger, remorse, or other emotional conditions. Association tests can show how common are such fears, and how they are repressed and kept unconscious in the mental hinterland. Such deep fears are caused either by the environment, and are transient, or by mental disintegration of the self. The first type is illustrated by cases of shell shock or fear of death from influenza; in the second type the fear is a symptom difficult to remove, e.g., fear of disease due to another person's death, melancholia, fear of being subject to authority. Many such fears can be found in the minds of savages, and are controlled by primitive taboos that serve to repress their emotional origins. In our civilization educational practices are like taboos, do the same work as taboos, and consequently do not help the child to develop. Although our civilization seeks to cast out fears, it has imported many, e.g., fears of sex, which have lead to sexual perversions and neuroses; fear of God and the growth of Satanism; fear of the future and the hatred of the world order. Such fears are often concealed by social movements that purport to raise the level of civilized life but are based on fear and hate. Studies in social psychology show that they are antisocial and detrimental to the normal growth of the individual.

Although Mayo's public lectures were successful in themselves, their value was limited because they did not involve systematic study, were disconnected and infrequent, lacked free discussion and interchange of ideas, and were delivered mainly in Brisbane, and then only to an audience of interested intellectuals. The Workers' Educational Association was situated so as to counter these drawbacks except that it appealed to only one section of the community. The university's Department of Correspondence Studies distributed lecture notes widely to people seeking professional qualifications, but the notes were little more than an inferior textbook. So in July 1920 a proposal was put to the university's Board of Faculties to raise the standard of adult education by bringing the university closer to the people. It recommended that the disconnected extramural activities should be reorganized with an emphasis on nonprofessional and nonvocational education. Proof of demand lay in the work of the WEA Workers' School of Social Science, scientific and literary clubs, and other private and semiprivate organizations. A committee was proposed of townsfolk in Brisbane, Toowoomba, Rockhampton, and Townsville to organize local activities. A lecturer would be appointed to each district, and a chief lecturer would be appointed to coordinate the work throughout Queensland. The person would have professorial status, be based in Brisbane, would lecture inside the university and out, tour the countryside, and generally supervise and direct district activities. The subjects should include history, economics, literature, philosophy and science. It was hoped that the centers eventually would develop with added staff into university colleges where the first year of a degree could be completed. The proposal was a clear expression of Mayo's plan to extend the university's work.[42]

During 1921 Mayo gave many lectures outside the university. In March he was asked to speak at a luncheon at the Advertising Men's Institute. He was writing articles on the psychological causes of industrial unrest for Ambrose Pratt's *Industrial Australian Mining Standard,* and agreed to deliver a lecture at a conference in Sydney, "The Spirit and the Working of the Present Economic Order in Australia." He decided to use the luncheon talk as a trial run of his Sydney and Melbourne material; he called it "Industrial Unrest and Psychological Research," and it served as a plea for psychological research in industry.[43]

The talk identifies the presence of industrial unrest and social movements that make for revolution, e.g., Satanism and its vicious hostility toward the world order, and warns that the problems are like those that emerged before the Great War. In industry careful attention and effort is needed to combat the social unrest arising from industrial ills. Arbitration courts are no longer able to help. Unrest means general dissatisfaction, suspicion, distrust, strikes, "go slow" practices, sabotage, bitter class divisions. It also means political organizations that exacerbate these ills by appealing to fear, rage, and hate. The imminence of destruction does not allow for creative reform of society. The press is mistaken in assuming that social ills can be resolved by rational discussion because psychological research has shown the cause of these ills lies not in the rational but the nonrational part of the mind. Thus it is necessary to study "fantasy compensations" as the cause of the symptoms of social unrest. In the eighteenth and nineteenth centuries theories of mind assumed that people were governed by the will to work and the will to be free. The latter determined political institutions, and was extended to industrial organizations. The former is expressed in the selfishness of the economic motive, demand for the security of tenure, and a sense of social function. These are important, but the more fundamental problem is that workers have lost the faculty to enjoy life because civilization treats them as mere items, and industry makes it impossible for them to participate in work simply because they want to. Instead too much emphasis is given to the material aspect of life and work, and little to intellectual pleasures. So long as civilization blindly disregards certain mental factors that contribute to the individual's development, society shall have many "lame dogs," i. e., people who find life and work dissatisfying, and whose mental disintegration and fear of life lead to an abandonment of effort and, eventually, nervous breakdown. Psychological investigation of problems at work is needed to prevent this.

The talk lasted about an hour, and Mayo believed that it had been received well enough for him to continue the theme at the Sydney conference, where he gave more time to the history of industrialization and its effect on the social order, and, presented more evidence of the causes of low morale among workers, and its consequences for human happiness. This point was drawn from *Democracy and Freedom.* At the Sydney conference he also joined the panel discussion "The Supremacy of Christ in All

Human Relationships." Here he took the position of a psychologist and set himself the task of showing how in human nature can be found all that Christ stood for in human progress. He did this by presenting his theory of mind, i.e., levels of consciousness, and by contrasting his ideas with those of the biologist. His message was modified further for a talk, "Deficiencies of Education," given under the auspices of the Australian Education Fraternity in Brisbane in July 1921. In it he outlined the psychological consequences of causes of industrial and social unrest, the importance of the human factor at work, and psychological research into the "mental hinterland," making a strong appeal to augment occupational and technical education training with education for living. "Commerce was made for man and not man for commerce" met with a round of applause![44] In another address, "Influence of Advertising on the Character of Business," Mayo made the same basic points, and sought to convince advertising men that they should take a professional approach to their work and join university researchers in modern psychology to learn what mental processes were involved when people made purchases.[45]

In the middle of 1921 Mayo gave ten lectures on abnormal psychology as part of the university's new policy to take adult education to the outside community. The first lecture criticizes the sensationists for omitting human instincts from a theory of mind. By separating traditional academic psychology from the new medical psychology, Mayo showed that instincts are fundamental, and the assumption that man thinks only rationally is clearly false. Medical psychology demonstrates that rational thinking, like sanity, is achieved through an education that develops rather than suppresses inherited mental capacities. So we need to know how complex is the mind if we are to help ourselves develop to a civilized stage. The second lecture on the complexity of the mind reviews the work of the early hypnotists— Mesmer, Elliotson, Esdaile, and Braid, whose work helps identify different levels of consciousness. Charcot, Krafft-Ebing, Forel, Delboeuf, Bernheim, and Wetterstrand had experimented on the complexity of the mind, and Mayo illustrated the effect of different states of consciousness with cases of shell-shocked soldiers and by hypnotizing a person from the audience. The third lecture shows that different levels of consciousness and varieties of dissociated thought are found not only in the clinic but also in everyday life. Each person's "mental hinterland" effects changes in behavior, and research illustrations of Charcot and Janet augment accounts of unusual daily activities of shell-shocked soldiers. In the fourth lecture appear Janet's theories of hysteria as a form of retraction of the field of consciousness and dissociation, and the processes of psychasthenia, e.g., doubts, obsessions, agitation, and other forms of fantasy thinking. Illustrations are from cases of disturbed children in families where excessive restrictions are placed on impulsive actions. The other five lectures are on Freud, and discuss the unconscious, sexuality, psychoneurosis, dreams, and compulsion neurosis. The final lecture restates the main themes of the earlier talks on the origins of social unrest and low industrial morale, and the importance of the individuals' struggles to understand and control their environments as well as themselves so that living becomes worthwhile. Mayo concluded with his frequent observation that modern democracies are in conflict with the developing will and freedom of humankind.[46]

Following the last of this series Mayo gave the second Douglas Price Memorial Lecture, "Psychology and Religion." Douglas Price (1874-1916) was born of a Quaker family in Birmingham, England, became deeply religious when young, but at eighteen rejected the coldness of Quakerism and was baptized into the Church of England. After completing theological studies and working for five years as curate of St. Mark's in Leicester, he came to Queensland in 1903 to be principal of the Brisbane Theological College and rector of All Saints Church. Within a few years he became a mystic, and fearlessly belittled the conventional doctrines of the Trinity, the Virgin Birth, and the Deity of Jesus, and the concept of atonement. He resisted subtle pressure to resign but the archbishop of Brisbane concluded that Price's sermons held so little positive emphasis on the verities of faith and had so much to condemn them, that in 1910 he called for Price's resignation. The congregation supported Price's views and asked the archbishop to reconsider. Although he admired Price's plainness and honesty, the archbishop refused to alter the decision, and Price left the country. He returned in 1911, became an active modernist and extolled a new religious spirit that sought to restate old religious faiths with the truths of science and criticism. The first Douglas Price Memorial Lecture had been given in March 1920 by Mayo's colleague Meredith Atkinson, who followed Price's ideas in his presentation, "The Place of Ethics and Religion in Education."[47]

Mayo's lecture also followed the general theme of Price's ideas by adopting a detached view of religion and religious practices, and referring to psychological research and anthropological studies to show that in many cases the adolescent experience of religious conversion involves an overwhelming conviction of sin, a sense of incompleteness, insecurity, and an unrealistic view of the social and material world. Brooding depression and morbid introspection ensue, real interest in the social world is withdrawn, the individual becomes preoccupied with self and has no concern for others. Suddenly interest turns outward; morbid introspection gives over to happy serenity, the self becomes part of the universe, the adolescent submits to God, old loves and hatreds are given up, faith enters, the outside world is received, and new mental currents stream forth. But this is not always the case. Mayo centered attention on the conviction of sin, its role in abnormal mental life, especially in compulsion neurosis, and asserted that if the conviction is accompanied by excessive repression of racial capacities and restriction of social life, then it may never be adequately understood and mastered, and mental ill health is likely to result. If religion is to contribute to the healthy development of normal adults, then it must help adolescents with the psychological problems of the conviction of sin and not exploit them during the process of religious conversion simply to gain adherents to the church. For this reason church leaders should study human experience, pursue the religion that gives a sense of unity with God and the universe, and therewith develop in people the vision to aspire to knowledge of themselves and to construct a better social order. On these final points Dorothea had specific ideas that Mayo used to improve the lecture for publication.[48]

At the end of 1921 he attended the annual reunion dinner for students and tutors of the WEA. In proposing the toast he traced the history of the WEA in England, told how Australian workers had overcome their early suspicions of the university's links with the association, and said that much good work had been achieved.[49] A week later he gave his last lecture in Brisbane at the Trades Hall. He wanted to do well because interstate delegates to the Australian Labour Party conference were to be present. He decided to make "a sort of summing up" and then restate the necessity for psychological research for industrial peace. He spoke for just over an hour and afterwards amused the audience with his replies to three critics. One tried to ridicule Mayo by saying that he was standing on his head. Mayo answered whereupon the critic tried to fire a further salvo but became so confused that Mayo said finally, "Well, sir, I agree with you that one of us is standing on his head!" The hall rang with laughter. Mayo wrote to Dorothea: "I always enjoy the discussion."[50]

Notes

1. Elton to Dorothea, 11-17 March 1919.
2. Elton to Dorothea, 15, 16, 19, 21, 23 March 1919.
3. Elton to Dorothea, 26, 29 March 1919.
4. Elton to Dorothea, 29 March 1919; Board of Faculties, University of Queensland, "Tenth Report" (1921), pp. 62-70.
5. Elton to Dorothea, 6 April 1919. This case is reported, with minor changes, in Elton Mayo, "Should Marriage Be Monotonous?" Harper's 151 (1925):426.
6. Elton to Dorothea, 20 April 1919. This case is like the soldier in Elton Mayo, "Civilized Unreason," Harper's 148 (1924):530.
7. Elton to Dorothea, 26, 27 April 1919.
8. Elton to Dorothea, 27 April 1919.
9. Elton to Dorothea, 19, 20 March 1920.
10. Elton to Dorothea, 29 February 1920; Board of Faculties. University of Queensland, "Tenth Report" (1921), p. 67.
11. Elton to Dorothea, 20 March 1920; Thomas H. R. Matthewson, "The Psychic Factor in Medical Practice," Medical Journal of Australia, 24 July 1920, pp. 73-77, 86.
12. Elton to Dorothea, 20 March 1920.
13. Elton to Dorothea, 7 March 1921.

14. Elton to Dorothea, 13, 14, 20, 23, 27 March, 3, 10, 23 April, 8, 13 May, 29 September, 15 October 1921.
15. Elton to Dorothea, 10, 19 May 1921.
16. Elton to Dorothea, 19 March 1920, 7 April, 6, 8, 9 May, 15 October 1921.
17. Elton to Dorothea, 19 October 1921.
18. Elton to Dorothea, 20 February, 19 March 1920; conversation with Patricia Elton Mayo, January 1974.
19. Elton Mayo, "The Secret Gardens of Childhood," MM 2.056.
20. Elton Mayo, *Psychology and Religion: Douglas Price Memorial Lecture, No. 2* (Melbourne: Macmillan, 1922), pp. 24-25.
21. Elton to Dorothea, 4, 23 March 1920.
22. Mayo, *Psychology and Religion.*
23. Elton to Dorothea, 28, 29 February, 1, 2, 4, 7-10, 12 March 1920, 7, 17 March, 23 April 1921.
24. Elton to Dorothea, 8, 9 March 1920.
25. Minutes, Senate, University of Queensland, 16 April 1920; Elton to Dorothea, 19, 21, 23 March 1920.
26. Elton to Dorothea, 3-27 May 1921.
27. Elton to Dorothea, 25 May, 9 November 1921.
28. Patricia Elton Mayo to Trahair, 12 January 1978.
29. Elton to Dorothea, 21, 23, 26 March 1919.
30. Minutes, Senate, University of Queensland, 14 April 1919.
31. Ibid., 16 April, 14 November 1919.
32. Elton to Dorothea, 26 March 1919.
33. *Brisbane Courier,* 18 September 1919, p. 8; ibid., 2 October 1919, p. 8.
34. MM 2.019.
35. Fritz J. Roethlisberger, Introduction to *The Human Problems of an Industrial Civilization,* by Elton Mayo (New York: Viking, 1960; London: Macmillan, 1933).
36. D. Crawford, *Thinking Black: 22 Years without a Break in the Long Grass of Central Africa* (London: Morgan Scott, 1913); William Kyle's notes on Elton Mayo, n.d. (from D. W. McIlwain, University of Queensland).
37. Crawford, *Thinking Black,* pp. 9, 72, 388.
38. MM 2.017.
39. University of Queensland, *Calendar,* 1922, p. 223; Elton to Dorothea, 1, 19 March 1920.
40. Elton to Dorothea, 28 March 1920.
41. MM 2.021.
42. Minutes, Board of Faculties, University of Queensland, 2 July 1920.
43. Elton to Dorothea, 29, 30 March 1921; MM 2.021.
44. *Brisbane Courier,* 19 July 1921, p. 7.
45. MM 2.021.
46. *Brisbane Courier,* 1 July 1921, p. 8; 15 July 1921, p. 6; *Daily Standard* (Brisbane), 11 July 1921, p. 6; ibid., 26 July 1921, p. 6; ibid., 13 September 1921, p. 5. The last five lectures were not reported.
47. A. Ralston, "Biographical Sketch" (of Douglas Price), in *The Place of Ethics in Religion and Education: Douglas Price Memorial Lecture, No. 1,* by Meredith Atkinson. (Brisbane: Cuming, 1920).
48. *Brisbane Courier,* 22 September 1921, p. 9; Elton to Dorothea, 27 September 1921; Mayo, *Psychology and Relgion.*
49. Elton to Dorothea, 29 September, 7 October 1921.
50. Elton to Dorothea, 10, 16 October 1921.

8

Crises and Career, 1919-1921

Although his reputation was growing Mayo was not satisfied with his career. He wanted to extend scientific research in psychological problems and find practical solutions to them, but administrative difficulties at the university commanded his attention. To overcome these as well as teach and do research meant that he overworked, and his doctor forced him to curb his activities. The university helped him, but he was nevertheless dissatisfied with his life in Brisbane because university support was insufficient and his colleagues were ambivalent toward him and his work. He tried to quit the university but could find no other job. He took leave to study and write. Writing was difficult, but eventually he published his ideas on the psychological origins of industrial conflict. He began planning to study in Britain in the hope he could work elsewhere and never have to live again in Queensland.

Between the middle of 1919 and the end of 1921 Mayo worked constantly on the task of establishing conditions for the scientific research into aspects of the new psychology and for putting that research into use. He believed psychological research would bring immediate benefits, and pointed to his own work with Matthewson's more difficult patients. In May 1919 Mayo drafted a proposal to the Walter and Eliza Hall Trust, an Australian foundation that supported academic research into the alleviation of human suffering, for a fellowship in psychology and psychotherapy to inquire into the applications of those disciplines to shell shock and kindred mental disorders.[1] He described how he and Matthewson had applied the techniques of psychoanalysis, suitably amended by the British neurophysicians, and that in Brisbane the Church of England had been so impressed with their successes that it had made available to them an outpatient department in a new hospital. Mayo wanted to do part of the work himself, so anticipating that he could be freed from teaching duties he requested half a professorial salary for two years. He closed the proposal with a typically hostile observation on current medical practice in Brisbane: "At present the neurasthenic and neurotic are all too often abandoned to the mercies of the quack and the charlatan."[2] In September the trust announced continued support for fellowships in engineering, and grants in economics, biology, and applied chemistry, but nothing was offered for Mayo's work.[3] Nevertheless, he was determined to carry it forward and continued searching for its financial support.

By June 1920 he knew that he had taken on far too much. He was treating patients, extending his lecture program, administering a growing department, and planning more research. Also, he had promised to write a book on his research for Macmillan during his forthcoming sabbatical leave. In June he asked the university Senate to grant him two weeks away from work and an assistant to take his ethics and metaphysics lectures for the remainder of the year. His medical adviser had recently forbidden him to combine any longer lecturing, publication, research, and administration. The Senate granted him relief from all lectures except those in psychology, and reduced administrative duties where possible.

But Mayo's work was held up in the following month by organizational problems inside his department. Seymour's work load too had become heavy; he was teaching first and second year students in logic, theory and the history of education, and taking tutorials for honors students in philosophy at second- and third-year levels. The breadth of the work was too great to engage students at anything but a minimum level of interest. Further, no time was available for research or for developing a real interest in his own work. Because there was no plan to appoint a lecturer in education, his temporary assignment seemed likely to go on another seven years! It had become impossible for him to lecture effectively in both education and philosophy, and at the same time, to know something of recent psychological and educational investigations. Seymour resigned.[4]

Mayo agreed with much of what Seymour had said. He suggested to the Board of Faculties that he also should resign and accept a two-year appointment to a research chair in psychology, with the vacated chair in philosophy going to Seymour. This would mean a sacrifice for Mayo because after two years he would be without a job, but he was keen to pursue his research in psychology, and this seemed the best way. After the board was assured that the suggestion was a true reflection of Mayo's wishes, it supported the idea because thereby the university would retain both his and Seymour's services, the standard of work in their department would be maintained by the hiring of a temporary lecturer, research facilities in both psychology and education would be enhanced, and the Senate would have two years in which to decide on a new teaching and research policy in psychology, education, and philosophy. A small salary increment was recommended for Mayo to offset his impending loss of employment. The Senate did not accept Mayo's scheme in its entirety but instead resolved to create a temporary research professorship in psychology and to advertise his chair in philosophy; Seymour could apply with others for the opening and be considered on his merits. The Senate would also advertise to fill the position from which Seymour had recently resigned. Seymour was asked if he wanted his resignation to stand, and Mayo was given a week to reconsider. Seymour informed the university that during the three months between lodging his resignation and the Senate's consideration of it, his situation had changed, and he was not free to withdraw it. He would return to Jesus College, Oxford University, to be a fellow and bursar.[5]

Without Seymour, whom Mayo had grown to regard as tiresome and bumptious, the Department of Philosophy was ready for complete reorganization.[6] Mayo would remain as its professor and increase its teaching staff by three: one each for psychology and philosophy, logic and ethics, and education and psychology. Salaries had to be raised. Seymour had been receiving £430 a year, while comparable positions in Sydney paid £500-700, and in Britain, £650-900. In Queensland even schoolteachers received £420. Because the university could not increase lecturer salaries, Mayo suggested that temporary lectureships be advertised at £300-450 a year until funds were available to hire full-time appointees. Also he wanted to introduce a diploma of education, which emphasized practical work, notably in abnormal psychology with casework and demonstrations, and training in the use of the Binet-Simon intelligence tests and Jung's association test. Such a course would help educationists manage backward children and improve methods of instruction for normal pupils. In all his psychology courses Mayo planned to augment the lectures with practical demonstrations, and give students the chance to complete minor research studies. To philosophy subjects he wanted to add a special course that would go deeply into the work of one great philosopher; classes would be open to the public for a fee, and would examine political philosophy, ethics, and metaphysics.[7]

Most of Mayo's requests were granted, and for 1921 he was given two temporary lecturers. Lewis D. Edwards would teach classes in logic and philosophy, and was also willing to take classes in psychology. A Melbourne scholar, Miss Flinn, would lecture in ethics and metaphysics, but shortly after her appointment, said she thought there were too few lectures given in the department, disapproved of the subordination of philosophical to psychological studies, was grieved she could not lecture for the whole subject of ethics, and showed no desire to extend her grasp of psychology. Mayo attributed her views to a "wounded *amour propre*," and did his best not to show how much he disliked her. Although these arrangements added administrative duties, Mayo was freed of the heavy teaching that he had had the year before.[8]

Now Mayo had time to work toward establishing conditions for scientific research on the application of the new medical psychology. While helping his sisters-in-law with their emotional problems, lecturing to the WEA and other outside groups, and counseling Matthewson, he was also making indirect contributions by writing, supporting the careers of some people, curbing the activities of others, and, whenever the opportunity arose, stressing the value of applying the new psychology to problems in industry and education.

In August 1920 Mayo had accompanied Matthewson to the Australasian Medical Congress in Brisbane, and, in the Section on Psychological Medicine, was the only discussant whose remarks were published. He commented on George Rennie's paper, "Psycho-analysis in the Treatment of Mental or Moral Deficiency," which describes the treatment of an adolescent boy who stole money. Rennie, who has been resistant to the idea of a sexual etiology for psychoneurosis, had changed his mind after examining the boy and observing the results of a psychoanalyst. Mayo stated that psychoanalysis must be based on clinical evidence rather than a psychologist's beliefs, especially those that assume that neurotic behavior is due solely to repressed sexual desires. Psychoanalysis was more valuable as a technique than a theory, and sex should not be introduced into the analysis until mentioned by the patient himself. Concepts such as "conflict" and "repression" were important, but they would be superseded as the working hypotheses of psychoanalytic theory were refined. Finally, Mayo summarized his own theory of personality, emphasizing its differing levels of consciousness and the prime motive of all individuals to achieve sanity by relating themselves successfully to their environment.[9]

Mayo's insistence that mental life be studied scientifically lay behind his attempt to curb and redirect activities of Brisbane's Psychical Research Society. He took a team of associates, including Matthewson, Ursula McConnel, and Miss Flinn to a discussion on the formation of psychic research groups. Followers of spiritualism wanted to establish investigations of psychic phenomena but were adamant that the investigators use no test that might injure mediums or to which the spirits of the other world might object. Two such members controlled the meeting with their reminiscences, which Mayo observed were based on experiences of twenty-five years ago. The dreary and unprofitable recollections led him to attack the two for their tediousness and gullibility. He stated that he would not leave until the character of the society was completely changed, and immediately the meeting got out of hand. Mayo challenged the group to consider the conditions he thought should be placed on the work. Good humored on the surface but fuming below, he proposed that a special committee be appointed for each test of a psychic phenomenon; that only one phenomenon be tested at a time; that the conditions for each test be agreed to at the university and not in the medium's room; that no test be done unless the medium agreed to the conditions; and that no vexatious or painful tests be administered to mediums. After the meeting Mayo and his associates, who enjoyed his performance as much as he, detached some of the younger members who had taken up the proposals. But a week later a "trance address" was canceled because the medium was indisposed. Mayo guessed that news of his attack at the previous meeting had circulated and the medium had lost courage, which served to strengthen his loathing for individuals whose "stunt" was to give "'sittings' at a guinea each to neurotics."[10]

In a more positive way Mayo helped establish the research and teaching of medical psychology in Brisbane through his association with the Red Cross Society.[11] In July 1920 the British Red Cross Society sent £10,000 to the University Senate for the endowment of a medical research chair that would promote inquiries into the application of psychology for the alleviation and cure of psychoneurosis, the psychological etiology of psychoneurosis, and the bearing of modern psychological discoveries on education. The applicants for the chair had to have both psychological and medical training. Mayo joined a subcommittee to determine and advertise the conditions of appointment, and he proposed that, contrary to the conditions that had accompanied the donation, the appointee should be allowed to practice medicine privately and not be restricted to research. Research for its own sake was never supported by Mayo.[12]

The two applicants were J.P. Lowson, a British physician, and Matthewson. Mayo was Matthewson's only referee. After extolling his diligence, competence, and experience in psychotherapy, Mayo wrote that "this University really owes the Research Chair indirectly to Dr. Matthewson. But for the facilities of research which he originally provided we should not have been able to advise in the work of the Russell Lea Hospital for Returned Soldiers (Red Cross Society) in New South Wales." Mayo's supporting letter veils his firm conviction that it was his own work, extended by Matthewson that had got the Red Cross money for the university.[13]

Lowson had testimonials from C.S. Myers, director of the Laboratory of Experimental Psychology, Cambridge University; Dr. E. Faquar Buzzard, physician to St. Thomas Hospital, London; Dr. Gordon Holmes, prominent wartime consulting neurologist; and Lt.-Col. R.H. Hall, deputy commissioner of medical services in the British Ministry of Munitions. Mayo's acquaintance, Professor James T. Wilson, formerly of Sydney University, and now professor of anatomy at Cambridge, interviewed Lowson and compared him with documents he had on Matthewson. Mayo's lone recommendation could not match the powerful support of four British referees. In December 1921, shortly after Mayo had begun sabbatical leave, the university announced that Lowson would occupy the new chair.[14] Five years later Matthewson would leave Brisbane for his psychoanalysis in London and the essential and much envied experience abroad that most colonials then needed to enter respected positions in their own country.[15]

Although Mayo knew that he had a "very good and very interesting job" at the university, he was largely dissatisfied with his work. He was pained by the wearisome board meetings at which university officials made every mistake possible, and disappointed by his failure to get support, even from Michie, to plan and work for higher education standards among Queens

land's high schools. Mayo was distressed by his colleagues' refusal to bring
new blood into senior academic appointments, and irritated by the am-
bitiousness of local incompetents who thrust themselves forward for promotion. He was appalled at the pettiness of the Senate's decision to double
salary raises for lecturers but not professors, thus saving the university a
mere seventy-five pounds. He was furious at colleagues who chose to face
students' demands with aggressive confrontation rather than positive cooperation. Mayo had come to the view that the "Queensland Enlightenment"
was led by very small men, and the university's policies were framed by
"congenital idiots."[16]

The future had spread itself without any immediate prospects of relief,
so Mayo planned to quit Brisbane. Meredith Atkinson, who was in Brisbane to give the first Douglas Price Memorial Lecture, suggested he apply
for the Challis Professorship of Philosophy at the University of Sydney
when Francis Anderson retired. Mayo believed he was such an obvious
candidate that he would not apply unless someone from Sydney suggested
that he should, so he waited. A year later he had heard no word from
Sydney except that applications were being considered. He thought then of
putting himself forward, but he was dissuaded by the prospect of once
more teaching logic, ethics, and metaphysics when he had firmly resolved
to work on problems of applied psychology.

He was troubled by doubts and hopes, and dominated by a strong need
to escape Queensland. He believed that men at Sydney would have a better
chance of success than he and reasoned that an offer of appointment would
be unlikely because Anderson had always seemed hostile to his work. Sydney would be swayed by no man but Anderson unless a strong campaign
from within the university were to press explicitly for Elton Mayo. Even if
Anderson wanted a psychologist to succeed him, and he had said he did
not, Sydney could always promote the local man, Tasman Lovell. Furthermore, Mayo held that the Faculty of Arts at Sydney comprised mainly
deadheads, a few able men, and no great scholars.[17]

Nevertheless he hoped that Sydney might call him; if not, then he
thought the pick would be a Scot or an Englishman, or a local candidate
like Bernard Muscio, whose work Mayo regarded as a collection of mere
"paper distinctions."[18]

Such thoughts, doubts, and hopes turned to bitter envy in October 1921
when Mayo learned that Muscio would succeed Anderson. "A good job for
an inexperienced man. . . . Anderson said he was opposed to the appointment of a second psychologist! All Muscio's special work has been done in
psychology—Good luck to him, anyway—and a deliverance for all of us."[19]
Had Mayo applied for the position he would not have won it. Muscio was
six years younger but had far more experience in psychology. He had also
enjoyed the advantage of the much-valued work at Cambridge University,
and unlike Mayo, had concentrated on the psychology of motor and sen-

sory process rather than the content and levels of human consciousness, had completed experimental rather than clinical research, and had published his research in reputable academic journals and his lectures in two books.[20]

While musing over possibilities at Sydney, Mayo had been roused further by a newspaper clipping from Dorothea describing the newly created directorship of the Commonwealth Institute of Science and Industry. With a colleague, he talked over his intention to apply for the post and the chances of success. Rumors were spreading that Prime Minister William Hughes had announced the post without proper or sufficient consultation with Australia's universities, and that of the three "certainties" for the job the first was an egotistical brute, the second was irresponsible, and the third was well past his best. Also because the newsclipping emphasized that the incumbant's duty would be to organize the institute, men in universities thought that a businessman rather than a scientist would get the job if the three "certainties" were passed over. For this reason it was unlikely that Australian academics would apply for the position, so Mayo applied. Because the federal cabinet ministers delayed their decision, he scoffed that they probably did not have the moral courage to appoint a psychologist. Perhaps he was right. Commonwealth Statistician George H. Knibbs, age sixty-two, was chosen, thus confirming that the job was merely administrative, that new ideas were not wanted, and that Hughes had appointed his old friend to the position. Mayo wrote bitterly, "Having a friend in court seems to be as important in a democracy as in a monarchy."[21]

The only remaining alternative for Mayo was to request leave of absence for further study; years before a similar request had been granted to a biologist in the university. In July 1921 the Senate decided that such leave was necessary for the ultimate efficiency of the university, and that if taken by Mayo would help him become conversant with all modern developments in his subject; however, he must be prepared to pay his own travel and living expenses, and accept less pay. Mayo agreed, and suggested a salary of £425 for himself in the plan he submitted for the organization of his department while he was away.[22]

Dissatisfaction with university affairs was not the only reason Mayo wanted to leave Queensland. He was sensitive to the way important people treated him. Often he was treated well, and he enjoyed the experience. Through Dorothea's family he received invitations to Government House, and because of his psychological work with Matthewson, Mayo had widened the circle of his and Dorothea's friends. He had become recognized as a man of superior talent, and was invited regularly to the monthly meeting of doctors, professors, clerics and lawyers at Matthewson's home. Mayo was a foundation member of the Thirty Club, an informal group of Brisbane's intellectuals among whom it was said that he, better than most, could state both sociological and biological problems. At such gatherings Mayo and

Dorothea left memorable impressions. He was known for his personal charm, pleasant voice, wit, and broadmindedness. She, unlike most of the wives, had the courage to take control of intelligent discussion as well as show a deep and active interest in her husband's work. Also she had a reputation for preferring to talk with men rather than women. Together they made an unusual pair: each could command a conversation, and if disagreed with, could state definite opinions loudly, and persist until the argument was won.[23] But in medical circles Mayo was not treated as well, and felt uncomfortable.

Mayo was becoming recognized for his psychotherapeutic practices, but because of their medical connection his sense of their recognition was often overshadowed by memories of his failure at medical school. Consequently the need for recognition became so distorted that he would overreact whenever a doctor accepted or rejected his work, or behaved indifferently toward him. This difficulty was exacerbated by the strong resistance among Australia's doctors and academics to psychological, especially psychoanalytic, explanations of disorders that had no conventional or clear cause.[24] Dr. J. Lockhart Gibson, a prominent Brisbane doctor, was skeptical of Mayo's work, so when another skeptic, Dr. Meehan, a surgeon, saw the value of light hypnosis for a patient whom Mayo had treated briefly and decided to attend Mayo's psychology lectures at the university, Mayo joyfully anticipated that he would now become "one-up on Lockhart."[25] Shortly before Mayo left Queensland he was one of only two academics invited by Sir Thomas Robinson to an important dinner of one hundred of Brisbane's notables. There a long-standing friend of Mayo's family, Dr. Espie J. Dods, snubbed Mayo not once but several times for no obvious reason. At the time he was tired, so the deeply painful snub combined with his ever-present and largely unconscious conviction of sin to drive home the old notion that because of failure at medicine he might never rise above his own unworthiness.[26]

At this time a report appeared in Sydney's *Sunday Times* on Dr. Ralph Noble's neurological work at the Russell Lea Hospital for neurasthenics in New South Wales. The article was illustrated with cases of shell shock. Although one of the cases was Mayo's, and another was treated successfully along lines he had recommended, no mention was made of his contribution. He was "amused" by the omission, and wrote that he was pleased to see "that perhaps I had helped. The atmosphere here [in Brisbane] is different—except among the working and middle classes who treat me very nicely."[27] On another occasion Mayo was happy to learn from his sister-in-law Barbara that her doctor had agreed with Mayo's advice as to the role vaccines should play in her treatment.[28] And he was most gratified to receive a letter from a Melbourne doctor asking if he could send Mayo a patient whom he had seen on his last Melbourne visit, and including a note from the patient's aunt stating that Mayo had understood the patient's problem far better than any of the doctors seen before him.[29]

Recognition of Mayo came from an unexpected quarter during the summer of 1921 in Melbourne when he met Captain George H.L.F. Pitt-Rivers, private secretary and aide-de-camp to Lord Forster, the governor general of Australia. Like Malinowski, Pitt-Rivers became a friend and much admired Mayo's work. Pitt-Rivers had been president of the Psychological Society when he was completing his B.Sc. at Oxford University. He then went to the war as a captain in the Royal Dragoons and was badly wounded. After recovering he became one of McDougall's research assistants and undertook special studies in psychology and social anthropology. From information given to him by the chief of intelligence on the Russian General Staff he wrote a preliminary essay on the Russian Revolution from the psychological point of view that attracted much public comment when it was published in 1920. He married the daughter of Lord Forster, whose personal staff he later joined. On his way from Melbourne to New Guinea and the Bismarck archipelago for an eight-month field trip, Pitt-Rivers dined with Mayo. He waxed enthusiastic about the uses of psychology in *Democracy and Freedom,* and said that he would quote the work in his future writings. He believed that Mayo's research was far ahead of similar work in England. Although Mayo was lifted by the appreciation given to his work he thought that Pitt-Rivers had concluded too quickly that the work was of value before knowing its details. "In any case I think I have a new friend—and a good one. It was rather exciting."[30]

Mayo's ambivalence toward Pitt-Rivers's interest in his work could not be fully explained at the time. Unknown to Mayo, Pitt-Rivers had come to Australia for the British Secret Service to report on the new formation of the Australia security operations; anthropology was his cover. Mayo's work was attractive because it supported Pitt-Rivers's feelings about revolutions and confirmed his suspicions about the use of democracy by Bolsheviks. Also, not long before Pitt-Rivers arrived, Mayo had exposed a communist who had been trying to induce trade unionists to become revolutionaries. During the day the man had worked as the lead writer for a conservative newspaper in Brisbane; at night he addressed unionists and began attacking Mayo's politics while he was on the WEA committee. Mayo exposed the duplicity by allowing the man to display his revolutionary aims to those who knew only his conservative cover. Once Pitt-Rivers posed as a communist sympathizer so that he could collect information at a public meeting in Sydney's Domain Park. He also saw threats from among theosophists, Rosicrucians, Masons, and supporters of feminists. He proposed as a countermeasure that the government establish an advisory bureau of social stability and research, quoting from Mayo's *Democracy and Freedom* to support the proposal. Pitt-Rivers was an anti-Semite, and during the Second World War he would become pro-Nazi and be imprisoned as a security risk. Mayo's uncertainty about him arose probably because he sensed a closed-minded extremist, not unlike the communist agitator who had posed as a conservative journalist. Eventually Mayo would learn about Pitt-Rivers's extremism, but not his espionage.[31]

In Melbourne during the summer of 1921 Mayo agreed to write five articles on industrial peace and psychological research for Ambrose Pratt's *Industrial Australian Mining Standard*.[32] He drafted and revised the articles that year while he was giving his public lectures for the university on the psychological causes of industrial unrest and aspects of abnormal psychology. The articles constitute the integration of Mayo's ideas on the role of the psychologist in resolving industrial conflict.

The first two articles draw heavily on his *Democracy and Freedom* but contain many new ideas. The first article, "Civilization and Morale," explains that the industrial unrest and economic burdens caused by the war continue to threaten civilized society, and that the usual remedies have failed to reduce industrial strife. Now unanimity and fresh efforts are needed. During the war psychological studies had showed that the strain of war could be reduced, and that morale and fighting effectiveness could be raised with the systematic use of rest and recreation. The same applies to industry. Research shows that morale—a mental attitude that is the source of human effort—is more important for success at work than are machines and office systems. Industrial morale is low because workers get little help from their leaders, who denigrate traditional forms of authority, condemn established social organization, and advocate anarchy and tyranny based on fear and suspicion. Economic and political theories cannot help because they assume workers are motivated by logic, and ignore nonrational human factors. Industrial peace can be restored by applying to industry the evidence from psychological research on morale.

The second article, "Industrial Unrest and Nervous Breakdown," says that most mental activity—the cause of either anarchy or civilized action—is out of awareness, and that mental attitudes toward life are determined by inherited racial consciousness and the opportunities for personal development. If the opportunities are incongruent with racial characteristics, then mental health declines and its place is taken by anxieties, obsessions, hysteria, and a loss of interest in living. Mental health is an achievement. Education promotes sanity by giving opportunities to people that help them understand and use their racial characteristics. While animals simply pursue immediate gratification by adapting to their environment, humans change their environments, raise their understanding of racial capacities, strive to collaborate with others, and work toward an integrated purpose. But many people have disintegrated minds because they lack self-control, have not achieved sufficient sanity, are forgetful, and are prey to nervous insomnia, melancholia, compulsions, and anxiety neuroses. Crime, war, and social revolution may ensue. Industrial and political practices exacerbate these mental states, and people pursue repressive and neglectful educational practices. These neglected mental attitudes and emotional complexes thrive in the unconscious mind—the mental hinterland—and feed industrial conspiracies and delusions that equally affect workers and employers.

Mayo seemed to have little difficulty in setting down these thoughts. The psychological ideas had been developed well in his university lectures on psychology, and the way that political leaders exploited the mental distress of people in a crowd had become a well-established theme of his. But the next article, "The Mind of the Agitator," gave him considerable trouble:

> I have spent the morning cursing roundly because of my absolute incapacity to express myself with a pen. I can talk and lecture well enough on occasion but when I take up a pen to write an article (or a text book) I become the most stilted pedant imaginable. I have spent at least an hour and a half over 20 lines or so of a Melbourne article and now the beastly thing reads like the dying croak of a strangled scholar. There is so much unadulterated bosh written about psychology that I want to take a hand. Yet I do no more than rage furiously together, like the heathen, and imagine a vain thing because of my lack of literary facility. At the present moment if I could express what I know on paper I could lift myself out of this soul-destroying University regime. Last night and early this morning I had four of our financial and political leaders reduced to unsightly lumps of quivering protoplasm by reason of the account I gave them of the psychological causes making for social revolution in our working class population. The Ad-men when I had finished with them were in a condition of lachrymose and impious petition. And when I came to write the d ——— d stuff it WON'T GO. How can I eliminate the factors that cramp my expression? Come over to Macedonia and help us.[33]

Reasons for Mayo's difficulty may be found in the subject of the article, circumstances in which the article was written, and earlier experiences. The article has four main points. The first states that psychological factors are important for explaining social ills; that if people lose control of their racial consciousness and fail to master all aspects of mental life, then irrational social actions may ensue. The second point illustrates the first by describing an unsettled, rebellious political agitator whose resentment of and conflict with authority is attributed to brutal treatment at the hands of an alcoholic father. The third point says that such agitators, many of whom are intelligent and burning to redress social ills, are a burden to the Australian Labour Party; their behavior is attributed to abuse and persecution but also to an education system that is constricted to preparing young people for a mere trade or profession, and thereby represses natural feeling and promotes neurosis. Consequently, the neurotic agitators, unlike the melancholics who wish to do away with themselves, read their personal misery into society and seek to obliterate it. The fourth point extends the third by asserting that the education system restricts youths so much that they value intellectual research and social service less than selfishness, sloth, and destruction; modern psychology could help alter this attitude if people understood that in healthy well-educated individuals, dispersed nonrational thinking and fantasies that compensate for distress are integrated purposefully with concentrated rational thinking about ways to resolve social and individual difficulties. Political agitators lack this integration, and, in an effort to realize their compensating fantasies, they pursue ideologies—socialism, guild socialism, anarchism—that justify destructive actions against society.[34]

These ideas were of intellectual value to Mayo. He had alluded to them in *Democracy and Freedom* and used them in his public speeches and university lectures. They also provided illustrations for lectures and discussions in the United States, and, at the end of his life, appear in the first chapter of *Some Notes on the Psychology of Pierre Janet*.[35]

At the time of his struggle to put the ideas on paper, their emotional value was clear. During an attack of dengue, the disease he had contracted seventeen years before in West Africa, Mayo wrote to Dorothea: "Directly I became feverish my anxieties all tended to come to the surface. I dreamed about social revolution all night and my three dearest in trouble. . . ."[36] The dream expressed simply the fear that all good things may be coming to an end, and that his dearest women, for whom he cared and who were a reliable source of self-esteem, were endangered.

When he had this dream and called to Dorothea to "come over to Macedonia and help us," Mayo knew his father's life was coming to an end. George was dying from tuberculosis, the disease that had killed his mother, and to which he had been exposed as a young man on the boat to England.[37]

During a visit to his dying father, Mayo struggled to follow the old man's ideas on the importance of women in a man's life. Later, when considering the fifth article, "Revolution," for Ambrose Pratt, Mayo began changing his view of women, those "dearests" in his life:

> I am beginning to understand what dear old George meant when he put loyalty so high as a quality of dear women. (The dear old fellow's suggestions come back to me everywhere). I am very glad I said what I did to the dear old fellow just before he crossed over. If there is anything on the other side, he will know how fortunate I have been in finding you to help my blundering passage, my dearest dear. . . . I realise how you have stood by me, helping me into the clear atmosphere of steadiness and devotion where you for ever dwell. Perhaps some day I shall become capable of making some return to you for all you have given me—your mental qualities and your dear delightful self.[38]

George's death aroused old loves, hatreds, fears, and hopes in Mayo while he lived alone and worked so hard during 1921. A father's death is a sign to his son that his own life must end, and that mortals are helpless in the face of death. More specifically, the death was a reminder to Mayo that doctors, who had often hurt him with their aloofness and arrogance, are rendered impotent by death, confused, as in West Africa, by their ignorance of disease, and culpable, as in his sister Olive's tragic death, for their false diagnoses. Mayo's probable anger, aroused by the death of George was turned back on himself. He felt guilty of failure to enter the medical profession, and shame for having let down the family. Although the death gave him the opportunity to say how he would make up for the disappointing past, his well-established conviction of sin and essential unworthiness agitated him, and he became sad and depressed.

George's death indicated, too, that life under the old order would end. At this point Mayo was in conflict. George had given him the gold watch that had belonged to old Dr. Mayo. The gesture meant clearly to him that his duty was to maintain the traditions of the family, and that he must answer to past generations in performing that duty.

Mayo's sense of loss, conviction of his unworthiness, and inner conflict between the duty to support old ways and the urge to carry forward new work were reminders of how once he had suffered at the hands of respected authority, been repressed by narrow-minded educationists, trained vigorously in a profession chosen for him not by him, and been banished to Edinburgh to make amends. In partial reparation he had turned to psychology, found its place in medicine, agitated for its use to overcome social ills, and used it to compensate for earlier rebelliousness and failure to follow convention.

Such thoughts and feelings may have constituted Mayo's inner conflict as he was composing the articles on society's ills and their psychological origins. That his difficulties in writing were associated with the death of his father is clear from the imagery in the letter to Dorothea likening his struggle to write to the "dying croak of a strangled scholar." Further, the inner conflict between the value of psychology and the authority it should enjoy appears in the letter's imagery. On one hand psychology is "unadulterated bosh"; on the other it is so omnipotent that it makes powerful leaders quiver and "Ad-men" weep. That he identified himself with the agitator and his mob can be seen from his description of himself as a heathen who imagines vain things. "Why doth the heathen rage?" was the first title he gave to what would appear as "The Rabble Hypothesis" in *The Social Problems of an Industrial Civilization*.[39] Finally, psychological tension was heightened by his strong wish to escape Queensland and retrieve some of the self-esteem lost in failing twice to find another job.

The conflict made heavy work of putting on paper the ideas that he could so easily otherwise express. And when George, who had always deprecated heavy effort, praised Hetty's loyalty, Mayo was reminded of what she had, so loyally, developed in him: the capacity to speak well in public.

In two months the conflict had passed, he achieved the sanity he sought, integrated nonrational thinking with concentrated and purposeful ideas, and wrote:

> I am slowly developing my ideas on "Revolution." I think the series is really good. I expected when I re-read them the other day to be disappointed or dissatisfied with patches. But I think I am quite content to leave them as they are. I hope, indeed, that they will definitely challenge the attention of our social scientists. I believe there is a certain "inevitability" about them that may "tune up" the quidnuncs. They were much rewritten—and "revolution" is undergoing the same process at present.[40]

"Revolution" and "The Will of the People" were the last of the five articles. Both draw heavily from *Democracy and Freedom,* and summarize the three earlier articles.

Mayo decided to take his study leave in Melbourne, but his future plans were still unclear. He wanted to spend a few weeks with Dorothea because they had been apart so often since their marriage. He wanted to speak with Ambrose Pratt and with Archibald Strong, associate professor of English, and other colleagues from the University of Melbourne.[41] He also hoped some sort of job would appear while he worked on "The Psychology of Sanity" manuscript for Macmillan. When a Brisbane friend asked if he wanted "to go home to England," he said that he could not afford the fare because the university had not allowed him sufficient salary while on leave.[42] He had hoped that Ambrose Pratt would syndicate the five articles and thus augment his Melbourne income, but Pratt had found that newspapers were loath to print anything that might offend their readers. Mayo's articles explained industrial conflict by pointing to psychological weaknesses in both labor and conservative parties, praising neither, and attacked the system of arbitration that had been used to curb and resolve the conflict.[43]

Three weeks before he left Queensland Mayo decided that after a stop in Melbourne he would go to Britain. The university had reconsidered the matter of salary for professors on study leave, and Mayo heard a rumor that he might receive a minimum of almost £500. So he began to reason why he should travel to London. In 1905 when Sir Charles Lucas was visiting the governor of South Australia, he had suggested to Mayo that he return to London and use his skills to handle meetings of working men. Mayo remembered that as a young man he had walked into the Working Men's College and was immediately taken into the men's confidence, interviewed by Professor Albert V. Dicey, the principal, and put onto many committees.[44] Mayo was also approached at this time by a "woolly-headed but decent" mathematics lecturer at the university, Kenneth Swanwick, who said he thought Mayo could be very useful in London because prominent scholars like Professor L.T. Hobhouse and G.V.H. Cole had failed to show a practical grasp of Britain's industrial relations problems. In the beginning

Mayo was inclined to think "that an assault on London, where the 'big men' are is advisable" even if he came back to Queensland afterward.[45] Inclination turned to firm resolve after discussions with "a clever old British Jew," the governor of Queensland, Sir Matthew Nathan, who also believed that Mayo could be of greater use in London than Brisbane.[46] Later that day, Swanwick, who had been secretly fired by the thought of Mayo's personal impact on British labor problems, presented him with an enthusiastic letter of introduction to friends to the effect that Mayo had a "very special task to save the Empire." With notable prescience Swanwick had imagined that Mayo would not be returning to Queensland, so he recommended Mayo drop academic life and take up politics as a member of no less than the British House of Commons! Swanwick believed Mayo was well known in Australia's major capitals and respected by both conservative and labor presses. He was the "right kind of Australian, with the gift of utterance," "and a man with a message for the world." Mayo was surprised and heartened by Swanwick's enthusiasm. So the die was cast, and London it would be.[47]

To confirm the London decision, Mayo talked with John Huxham, a businessman, member of the University Senate, and secretary for public instruction in Queensland. Huxham agreed that by cutting Mayo's salary while on leave the university had treated him ungenerously, especially because he had been largely responsible for the £10,000 Red Cross gift for the chair in medical psychology. Huxham offered to make Mayo the Queensland government's special representative to inquire abroad into applications of psychology to education and industry. Mayo welcomed the offer, for it would take him into high official circles and help him to meet influential politicians and industrialists.[48] Meanwhile, another colleague recommended that Mayo not waste his time in Melbourne but go directly to London as a leading exponent of psychoanalysis in Australia. He would be well paid for case work, and in the evenings he might teach sociology and economics at the London School of Economics.[49]

Mayo did not want another long separation from Dorothea. He thought she should come with him; the extra expense would not be great. They could take a cottage in Sussex, and, through his work, she could meet people like Barbara Drake, research worker for the women's labor movement, and the prominent sociologist, Beatrice Webb. These possibilities made Mayo feel that "the years are dropping from me now that my face is turned to London again." He imagined that a relative from Edinburgh would meet their ship, they would have a celebratory dinner at an expensive restaurant, and Dorothea could spend the winter at Bournemouth until he found a cottage. Lines from Kipling's *The Long Trail* came to mind and expressed his intense need for escape, new work, and an adventure with Dorothea.[50]

There's a whisper down the field, where
the year has shot her yield,
And the ricks stand grey to the sun,
Singing "Over then, come over, for the
bee has quit the clover,
And your English summer's done."

You have heard the beat of the off-shore
wind,
And the thresh of the deep-sea rain;
You've heard the song—how long? how
long?
Pull out on the trail again!
Ha' done with the Tents of Shem, dear
lass,
We've seen the seasons through,
And it's time to turn on the old trail,
our own trail, the out trail,
Pull out, pull out, on the long trail—
the trail that is always new.

Fly forward, O my heart, from the Foreland
to the Start
We're steaming all too slow,
And it's twenty thousand mile to our little
lazy isle
Where the trumpet-orchids blow.

The goal was clear even if the means were not yet available. Mayo did not intend to return to Queensland. Six years later he would describe the day of his leaving: "I rode out of Queensland in 1921 (my last departure) in the railway coach reserved for His Excellency (the Governor of Queensland, Sir Matthew Nathan) arguing as to whether or not Queensland was entirely stupid—Mayo for the affirmative."[51]

Notes

1. Elton to Dorothea, 7 May 1919.
2. Minutes, Senate, University of Queensland, 11 July 1919.
3. Ibid., 12 September 1919.
4. Minutes, Board of Faculties, University of Queensland, 20 September 1920; Board of Faculties, University of Queensland, "Fifth Report to the Senate," 12 November 1920.
5. Seymour to the Registrar, University of Queensland, 20 October 1920; Minutes of Special Meeting, Board of Faculties, University of Queensland, 24 September 1920.
6. Elton to Dorothea, 10 March 1920.
7. Board of Faculties, "Fifth Report to the Senate."
8. Ibid.; Minutes, Senate, University of Queensland, 10 December 1920.
9. *Transactions of the Australian Medical Congress,* 21-28 August 1920, p. 412.
10. Elton to Dorothea, 14, 15, 21 March 1920.

11. E. Jones, "On the Necessity for the Establishment of Psychiatric Clinics," *Transactions of the Australian Medical Congress,* 21-28 August 1920, p. 410.

12. Minutes, Senate, University of Queensland, 16 July 1920; ibid., 15 April 1921; Elton to Dorothea, 18 March 1921, 27 April 1921.

13. Mayo to the Registrar, 1 July 1921, in Board of Faculties. University of Queensland, "Tenth Report to the Senate"; Elton to Dorothea, 10 November 1921.

14. Minutes, Senate, University of Queensland, 16 December 1921.

15. Conversation with Matthewson, 21 August 1974.

16. Elton to Dorothea, 10, 18, 23, 30 March 1921.

17. Elton to Dorothea, 15, 23 March 1921.

18. Elton to Dorothea, 10 March 1920.

19. Elton to Dorothea, 11 October 1921.

20. A. A. Landauer and M. J. Cross, "A Forgotten Man: Muscio's Contribution to Industrial Psychology," *Australian Journal of Psychology* 23, no. 1 (1971):235-40.

21. Elton to Dorothea, 7, 16, 19 March 1921.

22. Minutes, Senate, University of Queensland, 12 August 1921.

23. Elton to Dorothea, 29 February 1920; W. M. Kyle, "The Psychologist in Industry" (University of Queensland, 1952, mimeographed), p. 10; S. Castlehow, "The Thirty Club" (1956, mimeographed; Robinson MSS, Fryer Library, University of Queensland); conversation with Matthewson, 21 August 1974.

24. Richard C. S. Trahair and Julie G. Marshall, *Australian Psychoanalytic and Related Writings, 1884-1939: An Annotated Bibliography,* La Trobe University Library Publications, No. 16 (Bundoora, Victoria, 1979).

25. Elton to Dorothea, 7 March 1921.

26. Elton to Dorothea, 1, 2 November 1921.

27. *Sunday Times* (Sydney), 29 February 1920; Elton to Dorothea, 4 March 1920.

28. Elton to Dorothea, 29 September 1921.

29. Elton to Dorothea, 9 May 1921.

30. *Who's Who, 1959* (London: Black, 1959), p. 2418; Elton to Dorothea, 24 March, 16 April 1921; Pitt-Rivers to Mayo, 22 July 1922, BLA.

31. Richard Hall, *The Secret State: Australia's Spy Industry* (Melbourne: Cassell, 1978), pp. 213, 218; Elton to Toni, 19 October 1932.

32. Elton Mayo, "Industrial Peace and Psychological Research," *Industrial Australian Mining Standard* 67 (January-June 1922):16, 63, 111, 159-60, 253.

33. Elton to Dorothea, 16 March 1921.

34. Mayo, "Industrial Peace and Psychological Research," p. 111.

35. Elton Mayo, *Some Notes on the Psychology of Pierre Janet* (Cambridge: Harvard University Press, 1948).

36. Elton to Dorothea, 9 May 1921.

37. Helen Mayo, "Biographical Notes on Elton Mayo," SAA.

38. Elton to Dorothea, 12 October 1921.

39. Elton Mayo, *The Social Problems of an Industrial Civilization* (Boston: Harvard University, Graduate School of Business Administration, Division of Research, 1945); Bingham to Mayo, 27 July 1942, MM 1.024; and Gregg to Mayo, 13 November 1942, MM 1.072.

40. Elton to Dorothea, 12 October 1921.

41. Elton to Dorothea, 2 October 1921.

42. Elton to Dorothea, 15 October 1921.

43. Elton to Dorothea, 18 October 1921.

44. Elton to Dorothea, 2 November 1921.

45. Elton to Dorothea, 11 November 1921.

46. Elton to Dorothea, 3 November 1921; Mayo to Ruml, 29 January 1928, RF.

47. Elton to Dorothea, 3 November 1921.
48. Ibid.
49. Elton to Dorothea, 8 November 1921.
50. Elton to Dorothea, 6 November 1921; Rudyard Kipling, *Verse* (New York 1939), pp. 164-66.
51. Elton to Dorothea, 10 November 1921; Mayo to Ruml, 29 January 1928, RF.

9

To America, 1922-1923

After delivering a series of public lectures on psychoanalysis and applied psychology in Melbourne, Mayo decided to apply for an academic position at the University of Melbourne and to take study leave in Britain to add overseas experience to his application. He would go via the United States, where a lecture program had been arranged for him at the University of California, Berkeley. The plans fell through, and, because he had little money, he sought work as a clinician and industrial psychologist, but with little success. He met important men in universities and research foundations who asked him to New York and Washington to discuss psychology applied to work. He was invited to address leading psychologists, psychiatrists and industrialists; they were much impressed with his style of public speaking and his idea that revery was a major source of human motivation. Because he was made so welcome, he decided to seek work in the United States but funds were not available until his friend Beardsley Ruml found sufficient money to support him for six months' work at the University of Pennsylvania.

In Melbourne Mayo prepared for study abroad. To augment his income he took psychological cases[1] and delivered public lectures. The *Herald* announced he was on his way to Europe, and that the public was invited to attend six lectures on psychology and psychoanalysis "by one of the foremost psychologists of the day," noted for special recognition by the British Red Cross Society in treating shell shock. Mayo also planned to conduct a parent-teacher study circle on problems among infants and adolescents, and a discussion group on techniques of psychoanalysis.[2]

The six lectures were so well attended that he received fees of £285, almost half his Brisbane salary.[3] There were several reasons for his success. First, he had already spoken to groups of professionals who knew his work well. At the Victorian Branch of the British Medical Association he talked on psychology, psychoanalysis, and applied psychology.[4] At a private girls school in Melbourne—with Dr. Eleanor Cissly Kemp, a New York psychologist, and Dr. Stephen P. Duggan of the Institute of International Education—he talked to specialists in education on how psychoanalysis clarified social problems. He talked to advertising people on the psychology of middle age, combining his theory of personality with the popular American success ideology, and concluding that "with concentration of thought and phantasy would come success in life."[5] Another reason for his success on the platform was skillful promotion by Mayo's friend from university days, Stanley S. Addison. Addison had completed a science degree, and after war service became the assistant registrar at the University of Melbourne. He enthused over Mayo's ideas on the structure of consciousness and the "mental hinterland." Because he appreciated the promise of modern psychology for resolving classroom problems and industrial strife, he advocated a chair in social or applied psychology at the university and arranged Mayo's appearance before the Melbourne University Association.[6] Thus, before the first public lecture Mayo's reputation was well established.

The first lecture, "The Two Psychologies," stressed the scientific status of psychology, distinguished academic psychology (the study of rational mental processes) from medical psychology (the study of irrational states of mind), and outlined levels of mental activity by contrasting deep unconsciousness processes in the "mental hinterland" with concentrated thought. The second lecture, "Dissociation and Split Consciousness," followed Janet's distinction between hysteria and psychasthenia, and showed ways in which the mind loses its unity and may disintegrate. The third lecture, "The Unconscious," described many neurotic disorders, and how ideas of Jung, Freud, and William Mitchell contribute to a four-level theory of consciousness. The fourth lecture summarized Freud's contributions to sexual theory (aberrations, infantile sexuality, libido); the fifth lecture set out Freud's theory of psychoneuroses; and the last outlined Freud's theory of dreams.[7] In keeping with the Australian attitude toward Freud's ideas, the Melbourne newspapers reported the substance of the first lecture but not the last three.[8]

Following the remarkable reception of his public speaking, and with the support of Addison, Mayo was invited to join the archbishop of Melbourne, prominent judges, and politicians in addressing the annual dinner of the Melbourne University Association. At the last minute the archbishop fell ill and could not give the major address. Asked to propose the ceremonial toast, Mayo turned his wit upon politicians: they controlled funding of the universities and would not allow them to save a portion of their income to gain some financial autonomy for development and planning. He also argued that although the tradition of lecturing at the universities was excellent, the Oxford and Cambridge tutorial or discussion system was far better.[9]

Mayo's success in Melbourne was followed by a change in plans. The directorship of tutorial classes at the University of Melbourne had become vacant and presented an opportunity for Mayo to escape Queensland and reach a wider audience. He felt more accepted in Melbourne than in Brisbane, and believed that Dorothea would be happier in Melbourne, but he knew that he did not have sufficient overseas experience to be certain of getting the directorship if he applied. So, at Addison's suggestion, Mayo planned to go to England by way of the United States. Addison arranged with Dr. Gillanders at the University of California, Berkeley, for Mayo to lecture there during the summer to augment his income. A.J. Tanza, an American psychiatrist in Australia on a Rockefeller grant to help establish the Commonwealth Health Department, gave Mayo a letter of introduction to Professor Stanley Cobb at Harvard University to discuss all phases of the promotion of mental hygiene. In England Mayo would associate himself with Professor J.T. Wilson, who had been at Sydney University and now had the Chair of Anatomy at Cambridge University.[10]

Mayo also had letters of introduction to senior executives of Standard Oil, two letters from the American vice consul, and a letter from Prime Minister Hughes that states quite wrongly that "Professor George Elton Mayo . . . occupies the position of Professor of Psychology and Physiology in the University of Queensland." The error could hardly have been an oversight, for the letter is countersigned by Mayo himself. In 1922 there were no chairs in psychology or physiology at the University of Queensland. At worst the letter was deliberate deception by Mayo to win respect from mental hygiene authorities, and at best an indication of the resources he believed that he needed to carry forward his work, i. e., "the application of psychology to social investigation, (e.g., the causes of social unrest) education, and industrial organisation."[11]

Before leaving Melbourne he addressed the Free Kindergarten Union on modern education practices, arguing strongly for a form of school discipline that was structured but not punitive so that "the individual was led to the appreciations of his own powers." He stressed the importance of peers in the child's education.[12] Also, when he was invited to speak on social psychology, he emphasized the value of studying the disorders of an industrial civilization, following the theme that Pitt-Rivers had taken up in public lectures for the Victoria League.[13] At the time *The Argus* was reporting industrial violence in the United States: the murder of mine workers, the use of troops to curb riots, and the death of a child in clashes between strikers and railway property guards.[14] So Mayo's plea for the study of the psychological causes of industrial unrest in Melbourne was preparatory for what he would say at the University of California.

At Scott's Hotel in Melbourne Mayo and Dorothea were given a farewell dinner by his brothers John and Herbert. Among the guests were the financier Edward C.E. Dyason and Mayo's mentor, Professor William Mitchell.[15] Carrying, among other things, fountain pens, the letters of introduction, and a good-luck telegram from Mayo's sister Helen, Mayo left Australia on July 12 aboard the S.S. *Sonoma* bound for San Francisco, via Pago Pago and Honolulu.

When Mayo docked at San Francisco, newspaper reporters beseiged his room at the Palace Hotel and demanded that he expand on his comments about the psychology of flappers that had appeared in the Honolulu press. He had said the activities of flappers indicated that society, like individuals, could have a "nervous breakdown." Women were not achieving self-expression nor the control of their destiny, so they substituted for this an imaginary world of dissociated reveries and an unreal social life in which they felt free. He asserted that modern literature, magazines, and musical comedies extended and strengthened in women the tendency to flapperism as a neurotic mode of adjustment.[16] What he had said had not been reported accurately.

Errors in the newspaper accounts irritated Mayo, and he much preferred that attention be given to his views on the psychological determinants of industrial strife in the United States. Examples were being reported daily: railroad executives had refused the president's proposals for industrial peace; strikers were being savaged by dogs; and duels, bombings, and deaths were increasing. He outlined his thoughts to a young woman from the *San Francisco Chronicle,* and was pleased when she took copies of his five articles on industrial peace and psychological research for possible syndication in West Coast newspapers.[17]

For the next three weeks Mayo's future was uncertain. Gillanders had made no arrangements for him to teach, so he had no income, and his expenses were unexpectedly high. His contacts at Standard Oil offered little advice or help. Dean Hatfield, deputy president of the university showed him the campus, and had him to lunch with local psychiatrists. Professor Alfred L. Kroeber, the psychoanalytically inclined anthropologist, advised Mayo that he could earn more money as a public lecturer on the East Coast than in California.

Because his funds were dwindling rapidly Mayo decided to see Jessica Colbert, a promotor of public lectures. He persuaded her to advertise his three talks called "At the Back of the White Man's Mind" in San Francisco. He then went to a conference of psychologists at Stanford, where he met Lewis M. Terman and Knight Dunlap. Among the rank-and-file psychologists Mayo found no one with special force and many who bitterly opposed Freud. He joined the discussion, and his amusing breezy style, which contrasted with the inarticulateness of most speakers, led listeners to tell him how good it was to hear English spoken so well. Harvard psychologist Herbert S. Langfeld, a colleague of William McDougall, assured him of a welcome in Cambridge, saying, "You are very different from an English professor—they can't talk." A doctor recommended him to the local neurologists as a "rattling good" speaker, and Kroeber wrote to a promoter of lecturers, he "can hold and please any audience." It was all very gratifying but furnished no immediate solution to his lack of money.[18]

On docking at San Francisco Mayo had hastily accepted an invitation from Dr. Blanche L. Sanborn to speak on the psychology of Australia at the

San Francisco Club of Applied Psychology. At the time he did not know that his lecture was one in a series that included such topics as earth's mysteries, the psychology of raw food, the power of the spoken word, and fulfillment of prophecy revealed through psychology. Dr. Sanborn herself would conclude the series with "How to Use Human Analysis and Attain, Retain and Maintain Health, Youth and Beauty."[19] Blasphemous prayers to the Almighty opened the evening, a senile violinist scraped through two excruciating solos, Mayo turned black with rage as he delivered an abominable lecture, and Dr. Sanborn's health-cum-success treatment finished the evening. "Another experience of that sort and I shall go back to Australia, steerage," Mayo wrote home.[20]

Mayo rued his association with such a pernicious charlatan, and squirmed with shame as he recalled that he had accepted fees for his Melbourne lectures on psychoanalysis. Was he also such a charlatan? Should he offer to call off lecturing on psychoanalytic ideas to the local psychiatrists, and cancel arrangements with Jessica Colbert? Such dark reveries brought back the habits of London twenty years before. Doubts about his ability and embarrassment led Mayo to walk the streets, brood, and, with intense curiosity, watch the people about him. This country was not for him: connections at Standard Oil had failed him; at Berkeley Gillanders had let him down; San Franciscans seemed provincial and to care little for anyone but themselves; and, worst of all, Jessica Colbert had objected to his favorite phrase, "mental hinterland." On August 15 Mayo would have gladly boarded the S.S. *Sonoma,* had he the fare.[21]

Resignation replaced rage, and the wish to return home gave over to the reality that no one would suddenly donate money for him to visit American universities and learned societies at his leisure. So he rested, came back into favor with himself, revised his lectures, and accepted invitations from local neurologists. One arranged a visit to the jail, where inmates were treated appallingly. Mayo saw that inadequate education in large cities meant "we build prisons and breed people to fill them." Another doctor told about plans for the purchase of a country estate to be used as a sanatorium for neurotics and mild mental cases, and then took him to a state home for defective children, where he saw vivid, bizarre mental disorders and the children's circumscribed lives.[22]

Mayo hoped that Jessica Colbert would promote his lectures so well that he would earn enough to go to Harvard University, then to England, and finally back to Melbourne. Suddenly the way east was closed by a Dr. Musgrove, who seemed to control much of the professional and public activities of the medical profession on the West Coast. Musgrove told him that he was not to lecture on medical psychology, and that to go counter to the fiat was ill advised. Mayo acted quickly; his lecture series would be called "The Problem of the Strike—in Australia and Elsewhere" but content would be unchanged. Musgrove was circumvented, and Jessica Colbert was pleased because the new title fitted in with newspaper stories about the rail strike.[23]

Then Mayo had a stroke of good luck. One of Dorothea's aunts arranged for a doctor to lunch with him at the exclusive Bohemian Club. They were joined by Dr. Vernon Kellogg. When Mayo learned that Kellogg had been Herbert Hoover's assistant during the war and was now on the National Research Council in Washington, he outlined for Kellogg his views about the psychological determinants of strikes and how research could help in their control. Kellogg suggested Mayo visit Washington to discuss his ideas further, but Mayo did not see how he could raise the fare. "I really want to see you," said Kellogg, "if when the time comes you are unable to get across, wire me, and perhaps we'll send for you." Mayo reached into his pocket for the letter of introduction from the prime minister and passed it across the table.[24]

Although the East Coast was again in sight, Mayo had only enough money to keep him for two weeks. Addison had sent £170 from Melbourne, but Jessica Colbert had not yet made firm plans for the lecture series. Mayo's first reaction was to ask Kellogg for industrial research work, and to ask the New York office of Standard Oil to back the request. Mayo believed that if he were invited to lecture in the East, he could convince psychologists to support him. A visit to the San Francisco office of Standard Oil seeking advocacy was unavailing.[25]

Family problems in letters from Dorothea, declining funds, vague anxieties, and nagging doubts were difficult to quash. Mayo asked himself, "I wonder what an energetic man of fiction would do?" Answer: "Repack his luggage, leave it with Gillanders, and go fruit picking." On impulse he cabled a friend in Australia for a loan of four hundred pounds; nothing came of it. Standard Oil offered no help from New York. In five days he would be penniless and have to register with the Community Placement Bureau.[26]

What he thought would be his last five days of respectable living began at the Pacific Union Club with a lunch at the expense of the British consul general. There an owner of a railroad and a corporation lawyer who were impressed with Mayo's "new gospel," as they called it, which denounced agitators who manipulated large groups. That evening he outlined the distinction between medical and academic psychology for a group of psychologists at Berkeley who called the presentation a restatement of psychology and asked why it had not been published. These two occasions showed Mayo he really could attract and hold the attention of both psychologists and businessmen. A medical friend offered him a psychological case, but he refused it because the five days were just about up and in any event he could not live on one case.[27]

At breakfast on the fifth day Mayo was handed a letter from Kellogg, who was going to urge his New York colleagues to give Mayo a chance at industrial research. Mayo quickly took on the psychological case at ten dollars an hour; asked the medical friend to write a letter of recommendation to Kellogg; and cabled his brother Herbert for a loan of two hundred pounds, putting up as guarantors Michie and Matthewson. In two days Herbert had wired the money, and Mayo was, once again, rising into favor with himself.

Kroeber visited Mayo, urging him to continue with lectures on medical psychology, offering to tell Jessica Colbert how he could not fail to interest an audience, and suggesting that six rather than three lectures were appropriate. Feeling confident, Mayo put aside the objections of Dr. Musgrove and rescheduled the lectures on psychoanalysis. And to Dorothea he wrote, "Three cheers for Freud and psychology . . . here's success to our adventure, sweetheart." He celebrated with a haircut.

On 23 September 1922 a letter summoned him to Washington. His expenses would be paid by the National Research Council, and, in New York, a representative of a "major foundation" would talk with him. The chairman of the council's Psychology and Anthropology Division was much interested in Mayo's work, and was sure other psychologists would be too. Mayo exulted: "This is the best thing that ever happened to us. . . . I am so overjoyed I cannot keep still. . . . Kellogg & co. are wonderful—to decide without knowing me, that this is worthwhile—I met him once, at lunch. . . ."[28]

Mayo speculated with Kroeber on Kellogg's letter, and particularly the part about one of "the major foundations." Mayo hoped he would have the chance to see leading psychologists and businessmen before he returned to Australia. "Let's hope I can outroar the lions. I shall be surrounded by them in Washington," he wrote. "I have an academic psychology that counts more among the psychologists than all the Freudian work."[29]

The call to Washington frightened him, but he also was sure that he would find something of value after enduring so much anxiety and fighting so hard to survive. What caliber of man would he meet in Washington? Large minded, generous men, or men absorbed in their own views? From the book he was reading, Theodore L. Stoddard's *The Revolt against Civilization,* Mayo planned to take some ideas, hit hard with them, and show the Washington people what road to follow.[30]

Kellogg arranged the first interviews, and assured Mayo that businessmen were ready for his psychological approach to industrial conflict, but before he could talk with the financiers of research in New York he had to satisfy the industrial psychologists in Washington. Mayo's old problem had followed him across the continent; he worried that by the time he was accepted and ready to start, he would be penniless, and have to work to get his fare home. He scolded himself that his "was a cheeky attitude to take, arriving here without any money and try to hold America up for a job."[31]

Mayo met Charles E. Merriam, a leading political scientist who was planning the structure and activities of the Social Science Research Council,[32] and on many points their thinking was similar. Both had optimistic views of democracy, despite its apparent failings, and agreed that, although it was easy to recognize and plan for continuing diversity of interests, cooperation could be engendered by the application of intelligent thought to problems. Citizens should be well educated, politicians and administrators should be well trained. Training should be based on scientific knowledge of society, and such knowledge would come from applied social and political research in the universities. Specifically, Merriam wanted research that used improved techniques of data collection and analysis, that called on practical political experience, and that turned to the insights available in sociology and Freudian psychology for help with political problems in modern democracies. Like Mayo, who had seen how a socialist government had dominated Queensland's industry, Merriam rejected socialism because it gave the state too much control over the economy. And, both men were dissatisfied with the free enterprise system because its unthinking and sometimes rapacious growth made for a source of great power outside a democratic nation's control. Merriam and Kellogg spoke of taking Mayo to see Secretary of Commerce Herbert Hoover. With James McKeen Cattell of the Psychological Bureau in New York, Mayo felt less impressive. Although Cattell was friendly, his profound dislike of Freud and medical psychology combined with a marked preference for his experimental research prevented Mayo from discussing his preferred topics. Mayo spent the next morning with Raymond Dodge, president of the Anthropological and Psychological Section of the National Research Council, and lunched with Robert M. Yerkes, who had once supervised the U.S. Army's psychological testing and, in Mayo's view was the country's leading psychologist.

Mayo learned that he was being compared favorably with the late Elmer Southard (1876-1920), a Harvard-trained physician whose neuropathological studies had led to his appointment as the first director of the Boston Psychopathic Hospital. Like Mayo, Southard developed a critical attitude toward the pessimism and emotional monism of Freud and his followers but fought antipsychologism among his own medical colleagues. The senior academics in the National Research Council considered that Mayo was the first person they had met who was familiar with the field of industrial sociopsychology since Southard's death.[33] And Louis L. Thurstone, a prominent psychologist, said that he wanted to consult Mayo on methods for studying causes of industrial unrest in Pittsburgh.[34] Because he had so impressed Kellogg and associates, Mayo was sent to New York with a letter of introduction to Beardsley Ruml and Raymond Fosdick.

Ruml had recently been appointed as stop-gap director of the Laura Spelman Rockefeller Memorial Foundation. He would become one of Mayo's closest American friends and the man largely responsible for Mayo's being so well established in academic life in the United States. Ruml was born in 1894, the son of a doctor in Cedar Rapids, Iowa. At Dartmouth College he was distinguished by a curious combination of high intelligence, playful loafing, and brilliant ideas. At the University of Chicago he completed a Ph.D. in psychology and education, and furthered his unusual technique of inventive thinking: alone, he would maintain a waking dream-state, and follow his reveries wherever they led. Ruml became an assistant to Professor Walter V. Bingham, and as codirector of the Division of Trade Tests during the war, became skilled in the development of mental tests. For a short time after the war, he worked with his former army supervisor, Dr. Walter D. Scott, and was an adviser to the management of the Armour and Swift meatpacking companies. In 1920 John D. Rockefeller, Jr., engaged Ruml to advise as to how the value to the public of New York's leading cultural institutions might be raised. The excellence of Ruml's work and his engaging personal style led to his immediate acceptance in New York society. At twenty-seven he was made director of the Laura Spelman Rockefeller Memorial Foundation. With customary energy and boldness, Ruml pursued a scheme to disburse $75-$80 million on long-term, large-scale research in sociology, political science, economics, psychology, and anthropology. The Rockefeller advisers had always preferred small, traditional projects on current issues, but Ruml overcame their resistance. Eventually he earned the reputation of a founder of American social sciences. In 1930 he went to the University of Chicago, then later became the treasurer of R.H. Macy's. His most notable idea would be devising the pay-as-you-go income tax plan in 1942.

Although Ruml was fourteen years younger than Mayo, of greater bulk, and American born, at this point differences fade. Both men had come from a medical family and valued clinical observations, and both had studied issues in education and the new medical psychology. They had also learned how to use their mental hinterland for imaginative thinking, and recognize the importance of a scientific base to reliable knowledge, and the value of applied knowledge. The overlap in their professional interests was augmented by a shared pleasure in conversation, wine, and gourmet cooking.[35]

Although Raymond B. Fosdick (1883-1972) would never become as close to Mayo as Ruml, he held Mayo's attention for his interest in novel ideas on labor relations and his efforts to prevent another war. Before the war Fosdick had been associated with John D. Rockefeller, Jr., through his Bureau of Social Hygiene, and studied European methods of police administration as part of a larger program to curb prostitution in the United States. In 1916 he was appointed chairman of a military commission on training camp activities. After the war he worked with President Woodrow Wilson on plans for a U.S. role in the League of Nations, and later helped create the Foreign Policy Association and organize the Council on Foreign

Relations. In these ways Fosdick involved Rockefeller in European politics. In industrial research, Fosdick encouraged Rockefeller to fund Industrial Relations Counselors, a New York agency that advised on means to reduce industrial conflict through raising worker morale, and to support scientific studies in industrial relations and have the subject taught in the universities. From 1936 to 1948 Fosdick was president of the Rockefeller Foundation.[36]

From his first contact with Ruml, Mayo learned that the decision to finance his research was "touch and go." Ruml suggested that meanwhile he write for magazines that were offering good fees to freelancers. Even though Mayo's notes were not at hand, he began immediately to prepare articles on failure of education, training in revery, and achievement in middle age.[37]

Mayo raised with Ruml, the matter of financial support for an institution to promote mental hygiene among industrial workers. He had had plans to set up such an entity if he became director of tutorial classes at the University of Melbourne.[38] Mayo decided that he wanted to work in the United States but if that was not possible he would accept the directorship if it was offered. If neither possibility came to pass, he would have to return to the University of Queensland in March 1923. Although he was making a network of valuable contacts, time was closing in. So he waited, hoped, wrote, and went to the theater.

News from home began ten days of misery. The Mayo family thought Hetty was on her deathbed, but Mayo could not bring himself to write to her lest his lack of achievement, which might appear between the lines, aggravate her condition. He sensed, too, that the Melbourne job would not be his. His luggage had not turned up, a calamity for such a fastidious dresser, and the notes he needed for his articles were in the missing steel trunk. Further, the editor of *The American* asked that his submitted articles be rewritten; it would be a week or two before he would learn if they would be accepted as revised. Angry and desperate Mayo considered asking his brother Herbert for more money, but instead sent a sharp reminder to Ruml that Kellogg had promised to pay the travel expenses he had incurred. Dark reveries developed: he should have stuck with Jessica Colbert and not believed Ruml's tales of easy money from magazine publishers; he wanted to be rid of both Freud and academic psychology; he would have to go back to Brisbane after vowing to himself that he intended never to return. The crisis was like that of 1905 when he was sent back from London, and had to face scorn at home.

Next day he found he had powerful friends after all. Ruml had received Mayo's note, and suggested to Leonard Outhwaite, professor of anthropology and psychology at Columbia University, that Mayo speak to his class. How unconscious mental processes contribute to problems of social organization was the theme of Outhwaite's course. Mayo took the class through his ideas on the mental hinterland to the ways of achieving sanity in the modern world, successfully, he believed. Afterward students consulted him on personal problems. Then Outhwaite took him to Yale to discuss the new psychology with President Angell, the president of both Yale and the American Psychological Association.

Mayo was becoming convinced that his old and well-worked integration of Janet's theory of obsessions and reveries with Freud's theory of unconscious mental processes appeared to be new to American audiences; they seemed to want him to repeat the ideas, and to examine scientifically the growth of irrelevant reveries in an individual's life.

In New York he was invited to a meeting of psychiatrists to open discussion of a paper on cryptomnesia (unconscious plagiarism) by Alexander A. Brill, founder of the New York Psychoanalytic Society and first American translator of Freud's works. Mayo impressed the gathering, and Brill said how pleased he was to find a man who knew what he was talking about. The psychiatrists obviously liked Mayo's use of case lore, and the psychologists seemed awed by the clinical experience it implied. He felt at ease in both camps and believed that he was being accorded a valued interstitial role. Whereas in San Francisco he had felt rejected as a Freudian, in New York he felt welcomed as a unique "mental hinterland" and "revery" psychologist among "mental foreground" and "stream of consciousness" psychologists.[39]

Although Mayo could see his reputation growing, a professional identity becoming clear, no money was coming in. In the past a lack of money had so undermined his self-esteem that black thoughts made it mandatory that he spend a few days in silence to recover. But this time outrage and indignation took hold, and he stormed at his acquaintances in New York. He attacked Kellogg for not having paid his travel fare. Then he went for Ruml, declaring that he had not come to New York to get magazine articles rejected. Results were promising. Kellogg said the expenses would be paid and hinted that Rockefeller might support Mayo's industrial work. But Ruml's help was more real. Firm offers of money as well as actual cash came for Mayo's articles; interviews were arranged with a senior executive in Standard Oil; invitations came to speak at a psychiatrists' dinner and before the National Council for Mental Hygiene;[40] Ruml and his psychologist wife became more friendly, and said they appreciated his distinction between academic and "revery" psychology.[41] But Ruml's most valuable assistance lay in introducing Mayo to Professor Joseph H. Willets, who welcomed the freshness of his ideas and offered two weeks at the University of Pennsylvania speaking to students, faculty, foremen from local industries, and managers from the local Chamber of Commerce.[42]

Mayo arrived in Philadelphia on November 15 at 4 P.M. At 5 P.M. he was speaking to Willets's graduate class in the Industrial Research Department of the Wharton School of Finance and Commerce because Willits had been called away. Next day Willits returned and heard Mayo lecture. After an informal desultory hour, Mayo moved at a more intriguing pace into what he liked most: discussion. A group of educators, businessmen, and medical men stayed behind for more discussion, some remarking that they hoped he would be available for consultation. Willits was so pleased with what he had seen and heard that he began immediately to rearrange plans for the academic year so that Mayo could be implanted at the university rather than spend only two weeks as a visitor.[43]

Willits, a Quaker born in 1889 and educated at Swarthmore College, had developed interests in economics that centered on labor relations and employment. In 1915 he began studies of unemployment in Philadelphia, and was granted a Ph.D. by the University of Pennsylvania in 1916, and then for two years was employment superintendent of a U.S. naval aircraft factory. This led to his current academic appointment and to studies of labor relations for the U.S. Coal Commission. In his professional life, Willits set himself the task of "hunting for, identifying and serving superior talent,"[44] and Mayo was one of his early discoveries.

The Wharton School was the first American school of commerce. It had been founded in 1881, and in 1908 began graduate education.[45] In March 1921 the Department of Industrial Research was established, and its aim was to be "a regional experiment station for the study of problems especially illustrated in the Philadelphia metropolitan area."[46] In its early days its growth was limited by the depression and by Willits's policy that it avoid becoming a service agency for any kind of industrial research without regard to ethical motives behind the request. As the department developed, it first upheld scientific research as the basis for sound community service and, second, established ties with Quaker employers who supported research with a practical and socially constructive character.

The main areas of study were wages and employment, executive leadership, effectiveness of personnel practices, and economic bases of industrial stability. Mayo's area would be "the group of problems of individual adjustment to [the] industrial environment whose solution involves cooperation among economists, psychologists, physiologists and kindred scientists."[47] But initially Mayo had to convince local influentials of the value of his work and that they should provide the university with money to begin it; Ruml could put such evidence to his foundation for funds to continue.

Willits hoped to introduce Mayo to influential businessmen and academics but shortly sicknesss intervened, and his assistant, W.E. Fisher, a young economist, planned Mayo's daily activities. Mayo taught Willits's class, and talked with Anne Bezanson, a Harvard graduate who shared his interests and was helping Willits with the Coal Commission inquiries. Fisher wanted to learn from Mayo more about psychology and anthropology. He was puzzled by Mayo's casual remarks about the aristocracy's characteristic agnosticism and fearlessness. Mayo explained that the conventional religious doctrines, which had been designed to keep the bourgeoisie at their social duties, were invalid for scholars and scientists, whose duty was to be tolerant of all views, even to the point of collaborating with the religious. Combined with comments on psychology and problems of authority, such talk aroused Fisher's conviction of sin, made him aware of the "apparatus of the restricted academic," and, Mayo wrote, stimulated him "to reading off his usual track in some excitement."[48]

A recovered Willits and Fisher took Mayo to a graduate seminar on "character analysis" at which he left a deep impression. Without professional training in clinical and social psychology, the leader of the discussion had acquired some grasp of the fashionable psychologizing that Mayo had seen purveyed in San Francisco. When he began touting phrenology, Mayo rose, and selecting evidence from biologists, physiologists, and anatomists, he roundly denounced all that had been said. The audience enjoyed this display, the speaker retreated, and Willits and Fisher praised Mayo for the repudiation. But, after some initial satisfaction, Mayo privately admonished himself for his aggressiveness.[49]

The forcefulness with which he was gaining associations in eminent circles brought Mayo personal satisfaction but anxiety, too. He was invited to give a conference paper on November 28 before the historical section of the Academy of Medicine on the development of psychopathology since Braid and its relation to educational theory and practice. Notable men would be there: John Dewey, the foremost educational pragmatist since William James; James H. Robinson, director of the New York School of Social Research; Everett D. Marton; and Charles L. Dana. To Dorothea he wrote: "In our personal history, yours and mine [the conference] is an historic moment."[50] Although he knew the usual route to success was from a low to a high position, Mayo deliberately used the reverse, attacking from above downward. The approach took its toll, for it aroused conviction of his own sin. First, he felt guilty because he had violated the rule of respectable men that one ought not to gain opportunities for distinction by thrusting; second, he felt ashamed because he thought he might fail to perform competently before those who had given him the opportunities. Thus, he was elated by his new associations with people of rank but also depressed by irrational fears of his own possible shortcomings.

Mayo's reaction to this conflict was to turn his attention to the current task, bringing to it a mixture of concentrated effort and comforting revery. He revised his paper, made an abstract of it, pondered it, and memorized it. "The thing now is to justify the opportunity they have given me," he wrote to Dorothea. "I expect just for a moment to be a little nervous when I stand up—but I shall look across the many miles of sea to you—and then turn to the attack." Reveries were becoming central to his personal experiences, his professional pronouncements, and his family life. "Watch little Patty's reveries and companions. Her daddy is going to be identified with 'revery.'"[51]

Mayo was anxious to impress the audience with his ideas on academic psychology and psychopathological revery and believed that if he could, "there is no doubt of a succes d'estime."[52] Afterward he thought the presentation had been too long and only moderately successful, even though it did result in an evening's discussion with Dewey, Robinson, and Pierce Clark. The medical director of the National Committee for Mental Hygiene wanted to publish the paper, but Mayo preferred to wait. Ruml had enjoyed the address, and invited Mayo to lunch with Joseph Hayes and Raymond Dodge of the National Research Council. Ruml revealed that he had cut through the red tape around a conference of the Americal Psychological Association and arranged for Mayo to take part in a symposium at Harvard University with William Healey, the Boston psychotherapist, Clarence S. Yoakum from the Carnegie Institute, and Edward L. Thorndike, a leading experimental psychologist. Ruml had even chosen the subject of Mayo's talk: the psychological analysis of industry. Without saying so, Mayo decided he would speak again on revery and its educational effects. Also, Ruml said that if Philadelphia's businessmen donated enough money to the university to attract his foundation's funds, Mayo's salary would be a hundred dollars a week. Mayo spent Thanksgiving Day with Hayes's party at the Vanderbilt Hotel enjoying violations of the Volstead Act, and feeling that he was "moving amongst the elite."[53]

Psychologists were beginning to note Mayo's illumination of work by Janet, Jung, and Freud. He emphasized the fundamental role of revery in normal life, and played down the sexuality in the psychoanalytic approach; impressed, Yerkes sent a representative of the Sex Research Committee of the National Committee for Mental Hygiene to consult with Mayo. When opportunities presented themselves, he would open discussion with his psychology colleagues—Ruml, Dewey, Clark—on reveries of murder and suicide, and, to his amusement, saw them collecting one another's suicide reveries.[54]

Although Mayo believed that businessmen wanted him in Philadelphia, it was not certain that they would donate enough money to the university before the date of his departure. The matter agitated him, but he could do nothing but wait. He did not have Dorothea to listen to his worries, and he had so much difficulty sleeping that at times he wandered restlessly through the streets, putting his worries aside, "thinking anxiously of you, and your troubles." Nights for a week he planned and reveried about his future, Dorothea's teeth, Patty's companions, the irresponsibility of black nannies, the possibilities of his taking a quick trip to Brisbane or of Dorothea's coming to Philadelphia, borrowing against his life insurance. In the daytime he taught, and pursued normal academic activities, for example, he attended a seminar on Robinson's *The Mind in the Making,* dominated the group, and led discussion to one of his favorite topics, the difficulties for women of combining education and marriage.[55]

At several meetings with Philadelphia's business leaders, Mayo put his case for psychological studies in industry and, at the same time, prepared his material for the Harvard symposium. For each meeting the procedure was as follows: Willits invited twelve to fifteen businessmen to dinner at the university's Lenape Club. After the meal, Willits introduced Mayo, who talked for about three-quarters of an hour and then for an hour fielded questions and developed the discussion. Each audience seemed interested, assessed his claims correctly, found something new in his approach, and many went home with the catchword "revery." All the men were courteous, sympathetic, and keen; no aloofness, no sneers; they treated him as a distinguished authority. "Such a change from Australia . . ." he wrote to Dorothea, "rather wonderful by comparison with the anxiety of Sydney not to have me." Mayo wondered what people in Brisbane would think if he did not appear there again.[56]

After one evening with a group of businessmen, the manager of Wanamaker's department store asked Mayo to see one of the department heads. Mayo found him suffering from a mild anxiety neurosis, of which the most incapacitating symptom was an intense muscular rigidity. Mayo suggested, among other things, that the muscular tension was causing many of the other symptoms, and as the afternoon wore on the man improved. He accepted and smoked a proffered cigarette. "That was very nice," he said. "I've been afraid to smoke for two years." Apparently the muscular tension had previously combined with the irritation of the cigarette smoke to produce incapacitating bouts of coughing.[57]

Willits and Mayo became closer. So that Willits would be free for consultation with the Coal Commission, Mayo lectured on mental testing to his class. Willits arranged a luncheon for Mayo with the professor of psychology Witmer, from whom Mayo's presence had been concealed for two weeks to prevent interference with Willits' plans; another luncheon was planned with a politician who was about to take charge of the state's administration of problems in labor and industry—Mayo felt he had created a favorable impression on both men but could see no clear purpose to the occasions. Witmer invited him to visit the children's clinic; the politician wanted to know him better, and, as their conversation developed, Mayo learned that Willits's plans would involve association with "some very big names." Worried by the vagueness of Willits' plans, Mayo told Willits later that unless his role became clearer, he would have to return to Australia. Time was short, and he was anxious about money. "After Xmas," laughed Willits.[58]

As Christmas approached Mayo's thoughts turned more often to money, Australia, and the paper for the Harvard symposium. From the university he had received board and lodging for almost two weeks, and two hundred dollars for his services, but most of the money went for his New York trip. To get cash for Christmas presents and a holiday for Dorothea and the girls he wrote to the magazine publishers asking for what he thought was due him. No reply. Willits promised to write, too. Still nothing. Apparently Willits was paying for Mayo's board: "If he hadn't I should have been in Queer Street," Mayo wrote.[59]

Around Mayo, families were celebrating. People hurried by with parcels, and wished him "Happy Christmas." All he could do was smile and mentally shrug his shoulders, tot up the cost of his forthcoming trip, and, back to his room, carry the shame of having let down his family. Sundays were his lonely days, his days for reveries of home. Once, for Dorothea's sake, he visited an art gallery; another time he went to a "so-called musical comedy, 'Blossom Time'" which delighted him, and "went far to 'sublimate' some of" his "unbelievable longing for" Dorothea's presence. Often he would walk and plan. He was looking forward to the day—January 3, Willits had said—when he could wire Dorothea to come. Perhaps they could live with the university crowd at Swarthmore, ten miles from Philadelphia's center. Dorothea could easily commute to the New York theater; American trains took only half the time taken by trains in Australia. Rent would be about eight hundred dollars; income, five thousand plus, or more, if summer teaching became available, even more if there really was a boom in applied psychology. Dorothea would like Philadelphia's shops. He needed her: "It cuts deep this absence . . . if I followed my desire I'd come flying back to Australia—cured of ambitions, if ever I had them. . . . I'm alone, and I have to count the paving stones as I walk the streets to keep myself from revery."[60]

Mayo worried about Dorothea's income. If he resigned in March at the beginning of the academic year the University of Queensland would be unable to staff his department adequately and have good reason to curtail salary payments to Dorothea. So he decided to request a twelve-month extension to his leave without pay—a similar request had been granted to a colleague—and resign within six months.[61]

With this decision behind him his thoughts turned to Harvard, where he imagined he would have to "cross swords with all the might of America on the Thursday after Christmas." The test would offer Mayo a critical audience for his psychology of revery; he was not anxious but did believe that because his ideas were still changing that perhaps he was not in as good form for speaking as the occasion might demand. It was most important that he keep the listeners' attention. He had something worthwhile to say, but the problem was to "put it over" as he heard Americans remark so often.[62]

On his birthday—he was forty-two—Mayo went to Harvard for the first time. "Red bricks, flat, white windows, with a dozen panes in each and green shutters. Everywhere snow, and boards above it to walk on." He called on Langfeld who was too busy to give him more than a minute but courteously suggested he stay on after the conference for a few days. The general secretary of the American Psychological Association made Mayo an official guest, which extended him some courtesies. He dined with some young Harvard men and their wives and discussed the sort of intellectual activity a woman can pursue and still be fair to her children, herself, and her husband. His "brutal onslaught" on the higher education of women was successful, so he thought.[63]

But Mayo needed cash. All the cheap hotels had been filled, so he had to stay at Boston's luxurious Copley-Plaza. He had only fifty dollars and at the week's end he would be asked for fifty-four! All he could do was send a desperate plea to the magazine publishers and hope that someone like Ruml would arrive in time to help him pay the account.

On the day before his address he went to the conference to hear how speakers delivered their papers; they simply read them at the audience. As he was leaving Yerkes introduced him to William McDougall and the two canvassed American psychology, psychopathology, and one of Mayo's favorites, the Nordic's conviction of sin. McDougall suggested Mayo write about the topic, and invited him for lunch the next day.

McDougall's courtesies strongly affected Mayo. He determined to speak well and to use few notes. He revised the talk as an attack on crowd psychology. Then he read in the newspaper that at the conference the day before, Dr. Thomas Baker of Pittsburgh had said: "Our system of education may not be able to check the growing power of the crowd. This is one of the disappointing symptoms of the age." Mayo decided to start there, and "Heaven help me (us) to 'put it over.'"[64]

At the McDougalls' house, the next day Mayo ate lunch with Knight Dunlap and other colleagues. He sat on Mrs. McDougall's right and contributed liberally to the flow of conversation about the friend they had in common, Pitt-Rivers, his work, his wife, and life in Australia.

Mayo began his address standing at the lectern, then, as was his habit, he moved toward the edge of the platform, and with a sheet of paper in his hand, delivered the body of the address without looking at his notes. When he finished the psychologists came forward, introduced themselves, and put questions to him. The psychotherapists attacked him—Healey, Emerson, H. Addington Bruce—but Elton came back at them. Bruce wanted Mayo to write a book in his *Mind and Health* series, and the editor of the National Committee of Mental Hygiene quarterly wanted to publish Mayo's address. It seemed he had "put over" his idea that all psychopathology from Braid to Freud could be regarded as a continuing investigation of the educational effects of revery. Chairman Raymond Dodge said, "Fine, splendid," as he shook Mayo's hand. Yerkes congratulated him; as did the president of the association, who remarked loudly to McDougall, "It's refreshing to see a man get the whole of a 35 minute address off a single sheet of paper." And later John B. Watson said: "It's a great method yours, much more effective to talk like that."

At dinner that evening Mayo was put beside Mrs. Walter Bingham, wife of the leading industrial psychologist, at the head of the table. During the conversation he got a laugh here and there, and much praise for having chosen his stories so well that afternoon. Even Cattell, the doyen of American psychologists, introduced him to Mrs. Cattell. "It really was quite a minor triumph . . . it was nice to be congratulated by the 'great names' in psychology—and to have said a new thing . . . altogether, you'll agree, much better than a triumph in Brisbane or Melbourne."[65]

At the peak of his triumph that night Mayo's conviction of sin set to work. He asked Dorothea not to take too much notice of the praise he had been given. After all, he was a stranger, and they had simply been very kind to him. The noted psychotherapist whom he had attacked, and consequently displeased, was really quite a decent fellow. And even though most people had been very nice to him, there were dissenters from his viewpoint. Fame does not come so easily. By the time he was ready for bed, the day's triumph had been reduced to a "good first step."

Next day Mayo was depressed; "many causes . . . no reasons." A mild touch of appendicitis forced him to decline a visit to the Boston Psychopathic Clinic, and an embarrassing shortage of money forced him to borrow fifty dollars to get back to Philadelphia. One cause of his misery was the imminent departure of an Australian friend, Mary Dods, whom he had known since they were youngsters. She and Mayo talked without end of Dorothea, Australia, the little girls, the United States. She offered to lend him money, but of course he could not accept. On January 28 the S.S. *Niagra* would leave for Australia; Mayo wished he could go too. "Things here are too big—3,000 scientists—in one city, talking—it gives me a feeling of futility." How could he educate the girls on a yearly salary of five thousand dollars? A year at Bryn Mawr cost two thousand dollars. If they did not go there, "we should have to send them to public schools with Niggers and Jews and so on." He thought the best decision would be to return to Brisbane to take up some special studies. He would have £810 net per year; with Dorothea's £300 they could settle down, and his American experience would establish him as an authority on psychology. "It wouldn't be a come-down because I would have refused work in America," he wrote. Reveries deepened his depressing thoughts about dragging himself back to Philadelphia to see the "old pussies" at the Sherwood Hotel, to hear the endless hymns emanating from the lounge outside his bedroom, to wallow in his solitude.

Mayo understood how the solitude, the absence of Dorothea, and the departure of a friend combined: "I get a conviction of sin—the contrasts are too evident—what I really need is regular work and the interest of it. I've just thought of that, and it's rather a solution." He left the Copley-Plaza room and, plodding through the knee-deep snow in the square, went to admire the mural decorations and the painting by Sargent at the Public

Library. "If it wasn't for you," he wrote to Dorothea "and your inspiration hovering over me I wouldn't do these things. My dearest woman—when shall we see each other again."[66]

On his return to Philadelphia Mayo read Dorothea's cable urging him to remain in the United States until he had money enough to support the family. Then she would come with a nurse and the children. He could not reply until after the last dinner speech to Willits's Philadelphia businessmen, when his task was to convince them that his research was so valuable that they should match the ten thousand dollars that it was hoped Ruml could convince his trustees to donate to the university. And it would not be until January 17 that the trustees' decision would be taken. On New Year's Day Mayo cabled Dorothea: "Yes. Expect Philadelphia decision soon. Greetings."[67]

The decision to cable Dorothea led Mayo into thoughts of the hurdles to their reunion. Among the hurdles was a shortage of money, which when overcome would be followed by difficulties in acquiring a passport; once she had that, she would be set upon by strange people aboard ship; and if she did reach the West Coast, immigration officials would not allow her in under the immigrant quota, so she and the girls would have to camp on Ellis Island. To facilitate her unimpeded passage, he suggested she sail to Vancouver, take a train to Montreal or Toronto, pretend she was a Canadian, and bluff her way across the border. The pessimism was accompanied by joy and impatience, and the conflict was resolved by his vow never again to leave his wife and children.[68]

While the welfare of his family occupied the back of his mind, Mayo's attention was given to how he could get work and the money that would bring them to his side. He imagined that with the Rockefeller money behind him he could do something for the future of civilization. He had attracted Ruml's attention through their shared interest in the application of the social sciences to industrial affairs. At every opportunity he tried to maintain Ruml's attention for the developing theory of reveries, but soon learned that Ruml appreciated him as much for his conversation and wit as for the professional discussion of psychology.[69]

While Mayo waited for January 17 and news from New York, the recognition that people were giving his concepts kept in perspective the haunting images of poverty and separation from family. His ideas were moving rapidly toward a theme of "education by revery" and an investigation under which he could subsume work from Janet to Freud. His thesis would be that mental health is determined by the relation between concentration and revery.

While Mayo was working on his revery thesis, Dr. Tartmeyer at the university clinic offered him the opportunity to study children with speech defects, and to visit the Children's Bureau directed by Dr. Jessie Taft. She seemed to Mayo to be "as frank as Havelock Ellis and as understanding."[70]

He expected that Dorothea would like her, and that on his say-so Dr. Taft would regard Dorothea as a competent psychologist and give her work at the bureau. A week later Dr. Taft learned of Mayo's own clinical skill, and was curious to know what he meant by relaxation. He obliged her by putting a twelve-year-old to sleep. He considered another difficult child, explaining how a child's show of temper was usually a response adequate to a situation; the problem then became how to understand the situation rather than the unacceptable behavior. This was his doctrine of the "total situation," which he had taken up in 1914 at Brisbane. In his black moments it comforted him to know that people in the United States appreciated his ideas, and that in the past he had followed the right line.[71]

Many opportunities helped to banish those black moments during the ensuing days. Dr. Taft offered him all the clinical work he wanted, but he had to say again that at present he was not taking any cases; Yerkes, chairman of the National Research Council, pushed men toward Mayo for consultation; he corresponded freely with McDougall on national welfare, social decay, and the Nordic race; he was asked to speak at a dinner for social workers; Willits was trying to arrange a place for him in the Coal Commission inquiries; and one day a faculty member said something flattering about him to Willits, and John Dewey agreed. It seemed to Mayo that he was becoming a member of a group of workers, and could expect to enjoy their backing.[72]

He began to take a favorable view of the world and himself. He kept in trim with exercise, and did not lose his eye for pretty girls, who were reminders of how he loved Dorothea. He wanted her to keep well, to look at life positively: "Head up sweetheart, use Coue's method 'better and better everyday'—it's a good revery."[73]

Mayo saw that his impact came mainly in the discussions after his talks, but several people wanted his ideas on paper. Willits had asked for a written statement of the scope and extent of his proposed research; Ruml said he would need something, too. And Leonard Outhwaite pressed him for articles for the *Journal of Personal Research*. So Mayo tackled what he had often found more taxing than anything else: writing.

To Willits Mayo proposed that his research should be of immediate help to industry, but not so restricted that it was concerned only with efficiency in office systems at the expense of valuable educational and social interests. He disdained the schools of social science that expounded ideologies of groups and classes without the support of specialized inquiries; he was sure he could make such inquiries into the real value of democracy.[74] Mayo asserted that the recent demands to democratize industry falsely identified democracy with majority rule. Society requires individuals to make moral decisions (e.g., voting, jury duty) and technical decisions (e.g., professional work).

Whereas it is probably best to decide who shall represent an electorate in Parliament by a popular vote, it is obviously impossible to decide the correct treatment of a typhoid fever by means of referendum. Now many of the current appeals for the "democratization" of industry, and many popular political theories, fail entirely to discriminate between these two types of . . . decision. Democracy . . . came into being, first, to protect industries and skilled professions from ignorant interference, and, second, to ensure that moral decisions shall be made by the community and not for it. . . . Congresses and numerical majorities are just as capable of ignorant interference with self-government as any monarch. . . . The "capitalistic" organization of society . . . whatever its faults . . . has served to conserve skill in the service of the community, to protect historic and professional traditions against the assaults of ignorant ochlocracy.[75]

To Mayo the Chartist riots had heralded defects in industrial society that in time became so widely felt that some people believed the world's economic structure would crack and civilization would fall. "There is, however, no need for such pessimism," wrote Mayo, and he warned, "our understanding of the human problems of civilization should be at least equal to our understanding of its material problems. In the absence of such understanding, the whole industrial structure is liable to destruction or decay. A world-wide revolution of the Russian type would completely destroy civilization."[76]

How did civilization get to this stage? With the industrialization of society no improvement had come in the social status of the worker. Once workers had had skilled jobs with necessary social functions but now they were dispossessed of decisions over their work, and its important functions passed to scientists and financiers. At the same time that workers became cogs in the machine, they were offered a vision of greater political freedom.

What wonder if he thinks little of the political freedom which is limited to a vote in the party organization, when he finds that his opportunity of directing his economic destinies is apparently irredeemably lost. Industrial research must be so far psychological . . . the investigator must discover the mental effect of this development and its expression in society. There is no question but that society will have to give back to the worker some opportunity for self-expression in work and of self-control. At the same time, it will be necessary to ensure that collaboration and skill in work are adequately conserved. We shall be unable to achieve this without considerable research, and especially psychological research. And without such development, civilization will have reached an impasse. This is the entirely practical research of the present which cries most urgently for attention.[77]

Mayo wrote that the alternatives, socialism and syndicalism, were "charlatan remedies" and "quack political medicines." Covering the same ground as he had at Harvard a month earlier, he concluded, "It was not only the real but also the imagined situation which determined individual development."[78] With the analogy "it is obvious that a society, like an individual, may suffer from 'nervous breakdown,'" Mayo argued that when "individuals are not achieving the direct experience of life which they are racially entitled to expect" they compensate with "'dissociated' reveries." "What else is socialism but a revery of this type? . . . The working class is failing to achieve that self-expression and control of individual destiny which racially it is entitled to expect. And it has substituted for such development a revery, an imagined social situation. . . . Socialism is a symptom . . . that all is not well with the industrial situation and that industrial research is required." But dissociated reveries were found not only among workers:

> The employer sits in his club and hears a lengthy tirade on the dangers of socialism. Returning to his office, he is faced with a request for increased wages, and replies by an indignant refusal. . . . So also with the employee. He hears constantly that he is being "exploited," that he is a "wage slave." These notions may seem to be forgotten but insofar as he has failed to achieve normal happiness they enter into his reveries. And some day a situation arises when they express themselves in action.[79]

In short, conflict was growing in industry, and, consequently, the danger of decadence or collapse of society was mounting. Through psychological investigation the irrational causes of conflict may be found and brought under rational control.

Willits had heard the arguments before, and asked Mayo to state how he would do his research. Mayo answered that he was accustomed to adapt the means to the situation; as a rule, he would begin by spending a few weeks among the workers, and talk later to assemblies of them. When he felt he had their confidence, he would administer association tests to a small group of people who worked together, take personal histories, analyze their reveries and dreams, and finally compare the development of the reveries with their orientation to life. He did not aim, as did the psychiatrist, to identify the mentally abnormal workers; rather, he sought to apply the psychiatric methods of study to normal people, and help identify the abnormality in their ideas and actions.[80]

Mayo's proposals to study the crises of industrial society were written during his personal crises. He desired intensely to be liberated from the constraints of his academic peers in Brisbane, and to be free to develop a career in the United States. He had gained valued recognition for his ideas but he had done all he could; the rest was in Ruml's hands. Without any control over the decision that would so deeply affect him, Mayo waited, plagued by doubts of his competence and old fears of failure, but buoyed by the slightest praise. Because he could recognize his personal difficulties, and the context in which they were exacerbated, he coped intelligently and productively by writing for Ruml, Willits, and Outhwaite, and pouring forth long abreactions, as he called them, in letters to Dorothea.

Whenever Willits was called to duties for the Coal Commission Mayo was left with no one to talk to and nothing to do. He preferred to be overworked than underworked. Among his reveries was the doubt that he would be able to do the work and handle the workers, and he felt guilty about discussing his anxieties and doubts in letters to Dorothea. Long days of solitude, inactivity, and Dorothea's absence mingled with the shame of not making enough money when lecturing on the West Coast, and the guilt of aspiring to become a charlatan who had lost the respect of scientists, the medical profession, academic psychologists and other colleagues.[81]

Colleagues helped him forget the personal crisis. At the Lenape Club academics would come up to his end of the table to hear him talk. In response to their attentions Mayo would expand not so much from conceit as from the relief of solitude and depressing thoughts. Once he and his colleagues were discussing Europe; a German approached the table, saluted, and announced that in his view the British race was the greatest on earth. This compliment struck to the center of Mayo's being. He had imagined becoming a naturalized U.S. citizen to facilitate Dorothea's entry to the country; the German's statement reminded him that "I don't want to give up being British at all."[82] He would always be a Britisher in the United States.

Mayo finished his "Irrational Factor in Society" and "Irrationality and Revery,"[83] the two main parts of his address at Harvard. The articles stated the problems of democracy in an industrial society, outlined the weakness of theories in crowd psychology to cope with the problems, and asserted that medical rather than academic psychology offers the best approach. The stream of consciousness theory was put aside for his theory of mind at four levels—concentration, revery, hypnoid state, and sleep—with particular emphasis given to reveries. Colorful examples were drawn from clinical experience, industry, and politics in Australia. The articles urge strongly the psychological study of reveries that people entertain at work. Mayo had a third article in mind, "Educational and Psychological Tests," which apparently he did not finish, but it probably would have indicated how he thought research ought to be done.[84]

Now there was little to do but wait for the decision of January 17. In a restless mood he wrote to his mentor Professor William Mitchell, and accused Australia of putting too many difficulties in his path. Little notice had been taken of his ideas and he regretted having to leave Australia. Mayo believed the University of Adelaide has allowed a mere bit of red tape to block his being awarded a master's degree. He wanted to have an M.A. to show his mother that he had become a credit to her, so he wrote to his friend Addison to see whether or not something could be done about it.[85]

The decision was postponed again. Fear struck Mayo that if such postponements continued his job in Brisbane would lapse before he had anything in the United States. In New York the trustees of the Laura

Spelman Rockefeller Memorial would not back Ruml's request to support Mayo, nor would they consider the matter further because his proposed work was clearly industrial and not medical. Ruml turned to Rockefeller, pointing to the modest sum needed, the work already in progress at the Wharton School, and the unusual opportunity given by Mayo's presence to explore how far local businessmen would go to support psychiatric research in industry. Ruml suggested giving three thousand dollars for use until July 1. If Mayo's work proved sound, then ten thousand dollars a year should be granted for two or three years; if it failed Mayo would return to Brisbane in July. Ruml added that since the death in 1920 of Dr. Elmer E. Southard of Harvard University, industrial psychiatry had suffered, and that Mayo would be his first replacement. Arthur Woods and Raymond B. Fosdick supported Ruml's personal appeal.[86]

While the people in New York were considering, Mayo waited, entertaining reveries on financial difficulties, problems of resigning from the University of Queensland, accommodating a family in Philadelphia, coping with traffic deaths on the road, nuisances on board ship, travel across Canada, and the immigrant quota at San Francisco. After ridding himself of these specific reveries with a lengthy abreactive letter to Dorothea, Mayo was beset again by the familiar blackness of general depression. But something his brother Herbert had said came to mind: Elton had more will to win than anyone Herbert knew, and Herbert's son Eric had inherited the same attribute. "And then I came back with the notion, that I may be beaten," he wrote to Dorothea "but I'll have a go—for you—first."[87]

On January 19, two days later than promised, Ruml phoned. The trustees had turned down his proposal altogether and allocated money instead to welfare work among disadvantaged children, but Rockefeller had promised personally sufficient money for Mayo to stay six months. "So we suffered a defeat and gained perhaps a greater victory," Mayo wrote to Dorothea. "We are 'placed next' (as they say here) to the richest man in the world, religious, interested in social and industrial investigations." Although the decision from New York was clear, Mayo was thrown into confusion. Should he cable Dorothea and the girls? Could they live on that amount of money? Would he have a job after six months? He decided to secure his job in Brisbane by asking officials at the National Research Council to request that his leave be extended another twelve months. He cabled Dorothea: "Satisfactory program. Details undecided." Next day Willits told Mayo there would be no problems about carrying on after July; and Outhwaite cabled that the two articles were accepted. Mayo could write to Dorothea: "Come over, then, come over. . . ."[88]

Notes

1. Dorothea to Henrietta, 1 May 1922, SAA.
2. *Herald* (Melbourne), 18 February 1922, p. 11; ibid., 22 February 1922, p. 22.

3. Mayo notebooks, Book 12, GA 54.4, BLA.
4. *Medical Journal of Australia,* 1 April 1922, p. 365.
5. *Argus* (Melbourne), 8 March 1922, p. 8.
6. *Melbourne University Magazine* 16, no. 2 (August 1922):67-69; Melbourne University Graduate House, Secretarial Files; Elton to Helen, 9 July 1922, SAA.
7. *Argus* (Melbourne), 16 March 1922, p. 8; ibid., 30 March 1922, p. 8, MM 2.020.
8. A search revealed no reports; see also Richard C. S. Trahair and Julie G. Marshall, *Australian Psychoanalytic and Related Writings, 1884-1939: An Annotated Bibliography,* La Trobe University Library Publications, No. 16 (Bundoora, Victoria, 1979).
9. *Argus* (Melbourne), 26 April 1922, p. 14; ibid., 1 May 1922. p. 8.
10. Lanza to Edsall, 10 July 1922, MM 3.026; Elton to Helen, 9 July 1922, SAA.
11. MM 1.099.
12. *Argus* (Melbourne), 28 June 1922, p. 6.
13. Pitt-Rivers to Mayo, 29 June, 2 July 1922, MM 3.085.
14. *Argus* (Melbourne), 6 July 1922, p. 8; 10 July 1922, p. 7.
15. Sir Herbert Mayo's Notebooks 557; Sir William Mitchell to Helen Mayo, September 1949, SAA.
16. Mayo to Willits, 17 January 1923; MM 1.099.
17. Elton to Dorothea, 1 August 1922.
18. Elton to Dorothea, 2, 3, 4 August 1922.
19. *San Francisco Chronicle,* 6, 18, 25 August, 1, 8, 15 September 1922.
20. Elton to Dorothea, 11 August 1922.
21. Elton to Dorothea, 15 August 1922.
22. Elton to Dorothea, 17 August 1922.
23. Elton to Dorothea, 22 August 1922.
24. Elton to Dorothea, 26 August 1922; MM 1.099.
25. Elton to Dorothea, 1 September 1922.
26. Elton to Dorothea, 8 September 1922.
27. Elton to Dorothea, 8, 11 September 1922.
28. Elton to Dorothea, 16, 19, 23 September 1922.
29. Elton to Dorothea, 24, 27 September 1922.
30. Elton to Dorothea, 3, 4 October 1922.
31. Elton to Dorothea, 5 October 1922.
32. Barry D. Karl, *Charles E. Merriam and the Study of Politics* (Chicago: University of Chicago Press, 1974).
33. *Who Was Who in America* (Chicago: Marquis)1:1157-58; John Frosch and Nathanial Ross, eds., *The Annual Survey of Psychoanalysis, Vol. 7* (London: Hogarth, 1956), p. 7
34. Elton to Dorothea, 9 October 1922.
35. *New Yorker,* 10 February 1945, pp. 28-32, 35; ibid., 17 February 1945, pp. 26-30, 33-34; ibid., 24 February 1945, pp. 30-34, 36, 38-39; ibid., 12 September 1942, p. 12; Karl, *Charles E. Merriam,* pp. 132.
36. Peter Collier and D. Horowitz, *The Rockefellers: An American Dynasty* (New York: Holt, Rinehart & Winston, 1976).
37. Elton to Dorothea, 12 October 1922.
38. A few days later the selection committee compiled a list of three applicants: Douglas B. Copeland, Herbert Heaton, and J. A. Gunn. Gunn was appointed. Minutes, Committee of Selection, Director of Tutorial Classes, University of Melbourne, 18 October 1922, Central Registry.
39. Elton to Dorothea, 12 November 1922.
40. Elton to Dorothea, 2, 4 November 1922.
41. Elton to Dorothea, 12 November 1922.

42. Elton to Dorothea, 7 November 1922.
43. Elton to Dorothea, 15 November 1922.
44. National Bureau of Economic Research *National Bureau Report,* No. 14, February 1975, pp. 12-13.
45. M. T. Copeland, *And Mark an Era* (Boston: Little, Brown, 1958), p. 15.
46. A brief account of the Department of Industrial Research, Wharton School, University of Pennsylvania (mimeographed), RF.
47. Ibid.
48. Elton to Dorothea, 19 November 1922.
49. Elton to Dorothea, 24 November 1922.
50. Elton to Dorothea, 12, 24 November 1922.
51. Elton to Dorothea, 25, 26 November 1922.
52. Elton to Dorothea, 17 November 1922. Notes for Mayo's talk are in MM 2.021 and MM 2.074. Many of the ideas and illustrations appear in Elton Mayo, "The Irrational Factor in Society and Irrationality and Revery," *Journal of Personnel Research* 1, nos. 10, 11 (1923):419-26, 477-83.
53. Elton to Dorothea, 29 November, 2 December 1922.
54. Elton to Dorothea, 1, 2 December 1922. Mayo collected suicide and murder reveries to illustrate his talks. He set down reveries of ten men and nine women. The cases were described by reference to the person's marital status, age, occupation, racial type (North European, Nordic), eye color, and complexion. Among men favored methods were a shot through the head, drowning, or jumping from a high place; among women, poisoning (gas, ether, morphine), drowning, shooting, and electrocution. Mayo noted whether or not the suicide reveries were accompanied by murder reveries. As a rule, murder reveries were denied; in exceptional cases the desire to hurt another person was found more among women than men. MM 3.013.
55. Elton to Dorothea, 4 December 1922.
56. Elton to Dorothea, 5, 7, 11, 13 December 1922.
57. Elton to Dorothea, 15 December 1922.
58. Elton to Dorothea, 18, 19, 20 December 1922.
59. Elton to Dorothea, 13, 17, 22 December 1922.
60. Elton to Dorothea, 17, 19, 20 December 1922.
61. Elton to Dorothea, 21 December 1922.
62. Elton to Dorothea, 9, 22, 24 December 1922.
63. Elton to Dorothea, 26 December 1922.
64. Elton to Dorothea, 27, 28 December 1922.
65. A summary of the address appears in MM 2.049; Elton to Dorothea, 28 December 1922.
66. Elton to Dorothea, 29 December 1922.
67. Elton to Dorothea, 31 December 1922, 1 January 1923.
68. Elton to Dorothea, 1, 8, 20 January 1923.
69. Elton to Dorothea, 3 January 1923.
70. Elton to Dorothea, 5, 6 January 1923.
71. Elton to Dorothea, 11 January 1923.
72. Elton to Dorothea, 1, 2, 3, 7, 11 January 1923.
73. Elton to Dorothea, 11 January 1923.
74. Mayo to Willits, 17 January 1923, MM 1.099.
75. Ibid. A few days earlier Mayo had sent a similar letter to Ruml; Mayo to Ruml, 10 January 1923, RF.
76. Mayo to Willits, 17 January 1923, MM 1.099.
77. Ibid.

78. When he wrote to Ruml on the same point the arguments were more emphatic. He claimed, "[my work] is going to sweep out of existence the social psychology of McDougall, Graham Wallas, psychologists of the crowd and herd (i.e. Tarde, Durkheim, LeBon and Trotter) when it shows in individual instances that we are dealing with highly organized irrationalities and emotions. The simple lists of instincts (McDougall), political impulses (Wallas), 'desires' (Knight Dunlap) all become irrelevant when it is realized that we are dealing with highly complex products of development by revery—different in each individual instance—though capable of being moulded to common action by a skilled orator." Mayo to Ruml, 10 January 1923, RF.
79. Mayo to Willits, 17 January 1923, MM 1.099.
80. Mayo to Ruml, 10 January 1923, RF.
81. Elton to Dorothea, 12 January 1923.
82. Elton to Dorothea, 13 January 1923.
83. See note 52 above.
84. Elton to Dorothea, 15 January 1923; Mayo to Ruml, 10 January 1923, RF.
85. Elton to Dorothea, 16 January 1923.
86. Woods and Ruml to Rockefeller, 17 January 1923, RF.
87. Elton to Dorothea, 17 January 1923.
88. Elton to Dorothea, 20 January 1923.

10

Industrial Studies in Philadelphia

Mayo had a salary that would keep him and his family for six months, and no guarantee of employment thereafter unless he demonstrated the practical value of applying his psychological ideas to problems at work. So he cabled the University of Queensland: "Opportunity lead in industrial research: ask year's extended leave without salary."

With supporting cables from the National Research Council and its associates, the precedent of two years leave without salary granted to the professor of biology at the university, and a reputation for having enhanced the university's public image, Mayo thought the Senate would do as he asked. It refused, and asked when he would return to duty. Mayo answered: "Refusal unanticipated owing to request National Research Council and Biology precedent committed four months work. Please suggest compromise."

There would be no compromise. The Senate cabled: "Special meeting Senate general dissatisfaction expressed existing temporary arrangements Philosophy Department. Necessary you resume duty forthwith or tender your resignation. Cable your decision immediately."

Mayo's reply: "Regret Senate action compels resignation."

In February 1923 Mayo resigned, and feared that by doing so his character would be so blackened in Brisbane that stories would cross the Pacific and hold up his attempts to become established.[1] However, in three years he became so well known for his ideas and research in industrial psychology that he was called to Harvard University. Industrial research, personal contacts, public addresses, lectures and informal talks, clinical cases, and publications would contribute to his remarkably quick, sure and authoritative rise to prominence in American academic life.

Mayo began to apply the new medical psychology to factory work. His approach was to assume the factory was like a hospital of shell-shocked soldiers who had to be examined for abnormalities in their attitude to life, especially those that affected collaboration at work. The approach proved to be too slow; it ignored problems in work organization as well as special difficulties of the employer, and risked arousing suspicion among both employers and employees.[2]

Mayo's first venture was in the noisy, filthy engine room of C.H. Masland & Sons, a textile manufacturer in North Philadelphia, where he told a small group of workers much of what he had been saying to managers and employers at Willits's special dinners: contrary to the popular view, shell-shocked soldiers, like mental patients, were curable; every year fifty thousand Americans were put into mental asylums because they could not care for themselves or achieve a satisfactory adaption to life; and, at that rate, in ten years half a million people who had been apparently normal children would be in an asylum before they were forty. Mayo asserted that work is affected by irritability, depression, and other irrationalities; for many individuals the irrationalities pass, but in the mass they cumulate and frequently cause breakdowns in group work. Psychopathologists showed that the irrationalities, once thought to be inborn, began during a person's lifetime, appear as socially maladjusted actions and brooding, and are exacerbated by poor opportunities for personal expression. Mayo argued that in industry the irrationalities and their consequences should be studied to determine the degree that social and industrial organization had contributed to them.

Mayo emphasized these observations, arguments, and proposals with his theory of revery. The mind operates at four levels of consciousness—concentration, revery, hypnoid state, sleep—and mental health depends on the relation between concentration, which we use to test ideas against observations, and revery, which we use to relax and allow the mind to work of its own accord. In a genius, ideas born of revery are tested at the level of concentration; but among neurotics revery is used as a refuge from concentration. Such individuals are led to a state of mental dissociation in which no cooperation exists between revery and concentration, and the two mental processes work in different directions. Two kinds of self develop, and unhappiness and maladjustments ensue; they can be corrected if taken in hand early by a psychiatrist. Conditions that cause the disintegration of the self are varied; monotonous work can contribute to hostile reveries, and work that requires close attention to detail can cause reveries of resentment against a society that sets such terms for employment. Overwork, then, is the result, not the cause, of nervous breakdown. When concentration and revery are well integrated overwork is impossible; when they are not, melancholic reveries can arouse feelings of insecurity, rebellion against authority and order, and radicalism. To help expose these irrationalities and, consequently, remove the effects of fear, part of the plant should be available for a modified form of psychopathological investigation that would collect data on mental problems at work and develop solutions for application in the plant and other workplaces.[3]

Managers had often been attracted to Mayo's ideas and presentation. On this occasion Masland workers were so impressed that, with their employer's consent, they called a meeting so more workers could hear Mayo.

They seemed keen for him to begin, so early in March he was given a noisy corner of the factory where workers could consult him. Few took the opportunity because most workers suspected he was there primarily to promote Masland interests. This worried Mayo, for if not many wanted his help and that fact was reported, Rockefeller funding would cease, he would be forced to quit the University of Pennsylvania, and he would not be able to support his family.

At the end of March Mayo was obliged to quit the factory anyway. A girl who had had her clothes ripped off by a machine fainted at the sight of her nakedness and was sent to Mayo to talk about her reaction. He first sought advice from a woman social worker, and when the girl revealed how ignorant she was of her body, he offered her a book on the physiology of sex.[4] One of the firm's partners objected to Mayo's action. Mayo saw his approach had overemphasized medical aspects of his work, and decided that in future educational factors affecting factory life should be given closer attention.

While he was at Masland Mayo had visted all departments, and some clinical cases had come to him, e.g., paranoia, excessive headaches, aural illusions, sexual fears, irrational radicalism. On a sociological level, he observed hostility among skilled Americans toward unskilled Italian newcomers who readily accepted low wages, general bitterness toward the company, and little or no interest or pride in work. And he believed that the company would worsen further its labor relations if it continued a hostile policy toward trade and labor organizations, and employee social life at work.

Mayo was next employed briefly by the Philadelphia Textile Employers' Association to study crime among workers, and the effect of Italian and Polish communities on American workers. He found that the industry's criminals were mostly petty thieves, and many of them were Italians, Poles, or European Jews; the few Americans among them tended to be hoboes, derelicts, or "white trash." He also found that members of the Italian colony worked for less yet lived well and maintained large families even so—a situation that aroused envy and hostility in American workers.

Two companies asked Mayo to reduce labor turnover, and in both he struck difficult personality problems among managers. Melville G. Curtis, president of Collins and Aikman Company, makers of plush, wanted to use a psychological test to select prospective employees with the mental capacity for work in the weaving department. It should be translated into German, French, Italian, and Polish, and its scoring and interpretation procedures so standardized that it could eliminate irrational factors from problems in the personnel department, and eventually remove the need for psychologists in the firm. Curtis instructed Mayo to tell his assistant to standardize interview records, and to define the position, pay, tasks, and hours of work of his assistant, Dr. Morris S. Viteles. Then Curtis accused one of the assistants of advising a former employee to return to work after having been dismissed for incompetence. Curtis wanted Mayo to be more businesslike in his approach, advice that was anathema to Mayo; he preferred to follow research wherever it led him. Soon it was clear to him that Curtis feared that he might uncover defects in company organization that led to high turnover. When Curtis actually closed avenues of inquiry that Mayo had opened and took charge of his work, Mayo asked Willits's leave to withdraw from Collins and Aikman, saying that in future "I'll know how to handle Curtises better."[5]

Mayo faced a conflict of personalities at the Miller Lock Company. E.S. Jackson, fifty-six, senior controlling partner, managed sales; his brother, A.C. Jackson, forty-one, controlled production. The latter had called in vocational guidance and time-study experts to solve the firm's problems by finding a psychological test to eliminate the unfit hands before their recruitment. Asked to discover why labor turnover was so high, Mayo found it was because wages and morale were low, productivity had declined, hours were long, most work demanded no skill and was monotonous, production schedules were confused, tools were inadequate, quality control was poor, and supervisors were frustrated and exasperated. And there was bad feeling between the sales and production departments.

Mayo found the elder Jackson poorly educated, someone who had learned business from his father. He regarded his brother—a civil engineer well trained in business but dour and intractable—as a failure. The enmity between the men put sales and producton at odds, to the detriment of profits.

Mayo persuaded the brothers to allow the formation of an advisory council composed of company executives to improve collaboration within the company. The Jacksons were not to attend its meetings. Mayo suggested to the council that, because the Jackson's were incompetent managers, any suggestions for improvements to the firm should be made by the council as a body, not by individuals, and then only after full and careful consideration of the probable consequences. After the council solved the problem of quality control and brought greater order to production, Mayo suggested several other managerial improvements, and it ended there.[6]

The most important of Mayo's research was done at Continental Mills, makers of woolen fabrics who had introduced a personnel department, bonus schemes, sickness benefits, a savings arrangement, and various recreations for workers. In the spinning department labor turnover was 250 percent, while in other departments the average was 5 to 6 percent. Why? "My first case in the industrial nervous breakdown field. Heaven help us," Mayo wrote to his wife, "my first case in Brisbane was not more important."[7]

At Continental Mills Mayo's approach differed from that he had used at Masland. With strong support from the management he began inquiries, not as a psychopathologist but as a visitor. Although he did not have to persuade employees to seek his advice, he met some minor resistance at first. So one day he brought a lunchbox and settled down to eat and talk with them. The few who mistrusted him very soon saw he was genuinely interested in their way of life.[8]

Mayo found that high turnover was typical of spinning departments in other factories, so he studied closely the work and conditions. Five ten-hour days a week spent at walking among machines, looking for broken threads and then twisting them together, was monotonous. The only variety was machine breakdowns and replacements. Workers complained that their legs were tired, and they showed neurotic disorders symptomatic of the inability to relax fatigued muscles. Alcohol consumption was higher among spinners than other workers, which indicated to Mayo that they were driven to achieve muscular relaxation by the wrong method. He found much evidence of pessimistic reveries. He concluded that the walking and stretching awkwardly across machines induced physical fatigue, and this was exacerbated by the reveries.

Mayo discussed his observations with Madison Taylor, a prominent psychiatrist, who diagnosed debility due to a sharp difference in blood pressure between the upper and lower body. He recommended a modification of a French army practice: soldiers marched in thirty-minute stretches interspersed with ten-minute rests, during which they kept their feet raised. Mayo's suggested variant of alternating work and relaxation was tried not in Continental's spinning department but in another department. Production rose 30 percent; the workers liked it; and the management praised its "splendid results."[9] In May 1923 the results were used to show Ruml how the research was progressing and he recommended to Rockefeller that he fund Mayo for three years. From then on Mayo's livelihood was secure.

Toward the end of September 1923, after working with the Jackson brothers at the Miller Lock Company, Mayo returned to Continental Mills to find that the rest-pause system had been adopted in several other departments. Although results were generally good, he observed that women sorters did not relax in the approved manner. Once they followed his instructions to lie down with their legs properly supported, their vigor and the quality of their work improved. During moments away from their work they would sit and talk with him. Mayo also learned that two months earlier in the spinning department his ideas had been used with good results all around: production increased; employee well-being improved; and turnover fell.

As a psychologist, Mayo was more attentive to irrational ideas and superstitions about work than to the immediate economic gains from regulated relaxation. Tired workers experienced anxiety reveries about their hearts, feet, arms, and knees; many went to quacks for treatment. Among managers also fatigue led to unproductive and wasteful reveries. The chief engineer, a good worker and normally popular, had violent temperamental outbreaks due to reveries about his health and domestic problems. The young and successful general manager reveried about his health to the extent that he could report details of minor illnesses as far back as five years. Even Colonel Brown, the senior partner, feared that trade unions conspired to destroy industry. Workers, especially middle-aged workers at monotous machine tasks dreaded the loss of health, and this was played upon by union organizers.

Mayo learned shortly before Christmas 1923 that some men in the spinning department had discontinued their rest pauses, and it was subsequently found that two head tenders had interfered with the system. During the period of their self-appointed control, employees became tired, pessimistic, and less efficient, and absenteeism rose.[10] Colonel Brown reinstated the rest periods, and cots were placed in the spinning rooms. He was so impressed with the consequent fall in turnover and rise in productivity that he put the whole firm at Mayo's disposal for the intensive study of individuals at work.

However favored a researcher Mayo had become, he soon learned the management of Continental Mills was not entirely motivated by a humane concern for workers. An uncertain market in the summer of 1925 curtailed orders while inventories climbed. Employees were laid off and the work week was cut. In most firms during slack times employees flocked to the dispensary and mentioned reasons that they should be kept on the payroll, but the Continental Mills dispensary was in the personnel department, and people did not want to bring themselves to the attention of officers in that way. Nevertheless, cases of tuberculosis, duodenal ulcer, and gangrene were identified at the dispensary, and referred for diagnosis and treatment.

When he studied the total situation of the worker Mayo found that problems at work often had domestic and curious cultural origins. For example, the American working wife of an Italian employee had refused to bear children for fear of being deserted during pregnancy, a not uncommon practice. The husband became ill tempered, unwell, and developed a hernia; because the symptoms were unusual, he was diagnosed as psychoneurotic. After further inquiry Mayo found the man feared an impoverished old age because, unlike most Italian fathers, he would have no children to support him. Further, Mayo ascertained that generally workers' sex instruction had been poor and that their attitudes toward sex were irrational, with guilt about sex extensive. This ignorance combined with superstitions about death, marriage, birth, and bad luck gave Mayo a fair picture of the human factors affecting work. He was reminded of the fear of Australian railway employees when management had uttered the words, "Taylor system," and effectively froze union members into a long strike in August 1917.

Union members and their education had concerned Mayo in Australia; in Philadelphia he followed this interest further and taught classes for the Philadelphia Labor College from late 1923 to 1925. His ideas were welcomed and accepted, and many of his students talked with him about their personal lives and business affairs. He learned from them how employers had curbed labor organizations in response to an irrational fear of their growth. As far as he could tell unions were not prospering to the extent that management thought, nor were they conspiring as a unit to take control of industry. Unions seemed caught between the general disapproval of managers and the specific irrational demands of communists for a dictatorship of labor. As a rule union members were looking to employers to develop career paths. Many union members had good pay and a home; few had cars. They could not be expected to follow militant communism as their employers suspected.

Rather than consider the expectations of unions, managers had tried to undermine unions wherever they began. For example, Mayo found that Colonel Brown, paid favored employees to join a union and to determine which employees attended meetings. One such employee, a steady worker, was dismissed, to the detriment of the spinning department. In Mayo's view such a policy, based on irrational fear rather than evidence, would go far toward duplicating the class warfare that long had dominated British and Australian industrial relations. Eventually the unions would become powerful in industry, and a political force that distorted the purpose of the economy. Mayo recommended intelligent handling of the situation rather than attempts at control by employers. The use of tests for intelligence, trade skill, or vocational interest had also exacerbated labor relations, as had the introduction of Taylorism for systematically defining tasks. Mayo believed that scientific study of individuals and of human relationships at work was required first; then the knowledge thereby acquired could be applied to manage work and make it both humane and efficient. Industrial leaders should take note of Graham Wallas's *The Great Society* or Brooks Adams's *Theory of Social Revolutions,* listen to what union members had to say, and heed advice from employment managers and social scientists.[11]

During the next fifteen months Mayo extended his industrial studies in Philadelphia in line with orientation of "total situation enquiry of a psychopathologist in a mental clinic."[12] His aim was becoming clearer. He did not intend to eliminate mentally distressed or psychopathological individuals from the workplace, as did most psychologists who limited themselves to techniques of selection and vocational guidance. Instead, Mayo intended to discover how far past experience, home life, and work conditions gave rise to obsessional reveries, which, in turn, eventuated in turnover, radical views of society, inefficiency, and emotional malady. His first problems had been those of management. Now he wanted to study workers, but there he was at a disadvantage. He was a stranger, had no office or rooms from which to work, no assistants, and, sometimes, his attempts to study some workers interfered with the productive work of others.

At the Miller Lock Company Mayo had seen how many problems could arise in the study of workers. The company employed a registered nurse and a doctor, but the doctor gave little attention to nonmedical aspects of the employees' lives. His special interest in heart conditions led to undue emphasis on heart ailments. Another firm's doctor was making a research career for himself in industrial medicine, but he did not apply his results to the factory workers at hand. Also, Mayo found that dispensary records were usually kept in the files of the personnel department and were thereby open to other office employees. Further, he considered the mental capacities of industrial nurses far too low. Mayo believed there should be a well-qualified, intelligent nurse to listen reflectively to employees appearing at the factory dispensary.

Mayo needed to establish his own employment conditions. At the Miller Lock Company he had met a registered nurse whose skills were not being used fully, so he tried to have her transferred to a similar post at the Continental Mills. He needed, too, the regular services of a medical practitioner because psychoneurotics required a medical examination before undergoing psychopathological inquiry. And Mayo needed rooms, for some of the people he was meeting wanted advice on private problems. His Labor College classes were held in the Machinist's Temple, and this was too noisy. In 1924 he received funds to rent rooms in the Otis Building in Philadelphia, to travel, and to hire secretarial and research assistants.

Mayo's first assistant was Mrs. L.H. Gilbert, and in the fall of 1924 she was succeeded by Emily Paysen Osborne, a registered nurse who would assist him until June 1937.[13] Miss Osborne joined the dispensary at Continental Mills and there recorded information about the personal attitudes, home life, and adaptation to work of the workers who came for treatment. Within eight months her confidential files contained one hundred cases. The information was to be used to identify the early symptoms of fatigue in specific departments, and to anticipate and help prevent widespread fatigue. Mayo did not publish this feature of his work because he believed that in its undeveloped form his work could be abused, and information might be misused and arouse employee hostility.

Mayo's ideas and practices attracted the interest of more and more industrialists in Philadelphia, and he and his staff were sometimes asked to study aspects of discipline. At the Chester plant of the Aberfoyle Textile Company a curious problem was drawn to their attention. The firm provided employees with amenities—country club, chiropodist, dentist, medical help, social welfare services—and was particularly proud of its democratic administration. Yet, the personal officer, Mrs. Stearns, was overworked, and her attempts to deal with personnel problems came to nothing. The democratization of work, which was of great interest to Mayo, was the origin of her difficulties. She was on a workers' committee whose task was to recommend changes in factory methods and to provide some control of the country club. There was no corresponding management committee so the committee had to make recommendations and give reasons directly to the executives involved, irrespective of their position in the chain of command. This unworkable devolution of authority created much busy work for Mrs. Stearns and showed her that the firm was not a democratic organization at all but a multiplicity of minor autocracies. Its amenities served to mask a conservative attitude to real changes in work methods, and its resistance to changes was maintained by the usual culture of the plant. Unknown to Mrs. Stearns, employees and executives tended to have long-standing intimate acquaintance with one another; whatever she recommended to raise efficiency would subsequently be blocked, presumably by actions occasioned by the friendships. Further, the country club was being used, especially by the many young women in the firm, for irregular liaisons, which, Mayo thought, was partly to blame for the unusually high incidence of psychiatric problems at the plant.

Inside the plant Mayo made interesting observations of the social control employees exercised over psychological problems of fatigue. In the cone-winding department the number of attendants was raised from two to three in the alleys between the rows of machines. Production rose but, because the piece-rate payment system was unchanged, the employees earned a little less. No one objected because the reduction in earnings was slight, the job market was tight, and a third attendant eased the task. Also, because mercerized thread did not break often during winding and thus close attention was not necessary, many young women habitually broke the monotony by congregating in the lavatory, where they scrawled obscenities on the walls, gossiped, and read magazines.

The quilling department saw similar practices. There each person attended one foot-operated machine that simultaneously wound 378 threads onto bobbins. When the quality of the yarn fell, breaks were so frequent that workers despaired, and to win in their contest with the machines would develop foot trouble, take unauthorized rests by lying prone on the foot board, of leave for another factory.

Mayo concluded that when appropriate rest pauses are not allowed for, workers take breaks on their own that frequently create waste and administrative chaos. And when he found that in the past efficiency had been highest when employees worked forty-eight instead of fifty-four hours a week, he began to experiment with the introducton of systematic rest pauses in one of the firm's similar plants. Mayo's assistant Rexford B. Hersey published the research.[14]

Among Mayo's early work in Philadelphia only the study at Continental Mills showed the value of systematic rest pauses for productivity and morale. And it was the willfulness of the two head machine tenders rather than Mayo's systematic control and observation of the study that had led ultimately to such dramatic results. Mayo's work for Masland, the Textile Employers, Curtis, and the Jackson brothers came to nothing, and Hersey wrote the Aberfoyle study. The early industrial work illustrates Mayo's interest in workers' behavior and their life away from work rather than in managers' technical problems. Nevertheless by the summer of 1925 he had established such a high reputation in industrial psychology that he was brought to the attention of the dean of the newly organized School of Business Administration at Harvard University. Mayo's status had been helped along by well-connected friends and acquaintances in a network that spanned industry, education, finance, and psychiatry.

Notes

1. Minutes, Senate, University of Queensland, 9 March 1923; Elton to Dorothea, 2, 7, 13 February 1923.
2. Elton Mayo, "The Method of Research to Be Adopted," n.d., MM 1.099.
3. Mayo to Willits, 14 May 1923, 2 RF; "Meeting of Business Problems Group," 24 February 1925, MM 2.060; Elton Mayo, "The Application of Psychopathology to Industry," Van Ordsell report, MM 4.011; Elton to Dorothea, 6, 8-12, 19 February 1923.
4. Elton to Dorothea, 23, 26, 28 March 1923.
5. MM 4.008.
6. Mayo to Willits, 28 December 1923, RF.
7. Elton to Dorothea, 12 April 1923.
8. Hockenberry to Trahair, 20 March 1975.
9. Elton to Dorothea, 28 May, 6, 7, 16 June 1923.
10. MM 4.034; Elton Mayo, "Revery and Industrial Fatigue," *Journal of Personnel Research* 3 (1924):273-81.
11. MM 4.008.
12. Richard C. S. Trahair, "Elton Mayo and the Early Political Psychology of Harold D. Lasswell," *Political Psychology* 3 (1981-82):170-88.
13. Mayo to Jurgman, 11 April 1944, MM 1.068; Balash to Trahair, 20 October 1975.
14. Rexford B. Hersey, "Rests Authorised and Unauthorised," *Journal of Personnel Research* 4 (1924):39-45.

11

Philadelphia to Harvard

By May 1923, shortly before his family joined him, Mayo had an established reputation in Philadelphia's medical, academic, and business community. He gave many addresses between 1923 and 1925 on the psychology of thinking, the role of physiology in mental integration, psychology and psychiatry applied to work, and the measurement of fatigue at work, many of which were published, as were popular articles on industrial relations and marriage. He saw patients whom doctors referred to him, and met Pierre Janet, whose ideas he would use for many years. Shortly before going to Harvard, he attended the first of the Dartmouth conferences on the social sciences.

Mayo's industrial work developed with help from influential people who respected his ideas and ability and sympathized with his feelings and clinical orientation. Three early contacts were particularly helpful. H.H. Donaldson, medical specialist at Wistar Institute and president of the Lenape Club at the University of Pennsylvania, and his wife often introduced Mayo to respected medical men and associates of senior administrators in prestigious universities.

Early in February 1923 Mayo began a close friendship with Frances Colbourne, an ascetic, well-dressed, and good-looking single Englishwoman forty years of age. She had been a governess, and during her twelve years in the United States had become a professional social worker. At first uncertain, she soon warmed to Mayo's English manner. He wrote to Dorothea that there was "something or other in her mental hinterland I can't describe." During their four-month friendship, she listened with genuine attention to his concern for his family's future welfare, his financial problems, hopes, and plans. She introduced him to other social workers and to sociology staff and students at Bryn Mawr, typed his papers, accompanied him to movies and concerts, and advised him on life in the United States as his family would experience it.[1]

Outside the university Mayo's most valuable early medical contact was S. DeWit Ludlum, who was a little older than Mayo, ran a private hospital, held a position in the Neuropsychiatric Clinic of Philadelphia General Hospital, and was one of the city's leading psychiatrists. He liked Mayo's ideas on the application of psychology to industry, offered Mayo private patients, and suggested that Mayo set himself up as a psychological consultant. He also arranged for Mayo to spend Tuesday afternoons at the hospital, insisted that he attend the clinic's neurology and psychiatry meetings, and put him up for membership in the University Club.[2]

Mayo did not become a consultant, but he did accept Ludlum's other suggestions and offers. Such sudden good fortune, especially in the medical field, took its inevitable psychological toll.

> If only this works out as it seems likely to—I'm so stupid, a foolish anxiety reverie makes me afraid to trust good fortune. I must eliminate it. It is only a revery, because when I'm in action I never question my capacity for fortune; it is only when I sit back "to think"—I've given much time to the development of a theory of revery since I got here, as you know. And I'm really trying to organize my own reveries, i.e. I'm trying to cut out the disaster "reveries" as useless. I'm no longer a Freudian, if I ever was one. We have to get beyond Freud. . . . Ludlum liked my methods of describing the psychopathologist's work and method—and said so—very nice of him. . . . It's very important to get the backing of the medical profession.[3]

Mayo's enduring doubts about his relation with medical men were banished one day when Ludlum was absent from the hospital. The other doctors walked the wards with him and talked over their cases, and the director of the clinic, Franklin Ebough, offered him as many cases as he could take. His joy at being accepted by them was doubled when he learned that they had been trained at, or were closely associated with, institutions that were highly respected by Brisbane doctors. Within a few weeks Mayo had a niche in Philadelphia that had been denied him in Australia. There were dinners with the "bloods of Philadelphia" and contacts with professional writers, architects, sociologists, anthropologists, industrial psychologists, rich businessmen, and politicians. By the time Ruml and his associate visited the University of Pennsylvania in May 1923 to see how Mayo's research had progressed, he was so well established that they recommended that Rockefeller give him funds for three more years.

Mayo's industrial work also benefited from the opportunities he was given to address informal groups and professional associations whose interest lay in applied psychology. Mayo read to the Franklin Institute a paper of a colleague on the relation between modern physics and psychology, and was able to handle discussion afterward, although much of the paper had been difficult to follow. He spoke, too, at Princeton, and at a conference on mental hygiene in Wilkes-Barre.[4] Mayo talked to a women's club, and attended a meeting on prison reform held by the American Academy of Political and Social Sciences.[5] A week after he had spoken to his first group of workers at Maslin's factory, he turned the ideas into an address that much impressed several audiences.[6] He had his thoughts mimeographed as "The Application of Psychopathology to Industry" for a university course for works managers.[7] He put the ideas to more of Willits's businessmen, among whom were the Pharisees, a group of elderly and distinguished Jews who held him for an hour's discussion. Also, Mayo spoke on psychology to students and professors at Byrn Mawr.[8]

One of Mayo's most important audiences was Philadelphia's Psychiatric Society; his topic, "Total Situation in Health and Psychoneurosis."[9] Although his ideas on mental life were unchanged, he introduced an element to his reasoning about linking psychopathology with an understanding of the individual's adjustment to the social and physical environment: physiology. For many years it was essential in arguments to gain support for his industrial work and was the means by which his approach won general respect in medical circles. Ludlum, at whose invitation Mayo had appeared, had expected a pro-Freudian address and was cheered that two elderly anti-Freudians congratulated Mayo.

The address assumes that psychological theories are not useful unless they are related to physiological evidence. Psychology concerns the person's relation with the environment, and physiology concerns the internal balance of the organism. Because the approaches supplement each other, their joint study is mandatory.

With regard to the internal balance of the organism, Mayo quoted studies by Sherrington and Head showing that the psychological state of consciousness is a physiologically integrated response of the organism to a stimulus. With regard to the relation of the organism to the environment, behaviorists Watson and Holt show that responses to stimuli are themselves an integration of reflexes functioning in relation to the stimulus situation. The integration of the response is, on its inner or subjective side, what is known as understanding of the surroundings. Accordingly, if functional disorders are seen as failures to respond adequately to one's early environment, the cases of many noted psychopathologists can be partly explained, e.g., cases where physiological changes are induced through suggestion. Among normal people in the civilization the inherited plasticity of the nervous system reaches a compromise with the particulars of specialized education. Thus, one is not born sane; sanity is a physiological and psychological balance that is achieved or missed by the individual in growth to adulthood.

Confusions in psychological research and theory are due to the lack of integration between competing claims of academic psychology, psychopathology, and behavioristic psychology. Physiology can help the integration because it depicts the individual's total situation rather than settling on one of the primary urges. But people find this integration difficult because it varies at each level of consciousness—concentration, revery, hypnoidal state, and sleep—e.g., the shell-shocked soldier who, afraid of the dark, sleeps when lights are on and wakes immediately when they are switched off. So even at low levels of awareness we are consciously directed to the total situation and then to a particular stimulus. Sherrington's ideas on nervous facilitation and inhibition correspond with the assertion that consciousness is an achieved orientation to the world rather than a thought process, as the stream of consciousness theorists imply.

In psychology, Mayo continued, the mind comprises everyday thought embedded in a field of consciousness or mental hinterland. The mind becomes unique when subject to concentration, attentive thought, discrimination, and habits over a lifetime. Failure to learn and overcome childish impulses means the individual has not achieved the necessary integration of levels of consciousness. This parallels Sherrington's idea on normal growth and physiological integration of the nervous system. Psychiatrists show that education comes by way of revery as much as concentration. Functional disorders are due to misuse of revery, and psychoanalysis is a way to discover unacknowledged and repressed reveries. Because of its close relation to physiology, the psychology of the total situation is the preferred approach in psychopathology.[10]

In the summer of 1924 Mayo was invited to Woods Hole to see the biological research of Dr. E.G. Conklen of Princeton, and to address Conklen's Sunday forum on "Primitive Thinking in Modern Society."[11] The address included material for his paper "The Persistence of Primitive Ideas in Industry," which, with Dr. E.A. Bott (University of Toronto) and Charles S. Myers (National Institute of Industrial Psychology, Britain), he would give at a conference of the Toronto Chamber of Commerce. The paper argues that because people respond adequately but differently to the same situation, only psychological ideas can account for variation in meanings people attach to the situation. Mayo distinguished academic from medical psychology, outlined the ideas of Janet, Jung, Freud, Sidis, and Morton Prince, and concluded that revery, or dispersed thinking, plays as important a part in determining behavior as does concentration. The first includes primitive ideas; the second, logical ideas. A sound mental life is achieved by a balanced integration of the two forms of thought and their respective contents. Mayo illustrated the primitive ideas of revery with case material from Freud, personal friends, and his daughter Toni and her imaginary playmates Ernest and Fred. He argued that revery of an experience rather than the experience itself provides the meaning of situations for an individual.

The ideas were not new, but the illustrations show him broadening his ideas to include anthropological as well as psychological research. He referred to the thinking style of savages studied by Pitt-Rivers and Malinowski, and his own observations in West Africa, and compared primitives' ideas with the superstitions of apparently civilized Philadelphians, the ideologies of communist agitators, children's nursery and fairy stories, and ancient Egyptian religious and magical ceremonies.

In September 1924 he was invited by L. L. Thurstone to discuss psychological methods of approach to political problems at the second annual meeting of the Political Science Association. There he renewed his acquaintance with Charles E. Merriam, and attracted his interest with a combination of anthropological, physiological, and psychological work that could be applied to politics.[12]

At Woods Hole Mayo had been introduced to Dr. G.H.A. Clowes, administrator of the research department of Eli Lilley and Company, a pharmaceutical manufacturer in Indianapolis. Clowes agreed that the methods of anthropology and psychopathology could be applied to industry, so he invited Mayo to look over the research department. Mayo found the same difficulties he had found in Chester and Germantown: the productive capacity of the worker was related directly to the amount of fatigue caused by the work and the type of revery it provoked.[13]

Central to Mayo's industrial research was the treating of cases that appeared in the factory. At the Neuropsychiatric Clinic of the Philadelphia General Hospital the director and chief resident psychopathologist, Franklin Ebough, wanted Mayo to take cases and join the staff in case discussion; in return for Mayo's assistance, Ebough agreed to handle pronounced problems of mental ill health referred by Mayo from industrial settings, and to arrange for help from social workers and welfare agencies.[14]

Mayo was also encouraged to take a few nonmedical cases for a fee. At Ludlum's private hospital, Gladwyne Colony, Mayo's first case was a melancholic in his sixties whom no one had been able to help. Mayo quickly established that an anxiety neurosis was making a sin of a sexual encounter with a spinster more than forty years ago. At Ebough's clinic Mayo helped a woman and two epileptics, and Ruml sent Mayo a twenty-year-old man from New York for counseling.[15]

Also, Mayo arranged for scholars to visit and exchange ideas on theory and problems in clinical work. Leonard Outhwaite, a former editor of *Journal of Personnel Research,* brought ideas from his practical knowledge of industry and anthropology. Josephine Gleeson (Vassar) and L.L. Thurstone (Chicago) learned about Mayo's techniques in clinical psychopathology at Ludlum's hospital. Mrs. Taber welcomed the visitors to the clinic at Philadelphia General Hospital.

At that time Mayo was beginning to clarify his ideas on clinical psychology by applying what he learned from clinical cases to current theories. He rejected as superficial and invalid the Bleuler-Jung labeling of hysteria as a form of extraversion, and dementia praecox as introversion. In hysteria, Mayo thought, the symptoms are determined by mental preoccupations, and the voluntary and autonomic nervous systems are so abnormally related that organic needs and physiological processes are not integrated. Mayo recommended the study of obsessional neurotics because, unlike hysterics and dements, they were better integrated mentally and physiologically, and could be more easily treated. He believed that the comparative study of obsessionals, hysterics, and dements would show the nature of the integration of their voluntary and autonomic nervous systems, their different patterns of mental preoccupations, and the various conditions under which cooperation of the patient could be achieved in psychotherapy.

Mayo wrote of his treatment of an hysteric, a twenty-eight-year-old factory worker, that the hypnotized man was put before a fluorescent screen: "His stomach was much relaxed, but when I began to talk to him about a fear he had of malignant disease in his wife his stomach went into a violent spasm. Judged by his outward appearance, he was apparently undisturbed and continued in the somnambolic conditions. I then explained away his fears and reassured him and his stomach returned to relaxation."[16]

In the factory Mayo found that separating the hysteric from the healthy person was a problem. Knowing the hysteric's voluntary and autonomic nervous systems were not well integrated, Mayo and Miss Osborne developed a technique that seemed effective: they watched the pupillary accommodation in the eyes of the worker; if it was out of relation with the light stimulus—and organic disorder was not indicated—there was the possibility of hysteria. In one case Mayo noticed that the small pupils in the eyes of a working girl dilated immensely when she went outside into bright light. In his experience such symptoms were not found in obsessional adults.

Mayo wanted to probe the origins of hysteria by studying how traces of the disorder in childhood persist into adulthood. He believed that principles governing the physiology of growth and the psychology of small adjustments interacted and produced a more or less functionally integrated organism. Here, he thought, was the fundamental problem of psychiatry. Physiologically the problem began once the myelinization of the nervous system was complete, and psychologically it began when surroundings were more or less suitable for the infant to integrate the autonomic and voluntary nervous systems. These ideas were not carried forward in Philadelphia but were essential to his early teaching at Harvard.

When Mayo began industrial research he was not certain that his ideas and skills would provide enough money to support the family, so he wrote for an income as well as to establish his professional position. His early professional writing included "Irrationality and Revery,"[17] the sequel to "The Irrational Factor in Society." The second article integrates the material from his report to Willits, addresses businessmen and psychiatrists, and uses illustrations from Australia and the United States. Both articles introduce his empirical research of later years. He also published "Superstitions," which asserts that many curious beliefs found in Africa, Australia, New Guinea, and Samoa may be found in Philadelpha, e.g., if a bird flies into and out of a house, a death in the family is imminent; if a visitor enters a house by one door and leaves by another, disaster will befall its occupants;

if a woman enters a coal mine, tragedy will ensue. Even educated individuals are prey to superstitions: a clergyman carries a potato in his pocket to ward off rheumatism; a basketball team refuses to launder its jerseys lest their luck be washed away. A civilized person stifles a yawn in the interests of good manners; a New Guinea male does so to stop his soul from leaving his body.[18]

The articles were summarized in "The Irrational Factor in Human Behaviour—The 'Night-Mind' in Industry."[19] The night-mind corresponds to the mental hinterland, and its role is illustrated with many examples, particularly from Mayo's first investigation in the spinning department of Continental Mills. The article was in a special issue, "Psychology in Business," of the journal of the American Academy of Political and Social Science, of which Willits was the associate editor. The other countributors were thirty of the leading American applied psychologists, among them, James McKeen Cattell, Knight Dunlap, Robert Yerkes, Arthur Kornhauser, Walter Bingham, L.L. Thurstone, Charles Yoakum, and Morris Viteles. So by the middle of June 1923, Mayo had become well-established in industrial psychology.[20]

Mayo decided to broaden his audience to include the readers of popular magazines. He engaged a literary agent, Mathilde Weil, under whose guidance he worked on five articles that would be republished as *The Secret Gardens of Childhood:* "The Invisible Playmates"; "The Perilous Adventure"; "Enchanted Forest"; "The Garden of Fear"; and "The Difficult Problem of Education."[21] The series was intended to help parents understand the context in which their children developed, and the material and drawn from anthropology and normal psychology. Mayo made extensive notes and outlines, but no articles were finished, nor was a book published. The ideas were an amalgam of observations on his daughter Patricia when she was recovering from her illness, the children of distressed parents whom he had helped in Adelaide and Brisbane, illustrations from his psychology lectures at the University of Queensland, and ideas appearing in his American publications particularly the "night-mind" summary of his work. Another article he planned was "The American Girl and Marriage," about problems of true romance for young women who worked in Philadelphia's textile industry.

The effort to establish himself was tiring and often during his absence from his family Mayo would reflect upon the appropriateness and value of his activities. Money worries overwhelmed him, and his inability to sleep made for pessimistic reveries about his own worth, especially in gaining acceptance of his factory work research and thus his ability to support his family. The circle of hard work, fatigue, pessimism, and either a conviction of his own sin or hatred of the people in Brisbane who had not wanted to recognize his work, was periodically broken when Frances Colbourne heard him out, or Ludlum arranged for some consulting for him, or Willits praised what he was doing, or a stranger remarked on his English characteristics.

Much of his anxiety was allayed by the anticipation of his family's arrival. He wrote to Dorothea each day, told her his money worries, outlined his scheme for her to land in Vancouver, cross Canada by train, and enter the United States from Toronto. To make them welcome, he rented a cottage at Cape May for the summer. Mayo went to meet them in Toronto, only to find nothing he could do would bend the official rule controlling entry to the country. For a month he went to see them there on weekends, then sought help from powerful political friends. He and the family were joined toward the end of June in 1923, after almost twelve months of separation. In Philadelphia they rented a furnished house, and about two years later, in August 1925, they moved to the Colonial Inn, Bryn Mawr, because Dorothea, who had become obsessive about tidiness and cleanliness, found the task of maintaining a house beyond her. The girls went to the Baldwin School.[22]

By the middle of 1925, when he was assured of a career in industrial psychology, Mayo began to integrate his ideas on the value of several disciplines for the study of work, particularly fatigue at work. His problem was to find a reliable and valid measure of fatigue that was independent of the individual's statement of feeling, and of readily observable behavior. Two colleagues helped him, Ludlum and Ellice McDonald.

In May 1925 Ludlum and McDonald published "The Mechanisms of Disease," an article to which Mayo would often refer in addresses, writings, and research reports and proposals.[23] The authors defined disease as a deviation from the proper balance between the vagus and the sympathetic parts of the vegetative nervous system that control the unconscious processes of the body, e.g., lungs, heart, pupils, intestines. The vagus inhibited heart action, and stimulated action of the intestines and pupils. The sympathetic stimulated the heart, and inhibited action of intestinal muscles. The authors asserted that mental disorders were correlated with the degree of integration of the two parts of the vegetative nervous system. Indicators of mental disorder that unconsciously affected the system were unusual dilation of the pupils, involuntary spasms in the stomach, or extremes of blood pressure.

Mayo used all three indicators in his case work, but became particularly interested in blood pressure. He needed a measure of how people differed in their response to similar work, how different work affected one individual, and how one individual's reaction to work varied as the workday progressed. Measurement of blood pressure provided an index of heart action, i.e., a physiological process related to work effort over which one has no conscious control.

To measure blood pressure two readings are taken: when the heart is forcing blood into the arteries, the systolic pressure, and when the heart is briefly inactive, the diastolic pressure. Normally they are about 118 and 78, respectively, and the difference, 40, is the pulse pressure. As a person begins to work, both readings rise; when the person is adjusted to work, they fall. Variations in rise and fall are determined by health. If the person is sick, unfit, or anxious, the systolic reading remains high, the diastolic pressure begins to fall, the tone of the arterial system decreases, and so does capacity for work. Increasing pulse pressure indicates this. Mayo knew that what people felt or said about their work was not always a good estimate of how well they were suited to it. So blood pressure was a way to find out how true fatigue could be measured, in the hope that, later, some methods of minimizing fatigue could be developed.[24]

Mayo also thought blood pressure readings would be useful in studying mental disorder. He believed Ludlum and McDonald had found that obsessive individuals could be identified by the failure of their blood pressure to rise when they got up from lying down.[25] And he found the same phenomenon among workers toward the day's end. This showed that during a day's work normal individuals could become like obsessives, and that this sometimes occurred even when no other symptoms of fatigue were present. From Pierre Janet's work, Mayo saw that as an individual became less able to maintain the organic tension needed for work he began to be obsessive, i.e., he perceived inaccurately events and conditions in the immediate work environment, he oscillated in his capacity to decide, hallucinated, and confused his experience of inner and outer reality. In summary, as working conditions diminished the normal individual's capacity for organic tension, measurable in terms of blood pressure readings, obsessive reveries could emerge. The appropriate treatment for fatigue among normal people is rest and proper relaxation, but in the genuine obsessive the symptoms would persist unless psychopathological treatment was given.

In integrating the work of Ludlum and McDonald with that of Janet, Mayo had a physiological and psychological theory of fatigue as well as a precise measure of bodily change to correlate with feelings, thoughts, and behavior about work. A further stimulus to Mayo's industrial work came when he learned that Janet would visit the United States.

In 1925 the French government delegated Janet to be an exchange professor to Mexico.[26] Early in August Mayo invited him to address doctors and psychologists in Philadelphia on depression and happiness. Although Janet had visited the United States three times before, his ideas had not been given the same publicity as had been given to those of the psychoanalysts. Mayo enthused over Janet's visit, and Janet agreed to allow him to check the translation, by one of Morton Prince's students, of *Les Nevroses*. When Janet arrived, credit for attracting such a notable was given not to Mayo but to the famous clinic at Philadelphia General Hospital where Ludlum worked. At the clinic Janet discussed cases, traced developments in psychiatry over the last twenty years, and raised topics essential to

Mayo's work by declaring that "many men who can make bargains and carry on mercantile activities, nevertheless lack the experimental mind and can neither reflect nor learn by experience."[27]

Before Janet's visit Mayo was invited to the first of six conferences that helped stage the development of the social sciences in the United States. Early in 1924 Beardsley Ruml had suggested an informal meeting of social scientists to discuss the directions that research might take. Mayo replied with a paper, "A New Way of Statecraft," that included his critique of modern democracy, a recommendation to study Machiavelli's *Prince,* and warm support for "an informal collection of appropriate men at some seashore or country place for purposes of conversation (no papers). . . . [It] needs a good clear-headed student of social happenings to hold the thing together . . . [and] beware of sentimentalists, socialists, reactionaries or anyone who knows the solution of anything." The discussions should lead to research, and the research should be used to train "diplomatists—international and industrial."[28] A year later the Laura Spelman Rockefeller Memorial Foundation planned for August the first of the gatherings variously called the "Dartmouth," "Hanover," or "Summer" conferences, to explore the social sciences for views that would advance both science and the common welfare. Mayo was one of the first invited to contribute by the organizer, L.L. Thurstone, who thought him to be an "excellent catalytic agent," even though he never got to the point of stating details of a research project.[29] Mayo was pleased to accept and, after discussion with Ruml, agreed to take up the general topic of psychology and social science.[30] Among the contributors were Angell, Wissler, and Dodge from Yale; Bott from Toronto; McFie Campbell, Gay, and Wells from Harvard; Walter Bingham from the Personnel Research Foundation; the New York psychiatrist G.V. Hamilton; Wolfgang Kohler from Clark; Charles E. Merriam and C.J. Herrick from Chicago; and G.M. Stratton and Robert S. Woodworth from the National Research Council.

During discussions Mayo contributed to a broad range of topics and demonstrated his skill as an intellectual catalyst and imaginative integrator of diverse fields of expertise. His colleagues clapped appreciatively when he outlined his ideas. He introduced the subject of orgasms among French prostitutes (Havelock Ellis), and the importance of orgasms for marital stability. Later he argued that psychopathological behavior, sexual or otherwise, was related to the adequacy of orgasm, and the conditions affecting both were medical, domestic, industrial, political, and social. Through his long discussions the general thesis centers on conditions promoting integration of the individual, i.e., the "total situation" viewpoint. He advocated scientific research, reflection, and discussion among scientists with clinical and experimental expertise in chemistry, biology, physiology, psychology, psychiatry, medicine, and anthropology. He used ideas from recent work in all the fields to identify critical differences between hysterics and obsessionals.

Mayo's address "Psychology and Social Science" was toward the end of the conference. He brought together his colleague's contributions to the conference, and recommended collaboration among his fellows for the general application of psychology to social problems from his "total situation" viewpoint. He used his characteristic technique of integrating opposites, turning common conceptions on their heads, and inviting fresh alternatives in frequent and sometimes outrageous combinations of ideas. His opening statement:

> To the many things that have been said this week of scientific investigation I have only one to add—not by way of criticism but as an insignificant addition. That is that science is a lunatic adventure—lunatic because the adventurer voluntarily leaves the paths of rest, commodity and reputation in order to voyage the unchartered seas of his own dark ignorance. Such a voyage inevitably involves privation in respect of comfortable thinking; the wandering knight is made to feel, socially, the consequences of his folly. So counsel with his fellows is of high benefit; it seems to extend and confirm the adventure. The greatest danger is always that paths of ease may lure the wanderer from his quest. The discovery of associates as in the Pilgrim's Progress cannot but intensify the depth and dream of his desire.[31]

Mayo closed with a strong recommendation that anthropologists could contribute to social sciences. He argued it was not the case, as Merriam had said, that anthropologists were wanting to be shown by psychologists the new and proper directions for research but, rather, that anthropologists were replacing psychologists, particularly the faculty psychologists with the "total situation" approach. Mayo's views were stong enough to ensure that his friend Bronislaw Malinowski was invited to the next Hanover conference.[32] Mayo enjoyed the conference, its content he found rewarding and entertaining, and its membership placed him with eminent men, many of whom he had known only by name.[33]

Mayo's reputation as an expert on the psychodynamics of family life was spreading. In October 1925 he was a speaker at a Child Study Association Conference in Philadelphia with David S. Muzzey of Columbia University, Miriam Van Waters, and C.W. Kimmins from Britain. Mayo spoke on the meaning of freedom for the child, advocating that parents furnish the unknown background to their children's lives with reassurance and a feeling of safety, thus ridding the children of fear and providing them with the ability to order their own method of managing reality.[34]

Success in public presentations and discussions was accompanied by success in writing. In the second half of 1923, when Ruml and associates decided that they would continue to fund Mayo's research, he published three papers.[35] In 1924 he published two professional papers, two popular articles, and an address, "Mental Hygiene in Industry," to Philadelphia's College of Physicians, which received laudatory comment from the discussant, Dr. Charles W. Burr.[36] The first research paper reports part of his address on research at Continental Mills and was delivered at the psychology section of the Toronto meeting of the British Association for the Advancement of Science. The second research paper emphasizes the psychology of the total situation and was originally presented to the Taylor Society in New York.[37] One popular article, "Civilization—The Perilous Adventure," repeats what he had said and written on similarities in the mental lives of savages, children, neurotic adults, and those who would destroy society because of the distressingly inhuman conditions of their work. The other article, "Civilized Unreason," repeats ideas in his 1919 book, *Democracy and Freedom,* i.e., it argues for a science of society, criticizes inept politicians, and raises the importance of parents and teachers in promoting normal development and controlling infantile reveries. It was reprinted in the second edition of K.A. Robinson's *Essays Towards Truth,* along with contributions from philosophers such as Bertrand Russell.[38]

In 1925 Mayo published two more popular articles and a disarming open letter to a critic, and saw his Toronto paper published in Britain.[39] The first popular article, "The Great Stupidity," includes ideas on industrial conflict and the need for research, and one of its points was sharply criticized by Robert W. Bruere, associate editor of *The Survey.*[40] First Bruere praised Mayo:

> No one has penetrated closer to the center of the industrial conflict than Mr. Mayo, no one has more luminously defined its character. The psychological technique of which he is master is as indispensable to the development of human relations in industry as the earlier technique of Frederick W. Taylor has proved to be in the development of the science and art of administration and management. . . . Mr. Mayo's work has been widely recognized as having much of the pioneering quality of Taylor's.

But Bruere could not agree with Mayo's conclusion that the happy future of American industry "would seem to depend upon the intelligence of employers and employers' associations . . . [in] anticipating the unionization of industry, by making it unnecessary." Bruere believed that the conclusion urged one party in industry to do away with its self-governing opposition, and that doing so would fuel, not extinguish, "the fires of obsessional irrationality." Here was the first critic to accuse Mayo of a bias against unions.

In reply Mayo admitted that his article could be misunderstood, agreed with Bruere's sentiments, and offered not a general but a specific solution to industrial conflict, i.e., scientific research of problems in industrial relations. The management "open shop" policy against compulsory unionization would only raise industrial conflict and support the historic development and purpose of unions. Mayo did not intend, as Bruere thought, that every right be conceded to employer organizations and that unions be ruled out; but, because the United States had not endured a long and bitter class struggle between labor and capital, it could "intelligently anticipate that dichotomy between employer and employed which vexed and vexes Europe" and encourage unionism to grow not from a base "of instability and uncertainty" but to a "continuing means of stability and security." This task, as Mayo would repeat often, may be carried out if executives improve their understanding of themselves and workers, and acquire the skills needed to administer cooperative rather than competitive relations in industry.

A fourth popular article earned Mayo a wider readership. "Should marriage be monotonous? Of course it should," he wrote in the September issue of *Harper's*.[41] In a breezy style he turned conventions about marriage upside down. He attacked rather than idealized romance, illustrated his points with psychoneurotic cases, and concluded that among young people unhappiness in marriage was due to their parents' repudiation of monotony. Also, marital unhappiness is a product of urbanization; women are isolated and lonely at home, domestic duties become drudgery, and they and their men lead distressing functionless lives that lack a sense of community. Finally, among young people an overemphasis on sex combined with its continous suppression confuses the proper relation between love and erotic experiences in marriage; and neither sexual promiscuity nor severe restraints on sex is a panacea. Mayo cited many women who were dissatisfied in love and marriage, blaming poor sex education at home and in the schools, and the obsessional reveries on sex in modern magazines and movies. By monotony in marriage Mayo meant the reliability, trust, sympathy, and understanding that he thought were essential for the great adventure of marriage.

The article drew many letters of praise. Distressed women sought Mayo's help, and he referred them to G.V. Hamilton, the psychiatrist whom he had met at the Dartmouth conference.[42] Congratulations came from Joseph Willits, who promised to save a copy for his wife, and high praise came from a doctor to whom Mayo had referred an anxious patient, and also from the editor of *Social Health*.[43] A nurse wrote recommending the article to all young people; another reader added more illustrative cases; an anxious woman asked Mayo whether or not her having masturbated as a girl would wreck her marriage; and another woman wanted to have the article enlarged for publication as a book.[44] The article was reprinted in the December issue of the *American Journal of Social Hygiene*. Those who liked the article said it was timely, interesting, much needed, of tonic quality, cleverly written, graceful, first-rate thinking, sane, sure, and authoritative. But others, like Pierre Janet's cousin, were merely "amused" and had "reservations".[45]

Except for a brief essay on the value of psychiatry for the study of human factors at work,[46] the "marriage" article was Mayo's last publication before he was called to the Graduate School of Business Administration at Harvard University.

Notes

1. Elton to Dorothea 2, 5, 11, 23 February, 3, 27-30 March, 4, 8, 14, 20, 23 April, 13 May 1923.
2. Elton to Dorothea, 23, 26, 28 February, 6 March 1923.
3. Elton to Dorothea, 26 February 1923.
4. Mayo to Ruml, 25 January 1923, RF.
5. Elton to Dorothea, 23 February 1923.
6. Elton to Dorothea, 1 March 1923.
7. Mayo to Willits, 14 May 1923, RF.
8. Elton to Dorothea, 10, 23 March 1923.
9. Elton to Dorothea, 8, 11 May 1923.
10. Elton Mayo, "Total Situation in Health and Psychoneurosis," May 1923, MM 2.049.
11. MM. 2.057.
12. Richard C.S. Trahair, "Elton Mayo and the Early Political Psychology of Harold D. Lasswell," *Political Psychology* 3, 1982, pp. 171-88.
13. Mayo to Willits, April 1925, RF; MM 1.099.
14. Mayo to Willits, 14 May 1923, RF.
15. Elton to Dorothea, 3 March, 3 April, 6 June 1923.
16. Mayo to Willits, April 1925, RF; MM 1.099.
17. Elton Mayo, "Irrationality and Revery," *Journal of Personnel Research* 1, no. 11 (1923):473-83.
18. Elton Mayo, "Superstitions," *Continental Pathfinder* (Continental Mills, Germantown, Philadelphia) 1 (1923): 5.
19. Elton Mayo, "The Irrational Factor in Human Behaviour: The "Night Mind' in Industry," *Annals of the Academy of Political and Social Sciences* 110 (1923): 117-30.
20. Elton to Dorothea, 13 June 1923.
21. MM 2.056 Elton to Dorothea 2, 5, 8, 15, 17, 23 April, 17 May 1923.
22. Elton to Dorothea, 2 March-16 June 1923; Patricia Elton Mayo to Trahair, 24 November 1975.
23. Stanley D. Ludlum and Ellice E. McDonald, "The Mechanism of Disease," *Medical Journal and Record,* 20 May 1925, pp. 1-14, MM 3.045.
24. MM 3.007.
25. MM 2.003.
26. Henri F. Ellenberger, *The Discovery of the Unconscious: The History and Evolution of Dynamic Psychiatry* (New York: Basic Books, 1970), p. 345.
27. Janet to Mayo, 19 September, 14 December 1925; Mayo to Allen, 30 September 1925; *Philadelphia Public Ledger,* 14 October 1925, MM 1.050.
28. Ruml to Mayo, 15 March 1924, plus enclosures, RF; Trahair, "Elton Mayo."
29. Ford to Thurstone, 1 July 1925; Thurstone to Ford, 7 July 1925, RF.
30. Mayo to Ford, 24 July 1925, and related documents, RF.
31. Transcript of the conference, pp. 58-61, 189-204, 243-41, RF; notes in MM 2.075.
32. G. W. Stocking, Jr., "Clio's Fancy: Documents to Pique the Historical Imagination," *History of Anthropology Newsletter* 2 (1978):10.
33. Mayo to Ruml, 25 September 1925, RF.
34. Elton Mayo, "Freedom for the Child—What Does It Mean?" *Child Study* 28 (October 1925), MM 1.060.
35. See notes 17, 18, and 19 above.
36. Elton Mayo, "Mental Hygiene in Industry," *Transactions of the College of Physicians* (Philadelphia), 3d series, 46 (1924):736-48.

37. Elton Mayo, "Revery and Industrial Fatigue," *Journal of Personnel Research* 3 (1924):273-81; Elton Mayo, "The Basis of Industrial Psychology," *Bulletin of the Taylor Society* 8 (1924):249-59.
38. Elton Mayo, "Civilized Unreason," *Harper's* 148 (1924):527-35; Elton Mayo, "Civilization—The Perilous Adventure," *Harper's* 149 (1924):590-97 (reprinted in *Essays towards Truth,* ed. Kenneth A. Robinson [New York: Holt, Rinehart & Winston, 1924]).
39. Elton Mayo, "Day-dreaming and Output in a Spinning Mill," *Journal of Occupational Psychology* 2, no. 5 (1925):203-09.
40. Elton Mayo, "The Great Stupidity," *Harper's* 151 (1925):225—33; Elton Mayo, "Open Letter to Robert W. Bruere," *Survey* (East Stroudsburg, Penna.) 54 (1925):644-45 (reprinted with R. W. Bruere's "The Great Obsession" in *Bulletin of the Taylor Society* October 1, 1925, pp. 220-25).
41. Elton Mayo, "Should Marriage Be Monotonous?" *Harper's* 151 (1925):420-27 (reprinted in *American Journal of Social Hygiene* 11 [1925]:521-35).
42. Mayo to Millstone, 9 September 1925, MM 3.057; Davis to Mayo, 10, 15, 26 January 1926, MM 4.013.
43. Carncross to Mayo, 9 October 1925, MM 4.013; *Social Health* 11, no. 1 (1925):2, MM 1.060.
44. Herzog to Mayo, 12 January 1926, MM 3.059; Schmidt to Mayo, 19 October 1925, MM 3.055; Strasswell to Mayo, 10 November 1925, MM 3.057; Bennett to Mayo, 30 January 1926, MM 3.058.
45. Whittman to Mayo, 22 September 1925, MM 1.050.
46. Elton Mayo, "Psychiatry in Industry," *Bulletin of Massachusetts Society for Mental Hygiene* 5, no. 2 (1926):4.

12

Harvard 1926-1932: Early Research and Associates

How Mayo was called to Harvard University in not known for certain. "I first met Dean Donham in 1925 at dinner in a New York Hotel," Mayo said.[1] And the popular view holds that the dean of the Graduate School of Business Administration was so greatly impressed by "Civilized Unreason?" "Civilization—The Perilous Adventure," and "The Great Stupidity" in *Harper's* that he hired him immediately. But inquiries show that Mayo's appointment was controlled by personal contacts and alternative job offers, and complicated by debates on the university's future employment policies.

Donham was attracted early to Mayo's ideas, and, once his work began, became one of its strong followers. In 1942, after his retirement as dean, he took an active interest in teaching Mayo's ideas. So, throughout his career at the Business School Mayo had strong support from Donham.

Lawrence J. Henderson, a Harvard biologist, was another influential man who supported Mayo. Under Henderson's direction, Henry A. Murray and his brother Charles studied at Cambridge in the summer of 1925. Henry Murray returned to Bryn Mawr in the fall, and was visited by Charles, who had recently been so impressed by Mayo's work that he spoke of it to his brother and Henderson. At first Henderson was skeptical, but after meeting Mayo recommended him to Donham.[2] In November 1925 at the Boston Chamber of Commerce Donham heard Mayo talk on psychology applied to industrial problems. Other speakers were McFie Campbell, director of the Boston Psychopathic Hospital, and Abraham Myerson, a neurologist from Tufts Medical School. Mayo spoke last, so he had the opportunity to summarize the others' ideas. A few days later Mayo was invited to lecture on industrial management at the Business School. At the end of November Donham asked Mayo to join the school.[3] Mayo was considering an offer to establish experimental psychology at McGill University, but when Donham outlined his plans Mayo believed the Harvard research setting would be superior.[4]

On December 7 Mayo and Donham met to reach a decision. Mayo was happy, relaxed, and talkative; he reminisced about his Australian experiences and outlined the shortcomings of recent British research on industrial fatigue. Donham needed evidence of Mayo's qualifications and past academic achievements, so Mayo gave him the letter signed by the prime minister of Australia saying that Mayo had been a professor of psychology and physiology at the University of Queensland, and that he enjoyed "a very high reputation in the particular branch of study in which he is engaged." Ludlum would send a supporting reference.[5]

Donham sent the letter to Harvard President A. Lawrence Lowell, and with it an erratic statement of Mayo's academic experience that suggested that he had qualified in medicine during his four years at the Universities of Adelaide, Edinburgh and London; that in 1910 he had been appointed reader in psychology at the University of Adelaide, which had awarded him an M.A.; that in 1911, Mayo had been a lecturer in psychology at the University of Queenstown (*sic*), and that in 1918 he had been promoted to professor of psychology; and that "in recognition of Dr. Mayo's work" on shell-shock cases between 1914 and 1922 and "on the recommendation of Professor J.T. Wilson, Cambridge University these studies had led to the endowment of a Chair in Medical Psychology." Lowell "talked with Dean Edsall [Medical School] and Dr. Henderson about Dr. Mayo and [got] the opinion that he [was] a very valuable man."[6]

Lowell did not support Donham's proposal to hire Mayo because it was an expansion within a new field for which funds were available for only three and a half years, and should Harvard want to offer tenure to Mayo, then the financial burden would be too heavy. Donham replied that Mayo's work was not a new discipline, that human relations in industry was important for both teaching and research, that A. Lincoln Filene, the Boston retailer, would guarantee enough money to support Mayo's work, and that Mayo understood clearly his appointment as associate professor of industrial research was for no more than five years. Donham also mentioned that McGill was keen to have Mayo on the same terms, and that Ruml wanted the matter settled before the year's end. Lowell would not assent because he understood the Laura Spelman Rockefeller Memorial Foundation intended to establish an enduring study of Mayo's subject and, after five years when Filene's gift came to an end, funds would not be available to decide whether or not to continue the work. At this point Donham was faced with a series of complicated negotiations with senior Harvard academics and officials who distributed the Rockefeller funds.

Donham wanted $200,000 to finance studies on human relations in industry and related medical research. Dean Edsall said the Medical School could not help. Mayo agreed to postpone his reply to McGill because he appreciated Harvard's prestige, believed that among American industrialists Harvard-trained disciples would be accepted more than would others, and anticipated that collaboration with physiologists and psychiatrists in Cambridge would be rewarding. Meanwhile Donham learned that a sensitive official in the Rockefeller Foundation felt slighted because he had not been kept fully posted on discussions regarding Mayo's intended move. At the same time Mayo received an offer from University College, London. Donham was caught between the employment needs of Mayo, the demands of Harvard to choose its own research directions, and the expectations of the Rockefeller Foundation officials that its philanthropy be both limited and highly praised.

At the end of March 1926 Donham spoke with Lowell and resubmitted the proposal to employ Mayo. It was to be experimental, to last only five years, and to be fully funded by the Laura Spelman Rockefeller Memorial Foundation. Lowell agreed, and in September 1926 Mayo took up appointment as associate professor and head of the Industrial Research Department in the Harvard Business School. Emily Osborne came with him as his secretary and research assistant.[7]

Mayo wrote of his appointment to Sir William Mitchell, his mentor at the University of Adelaide. Immediately Mitchell personally arranged for Mayo to receive a Master of Arts degree. It was awarded for a thesis, presumably, on Mayo's research at Continental Mills.[8]

In the early years at Harvard Mayo had four young men assist him with studies of industrial problems in Massachusetts and with clinical work: Harold D. Lasswell, Osgood S. Lovekin, Fritz J. Roethlisberger, and W. Lloyd Warner. In 1926-27 Mayo worked with Lasswell, who was twenty-two, on his personal problems, interviewing skills, and aspects of politics and psychoanalysis, which Lasswell would later make central to his career.[9]

Osgood Lovekin, twenty-four, had completed undergraduate requirements for a medical degree at Stanford University but decided to enter the Harvard Business School in 1925. Late in 1926 Lovekin attended one of Mayo's lectures to second-year students. Mayo fascinated the class as he sat cross-legged on a table, lecturing effortlessly without notes or any form of preparation. He moved from the classics to recent scholars—Janet, Freud, Malinowski, and Pitt-Rivers—whose work was unfamiliar to most students. He spoke like quicksilver, lighting pathways of ignorance, darting from one discipline to another with anecdotes, homilies, crisp stories, and brilliant illustrations. At the time students were stimulated and excited by Mayo's insights; a week later, when the charisma faded, they looked at their notes and asked, "What does it all mean?" As always Mayo aimed to raise curiosity to an intensity that would lead a young student to join him in the adventure of industrial research.

Osgood Lovekin joined Mayo's department in February 1927, and, with Emily Osborne, took blood pressure measures and conducted interviews in New England factories. Their research was more an exploration than a task with specific hypotheses, so, once data were collected, Lovekin analyzed them and wrote reports. To learn interviewing, he attended the clinic at

Boston Psychopathic Hospital with Mayo and McFie Campbell, the city's eminent psychiatrist. Shortly before leaving Mayo, he assisted with research at the Hawthorne Works of Western Electric Company. At the Hawthorne Works Lovekin interviewed the plant supervisors because the staff had neither the status nor the objectivity to win and keep respect from their interviewees. Later Lovekin interviewed the inmates of the Norfolk Prison Colony, where progressive and humanitarian policies were followed in rehabilitating criminals. During his last year with the department, Lovekin assisted W. Lloyd Warner at Newburyport in a study of consumption habits and control of household expenditures. In 1933 Lovekin entered business, later studied medicine, and at the outbreak of World War II became a senior hospital administrator.[10]

Fritz Jules Roethlisberger became Mayo's most notable student, clinical assistant, and follower, and contributed much to the application of Mayo's ideas to American industry. Although he was not appointed as Mayo's research assistant in industrial research until September 1927, Roethlisberger began working with Mayo on clinical cases referred to him in May 1927. With a science degree from the Massachusetts Institute of Technology and two years of industrial experience, Roethlisberger entered Harvard to study philosophy but did not complete the requirements for the higher degree. His life had become "dust and ashes," and he was so deeply depressed that even psychiatric help was valueless. A. North Whitehead, the retired English philosopher who had joined Harvard's Department of Philosophy, advised him to see Mayo.

When he first met Roethlisberger, Mayo was "curious and amused"; no doubt he saw himself as an immature young man in the sad young philosopher. When next they met, Mayo offered him a job assisting in research and interviewing unhappy young students. In April 1927 Roethlisberger wrote up the case of a woman from a local manufacturing company who had become addicted to heroin. Later Mayo considered giving one of his own cases to the young man because, as he wrote to Ruml, "Rothlisberger [sic] . . . is doing well. Having apparently mastered his own obsessions, he is proving himself very much able to capture the obsessions of others—all this in a week or two." By January 1928 Mayo was pleased with Roethlisberger's developing clinical skills and effective methods of therapy with distressed students from the Business School.[11]

Roethlisberger made his career with Mayo. Between them grew an emotional bond so strong that Mayo was seen as a father, miracle worker, healer, admired and envied colleague, and, eventually, a respected man with faults. Mayo saw Roethlisberger as an intelligent obsessive, and helped the young man through his emotional problems with work, and through squabbles with peers and colleagues, and enabled him to make a valuable contribution to industrial research. But in 1942, Mayo was shocked when Roethlisberger's resistance to taking charge of some of Mayo's work led to effort syndrome, which made for a long recuperation and self-renewal away from Mayo.

Until the summer of 1930 Roethlisberger was largely responsible for psychological cases that came directly to Mayo's department. Most cases were Business School students whose preoccupations, misunderstandings, and distresses had interfered with their studies; others were people on the administrative staff, and a few came from outside the Business School. At the same time Mayo was seeing cases referred to him by doctors, and talked about them with Roethlisberger. In August 1930 Roethlisberger visited the Hawthorne Works of the Western Electric Company and discussed the evaluation of interview data collected from employees.[12] In March 1931 he was engaged to interview executive staff and supervisors at the Hawthorne Works, and Mayo was planning to write a book on the earlier research.[13] That year few students needed counseling, so Roethlisberger spent most of his time in Chicago discussing plans for further research at the Hawthorne Works.[14] In the winter and spring of 1932 when glaucoma prevented Mayo from writing the planned book, Roethlisberger and two Western Electric staff members, Harold A. Wright and William Dickson, began collating material and writing *Management and the Worker.*[15]

In April 1930, W. Lloyd Warner, a young follower of Malinowski and Radcliffe-Brown, joined Mayo. Supported by the Laura Spelman Rockefeller Memorial Foundation in the late 1920s, Warner had studied aborigines in Australia, and when the foundation increased Mayo's funds, Warner, who had gone to Harvard's Department of Anthropology, was attracted to work with Mayo.[16] Warner decided to study the problems of industrial civilization by making a general survey of Newburyport. The community's leaders and citizens were keen to be studied, and the town was both representative of small American towns and within commuting distance of Harvard University.[17] At first Warner had help only from students in anthropology, but later Mayo and his staff, and even Dorothea, became involved in training research assistants and in data collection. By the end of 1931 Warner was an assistant professor in Mayo's department, had extended his anthropological studies to Ireland, and had become a contributor to research at the Hawthorne Works. Much of his support came from funds available to Mayo.[18]

In April 1926 the Laura Spelman Rockefeller Memorial Foundation gave $12,000 a year for five years for Mayo's work at Harvard. The following year a supplementary grant of $155,000 was made: $35,000 to equip Lawrence Henderson's Fatigue Laboratory in the basement of the Business School, and $30,000 a year for four years to continue industrial research in physiology and related areas. By April 1930 Mayo's work had so effectively joined with that of Henderson and associates that the earlier grant was cancelled and replaced with a seven-year grant of $125,000 a year for a comprehensive program of research in industrial hazards. A special committee—Mayo, Henderson, and Dean David Edsall—administered the funds independently of faculty control. Each year $25,000 to $35,000 was used as fluid research funds for whatever projects emerged within the overall program, and the remainder was divided equally between Mayo and Henderson. Mayo's estimated annual budget was $68,000; the Fatigue Laboratory's about $54,000. Reasons for extending the grant over seven years center on the remarkably cooperative relations that had grown between Harvard's Schools of Business, Medicine, Public Health, and Engineering, and the likelihood of further collaboration with other schools. Also, Mayo planned to augment his psychological work with sociological investigations of living conditions in industrial centers, e.g., Newburyport, and Henderson wished to study more physiological factors and increase the subjects used in experiments. The support was liberal so that Mayo and Henderson would pass quickly beyond the early stages of their research.[19]

A few months after he joined the Business School Mayo found a friend in Lawrence J. Henderson. The friendship lasted until Henderson's sudden death in February 1942.[20] He was one of Harvard's most able, respected, and influential academics, a masterful man who set high standards of excellence for his students and colleagues. The relationship between Mayo and Henderson was based on more than shared academic interests.[21] In many ways the men themselves were similar. Both had been reared in families in which the businessman father had little influence and the mother showed good sense, adaptability, and strong independent judgment. As adolescents both had been prize-winning students who willfully pursued their own interests, but in the early stages of education Henderson enjoyed greater freedom from family constraints. Both studied medicine, not to become physicians but rather to follow an interest in related research; later they would join in criticism of medical training because it omitted concern for the social relation between physician and patient.

Mayo and Henderson had diverse wide-ranging academic interests, e.g., philosophy, history of science, physiology, psychiatry, sociology. As a young man Henderson had studied philosophy under Royce and with a close friend, Elmer E. Southard; when Mayo first came to the United States his style was likened to that of the late Southard. In 1925 when Henderson and Mayo first met they shared similar conceptions of how the organism's functioning related to its total environment. Also, both men attributed order to the apparent chaos of natural phenomena by first assuming a strain toward balanced, harmonious integration between elements and their interaction within the total social and physical context. To the study of humans both men applied the methodology of the medical sciences, i.e., close continuous observation and experiment to refine, clarify, and extend firsthand knowledge. Only this approach, they believed, would raise psychological and sociological work from sentimental, biased, and philosophic inexactitudes to the level of a respected science.

The two men differed in their approach to research problems with students.[22] Mayo was humanistic, and cared as much for the students' experience of the research problem as for the problem itself; Henderson seemed to use his personal force to conceal any sympathy for the student lest the problem remain unclear. Mayo enjoyed giving to some unexpected research finding or half-baked proposal a thought-provoking, hypothesis-generating, adventurous twist. With a joke he would turn a problem on its head. But when a student took a problem to Henderson, either he was castigated for stupidity in not seeing an obvious solution or Henderson demanded, then and there, that the elements of the problem be defined, the variables be stated exactly, and from their relations he deduced scientifically testable propositions. And Henderson did not joke. Along these quite different paths Mayo and Henderson followed their creative imagination in science.

When they met first, Henderson was troubled by two matters that a scientist could not quickly clarify. Following World War I many intellectuals began to believe that organized society was in danger. Mayo had feared as much—and had had nightmares about it—years before; he supposed the origin of the danger lay in the minds of men and, especially, the uncivilized hostility of agitators, revolutionaries, and incompetent leaders who, in democracy's name, manipulated the obsessions of people in crowds. For help Mayo had turned to the new psychology. Henderson, following a colleague's advice, read Pareto and thereby brought order to his fear of chaos in society. He eventually taught Pareto's ideas to Harvard's sociology students and selected faculty, and vigorously upheld Pareto's approach as the clearest approach to the study of concrete rather than intellectualized social problems. Mayo reinforced Henderson's interest in Pareto, proved a good listener when that was expected, and felt the sociological perspective tempered Henderson's interpersonal relations and helped him become more understanding, sympathetic, and caring for humanity.

Early in their association Mayo noted that Henderson's "relapse into common humanity" was accompanied by a positive attitude toward psychiatry.[23] The attitude may have been established by Henderson's earlier friendship with the psychiatrist Southard, banished when the latter died, and returned when Mayo appeared. The concern for psychiatry may also have been reawakened by Henderson's wife Edith, who was committed to an institution for the insane.

Sometimes Mayo was a guest at Henderson's summer home in Vermont, and often Mayo's dinners included Henderson. Both relished good food—Henderson's coq au vin was more a celebration than a dinner—and were delighted with French wines. And when Dorothea and Mayo decided she should live in England with their daughters, the loneliness of the two men would draw them even closer. At work they seemed very close; their offices were together, they ate lunch together, and they shared a large research grant and controlled the committee for its disbursement. In the Business School their personal influence was impressive; they were the only faculty members seen to have the privilege of strolling into Donham's office without appointment and joining immediately in discussions, regardless of who was with the dean.[24]

During his first four years at the Business School Mayo tried to interest local businessmen in his approach to the human and social problems of industrial life. He was not successful because of the resistance to his ideas, which came from within both the Business School and the firms that sought Mayo's help. Colleagues at the Business School thought the study of fatigue, monotony, and morale had no proper place in the training of men of business. Further, special, close, and time-consuming instruction was needed for the understanding of human problems in the workplace, instruction that was costly, the return on which was difficult to see and to justify in business terms. Students resisted the study of human problems in industrial organization because it was a new and undeveloped field in business administration, and higher salaries could be earned in other fields.[25]

Within industry Mayo's ideas were resisted by those whose influence would be most affected by the changes he advocated. "Our main problem," wrote Osborne to Donham two years after Mayo had joined the Business School, "is to gain the confidence and cooperation of leaders in industry . . . [however] we have been unable to work in any plant where we have received the cooperation of the management and heads of departments."[26]

In a firm Mayo could gain the confidence of higher management and the cooperation of employees but little help from middle management and foremen, who were fearful of his research and obstructed it. As a rule Mayo aimed to study fatigue and its effects by first seeing employees who came to the dispensary for medical attention from the industrial nurse. While she took the employees' blood pressure readings they would talk about their preoccupations. Such information revealed to Mayo the human problems at work and the production, labor, and organizational difficulties in various parts of the plant, and he could then identify where his research would bring most benefit. But middle management and foremen, sensing that organizational changes arising from Mayo's work would undermine their control, saw no utility for themselves in cooperation with the dispensary. They kept it well away from their administrative problems, tolerating it only to satisfy the firm's insurers.

Mayo's research with the United States Rubber Company illustrates the course taken by his early industrial work. On February 20, 1928, the company's supervisor of industrial relations, C.S. Ching, a leader in the United States in the development of personnel management, sent Mayo a report,

"Study of Fatigue in Relation to Work Places" by Marion Lee, the assistant industrial relations manager of one of the company's East Cambridge factories, the American Rubber Company. Mayo complimented Ching on the research and sought to augment the study with one of his own that would aim to improve selection of workers. Medical criteria, he wrote, are not adequate; and because even fit people differ in work performance, one must study workers' capacities by continuously examining them on the job. Mayo mentioned research findings showing that low efficiency and poor morale are symptoms of pessimistic preoccupations, which in turn indicate organic fatigue due to metabolic disorders arising from unsuitable work conditions and lack of vocational aptitude. He thought the Addis Index (pulse rate $\times$ pulse pressure/100) would help identify workers who were subject to such adverse work conditions, and those who lacked interest in their work. During the day the Addis Index curve of the efficient and highly productive worker is steady, but "marked variations are significant of a production 20-30% below the individual's average. Such variations indicated lower production and lowered organic fitness (e.g. thyroid inadequacy, menstruation) often when the worker was not aware of reduced fitness," and lowered work capacity. Mayo proposed to use Marion Lee's workers to see whether or not the Addis Index would measure changes in the worker capacity for and attitude toward work.

Ching supported Mayo's proposal, and through G. Woodward, the company's works manager, arranged for Osborne to visit Marion Lee and her boss, D.F. Ohlstrom, at the plant in January 1929. First-line supervisors were expected to resist the proposal, so Mayo addressed them and the Factory Council before beginning experimental work. Meanwhile Osborne befriended the company doctor and his nurse, who understood and had sympathy for Mayo's plan but said that the management had given no cooperation on similar and related matters in the past. She also found that the work force included many Irish and Portuguese, whom the foremen mixed lest they fight among themselves in their own groups and become troublemaking socialists.[27]

Mayo spoke three times on his scheme, each time pitching his talk to the interests of the specific audience. He said that mechanization of work advances faster than knowledge of human behavior and experience, and work fatigue is a recurrent issue that requires scientific study and raises many unknown psychological and physiological problems that affect production, absenteeism, and labor turnover. The problems are best approached by studying how people change during a day's work.[28]

Late in February 1929 Osborne and Roethlisberger took blood pressure readings, and listened to workers who needed help from the dispensary. During March and April, Lovekin joined them. At set times during the day blood pressure readings were taken on the job as well; the average Addis Index was calculated for each department and the individual deviations from the average were noted. These measures were related to production figures.

Lovekin wrote the report on this study. The Addis Index correlated with energy expenditure, and could show the rate of energy expenditure on mentally and physically exacting work. Lovekin planned more studies, but in May 1929 demand fell for the company's goods, and subsequent reorganization made research impossible. As the business depression advanced, morale among workers fell. Partly to remedy this Mayo was asked to return and talk to the industrial relations officers on the implications of the report. He advocated systematic rest periods and interviewing that he had seen at the Western Electric Company in Chicago, but the production manager of the American Rubber Company had no time for such recommendations. By May 1930 the depression had all but closed the plant, and Mayo's association with the firm ceased.[29]

Another company that sought Mayo's help was the Boston Manufacturing Company of Waltham, producers of yarn and fancy cloth. In December 1926 Osborne and Lovekin, and later Roethlisberger conducted clinical interviews, took blood pressure readings, and related these to the production of a hundred employees. The research problems were: Why do young girls adapt easily to silk winding while older women prefer beaming? What are the physical characteristics of successful employees? Is a particular physical or mental type better suited to monotonous work? How is the worker's mental attitude related to fatigue? How can monotonous work be defined?

Before Mayo and his associates could advance their work a report was made on the firm's operations in April 1927; it indicated that central control was lacking, morale was low, and the executive staff was seeking, at no cost to the firm, modern techniques of scientific management. Mayo's work was unsuited to such expectations, so his association with the firm came to an end in May.[30]

In November 1927 the application of modern scientific management to knitwear production at the William Carter Company led to a call for Mayo's help. The standards department had learned of the initial benefits of rest pauses, and also that upon their cessation production fell. The management feared that rest pauses would slow production and cause carelessness. Lovekin studied seven young women at work and reported the production curves did not support the management's fear. He argued that whether or not rest pauses are given, people adjust to increasing fatigue by slacking off, voluntarily or not. Production stops and, if the employees drive themselves to maintain it, inefficiency and organic damage follow. He advised the firm to accept the slack periods and organize them into controlled rather than uncontrolled rest pauses, thus maintaining smooth production curves for the firm and achieving an evenly fluctuating energy expenditure among employees.[31] Mayo did not learn if the firm followed this lead.

Early in 1930 Osborne and Mayo discussed the Industrial Research Department and Mayo wrote answers to Osborne's questions about their future. In Mayo's view New England industries needed extensive economic reorganization. Some of those he studied had liquidated or shut down, thus making his work inappropriate. Only two of the twelve firms he had studied—Continental Mills (Philadelphia), and Western Electric (Chicago)—had fortunate results; and in the American Pulley, American Rubber, Hood Rubber, and Carter companies some fruitful inquiries had been conducted. Negative results marked the studies of the other six firms. Mayo believed his work had been impeded by middle managers and foremen who, he thought, were too much devoted to rituals and were constantly looking for easy rules of thumb instead of a genuine understanding of work.

Mayo concluded that the work of his department could not continue for more than another year or so unless industries in Massachussetts became available for research and "apprentices" could be persuaded to join him. The department had sound financial support from the Rockefeller foundation and willing collaboration from Harvard's Law and Medical Schools and the Departments of Bio-chemistry, Economics, Abnormal Psychology, and Psychiatry. Because of these strong associations Mayo did not see the department's being absorbed by industry, but he expected his staff to become consultants to a few firms.[32]

In a search for industries that might follow his lead, Mayo was directed by Dean Donham to consult with executives in the movie industry. Early in 1927 Mayo was asked to see Mr. Brownell of Kennedy's Moving Picture Corporation and report to Donham, who saw the need to train businessmen in that industry because of its rapidly growing influence in the economy. Mayo's report was harsh and critical, and reflected his personal loathing of people who manipulate the ignorant and waste opportunities to advance socially responsible and civilized behavior.

Mayo reported that three major defects in the movie industry led to the waste of millions of dollars. First, the criteria for selecting a movie plot that would appeal to a large audience are applied unsystematically, and the decision to "picturize" conventional novels or magazine stories makes new developments for movies impossible. Second, the criteria are applied in Hollywood, where the movies are made, rather than in the New York head office, where the initial decisions are taken, which makes for administrative chaos in the industry. Third, alterations to plots made between New York and Hollywood are based on whim, not consultation with writers or producers. Three consequences follow: there is no chance of learning from successes and failures, and this leads to the creation of a bored public; if control of movie making is left to the creative inspiration of a Hollywood director, this may lead to a brilliant success but no one will know why, and costly failures will certainly ensue; if individualism rather than planning controls the industry it produces strong directors, star actors, favorite authors, and, perhaps, excellent movies, but such actors and directors burden the industry when they believe their renown will redeem a poor plot. "In the long run even . . . brilliant individuals would be unable to meet competition from better organised institutions."

Mayo believed the chaos in the movie industry could be overcome by defining functions and their relations. The selection of a plot should be determined by what is known of the human appeal of issues, events, and their background. In cooperation with the authors, the directors should control actors and acting but never drastically alter the script lest effective collaboration within the industry be destroyed, learning be limited, departmental dictators emerge, few artists find expression for their talent, and the industry have more failures than successes.

Mayo enjoyed movies, and was concerned about their impact on society. Some years later a student of his would join the industry and attempt to have the ideas realized, but with little success. As Mayo predicted, individualism and the star system would dominate the economy of the movie industry.[33]

Donham understood that charlatans applied psychology to business and even well-meaning individuals used the results of psychological studies in industry loosely and unprofessionally. Mayo's work had to be protected against such misuse, and his ideas had to spread and be directed through sound reputable business connections. One such connection was made at the Harvard Club in New York in October 1927 when Mayo spoke on what psychology could do for industry in the next ten years to The Lunchers, a group of prominent industrialists. The invitation had come from Arthur H. Young, the director of Industrial Relations Counselors, an organization, that Donham hoped would be helpful.[34]

Industrial Relations Counselors was incorporated in 1926, and had emerged from a small staff of industrial relations specialists directed by Raymond B. Fosdick of Curtis, Fosdick and Belknap. John D. Rockefeller, Jr., provided the funds for Fosdick's work and was the sole support of Industrial Relations Counselors. The original purpose of this nonprofit organization was to keep Rockefeller informed on industrial relations in his firms; companies other than Rockefeller's would later support the organization and benefit from its work "to advance the knowledge and practice of human relationships in industry, commerce, education and government."[35]

Mayo's talk impressed The Lunchers and led to many valuable connections with senior industrialists and managers.[36] Among the listeners was T.K. Stevenson, the personnel director of Western Electric Company, who would ask Mayo to read reports he had received on the company's research in its Hawthorne Works at Cicero, Illinois. In January 1928 Rockefeller entertained Mayo, and in October he was commissioned to research industrial relations problems at Rockefeller's Colorado Fuel and Iron Company in Pueblo.[37]

The Colorado Fuel and Iron Company had established its industrial plan in 1915 with personal support from Rockefeller. The plan aimed to reduce industrial strife and promote a cooperative relation between management and labor in the company's mines and steel works. Its cornerstone was the Committee on Conciliation and Wages, which included members from among managers and workers. Despite the intervention of Rockefeller, the plan had not been entirely successful.

Accompanied by Arthur H. Young, Mayo spent three weeks at the plant in Pueblo studying the human situation and the adequacy of management's information, and evaluating the efficacy of the plan. Mayo found the plan deficient because top managers were autocratic and unbending, middle and first-line supervisors felt the plan had diminished their influence, and employee representatives and associates used the plan to unionize the work force and promote socialism. Notwithstanding, on many occasions the committee had resolved conflicts. Mayo concluded that conflicts had arisen because management was not adequately prepared for such a radical change in the company's industrial relations policy. Worker representatives, seeing some managers were hostile toward the plan, had avoided important matters, pursued trivialities, raised legalistic arguments, and neglected the spirit of agreement. Mayo recommended that a full, precise account be made of the human problems associated with the plan; that managers be given the account to help them understand and accept the plan. Their understanding should be shown to the workers, who would then accept and use the plan because they would know managers were no longer hostile toward it.

Mayo used his report to examine and criticize the work of the former investigators of the plan, Benjamin M. Selekman and Mary Van Kleck, who, with support from the Russell Sage Foundation, had favored worker participation in management through representation and joint committees, or collective bargaining. Mayo agreed that if industrial relations were cooperative workers could make constructive suggestions, but wrote that such contributions should be evaluated correctly by management. There was evidence that in Britain and Australia worker participation in management had created disastrous industrial relations whenever management had not evaluated such participation accurately, and both unions and management had not substitued mutuality of interests for class conflict.

On a more general level, Mayo's thesis was that between workers and management there must exist a knowledge of common interests from which would emerge mutual confidence, trust, and effective collaboration. On that basis a business would thrive. An independent investigator could provide an intelligent understanding of mutual interests and initiate action to achieve collaborative relations at work.

When Van Kleck assumed industrial democracy and modern political democracy were alike, Mayo became severely critical, and illustrated his argument by again pointing to Australia, where the arbitration system had raised rather than diminished the incidence of industrial strife. Mayo preferred the American approach, which did not allow economic areas to be debased by the modern developments in democracy. In this regard, Mayo held that success in industry depended upon management's being so well informed on the human situation at work that grievances can be understood and their origins eliminated before they create strife.

Mayo carried his work beyond the conflict and squabbling within the organization of the mines and steel works to the sociological problems in the community. Following the anthropological work of Malinowski and Pitt-Rivers and Ruth Cavan's studies in Chicago, Mayo assumed a direct relation between a community's social organization or disorganization and its industrial content or unrest. "Directly the major significance [i.e., the social] of an individual's life disintegrates, his interest in his work must diminish also. . . . The social ailment which affects the cities of our civilization has made its appearance in . . . Pueblo." Mayo's solution to social disintegration lay in extending the community's recreation facilities and providing skilled leaders to turn disaffected youth from hostile gang activities to constructive sport and cultural pastimes.

Mayo was appalled by the illiteracy, overcrowding, ill health, and sexual promiscuity in Pueblo's Mexican community. He recommended that the Rockefeller Foundation support a sociomedical survey of these problems in preparation for a systematic change in community welfare services.[38]

Two months after the Colorado study Mayo and Osborne received fees from Industrial Relations Counselors: Mayo, $1,000 a year retainer as a consultant; Osborne, to write a monthly report for Arthur Young on the work done in Mayo's department.[39] A few months later Dean Donham invited Young to lecture at the Business School.[40] Thereafter Mayo and Young were close working associates; Mayo benefited from the connections made through Young, and Young admired Mayo's "natural gift (for colorful, persuasive expression) which needs no further cultivation."[41]

Notes

1. Elton Mayo, "The Study of Human Problems of Administration," *Harvard Business School Alumni Bulletin,* Sumer 1942, p. 232.
2. Conversation with Henry A. Murray, 17 April 1975.
3. Biddle to Mayo, 4 December 1925; Mayo to Donham, 3, 8, 25 December 1925; Donham to Mayo, 2 December 1925. Donham file, GC 332, AFFD1, AB4, BLA; MM 1.060.
4. Martin to Mayo, 17 December 1925, MM 3.079.
5. William M. Hughes, 26 June 1922, MM 1.099; Donham to Lowell, 14 December 1925, Donham file, BLA.
6. Lowell to Donham, 15 December 1925, Donham file, BLA.
7. Donham to Edsall, 24 December 1925; Edsall to Donham, 30 December 1925; Downey to Donham, 7, 8 January, 8, 16 March 1926; Mayo to Donham, 9 January 1926; Donham to Ruml, 30 March 1926; Donham to Lowell, 23 March 1926, Donham file, BLA.

8. No details of the theses can be found; Wesley-Smith to Trahair, 5 June 1974. Sir William Mitchell "reported verbally on work received from Mr. G. Elton Mayo . . . the Faculty approved his suggestion that the matter be left" to Professor Stewart and him. Minutes, Faculty of Arts, University of Adelaide, 17 November 1926. The degree was awarded 25 November 1926.

9. Richard C.S. Trahair, "Elton Mayo and the Early Political Psychology of Harold D. Lasswell," *Political Psychology* 3 (1982):171-88.

10. Conversation with Lovekin, 18 September 1975.

11. Fritz J. Roethlisberger, *The Elusive Phenomena* (Boston: Harvard University, Graduate School of Business Administration, Division of Research, 1977), pp. 26-33; Mayo to Ruml, 16 May 1927, 28 January 1928, RF; MM 3.008.

12. Osborne Reports, October 1930, April, November, December 1931; Roethlisberger, *Elusive Phenomena,* p. 49.

13. Mayo to Pennock, 24 March 1931, Mayo to Putnam, 25 March 1931, MM 1.090.

14. Osborne Reports, November, December 1931.

15. Wright to Mayo, 25 April 1932, Mayo to Putnam, 27 April 1932, MM 1.091.

16. Osborne Reports, May, November, December 1930.

17. Osborne Reports, November, December 1930, January, February, December 1931; Roethlisberger, *Elusive Phenomena,* p. 54.

18. Osborne Reports, November 1931; Streiber to Mayo, 16 October 1931, MM 1.081.

19. "Harvard University Research in Industrial Hazards," 16 April 1930, Doc. No. 30108, RF; Mayo to Donham, 22 January 1927, ARIP.

20. Mayo to Ruml, 9 February 1927, RF.

21. For this comparison the material on Henderson comes from Walter B. Cannon *Biographical Memoir of Lawrence J. Henderson* (Washington, D.C.: National Academy of Sciences, 1943).

22. Conversation with Homans, 3 June 1975; conversation with Chapple, 28 August 1975.

23. Mayo to Ruml, 20 April 1927, RF.

24. Lombard to Trahair, 1 April 1975.

25. Trahair, "Elton Mayo and the Early Political Psychology of Harold D. Lasswell."

26. Osborne to Donham, 14 June 1928, MM 3.071.

27. Osborne Reports, 1 February 1929.

28. Osborne Reports, March 1929; Factory Council minutes, American Rubber Company, 11 February 1929, MM 3.001-2.

29. Lovekin to Woodward, 16 May 1929, MM 3.049; Osborne Reports, May, November-December 1929, May 1930.

30. MM 3.008-10, 3.047.

31. MM 3.001.

32. Mayo to Osborne, March 1930, MM 1.068.

33. Mayo to Donham, 9 May 1927, MM 1.033; ARIP.

34. Donham to Ruml, 14 December 1926, RF.

35. *Industrial Relations Counselors, Inc.* (New York: Industrial Relations Counselors, 1951), MM 1.102.

36. Young to Mayo, 22 November 1927, MM 1.102.

37. Mayo to Ruml, 29 January 1928, RF.

38. Mayo to Woods, 20 November 1928, MM 3.016.

39. Young to Mayo, 23 January 1929, Young to Fosdick, 24 January 1929, MM 1.103.

40. Young to Mayo, 29 May 1929, MM 1.103.

41. Young to Mayo, 21 September 1929, MM 1.103.

13

Harvard 1926-1932: Teaching, Clinical Work, Writing, and Travel

Dean Donham and Mayo agreed that scientific studies of human relations in industry should be the basis of Mayo's contribution to the Business School. For this reason, research had first priority and Mayo did little teaching in his early years. Each year Mayo gave three lectures on his research to students in the Business School. For his research assistants and special students he held informal discussions of set texts.[1]

Malinowski's functional theory of society guided Mayo's teaching of the industrial problems of civilization. Mayo assumed that in primitive communities if social functions are clear then individuals can identify with them easily and, consequently, society is well integrated. In the United States social functions are unclear and individuals are unable to identify readily with their occupations, are thrown onto their own resources, and have no communal support or guidance other than psychiatric help.

The disintegration began when industrialization increased labor mobility and weakened communal ties, isolated family life, organized work so that obsessions dominated mental life, and justified all these changes by placing a high value on economic growth. The practical consequences of destroying social functions for individuals are divorce, crime, irregular living, resentment, and paranoia. To manage these problems an education is needed that gives people control over their own preoccupations, and helps them to discipline themselves by subordinating their needs to a social function. Mayo had made these points often in his lectures on industrial psychology in Australia, in *Democracy and Freedom,* and in the articles for *Harper's.*

In his teaching of psychology, Mayo's topics included elementary physiology and psychopathology. In physiology students studied muscular and mental fatigue and body metabolism; in psychopathology, obsessive thinking and its origins in psychogenetic fatigue. Students applied academic and research studies to problems in industry and among criminals, and to fellow students' incapacity for concentrated work and decisions. They learned the use of physiological measures in distinguishing personality

214 The Humanist Temper

types, methods of interviewing to identify individuals' productive capacities, the role of the industrial dispensary, organization of personnel work, education in industry, problems of adolescent girls at work, and the difficulties work made for normal, intelligent adults.

Readings included Freud on hysteria, sexuality, dreams, and primitive thinking, and works by related authors: Jung, Janet, Bramwell, Bjerre, Morton Prince, William James, Starbuck. Social theory was from Malinowski, Wallas, Westermarck, Durkheim, Barker, Frazer, Ginsberg, and MacIver. Industrial studies were from Goldmark, Vernon, and Watts.[2] Often Mayo illustrated his teaching with cases of patients he had treated.

Until late in 1928 Mayo saw patients, but thereafter they were directed to Roethlisberger. Most patients suffered from obsessional neurosis. In 1927-28 Mayo's department received forty-seven cases; of the forty-two on which some clinical comments were made, twenty-six had clear symptoms and seven showed less serious indications of obsessional neurosis.[3] The substantive problems centered on marital relations, overwork, or a lack of purpose and personal identity. Local doctors referred cases to Mayo from among Business School students, office staff, and colleagues; he saw patients referred by Ludlum in Philadelphia and Harvard's Department of Mental Hygiene, and institutions where he talked.[4] Mayo treated most cases quickly, but two lasted many years because they were probably psychotics.[5]

A case that illustrates both Mayo's technique and ideas was a businessman whom Mayo first saw at Philadelphia General Hospital. A young, bright, and vigorous bachelor, he was promoted to store manager just as the depression was beginning. He enjoyed gambling and the company of young people but his pleasures gave way to bouts of melancholia. He considered marriage seriously because his sexual urge was strong and quickly aroused; masturbation, the only outlet, depressed him. Neither reasoning with himself nor psychiatric advice helped. Mayo advised him to read Malinowski's *Sex in Primitive Society* to extend his understanding of his instincts and society's attitudes toward them. The treatment was successful, until two years later when a business takeover left him unemployed. He became depressed again by the daunting problem of finding a managerial position. He wanted to see Mayo because a psychologist he had seen would not listen to his sex problems. Henry A. Murray took him as a patient, but the man could not bring himself to pay the fees; he could make no financial sacrifice without evidence of progress. He became disgusted with himself because his inner life was too complex to understand. He found a promising job, and then the Wall Street crash ruined his hopes for success in business. He returned to Philadelphia General Hospital, for the old habit of overthinking problems was returning. Mayo could help no more because he was now in Boston.[6]

When Mayo came to Harvard many organizations wanted him as a public speaker, lecturer, and adviser on the application of psychology to industrial, social, and family problems. Several of his addresses were published between 1927 and 1932; two report the work at Continental Mills: "Fatigue in Industry" and the "Surrey Textile Company." In the first paper Mayo integrated clinical, laboratory, and industrial research on fatigue, using Janet's theory of obsessional neurosis, Kleitman's studies of sleep deprivation, and Ludlum's work on the physiological correlates of fatigue and obsession. As general fatigue increases during the working day, normal people begin to react, especially in the afternoon, as if they were obsessional neurotics.[7] In the second paper, the "Surrey Textile Company" is Continental Mills; the article describes Mayo's research in Philadelphia and summarizes his ideas on fatigue for the collection of cases for classroom work at the Business School.[8]

In March 1927 Mayo spoke on industrial fatigue to industrialists at the Cambridge Chamber of Commerce.[9] Between September 1927 and August 1929 at Silver Bay on Lake George, Mayo attended four conferences on human relations in industry sponsored by the New England Committee of the Y.M.C.A. About three hundred prominent workers in industrial relations attended each conference, thus providing Mayo with an excellent opportunity to publicize his ideas and research on control of people and situations, fatigue, and the scientific approach to industrial relations.[10] The first of the talks was published, and shows that Mayo's approach to industrial relations was becoming clear and definite. With the introduction of mass production and long working days, output falls, discontent increases, and morale diminishes. Little is done to learn about fatigue and repetitive work, problems of organization and control, class consciousness, and strikes. The latter two emerge with the obsessive belief of no identity of interest between employers and workers. Research on fatigue should broaden to include the relation of emotional needs to social issues. Finally, problems of industrial control arise because complex organizations curb craftsmen's initiative and autonomy, devalue their intelligence and skill, create monotonous tasks, and, as compensation, offer only money and leisure time. Mayo pointed to research at Harvard on the relation of metabolic disturbance to fatigue, and the relation of fatigue to irrational preoccupations and their role in determining class consciousness and radicalism. He recommended that proper rest periods break the vicious circle of poor work conditions producing poor industrial relations.[11]

In December 1928 Mayo joined a group of distinguished scholars, including Joseph H. Willits and Harvard's Frank W. Taussig, to deliver the Wertheim Lectures on Industrial Relations. The first part of his lecture repeats the address at Lake George. The second part argues that social integration is vital to an individual's contentment, and illustrates this thesis with theories and research from anthropology, sociology, and psychopathology. The theme from *Democracy and Freedom* is repeated: when individuals identify with their occupations and this in turn with social functions, then they are adapting themselves to society. In the United States, because labor is highly mobile, the society disintegrates, social functions blur, and, consequently, individuals become maladjusted. Mayo illustrated the process with the life he had seen in Pueblo. He outlined the work of Charcot, Janet, and Piaget to show that the relation of the individual to society is, as Spencer wrote, a "moving equilibrium" that could be thrown off balance by the eruption of pessimistic reveries at work. Finally, he again summarized the Continental Mills research, and cited the value of the Addis Index of blood pressure for identifying fatigue.[12]

In the summer of 1928 Mayo went to England to study recent research in his field, and used much of the above material in "The Practical Outcome of Psychopathology," an address to the Industrial Section of the British Psychological Society.[13] In January 1929 he published the same ideas in "What Is Monotony," illustrating the thesis with the case of telegraphist's cramp. In England, telegraphists have job security, perform an obviously fatiguing task, and, consequently, suffer cramp; but in the United States, where labor mobility is high, telegraphist's cramp is rare because the individuals are not tied to a job they detest.[14] This was Mayo's last publication in industrial psychology before he became associated with studies at the Hawthorne Works of the Western Electric Company.

Although he was an applied psychologist, Mayo occasionally made theoretical psychology a point for discussion. In August 1926 he spoke on his approach to psychology at the Social Sciences Council conference at Dartmouth College in Hanover, New Hampshire. Following recent publications by Wallas and Poincaré, Mayo saw a place in scientific thinking for creative reveries and the principle of equilibrium and synthesis among natural phenomena. He criticized the stimulus-response theory of psychology, and with evidence from anatomy, chemistry, biology, adult and child psychiatry, and speculations of the early philosophers in psychology, he advocated the use of the concept "organism" to mediate between the stimulus and response in psychological theory. Mayo argued that such a concept was needed to integrate recent work emerging from the disciplines cited, and took the points further in discussion with two young psychologists, Robert S. Woodworth and Gordon Allport.[15]

Clinical psychology was Mayo's topic in an entertaining address he gave in New York to the First Colloquium in Personality Investigation. He used cases that he and Roethlisberger had collected from their psychological investigations and counseling. "Obessions in Students" follows the ideas of Janet, and uses jokes and witty remarks to keep up interest in the catalogue of cases.[16]

Mayo was often asked for his opinions on child and family psychology. Early in January 1927 he read a paper on the place of father in the present-day home. After an erudite review of anthropology's contribution to defining sex roles in various societies, Mayo selected three problems in the modern family: sexual, economic, and social. He stated that between men and women sexual intimacy was "the highest relation of all and must be the basis of any successful social order." Then he argued that in modern families women had lost their economic functions; attempts to regain the pride and pleasure of these past activities had often led to great unhappiness, which was exacerbated by the growth of an abnormally intense and overprotective concern for children. Mayo recommended that, for the sake of their sanity, all family members should develop direct relations with social groups outside the home; but to cope with complexities of civilized society each family member needed personal comfort and affection inside the home. Within the family each member must learn that affection and security is more important than strict discipline and obedience.[17]

Late in January Mayo delivered "The Dynamics of Family Life" at the Institute on Parent Education in New York, attending to issues arising between generations. He combined his theory of mental life with his experiences as a child and as an adviser on child rearing to friends and worried parents. Children become normal adults if anxious and overprotective parents do not stop them from developing ordinary social relations outside the family. Children need a well-ordered, simple, and secure home in which they not only can learn skills with other people but also revery and daydream by themselves; this allows their egocentric, primitive ideas to be differentiated from and change into communicable social thoughts. If family life is chaotic and insecure the difference between the two will never be learned, the change will be impaired, the children will fear and never fully trust others, and then regress to infantile and obsessive modes of thinking. Such modes arise in homes where children have been either ignored or overprotected. In the first, obsessional thinking arises from infantile terrors and distrust; in the second, incomplete and childishly logical thinking among parents provides for the compulsion to overthink problems. For normal childhood development, Mayo recommended that parents always be affectionate toward children, and reformulate intelligently the children's preoccupations rather than restrict the children with such false dichotomies as good versus bad, or authority versus repudiation.[18]

Mayo's reputation as a family psychologist spread. In September he summarized discussion on the free-time problems of the housewife for conference delegates at the American Association of Social Workers at Wellesley College.[19] In March and April 1929 he spoke to members of the Illinois Society of Mental Hygiene, the Chicago Foundation for Child Study, and the Child Guidance Association of Chicago. And in April 1930 he presented a paper on Jean Piaget's work to the Ohio State University's Educational Conference in Columbus.[20]

Mayo and his sister Helen believed that as youngsters they had not experienced sufficient direct social relations outside their home in Adelaide, and he had concluded his own tendency to melancholic reveries stemmed partly from that defect. Such experiences and their rationalization in his theory of the individuals' adaptation to society contributed not only to his talks and publications on the social psychology of the family but to advice he gave to the troubled wives of industrialists, and to his own decision to accept Dorothea's plan to send their daughters to be educated in England.[21]

Other topics on which Mayo lectured and wrote included sin, eugenics, and the business depression. "Sin with a Capital 'S'" notes the widespread alarm in 1927 at the behavior of youth and the anxiety of members of the older generation toward their children's deviance. Forty-year-olds should understand youth better, Mayo argued, and youth should be congratulated both on its progressive and civilized morality and its demonstration to the older generation that moral restraints on and condemnation of youth arise from ignorance and an obsessive thinking. Mayo outlined his ideas on religious conversion that he had given in *Psychology and Religion,* and described again Janet's theory of obsessional neurosis. In that description Mayo found the theme for his article: "It is not the sin [the obsessive] has done that distresses him . . . it is the indefinable sin he might do." The thesis: in a person who feels distant from the real world there emerges a conviction of sin that combines a sense of inferiority with personal depression. In Mayo's thinking, the person becomes preoccupied with oversimplified attitudes, and substitutes false dichotomies for complex well-formed opinions. Adolescents have a strong attachment for false dichotomies, particularly in regard to what affects them most, i.e., sex, authority, and changes in social relations. Because of its ignorance of sex and young peoples' values, the older generaton provokes in the young a morbid sense of sin; they respond by using false dichotomies to master their sexual and social problems and conflict radically with the older generation. Although the article was a popular exegesis of life during the 1920s, it contained many ideas that would be used in teaching at the Business School.[22]

Interaction between generations always interested Mayo. When he first undertook the study of psychology in Adelaide he had been attracted to eugenics because it promised help in deciding who was fit, psychologically, to undertake political leadership in modern democracy. The promise was never kept, and the idea that control could be exercised through biogenic selection of authorities became discredited. Nevertheless, Mayo maintained a passing interest in eugenics, and in September 1930 when he was visiting Pitt-Rivers in Dorset he accepted an invitation to meet with the International Federation of Eugenic Organizations and to introduce a film, "The Evolution of Social Consciousness."[23]

By 1931 most Harvard Business School faculty had become concerned about the business depression. Mayo set down his ideas in *Economic*

Hygiene, a report that included four essays: "The Problem of the Administrator," "Economic Stability and the Standard of Living," "Economic Health and Balance," and "Economic Hygiene." Mayo sent copies to the Rockefeller Foundation, and to Arthur Young and Joseph Willits.[24] In April 1931 Mayo addressed the Industrial Relations Association (Chicago) on human factors related to economic stability.[25]

"The Problem of the Administrator" quotes extensively from *Theory of Revolution* by Brooks Adams, argues for raising administrators' intelligence to the level of other major occupations, and goes as far as to suggest that the business depression was caused by "the inferiority of . . . administrative intelligence." Mayo distinguished between two kinds of scientist: those who develop knowledge logically according to precise rules, methods, and techniques, and those with a broader view, who look on science as an adventure. He applied the distinction to administrators: sound administrators need some scientific training and experience at first, but later, if they are to be effective, they must be alert to the new, the changing, and the half-known, and the continuing need for fresh enquiries. The ideal man would be "capable of any intensive study [which] the situation may demand but with undimmed perception of the relevant facts at the experiental level." The tasks allocated to such men are to make decisions when precise knowledge is lacking, recommend action without knowing its full effect, and act on premises they know are insufficient or wrong. Such men must be alert to symptoms of error in their decisions, be constant in their method so they learn from it, and maintain normality in social and economic development. Mayo placed great importance on these attributes and tasks of the administrator, recommended them to the Western Electric management, and repeated them in his Lowell lectures.[26]

"Economic Stability and the Standard of Living," published for distribution to the Business School alumni in the summer of 1931, was the main part of Mayo's address of July 1932 to a London meeting of the International Management Institute. The paper was translated into French in 1933. When it was published it included the main ideas from the other two parts of the report, "Economic Health and Balance" and "Economic Hygiene." He used the ideas for several addresses in the United States and England.[27]

Mayo asked what external, noneconomic factors determined the imbalance between production and consumption in the depressed American economy. He looked to France first, and showed that its economy had resisted depression better than had either the British or American. The French economy was relatively stable because its industry had developed slowly and retained the nation's social determinants of living standards; American industry had grown rapidly, abolished the social standards of living, replaced them with the compulsions of advertisers and salesmen, and, consequently, produced goods for individual display rather than goods with a stable social function. The business depression was a result of a declining demand for goods that individuals use for show—cars, fur coats, candy, fountain pens, and so on—and that do not always bring an increase in the standard of living. Such materialistic industrialism, abetted by mass production methods, discounted individuality, and, as anthropological and sociological studies in cities like Chicago showed, social pathologies and personal disorganization ensued and thus led to an imbalance in the relation of consumption to production.

Mayo explained the imbalance by using his thesis on the social consequences of rapid industrializaton. Before such industrialization, although travel and intellectual growth were restricted, people lived a full communal life and served a necessary social function. After industrialization labor became highly mobile, families lived in temporary quarters, travel to work used much more time, apartment life restricted the family's physical world, and every five years the neighborhood population changed. All of these factors affected internal markets because people began to purchase for material gain rather than for social use and enjoyment. The production of material goods rose as people began to use them to compensate for the disintegration of communal life. Mayo asserted: "The demand for material goods as a substitute for social values is not indicative of a high but of a low standard of living" and implies uneven economic growth. A satisfactory market cannot be found in a poorly ordered community, because its members have become highly susceptible to persuasive advertising and calamitous rumors, and act as if they lived in a state of either high prosperity or deep depression. As a general conclusion, Mayo stated any diminution of social integration leads to a retraction of socially required expenditure and so converts what was necessary income into surplus for extravagant use and excessive speculation on stock exchanges. Mayo recommended that society should give as much attention to organizing consumption and the social problems of economic stability as it does to financing and producing goods and services.[28]

Anthropology and sociology have much to contribute to the understanding of economic behavior, Mayo believed, and action should follow from that understanding. He wrote a short paper on such action, "The Dynamic Pose," which distinguishes dynamic or latent capacity for action from energia, or actuality of action. The dynamic pose is found in business, art, and science. Mayo considered the dynamic pose was false and condemned the professional who adopts a dynamic pose, pretending to be knowledgeable and wise when he is not. But the falsity of the dynamic pose lies not so much with man himself as with the popular attitude to the field of study. Mayo used economics as his example, for this was the field of study that it was widely believed would eliminate business depression. The dynamic pose had been foisted on the economist by promoters of popular opinion. Mayo asserted that scientific study, not popular opinion, should underpin the economist's ideas, and that only scientific research could show how valid were the assumptions that economic theory makes about human nature and social organization.[29]

In the summer of 1928 Mayo planned to visit Britain. He had not been there since 1905. He wanted to see Bernard Hart, London's leading psychopathologist, and Dr. Charles S. Myers of the National Institute of Industrial Psychology (N.I.I.P.), "a personal friend . . . interested in our . . . diverse approaches to" industrial inquiries. He planned to return to the Working Men's College, where he had taught, to collaborate on adult education policies among workers with Albert Mainsbridge, whom he had met in Queensland. Mayo hoped to have discussions at the London School of Economics with Malinowski, and at University College with A. V. Hill, the physiologist; to renew his acquaintance with Sir Matthew Nathan, former Governor of Queensland, and discuss industrial questions in the United States, England, and Australia; to canvass work done by the British Industrial Fatigue Research Board; and to visit Jean Piaget in Geneva and Pierre Janet in Paris.[30] The plan was too ambitious. He did not stay long enough to visit Janet and Piaget; Hart and Mainsbridge were unavailable; and he did not see the Working Men's College.

The travel plan was a response to several pressures that had arisen in 1928. Mayo's research was not advancing as he had expected,[31] and, by extending associations abroad, he hoped his local reputation would grow and he could gain the cooperation of industry. By contrast, Henderson's work was progressing—the new laboratory had just been named, "the Fatigue Laboratory"[32]—and Hetty, Mayo's mother, had written of the Adelaide family members' successes and her high hopes for her eldest son's future. She wanted copies of his lectures, books and articles, something tangible to show for what he was doing at Harvard, but she also wanted him to go "home" to England. "I think I should like it better if you were in England than in America other things being equal. . . . I hope the new Chair at Harvard is making itself felt. . . . It would be a joy if you would go home to England in a short time and stir them up."[33]

Mayo tried to do as Hetty wanted. In his report on the English visit, Mayo listed the many firm and important associations he had made.[34] At the insistence of Sir William Beveridge, Mayo was made an honorary member of the Senior Common Room, London School of Economics, and thus enjoyed the privileges of faculty at the University of London. He renewed acquaintances with Malinowski and Pitt-Rivers; associated with Westermarck, J.G. Frazer, Seligman, Marcel Mauss, and Sir Arthur Keith; worked with Myers and Miles of N.I.I.P.; lunched with Sidney Webb, Allyn Young, and Harold Laski; held discussions with fatigue researchers Eric Farmer, May Smith, Millais Culpin, and, D.R. Wilson and spoke at a special meeting of the British Psychological Association.

In the years to come Mayo would travel to Europe every summer, and on returning give his Cambridge colleagues and young associates a deep impression that in Europe he was well connected, particularly within Britain's aristocratic circles and among academics.[35] Because he had enjoyed so much regular contact with these people, Mayo could report on many aspects of British work in anthropology, sociology, and economics; developments in medical and industrial psychology; the appropriateness of his thesis on the changes to society that accompanied rapid industrialization; the importance of equilibrium both within the organism and in relation to its environment; psychopathological inquiries; and the recent developments in psychoanalysis and related psychologies.

At the end of his report Mayo compared British work with a study he had recently joined at the Hawthorne Works of Chicago's Western Electric Company. George Pennock, the officer in charge of the study, had reported on a year's observation of five girls at work. He found that when they were in a state of organic equilibrium their production was high. After rest pauses and proper diet, organic equilibrium improved, production rose, variability of output fell, and the girls' mental and physical health improved. Mayo was reminded of what he had been told in 1915 by a Labour politician in Queensland: fatigue among workers leads to morbid preoccupations and class consciousness, and is followed by diminishing interest in work and job skills. Mayo believed that Pennock's research illustrated what could be done when fatigue was eliminated, and showed that it was better for production and for workers when supervisors listened attentively to subordinates.[36]

The month in Britain served personal ends also. He learned the sad news that Malinowski's wife Elsie was afflicted with multiple sclerosis. Pitt-Rivers entertained Mayo royally but showed little interest in his work—apparently because it was being done in the United States rather than England. Mayo had the impression that Sir Matthew Nathan held the same attitude.

Ambivalent attitudes and associated preoccupations emerged during Mayo's absence from Dorothea. He bought new clothes, and was pleased to find a jeweler to repair his late father's watch but he loathed spending the money. He looked forward to visiting Dorothea's relatives, but when he was with them he found their company more dull than entertaining. In a restaurant he enjoyed playful persiflage with two "ladies-of-the-street," but his black anger rose when he remembered how uncivilized was the society that had produced such human distress.

He heard gossip about the intimate life of noted psychologists, the background to factions among anthropologists, and the details of the Savidge Case (indecent exposure combined with zealous police work). He attended plays, movies, horse races, and a risque musical: "I'd never seen so many naked feminine legs" he wrote to Dorothea. After an informal meeting of industrial psychologists he enjoyed tackling the criticism of his ideas; and at dinner with Ruml listened patiently to the exasperation of a man who felt harassed by the demands from Britons for nothing more from him but Rockefeller's money. At the end of June Mayo sailed to Nova Scotia for a short holiday with Dorothea and the girls and to write his report on his first month in London since 1905.[37]

For three years in Boston, Mayo's family life was normal. In September 1926 he had brought the family from a holiday at Les Eboulements in Quebec to live in Cambridge at 11 Trail Street. After a year they moved to 43 Larch Street. In the summer of 1929 this house was vacated when Dorothea and he took Gael and Patricia to Europe. On the boat the girls were told they were unlikely to return because they would be going to school in England.

The girls where to be educated at Bedales, a progressive school. Dorothea, an anglophile, was determined her daughters would not be raised as Americans. Also, she was fifty-three that summer and did not have sufficient patience to deal with teenage girls. She feared she might reproduce her past miserable family life by becoming a domineering matriarch and dispensing adult tasks to adolescents. And she wanted to further her intellectual interests. So Dorothea persuaded Mayo that better opportunities existed for the girls' proper education in England, and in summer they could join them for a holiday in the hotels of Europe. At the end of every summer the girls would cry when the leaves began to turn because they were reminded that their two months of regular family life were coming to an end.[38]

Notes

1. Osborne Reports, February, May 1929, March, April 1930, January, February, April 1931.
2. Miscellaneous notes, 1927-28, MM 2. 019.
3. MM 2.019.
4. MM 3.056, MM 3.060, MM 3.099, MM 1.099.
5. MM 3.052-3.
6. Halbkrain to Mayo, 20 October 1926-24 November 1929, MM 3.031.
7. Elton Mayo, "Industrial Fatigue Studies," or "Fatigue in Industry," Winter 1926-27, MM 2.033.
8. Elton Mayo, "Surrey Textile Company," Harvard Business Reports 4 (1927): 100-15.
9. Boston Herald, 17 March 1927.
10. Mayer to Mayo, 27 May 1929, MM 1.105.
11. Elton Mayo, "The Scientific Approach to Industrial Relations," Proceedings of Y.M.C.A. Conference on Human Relations in Industry, September 1927, pp. 19-23.
12. Elton Mayo, "The Maladjustment of the Industrial Worker," in Wertheim Lectures in Industrial Relations, ed. O.S. Berger et al. (Cambridge: Harvard University Press, 1928), pp. 165-96.
13. Elton Mayo , "The Practical Outcome of Psychopathology," address, Industrial Section, British Psychological Association, 21 June 1928, MM 2.019.

14. Elton Mayo, "What Is Monotony?" *Human Factor* 5 (1919): 3-4.
15. Elton Mayo, "The Approach to Psychological Investigation" (transcript), Social Sciences Research Council's Hanover Conference, August 27, 1926, pp. 401-32, MM 2.007.
16. Elton Mayo, "Obsessions in Students" (transcript), address, First Colloquium in Personality Investigation, New York, December 1928, MM 2. 028.
17. Elton Mayo, "The Place of the Father in the Present Day Home" (transcript) , MM 2.045, MM 3.059.
18. Elton Mayo, "The Dynamics of Family Relations," *Child Study,* May 1927, p. 6.
19. *Boston Herald,* 17 September 1927, MM 1.060; *Northampton Gazette,* 23 September 1927, GC 563, BLA.
20. Osborne Reports, March, April 1929, April 1930, GB 2.563, BLA.
21. Mayo to Woods, 23 September 1928, MM 1.100.
22. Elton Mayo, "Sin with a Capital 'S'," *Harper's* 154 (1927): 537-45; excerpts, HP 267, BLA.
23. *Western Gazette* (Dorset, England), 19 September 1930, MM 1.060.
24. Elton Mayo, "Harvard University—Economic Research Report on Economic Hygiene," n.d., RF; Young to Mayo, 27 March 1931, MM 1.104; Willits to Mayo, 25 March 1931, MM 1.099.
25. *Daily News* (Chicago), 15 April 1931.
26. Mayo to Pennock, 9 February 1931, MM 1.090; Elton Mayo, *The Problems of an Industrial Civilization* (New York: Macmillan, 1933).
27. Elton Mayo, "Economic Stability and the Standard of Living," *Harvard Business School Alumni Bulletin* 7, no. 6 (1931): 290-94; Elton Mayo, "The Study of Consumption and Markets," *Bulletin of the International Management Institute* 6, no 11 (1932): 3-15; Elton Mayo, "La Stabilité Economique et le 'Standard of Living'," *Travail Humain* (Paris) 1 (1933): 49-55; *Daily News* (Chicago), 15 April 1931; *Oak Leaves Weekly* (Oak Park, Ill.), 17 April 1931.
28. Mayo, "Economic Stabilty and the Standard of Living."
29. Elton Mayo, "The Dynamic Pose," *Harvard Business School Alumni Bulletin* 9, no. 3 (1933): 95-97.
30. Mayo to Biddle, 6 April 1928; Mayo to Biddle, 11 April 1938; Elton to Dorothea, 15 May-26 June 1928.
31. Osborne to Donham, 14 June 1928, MM 3.071.
32. Henderson to Ruml, 31 March 1928, RF.
33. Hetty to Elton, 17 April 1928, MM 1.007.
34. Mayo to Donham, 25 September 1928, RF.
35. Conversation with Homans, 3 June 1975.
36. Conversation with Homans, 3 June 1974.
37. Elton to Dorothea, 15 May-26 June 1928.
38. Mayo to Donham, 9 September 1926, AFFDI; Anon. to Dorothea, 14 August 1929, MM 1.004; conversation with Gael Mayo, 12 February, 22 July 1975; conversation with Patricia Elton Mayo, January 1975.

14

Mayo at the Hawthorne Works: 1928-1931

This chapter describes industrial research in the test rooms, interviewing employees and supervisors, and the bank wiring observation room at the Hawthorne Works of the Western Electric Company in Cicero, Illinois, and how, between 1928 and 1931, Mayo advised the researchers and helped them bring their work to the attention of industrialists and social scientists in the United States and Europe.

The Western Electric Company, manufacturer of telephone equipment at its Hawthorne Works, had a policy of high wages and good working conditions for employees and of using modern placement techniques. For twenty years before the research began, managers considered general morale was high among employees and the incidence of industrial conflict infrequent.[1]

In collaboration with the National Research Council the company studied the relation between intensity of illumination at work and the output of workers. No simple direct relation appeared because many psychological factors interfered. To control them, especially the factor of fatigue, researchers asked six girls to work in a test room away from their regular department; to be subject to changes in working hours, rest pauses, and other conditions; and to have their comments on work recorded while their output was measured. The girls agreed. Five girls assembled telephone relays, one supplied the parts. For five years, beginning April 1927, accurate records were kept of the number of relays made, temperature and humidity of the test room, medical and personal histories, eating and sleeping habits, and snatches of conversation on the job. No one supervised the girls; instead a test room observer, and later his assistants, kept records, arranged work, and tried to keep up the spirit of cooperation among the girls. The girls were told to work as they felt and at a comfortable pace, and only with their consent would changes be made in their work.

First, the researchers measured productive capacity by recording the girls' output for two weeks before the test-room study began. Then, for the first five weeks no changes at work were made so that the mere effect on output of being transferred was known. At the third stage, a pay system was introduced that ensured each girl's earnings were in proportion to her efforts, thereby centering her financial interests on the study. Eight weeks later, two five-minute rest pauses—one at 10 A.M., the other at 2 P.M.—were introduced; subsequently they were extended to ten minutes, then six five-minute rests were established. Next, the girls were given a light lunch in the mid-morning and afternoon rest pauses. In the eighth phase, the workday ended a half-hour early; in the ninth, the girls finished work an hour earlier than usual. In phase ten, work conditions returned to what they had been. Then a five-day week was introduced and it ran through the summer of 1928. Results showed an unexpected gradual rise in daily output. The researchers, believing that something other than the changes had affected the output, asked the girls if they would return to the original work conditions, i.e., no pauses or lunches and a full work week. The girls agreed, and for twelve weeks output declined, but not to its original level.

The researchers expected that if output rate were directly related to the physical conditions of work, then identical conditions would produce similar output rates. Instead, the girls' output rate rose from one phase of the study to the next. It remained on a high plateau until the depression ended the study in 1933. Detailed analysis of the data would show that there may be an association between output and physical environment in extreme conditions, but within the limits of the test room physical changes appeared to have no definite effect on output rate.

Why? The girls' comments recorded during work offered an answer. They knew that without consciously putting themselves to it they where producing more in the test room than they had elsewhere. Also, they valued the idea of doing work that might lead to improving their fellow employees' working conditions. Moreover they liked not being supervised. In time friendships grew and continued after work. The girls made a ceremony of their regular medical examinations by having the company serve ice cream and cake, they celebrated birthdays, and helped any one among them who was fatigued. Also, leadership developed, centering in one ambitious member. Researchers concluded that changes in output could be attributed to changes not only in work conditions but also work attitudes and social relations.

In the test room the girls' attitudes to work differed from those in the original workplace because there supervisors had been particularly irksome. But managers had thought the supervisors quite capable. Because of this sharp difference, the researchers decided to interview many employees, and from specific questions learn attitudes toward company policy and supervisory methods in the hope the information would improve supervisor training.

In September 1928, eight months after the test-room studies had begun, the interviewing of five supervisors in the Inspection Branch was initiated. Completed early in 1929, results were so useful that interviewing was extended to the Operations Branch. On February 1, 1929, the Division of

Industrial Research was founded to interview all forty thousand employees to discover attitudes toward work, to correct causes of discontent and enhance favorable work conditions, and to study fatigue, efficiency, and employee relations. By 1930 over half the employees had been interviewed and the team of interviewers had grown to about thirty.

Workers and supervisors accepted the interviewing. Workers enjoyed the opportunity to express their feelings and ideas about their work; such expression often allowed discharge of irrational impulses, and consequently attitudes toward work became more accepting and tolerant. Supervisors found they were not embarrassed or fearful of the interviewers' findings, but instead learned much about effective supervision when the transcripts were used for training.

Interviewers found their specific questions were frequently unrelated to opinions workers wanted to express, and that worker comments were often merely subjective views about individuals and situations rather than objective and accurate statements. So the interviewers' noting of replies to questions about what was liked and disliked about work gave over to directed conversations, recorded *verbatim,* following topics chosen by the interviewees. Consequently, a seemingly quiet interviewee would become talkative, and another would become unexpectedly preoccupied with a single topic. The preoccupations were like obsessions or compulsions of the mentally ill; many workers who complained of feeling overtired seemed to think like obsessives: no control of reflective thought, compulsive rituals, indecisiveness, elaborate reasons for not acting, complaints of nervous tension, and anxiety about nothing specific. Often interviewers could trace problems to home life as well as to work conditions.

Researchers saw that responses in interviews were the result of the individuals' social lives, e.g., families, communities, and work group. Interviews showed employees followed their own practices at work, e.g., a standard daily output, rules for punishing workers who exceeded or failed to meet the standard, leaders who united workers and enforced standards, and clear beliefs about the futility of promotion and the domineering manner of supervisors. So, in May 1931, interviewers were assigned to particular work groups and talked with each member frequently. Results were surprising. Whereas managers had always believed specific tasks were difficult to master, workers had found them easy to learn and considered themselves clever to have fooled the managers. To do this the workers had formed groups in which one man had the task of keeping visiting managers ignorant and an other man of teaching new members how to restrict their production. And the group supervisor had no real authority over the men's work practices. And most members were dissatisfied because they thought it futile to be serving opposed interests.

To study social norms and satisfaction the Division of Industrial Research assembled a work group of fourteen men that from early December

1931 to May occupied a special room and wired banks of telephone exchange terminals. An investigator noted what the men said and did. At first
the men formed two friendship groups that together undermined wage
incentive systems that assumed employees work to maximize pay and pressured fellow employees to cooperate toward this end. But the workers restricted output for fear of management's lowering the pay rate, demanded a
minimum of output from one another to stop some workers from being
paid for work they did not do, and allowed no worker to behave officiously
toward a fellow worker or say anything to supervisors that might affect any
worker's standing on the job. Anyone breaking the rules was punched on
the upper arm or insulted. Also, management's assignment of employees to
jobs according to skill was violated; men swapped jobs and otherwise
helped each other. Accounting controls were broken when the group chief
recorded claims for pay that the men were not legally entitled to make.

Researchers believed that the workers' actions were logically related not
to the technical but to the social organization of work; and that changes in
the technical organization often attacked routines of human association
that give value to work. In response, workers protected themselves against
such attacks with what appeared to be illogical sentiments and practices.

Work for the girls in the test room differed from that of the men in the
observation room. The girls had no close supervision, and always had the
chance to originate and participate in decisions affecting their work; the
men were under close supervision, disliked it, and were never given the
chance to participate in decisions about their tasks. The researchers concluded that different social relations within the two groups helped explain
why the girls cooperated to raise output while the men collaborated to
restrict it.

In 1932 the business depression ended most of the research at the
Hawthorne Works, but in January 1936 the researchers were able to begin
with a new approach. They proposed a counseling program based on what
had been learned from the interviews. It aimed to study personnel problems, to give nonauthoritative support to employees and supervisors in
understanding individuals' difficulties, and to provide managers with information on how relevant their practices and policies were to those of the
work groups under them. The study would be done through counselors. By
April 1936 the program was in place. Recent college graduates and high
school graduates were hired and trained for the position of counselor or
"personnel man" in each department. The counselor assumed none of the
supervisor's duties; he helped both supervisors and workers to speak freely
with him, and he treated personal information in confidence.

Initial resistance to the counselors was overcome when they dispelled
fears about the anonymity of interview material, forestalled objections that
they would duplicate the functions of union representatives, and allayed
anxieties that they constituted a spy system to help managers oppose

worker demands. In consequence, the counselors were free to help individuals adjust to personal problems at work and home, to give supervisors an appreciation of those difficulties, and provide general information about employees' feelings and activities that managers could incorporate in the firm's policies.

Following his talk to The Lunchers on psychology in industry, Mayo received a letter in March 1928 from the Western Electric Company comptroller of manufacturing, T. K. Stevenson,[2] enclosing a copy of the report on the six girls' work in the test room and asking for comments. From data collected during the first seven periods of the study, the researchers could see that as rest periods were introduced Theresa Layman and Ladislas Blazijak produced consistently more and more relays; Anna Haug had kept her output at an even level, and then raised it suddenly after her vacation, and continued at the higher level; Adeline Bogotowicz and Irene Rybacki had similar output records that fell, rose, jumped suddenly, and later dropped. The differences could not easily be explained. Relations with supervisors, friendships, differences between tasks, and organic variations among the girls all played a part.

Mayo's task was to see if organic differences could explain variations in output. He thought the Addis Index, a measure of pulse product, indicated organic differences because it varied with oxygen consumed for tasks requiring muscular effort or attentiveness and during emotional arousal. Such energy levels were determined by the individual's constitution, demands of the task, and food intake. When pulse product was related to output, four types of worker emerge: worker under strain—high pulse product and high output; sluggish worker—low pulse product and low output; fatigued worker—high pulse product and low output; and efficient worker—low pulse product and high output.[3]

Dissatisfied with his previous attempts to establish industrial research in New England, Mayo was hoping that late in 1928, when he returned from the summer in Europe, he would be able to "secure a convenient niche in the industrial structure from which to push investigations and experiments." For this reason Mayo was strongly attracted to the problem at the Hawthorne Works.[4]

On April 25 and 26 Mayo, Osborne, and Lovekin took blood pressure readings of Layman, Blazijak, Haug, and two new girls who had joined the group, Mary Volango and Jenny Sirchio. Also, readings were taken of three girls in the coil winding department: Mary Ganski, Eloinia Markovitch, and Allika Kacikek.[5] Bogotowicz and Rybacki had been asked to leave the test room because of uncooperative behavior. A few days later Mayo wrote to Ruml, "Once again the highest producer was . . . [Sirchio] who achieved an organic equilibrium—and kept it."[6] The report was more cautious. Although the researchers had expected that a low steady index—a desirable state of equilibrium—would be associated with high output, no constant relation between the two variables emerged. Results showed that all operators were working well within their physical capacities, and that differences among them could be attributed to variations in work habits and differences in constitution generally.[7]

Mayo's results could not be used to explain the unexpected uncooperative behavior of Bogotowicz and Rybacki. The former had married, and after being dropped from the study and taking an assembler's position elsewhere in the plant, left the company in August. Rybacki had lost interest in her home life and work during the months leading up to Bogotowicz's marriage. Both girls' output had fallen, and the other girls teased her about it, and she became irritated. Also, despite the assurance of company officials to the contrary, she began to believe her friends whom she had left in the regular department when they told her that the test-room study was a management scheme to maximize profits. In management's eyes she turned "Bolshie," and in December 1927 was asked by George Pennock, assistant works manager, and his associate Mark Putnam to explain her change in attitude. She could not, complained of fatigue, and said she wanted to leave the study. Ten weeks later when Mayo visited the Hawthorne Works, he asked to see her medical report, noticed immediately that she had symptoms of secondary anemia, and suggested referral to one of the company doctors. He put her on a special diet, and a two-week vacation was planned for her in the summer. Her blood count improved, and she regained weight and began to take a positive interest in life at home. She continued as an assembler in the regular department until she quit the company in September 1930 for health reasons about five months after her marriage.[8]

During his first visit Mayo discussed general personnel issues with Pennock, and made some suggestions for which Pennock was grateful. Mayo was assured that in November he would be sent further blood pressure readings when the rest pauses and the girls' lunches had been discontinued.[9]

In September 1928, on his way back from observing industrial problems in Colorado, Mayo spent two days at the Hawthorne Works. He learned from Pennock that the research was being extended to include an interview inquiry into the effects of various supervisors on the preoccupations of workers. Mayo thought that such a radical approach could lead to changes in the company's policy on supervision. He read the most recent progress report, and wrote to Pennock that his study "will be almost a classic in the literature of industrial investigation," suggested that Osborne go to the Hawthorne Works as an observer, and recommended the research be published at a conference to be held by Walter Bingham's Personnel Research Federation early in December.[10] Pennock agreed, and added that the interviewing and the use of conference groups to train supervisors was rapidly producing good results.[11]

In January 1929, Pennock told Mayo that over the next two years the company planned to spend $200,000 on a scheme to interview all employees at the Hawthorne Works. Results would be used to identify unsatisfactory working conditions and to train supervisors.[12] Early in March Mayo visited Pennock to consider the method and the theory of interviewing, and to propose that indirect methods of interviewing be adopted.[13] Pennock wanted Mayo to join the firm and take full responsibility for the interviewing program, but Mayo declined, saying that he preferred his present position because, although he might have to earn extra money with occasional lectures and magazine articles, he enjoyed the freedom of academic life and had no mind for the "unpleasant emergencies of earning" that employment elsewhere often required. He told Pennock that Industrial Relations Counselors gave him an annual retainer for his services, but rather than have Western Electric Company follow suit, he proposed it simply bear the expense of his occasional visits, during which he would "extend and intensify your enquiries . . . help to train your interviewers," adding, "I have in fact done this in many places." Pennock agreed and began building his team of interviewers, while Mayo prepared an evaluation on the work done so far.[14]

Mayo's evaluation centered on the interview, and argued that training in how to interview would produce "an entirely superior technique of selecting and training administrators."[15] To support his approach, he offered a long quotation from Brooks Adams's *The Theory of Revolution* but replaced the word "capital" with "manager," "businessman," "industrialist," and "employer." Mayo preferred an interview technique that required the interviewer to listen sympathetically, to probe for information rather than ask for it directly, and to follow the course of the respondent's interests rather than the concerns of the interviewer. Two months later, in July 1929, the interviewing method was changed along the lines that Mayo had suggested.

Mayo could see that all the interviewers were capable of following the ideas he was advocating; some understood from firsthand experience the indirect interview style, but most were badly confused as to the precise research objectives. He recommended that all interviewers adopt his suggestion, and then, in time, their own preoccupations about the aim of the research would diminish. In fact, the vagueness of purpose was, to Mayo, a sign of good health in research. Taking as his authorities, Poincaré and Peirce, he asserted that scientific inquiry follows a question, and as it does so, the question changes. If the question does not change, then inquiry becomes merely a technical exercise and no longer of scientific interest. Feelings of awkwardness, doubt, ambiguity, impatience all come before a new illumination casts itself on an inquiry. Mayo wanted the researchers to keep in mind two questions: How are production, organic balance, and mental attitude related? And, what does that relation hold for industry? Mental attitudes could be explored through nondirected interviews, while organic balance could be assessed through extending the experimental work to more groups and refining the technique of continuous pulse-product measurement during the working day.[16] Lovekin took up the second task, while Mayo worked to have his views on interview technique take hold.

In September 1929 the influence of Mayo's views extended at the Hawthorne Works when he accepted Pennock's invitation to address company executives on his evaluation of the Hawthorne research. But Mayo's obsessive cycle of personal doubts was turning. Weeks before, he felt that he had spoken poorly at several meetings; a few days earlier at the Silver Bay conference on industrial relations he had been cheered each time he rose to speak. Now, exhausted, sweating, and grimy from hours of train travel he was entering a heat wave that had engulfed Chicago. Would he be able to show the old spontaneity? Did he have the capacity to push the audience before him? The cycle of self doubts had begun when, at summer's end, he sailed to Boston leaving Dorothea in England to help the girls with their first few weeks schooling at Bedales. Also he had recently been promoted to a tenured professorship at Harvard. So he feared for his family's welfare, was anxious to meet the new and unclear expectations from his colleagues, and wondered if he could hold his audience at Hawthorne. "There is at the back of my mind a loss that is perpetual and an anxiety for the letter I cannot get until Chicago . . . if I wasn't moving actively, I should go morbid. . . . If Chicago goes well, then we are ready for the year."[17]

Chicago did go well. On his first night Mayo dined with Pennock and Fred W. Willard, the personnel director. The next day Mayo received princely treatment:

> At 8:30 the doorman clears the taxis away from the Wabash Street entrance of this hotel [The Palmer House] and a large limousine with a uniformed chauffeur slides noiselessly in. The door is opened and Elton Mayo, formerly of South Australia, gets in and glides off to his alleged industrial researches. At 5:45 in the evening the event is repeated—the large limousine glides in and the afore-said E.M. gets out after his alleged industrial researches. The door snaps shut, someone says 'Good night, Sir'—and the porters and the doormen grievously misjudge E.M.'s financial (and therefore social) status. The . . . Western Electric Co. . . . are very nice to me—and the work is going very well. My apprehensiveness . . . the superstitions of an obsessive . . . were groundless . . . after all.[18]

The industrial Research Division had been established in February 1929 with Mark Putnam as its chief, and a well-educated and intelligent staff to be responsible for interviewing, analysis of interview data, training of supervisors, and experimental studies of employee reactions and efficiency. Mayo was concerned in all these functions, but on this visit was expected to discuss the new interviewing technique, and help the interviewers understand the value of replacing interrogation with indirect questioning and sympathetic listening. The interview program had been such a success in a short time that the plan to interview the forty thousand Chicago employees was extended to include twenty thousand more at the Kearney plant in New Jersey. "So we are affecting the lives of 60,000 people already," he wrote to Dorothea. Also a new series of experiments was planned that would use "the Piaget Method," which meant "taking down any remark that a worker makes, and . . . comparing preoccupations with production."[19]

On personal as well as technical grounds Mayo's relations were beginning to become stable at Hawthorne. He had been asked to talk with Pennock's teenage son, whose low grades at college were putting his education at risk. Mayo quickly identified poor study techniques and advised on how to improve them; the youth worked better and was allowed to continue at college. A year later Mayo would arrange medical aid and counseling for him in Boston. Also, Pennock liked Mayo personally, and tried again to entice him to join the firm, but without success.[20]

The September visit was the first of three in 1929 that would secure for Mayo the niche he wanted in the American industrial structure. But success brought back the painful doubts of childhood. At first he enjoyed a heightened sense of personal worth; he wanted that, but as soon as he began to enjoy it the doubt swiftly returned. Early in his working life the doubts had weighed heavily; in the United States he lifted them by writing to Dorothea. No matter how successful his achievements, the doubts merely changed form and would never be banished because he was ashamed of needing Dorothea to assuage the moral anxiety that gave rise to them.

> I have to struggle with the sort of superstitious reluctance to admit that all goes well—those people who believe they did well to shake my 'self confidence' in childhood were gravely mistaken. Of course I fought back and in some degree perhaps conquered. But even now—and in success rather than failure, the doubts returned . . . it is shameful to inflict this on you—except that my dear lady should know all there is of me.[21]

While in Chicago, Mayo was consulted by C.G. Stoll, vice president of Western Electric, on the management of time lost among office workers. Mayo had no opportunity to study any specific instances, but, flushed with the success from discussions with Pennock and Putnam, and their associates, he considered the problem to be one of inadequate supervisors, and suggested presenting them with the problem and having them discuss frankly the alternative methods for using time in the office.[22]

In October Mayo returned to the Hawthorne Works to discuss with 250 division chiefs of the company the methods of employee control that he had introduced to the staff in the Industrial Research Division a month before. This was his first meeting with the senior executives. He sat with

Stoll, C.G. Rice, manager of the Hawthorne Works, Pennock, Putnam, and the senior doctor. Two hundred of "the most hard bitten and experienced engineers in the country" constituted his audience, he wrote to Dorothea.[23] Surrounded by microphones Mayo spoke at high speed for ninety minutes without faltering, and drew on many humorous images and stories to build a theme on the value of administering work with human understanding and insight that comes from effective listening and careful observation of employees. It seemed to Mayo that he held the audience. For the next few days he was cross-questioned by the "hard-bitten" executives in small groups, and by Putnam's staff, who asked for advice on two difficult cases.

The October visit had three important results. First, it raised the status of Pennock and Putnam in the company especially when Rice publicly supported their past research. Second, it left Mayo with the impression that he was at the center of a great change in industrial administration.[24]

> I have come to the conclusion that we are 'sitting in' at a major revolution in industrial method—a revolution that will probably be as far reaching in its ultimate effect as the so called industrial revolution of the latter eighteenth century. I really think that the work has just assumed this magnitude—or threatens to do so shortly. It is amazing—the effect of the interview programme (when backed by courage, intelligence and energy.)[25]

This paragraph to Dorothea became the main point in a letter to Pennock that Mayo wrote immediately on his return to Cambridge. He thought that although the revolutionary changes would have humane rather than mechanical implications for industry, they would deal more precisely than ever before with human problems of industrial civilization, raise self-control, and diminish irrational and unnecessary conflict. Why? First, the workers approved of the interviewing because they believed their morale and sense of cooperation with the company improved with the opportunity to state their complaints and see some of them removed. Second, the test-room researches showed that work performance, personal health, and individual morale all benefited when methods of control were altered and interviewing was continuous. Mayo's favorite illustration was an operator from a group of mica-splitters who, during a talk on her unhappy home life, decided to quit living with her mother; she began to produce more at work, and then when she had to return home to nurse mother, her output fell. The guiding principle, which Mayo himself had lived through and was now abstracting from the research findings, was that everywhere, from medical clinics to industrial workshops, mental health varies with the association between one's preoccupations and actions; as soon as one decides to act instead of pitying oneself, life improves and work becomes productive. And Mayo liked to cite the case of "even a Bolshevik" who agreed with his view on the proper changes in methods of control: "If all fear of bully-ragging can be taken out of supervision, and if a majority of supervisors are trained interviewers . . . industry will enter upon a new and undreamed era of active collaboration that will make possible and almost incredible human advance."[26]

The third result of Mayo's October visit was better interviewers. They began to understand the purpose of their work, which a month earlier had been vague, directionless, and worrisome. They saw that when the interviewee was encouraged to control the course of the interview, this improved the interviewer's own technique of eliciting information and enhanced his grasp of its pattern. Putnam, himself, had had such experiences, and Mayo could see that he now believed the Industrial Research Division's work was objectively valuable where once it had seemed nebulous, with little to contribute.

In teaching how to interview at work, Mayo gave a simple set of instructions taken from the introduction to Jean Piaget's *The Child's Conception of the World* and from Andreas Bjerre's *Psychology of Murder*. The method was a clinical sociological technique that Mayo assumed would be appropriate to the tasks of administrators, social scientists, and scholars. The instructions that he set down for the interviewers at Hawthorne covered two main elements: rules to guide the interviewer, and patterns to note in the respondent's life.

The rules were: give full attention to the interviewee, and make it evident that you are doing so; listen and do not talk; never argue or give advice; listen for what the interviewer wants to say, does not want to say, and cannot say without help; as you listen, plot tentatively and for subsequent correction the pattern that is being set before you, and to test the pattern summarize cautiously and clearly what has been said without twisting it; treat what is said in confidence.

From following the penultimate rule, a pattern emerges that shows the relation between the person's present beliefs and past experiences. To complete the pattern the interviewer should ask about the person's family of origin—neighborhood, economic and social prestige, geographical and social mobility—and personal life, i.e., relations with family members, friends at school and work, and effects of illness on social life. Questions should center on habitual preoccupations and assumptions, and these should be related to events in the person's life, whether or not he is solitary, and if so, by preference or circumstance. Other questions should elicit his rituals, i.e., his nonlogical social skills, his social mana based on his unique skills, and his irrational or obsessive compulsions that constitute his social rituals. Estimates should be made of the proportional balance between these three in a day, and ultimately of the person's degree of independence or dependence in relations with others.

The teaching staff in the Industrial Research Division would use Mayo's ideas to give weight to the instructions that their pupils were expected to follow; "(Until Doctor Mayo came along the interview was used mainly for supervisory training and research, but) . . . as we know, he revealed what seems to be the greatest use of all—emotional release . . . the employee is given freedom to unburden himself and a chance to express his thoughts."

In addition to laying out the technical procedure for "catharsis," Mayo told how the modern theories of abnormal psychology related to the interviewing technique. He taught the various psychoses and psychoneuroses, and drew attention to obsessions, compulsions, and preoccupations or reveries and how they accompany organic and psychological imbalance at work. To the company's officials Mayo's thesis was "as interfering reveries are expressed and gotten rid of underlying normalcy returns."[27]

On a personal level, Mayo's rules stemmed from his lonely period in London when only his sister had helped him overcome depressing preoccupations; the areas of substantive questioning take their origin from defects Mayo believed he had suffered in his own childhood. These personal experiences were refined, clarified, and extended through his reading of the psychopathologists Janet, Freud, and Jung, reflections on his own thought processes, theories of personal and social maladjustment, and patients he had seen in Queensland, Sydney, Philadelphia, and Boston.

He thought the first rules were appropriate to use alone for studying people at work because, in his view, at work no one had the right to ask direct questions. The substantive questioning, however, was suited to, say, hospitals where time is short and direct questions are normally asked because responses to them are treated confidentially. Generally, Mayo considered the rules sufficient in themselves inasmuch as they constituted a superior method from which emerged, at the pace the interviewee could control, a valuable pattern of his own experience rather than of the interviewer's expectations. This enhanced the interviewer's understanding of the person and gave a sounder base on which to offer advice or otherwise help.[28]

Mayo's own interview shows his technique. A worker who had suffered exposure to mustard gas during during the Great War is allowed to direct the substance of the interview until he is ready to learn that his obsessional attitude to health and financial problems at home could be partly resolved by recognizing his capacity to acquire new skills and get a better paid job. Mayo's first impression of the transcript of this interview was that he had "broken all the principles that I have so carefully inculcated into the interviewing group."[29]

When he returned to Boston, Mayo received not only a copy of his own interview but a letter from Stoll that included some comments from a supervisor, J.D. Watson, in the machine construction department: "The interviewing system was certainly not on trial. . . . It seemed like a full fledged competent kind of bird showing itself for criticism and gathering only approval. It works. . . . It is a humanist movement and at the same time, as Mr. Pennock said, a sound commercial proposition."[30]

Mayo also undertook to draw the attention of industrial psychologists and businessmen to the importance of the Hawthorne studies. Already in the summer of 1928 he had mentioned the research briefly at discussions with British academics, and during his September visit to the Hawthorne Works, when he learned of the radical innovations in the use of interviewing for supervisory training, he suggested that Pennock begin reporting the research to scholars and colleagues outside the company. Mayo recommended Walter Bingham's Personnel Research Federation, a loose grouping of prominent colleges, universities, labor organizations, government agencies, and large business corporations. The federation encouraged scientific research into personnel problems, published a personnel journal in which Mayo's first American writings had appeared, and was to hold its autumn meeting in December 1928. Pennock agreed, and Bingham set aside almost a whole morning for Pennock to present, and for Mayo to open formal discussion of, the Hawthorne studies.[31] However, Fred Willard, with Stoll, Stevenson, and a company vice-president, William F. Hosford, decided publication of the research should be delayed. Hosford wanted to discuss the work with a regular meeting of personnel executives he attended,[32] and Willard wanted Pennock to report the research to a group of competent managers and professionals for their constructive criticism. Mayo and Arthur Young would be among them, because, after their recent study of an employee representation plan in Colorado, Willard thought they could bring their experience and open-mindedness to bear on that aspect of Pennock's presentation that others might think could limit supervisors' authority and concede too much control to employees. Willard made peace with Bingham, who was overly keen to be associated with and even claimed responsibility for the work at Hawthorne. So Pennock's publication of the studies was held up until early in 1929,[33] but this decision did not bind Mayo.

Mayo's first statements in the United States were made early in November 1928 to Willard's group, the Conference Committee, an exclusive and confidential monthly luncheon meeting of leading American industrialists who discussed one another's plans and policies before they were to be implemented. The committee comprised influential men from American Telephone and Telegraph, Union Carbide and Carbon, U.S. Rubber, New York Central Railroad, Standard Oil, General Motors, Tidewater Oil, U.S. Steel, Bethlehem Steel, and Industrial Relations Counselors. Willard heard Mayo speak, and reported to Pennock that Mayo had mentioned Pennock's research, offered no criticism, gave Pennock full credit, seemed a wholly disinterested account, and reflected a truly scientific spirit. Willard was much impressed, and recommended Pennock maintain a close working relation with Mayo for both his technical competence and sensitive discretion.[34]

In March 1929 Pennock himself addressed Willard's associates, and won

Mayo's congratulations for the presentation. And in July Willard spoke on the work at a summer school for engineering teachers at the Hawthorne Works.[35]

On November 15, 1929 Pennock, Putnam, and Mayo made the first major public statement about the Hawthorne studies to the New York conference of the Personnel Research Federation. Mayo's task was to evaluate the work, so he read beforehand what Pennock and Putnam were going to say, and immediately encouraged both men by praising their papers as "immensely interesting . . . excellent . . . intriguing," and told them that in the audience they would find L.J. Henderson and McFie Campbell.[36]

Pennock reported the test-room studies, outlined the benefits that accrued to employees, discussed his firm's modern personnel practices, and emphasized that never before had the company based its programs on facts derived from employees' experiences but only from the ideas of executives. The experiments showed how inadequate the latter programs were, and at the same time provided criticism and constructive suggestions for training managers.

The research began with the illumination studies, which had found that many rather than only one factor affected work behavior, and that controlled experiments and careful observation could study many factors. Six were chosen; tiredness, rest, hours of work, attitudes to the company, equipment changes, and production levels. After two years the research question changed to: What effect do right and wrong methods of supervision have on worker performance and morale? From the test-room studies and their results, it was concluded that because relief from fatigue and raises in pay had not wholly determined production changes, they must be due to changes in employees' mental attitudes—"the major accomplishment of our entire study."

Supportive data were: a friendliness toward supervisors that indicated how unnecessary were the urging, driving types of supervisor; a feeling that production rose without conscious effort; a belief that the man in charge was not a boss; and the discovery that output is associated with freer, happier, and more pleasant work conditions. Also, work performance was seen to be affected by the emotional tone and the quality of home life.

Then Putnam told how the findings were used to train supervisors and otherwise improve working conditions. He outlined the interview program, the way it changed, and how the transcripts were used to show supervisors more humane and insightful ways to manage subordinates.

Mayo praised the papers for heralding two important changes in industry. The first lay in the relation between industrial organization and biological inquiry. This point gave him the opportunity to upbraid industrialists who expect the "rags and tatters of physiology and psychology coupled with oddments of technique . . . to yield increased production and diminished turnover." The experiments, he said, aimed not merely to furnish

material benefits but primarily to advance understanding of human situations, to provide precise biological knowledge, and to give more general
information on conditions that affect the capacity for work. To achieve this
aim the research studied organic, production, and attitude changes among
workers.

At the Harvard Fatigue Laboratory research provided an hypothesis to
guide studies of organic change, especially fatigue, at work, i.e., individuals
cannot continue productive work unless they maintain an organic equilibrium. Because the sources of fatigue at work are not merely physiological, external factors must be studied. At the Hawthorne Works researchers
found that workers differ in organic equilibruim, and the differences could
be attributed to health, personal history, and social situations outside work.
Researchers found, too, that when given the chance to talk in confidence
with interviewers the troubled workers were emotionally relieved, found
they could state and realize the origin of their troubles, and, subsequently,
their lives became more readily manageable and work performance
improved.

The second change the papers heralded lay in the methods of supervision and arose from the use of confidential interviews. The identity of the
interviewee was protected, the interview material was collated, and the
information was used to show supervisors the facts of human experience.
Also, unlike other studies, this drew the interviewers from among the firm's
employees rather than from outside. Finally, the company used the facts to
train a new kind of supervisor, i.e., one who valued human work experience and the skill of attentive listening, and who did not feel impelled to
moralize or become emotionally involved with workers. In consequence,
employees were willing to speak openly because they knew their views
would not be abused and they felt more confident themselves with this new
form of supervision.[37]

To Mayo, November 15, 1929 was a celebration as much as a report of
the Hawthorne studies, and over the next three years he took many opportunities to repeat the presentation of the work himself. On December 30 in
Washington he delivered "The Human Effect of Mechanisation" to the
annual meeting of the American Economic Association. He integrated the
research at Hawthorne with work done by Lovekin and Henderson's associates in the Fatigue Laboratory. He drew five specific conclusions: rest periods raise total output; daytime work conditions affect production more
than does the number of days worked each week; factors outside the plant
affect the worker's emotional life, which in turn affects production; supervisory method is the most important factor affecting production; if working conditions are poor, then pay incentives do not stimulate production.
He recommended that in the future "industry should give as much attention to human as well as material enquiry." A discussant, Elizabeth F.
Baker, made the first public criticism of the Hawthorne research when she

asked if it was desirable for employers to be concerned with anxieties that arose in conditions outside the workplace, asserted that it would be difficult to find enough supervisors competent in listening to do the work normally expected of them, and suggested the costs of employing such supervisors could not easily be borne by industry during the "ups and downs of competitive businesses."[38] Three weeks later Willits asked Mayo and Pennock to attend a conference of Quaker businessmen and discuss the Hawthorne research.[39]

In the January 1930 issue of *The Human Factor* the editor stated: "This issue is the most significant yet published [because it includes] . . . a summary of ELTON MAYO's recent work on supervision and production in the Hawthorne Works. . . . Elton Mayo's work tells of a new and practical method of supervising employees based on good mental hygiene principles."[40] The March issue of Bingham's *The Personnel Journal* included the addresses by Pennock, Putnam, and Mayo.[41]

Mayo not only spoke about the Hawthorne research but also arranged to distribute the printed accounts of the work. In December 1929 he sent Pennock a list of people who should be interested in the research. The papers were to be accompanied by a personal cover letter from Mayo that would indicate the relevance of the studies to the recipient's own interests. A similar note was sent to Edmund E. Day at the Rockefeller Foundation. Mayo's list included: Britain—Sir Josiah Stamp (statistician), Seebohm Rowntree (businessman), Henry Clay (Bank of England), Malinowski, and Pitt-Rivers; League of Nations—Sir Arthur Salter (economics), Albert Thomas, and E. J. Phelan (I.L.O.); Geneva—Jean Piaget; Paris—Pierre Janet, J.M. Lahy (industrial psychology), and André Siegfried (politics); New York—Edmund Day, Arthur Young, Wesley Mitchell (Columbia University), and C.S. Ching (U.S. Rubber); Cambridge—Donham and George F. Doriot (Business School), Edsall, and McFie Campbell; and Pennsylvania—Morris Viteles (industrial psychology). To this list Day added Robert S. Lynd of the Social Sciences Research Council.[42] In response Pennock decided to print the three addresses of November 15 in a special monograph, and Arthur Young proposed to print the "mechanisation" paper and distribute it through his organization.[43]

In April, before leaving for Europe, Mayo reported the work, calling the paper "Psychology in Industry," to the Ohio State University Education Conference.[44] And in September, while in England at a conference at Balliol College, he repeated the "mechanisation" paper under the title "Recent Industrial Researches of Western Electric Company in Chicago." It was published shortly after, and an amended version with photographs appeared in 1931 as "Supervision and Morale."[45]

On his return from Europe Mayo repeated the talk, calling it "A New Approach to Industrial Relations," to colleagues at the Harvard Business School. Donham wrote that "of the various researches that have been undertaken from time to time at the School, this represents the largest single development of a long term project; it is the best available 'case' on the question of the value of research to business."[46] In December at the first meeting of Associates of the Harvard Business School, a group of 250 businessmen who each paid annual dues of $1,000 to further the school's scientific research in business, Mayo presented the Hawthorne studies as "An Experiment in Industry."[47]

During his next visit to Europe from June to October 1930 Mayo had more chances to publicize the research and report its impact among businessmen he knew. He spoke to a group of thirty at the British Association for the Advancement of Science, and, in general, the industrialists seemed to favor the work, particularly Seebohm Rowntree, Lord Amulree (Economic Advisory Committee), and Johnstone of the International Labor Office in Geneva. Also, Major Lyndell Urwick, who would become one of Britain's leading management consultants, wanted to reprint in three languages Mayo's "mechanisation" paper.[48]

Notes

1. The summary of the Hawthorne studies is based on Fritz J. Roethlisberger and William J. Dickson, *Management and the Worker* (Cambridge: Harvard University Press, 1939), and National Research Council, Committee on Work and Industry, *Fatigue of Workers with Relation to Industrial Production* (New York: Reinhold Publishing Company, 1941).
2. Stevenson to Mayo, 15, 23 March 1928, Mayo to Stevenson, 19 March 1928, MM 1.087.
3. Roethlisberger and Dickson, *Management and the Worker*, p. 119.
4. Mayo to Ruml, 11 April 1928, RF; Mayo to Donham, 14 June 1928, AA 924.41, BLA.
5. MM 3.101.
6. Mayo to Ruml, 30 April 1928, RF.
7. Western Electric Report, Section V, p. 6, MM 5.001.
8. See notes 6, 7 above; Mayo to Stevenson, 7 May 1928, MM 1.087; Mayo to Pennock, 7 September 1928, Mf 159.
9. Pennock to Mayo, 11 May 1928, MM 1.087.
10. Mayo to Pennock, 7 September 1928, Mf 159.
11. Pennock's introduction to the interviewing program, 13 September, 1928, Mf 107; Pennock to Bingham, 24 September 1928, MM 1.087; Mayo to Donham, 1 October 1928, AA 929.41, BLA; Pennock to Mayo, 20 November, MM 1.087.
12. Pennock to Mayo, January 1929, AA 929.41, BLA.
13. Osborne Reports, pp. 10, 12.
14. Mayo to Pennock, 25 March 1929, Pennock to Mayo, 3 April 1929, MM 1.088.
15. Roethlisberger and Dickson, *Management and the Worker*, p. 208.
16. Putnam to Mayo, 22 March, 2 April 1929, Mayo to Putnam, 1 April 1929, Mayo to Pennock, 23 April 1929, Pennock to Mayo, 6 May 1929, MM 1.088.
17. Elton to Dorothea, 2 September 1929.
18. Elton to Dorothea, 3 September 1929.
19. Elton to Dorothea, 8 September 1929. Interviewing at Kearney was delayed until the early 1940s.
20. See notes 18, 19 above; Elton to Dorothea 11, 12 September 1929; Mayo to Pennock, 12 May 1930, MM 1.089.

21. Elton to Dorothea, 12 September 1929.
22. Mayo to Stoll, 30 September 1929, MM 1.088.
23. Elton to Dorothea, 23 October 1929.
24. Pennock to Mayo, 15 October 1929, MM 1.088.
25. Elton to Dorothea, 26 October 1929.
26. Mayo to Pennock, 28 October 1929, MM 1.088.
27. Davidson's memoranda: 15, 27 November 1929, Mf 107.
28. Roethlisberger and Dickson, *Management and the Worker,* ch. 3; National Research Council, Committee on Work in Industry, *Fatigue of Workers,* ch. 5; memorandum, 16 December 1929, MM 3.063.
29. Mayo to Pennock, 14 January 1930, MM 1.089.
30. Stoll to Mayo, 20 December 1929, MM 1.088.
31. Pennock to Bingham, 24 September 1928, MM 1.087; Bingham to Pennock, 8 October 1928, Mf 159.
32. Hosford to Rice, 11 October 1928, Mf 159.
33. Willard to Pennock, 3, 11, October 1928, Mf 159; Willard to Pennock, 28 February 1929, Mf 160.
34. Willard to Pennock, 2 November 1928, Mf 159.
35. Mayo to Pennock, 25 March 1929, MM 1.088; conversation with Holmes, 11 November 1975.
36. Mayo to Pennock and Mayo to Putnam, 6 November 1929, MM 1.088.
37. George A. Pennock, "Test Studies in Industrial Research at Hawthorne"; Mark L. Putnam, "A Plan for Improving Employee Relations on the Basis of Data Obtained from Employees"; and Elton Mayo, "Changes in Industry," in *Research Studies in Employee Effectiveness and Industrial Relations: Papers Presented at the Annual Autumn Conference of the Personnel Research Federation at New York, November 15, 1929* (New York: Western Electric Company, 1930).
38. Elton Mayo, "The Human Effect of Mechanization," *American Economic Review* 20, no. 1 (1930):156-76 Elizabeth F. Baker, "Economic and Social Consequences of Mechanization in Agriculture and Industry—Discussion," ibid., pp. 177-80.
39. Willits to Mayo, 23 January 1930, MM 1.099.
40. *Human Factor* 6 (January 1930):1-2.
41. *Personnel Journal* 8, no. 5 (1930) includes the papers listed in note 37 above.
42. Mayo to Pennock, 2 December 1929, MM 1.088; Mayo to Day, 3 December 1929, Day to Mayo, 5 December 1929, RF.
43. Pennock to Mayo, 16 January 1930, Mayo to Pennock, 17 January 1930, MM 1.089; Young to Mayo, 8 January 1930, Mayo to Young, 6, 9 January 1930, MM 1.104.
44. Elton Mayo, "Psychology in Industry," *Ohio State University Bulletin* 35, no. 3 (1930):83-92.
45. GB 2.563, BLA; Elton Mayo, "Supervisor and Morale," *Journal of Occupational Psychology* 5 (1931):248-60.
46. Elton Mayo, *A New Approach to Industrial Relations* (Boston: Harvard University, Graduate School of Business Administration, 1930).
47. Elton Mayo, "An Experiment in Industry," *Proceedings of the First Annual Meeting of the 250 Associates of the Harvard Business School, December 6, 1930,* pp. 59-65, DE 5.83, BLA.
48. Mayo to Pennock, 10 September 1930, Mf 159.

15

Collaboration at the Hawthorne Works: 1929–1932

Effective collaboration with researchers at Hawthorne increased Mayo's influence at the Western Electric Company, and enabled him to integrate the Hawthorne studies with the interests of his associates at the Harvard Business School. Between 1929 and 1932 he nurtured that relationship, publicized the work, and protected it against professional criticism and the effects of the business depression.

When he began publicizing the Hawthorne studies Mayo's influence with the Western Electric Company began to change. In February 1929 he and Willard had agreed that researchers from the Hawthorne Works would benefit from a visit to the Fatigue Laboratory and related areas, while Mayo's associates would learn much from time spent at the Hawthorne Works.[1] A year later, and only a few months after the presentations on November 15, Stoll approved a visit to the Harvard Business School by William Dickson and Harold Wright. They had been working under Putnam, who released them for two weeks to study interviewing with Mayo and Roethlisberger. Putnam was much pleased with the results of the visit, and encouraged further contact between the two men and Roethlisberger.[2]

In the summer of 1930 three of Mayo's associates visited the Hawthorne Works: Roethlisberger, Richard S. Meriam, and William Lloyd Warner. Meriam was an economist in the Business School, and Warner had recently accepted a joint appointment in the Business School and the Department of Anthropology. Roethlisberger and Warner would have close and long association with the research at the Works.

After working for two years with the clinical problems of Business School students, Roethlisberger had given a definition of his job for 1929–30 to Mayo. The young man wanted to develop a technique to assess adult situations so a person could understand and control them better. To do this Roethlisberger would use psychological tests and interviews, the results of which should be evaluated within the available knowledge of the person's total situation. Experiences with troubled students and discussions with Mayo had brought Roethlisberger to where he could draw a parallel between the morbid preoccupations of the unproductive student who had learning problems and the eccentric attitudes of fatigued workers whose productive capacity had diminished. And from this parallel he noted how similar were his ideas on research method to the techniques practiced at the Hawthorne Works.[3]

Roethlisberger did not know precisely Mayo's early relations with the Hawthorne Works; later he saw him as an adventurous, informal adviser to Pennock, Putnam, Stoll, and their associates, as a teacher of interviewing, and as an interpreter of puzzling data who could lead others to fresh research. He knew of Mayo's visits to the Works in 1928 and early 1929 and could see vaguely how they related to his own interests. His view sharpened in March 1930, when Dickson and Wright came to see Mayo for two weeks, and Roethlisberger was asked to join them in reading and training in interviewing technique.[4]

In the summer of 1930 at the Hawthorne Works, Roethlisberger learned something of the confusion and anxiety among Putnam's research associates. They were unclear about their research aims and worried that they had poor qualifications for carrying their work forward, wondered about their future with the firm, and felt caught in the dilemma of either striving for efficiency or pursuing humanism in industrial organization.[5]

A year later, when the interviewing program was under way and following principles that Mayo had enunciated, Roethlisberger was given leave to return to the Hawthorne Works and interview executive officers and supervisors. In October he called for assistance from Lovekin because the number of people seeking interviews was far greater than had been expected.[6] While he was conducting the interviews Roethlisberger offered to write regular reports and memoranda telling Putnam how he was doing the interviews, and what he was learning that might guide Putnam's staff in their tasks.

Only after he had seen fourteen supervisors did Roethlisberger discover what his interviews might cover: terms of employment, major problems, qualities of an able supervisor, reasons for seeking the position of supervisor, and relations between a supervisor and subordinates.

As the work progressed Roethlisberger was struck by a curious case in which being diplomatic had made unexpectedly for confusion rather than improved understanding; he noted how the supervisor role had changed from hard-boiled autocrat to jargon-ridden and friendly follower of nonaggressive rituals who sought increased control through either a new tricky formula or scientific facts. Four types of interviews emerged: informal, diagnostic, therapeutic, and educational. Each had value in training supervisors. He began to see that "projection," a mechanism of defense whereby unacknowledged impulses are imputed to others rather than being accepted by oneself, distorted a supervisor's view of reality and should be clearly seen or else his control would seriously deteriorate. This observation led Roethlisberger to write on the total situation—one of Mayo's favorite concepts—and its use in noting what supervisors do, e.g., blame fate, play safe, avoid facts, resist learning, separate earnings from performance, maintain an infantile view of authority, and become preoccupied with objects and attitudes they cannot change. From these considerations Roethlisberger was able to compile a list of topics for interview training, many of which reflect Mayo's influence, e.g., irrelevant syntheses like superstitions, false dichotomies, interview techniques, self-observation, and the approach by way of the "total situation."

After returning to the Business School, Roethlisberger reported extensively on the 253 supervisors interviewed in the Operating Branch at the Hawthorne Works. He presented evidence and conclusions about their preoccupations and attitudes toward authority, foreman and higher bosses, company policy, and how they saw their tasks, themselves, and their relation to the Western Electric Company. Immediately after sending the report to the Hawthorne Works, Roethlisberger arranged to return to Chicago to help analyze the interview data collected from workers. And in June 1932, with help from Shirley Taylor, Joseph Kish, Jr., presented a statistical analysis of 522 interviews that studied the correlates of dissatisfaction at work, and found that among both men and women it varied with departments, and that only among women work dissatisfaction was associated with personal situation and the individual who had conducted the interview. Reasons for the findings were not clear and further research was needed.[7]

Meriam reported to Mayo on Stoll's interest in using interviews to anticipate workers' grievances, Putnam's concern with the role of case studies in pedagogics of supervisor training, problems of noise in the test rooms, the importance of financial and economic incentives to workers, and the general interest at the Hawthorne Works in regular employment and employee representation. Meriam's interests were primarily economic, and although for almost two years he did help Putnam with case material for the supervisory training, his association with Mayo was not as close as Roethlisberger's.[8]

In May 1930 Mayo sent Putnam and Pennock a letter of introduction to Warner, and he also visited the Hawthorne works that summer.[9] On Warner's return to Harvard, Putnam sent him reports of the research, and Warner promised to offer specific proposals for its direction once he had decided upon them with Mayo, whose ideas Warner believed were similar to his own. Warner was interested in a course of instruction for supervisors but was much taken by Putnam's idea of using Harvard anthropology students to investigate the Hawthorne Work's environs in Cicero according to Warner's plans for studying an eastern city. Warner agreed: "Social anthropology has a lot to offer the kind of work you are pioneering."[10] At Christmas he returned to Hawthorne to discuss the plan further. By that time he had chosen Newburyport as his eastern city. The seventeen thousand inhabitants constituted what Warner considered a well-integrated, well-adjusted community where family life seemed stable; he wanted to study Cicero, too, because then he could "see how the relationship of a community to a large industry . . . [different from] that of a small industry in a town that has adjusted the industry to its larger social structure."[11]

During the next month Warner helped clarify the central idea that supported the bank wiring room study that would begin later that year. While telling stories about his field experience he had mentioned to Dickson that in the study of families the researcher concentrates more on relations among members than on the members themselves. Dickson asked: Could this be applied to the study of work groups, too? Warner said: Yes, the principle applies to any social structure, to relations among people within a group, and to relations between one group and another, i.e., internal and external relations are central to understanding group research at Hawthorne. Warner suggested that in the study of work groups Dickson and associates note the antagonisms and solidarities between persons, how the relations become balanced and then organized. Also, he said, groups contain three types of social cohesion on which the balance turns and the organization rests: superordination, subordination, and coordination. The first two are obvious from supervisor-employee relationships, and the third appears in the equality of relations among workers. Warner believed that if the Hawthorne researchers looked at these three from the viewpoint of the principle of antagonism-solidarity, then much work group behavior would be explained. Evidence for these ideas comes from interviews and direct observation, which are the primary techniques of the social anthropologist in the field as well as those discovered independently at Hawthorne. "The big thing to look for is the attitude" of those under observation, Warner wrote. The attitudes are often unconscious and prejudiced; to the psychoanalyst they are latent content, to the sociologist they are the elements of social structure. With these principles, observations began in December 1931 in the bank wiring room.[12]

At the same time Putnam reminded Warner about extending the study to the environs of the Hawthorne Works. Professors Binger and Newcombe of the University of Chicago, were anxious to begin research along the lines that Mayo and Ruml had been discussing with Putnam. But Putnam saw the Chicago school as too oriented to studies of delinquency; he much preferred Warner and Mayo to begin researching fully the social structure surrounding the Hawthorne Works, but this was prevented by the downturn of the depression early in 1932.[13]

Mayo had a hand in facilitating visits to Hawthorne by people further from his field of direct influence. Dennison, the prominent welfare industrialist in Framingham, sent two men to study the work under Putnam's control. Arthur Young was sufficiently interested to visit. Mme. Zimmern, following Mayo's suggestion, visited the plant and said she wished European industry would follow the Hawthorne methods. She declared her intention of using the interview techniques for handling visitors to her work in Geneva. And on Mayo's fiftieth birthday, he arranged for Henderson to make his only visit to the Hawthorne Works.[14]

Mayo supported the Hawthorne research staff with praise, protected them from their critics, and, for as long as he could, spared them the effects of the company's policies on how best to cope with the depression. He congratulated Pennock, Putnam, and associates on their foresight, excellent attitude toward the studies, and the value of their findings. At the same time he encouraged them by reporting back favorable impressions of their work, and by countering any criticisms of it.

One of the early critics was Arthur W. Kornhauser, a young industrial psychologist who would become an American academic leader in the field. In a report for the Industrial Relations Association of Chicago, he commented on Putnam's paper "Improving Employee Relations."[15] His remarks were offered hesitantly and interlarded with much praise for the Hawthorne studies as a whole, which he viewed as "extremely valuable [and] highly important." Nevertheless, he identified many weaknesses that would occasion many attacks on the research for almost fifty years.[16]

Kornhauser compared the test room studies with similar work from Germany and the British Industrial Fatigue Research Board, and concluded that the results were "rather fruitless" because the tests had been conducted with inadequate experimental controls. The interpretations were not "too clear," and the conclusion that "supervision is *the* important thing" was unconvincing, i.e., the effects of variations in wages and of removing the women from their regular workplace had not been properly eliminated. Kornhauser preferred systematic experimental control to weak control through observation of "the multiple free variation of factors."

Interview findings were not representative of the employee population, and Kornhauser was bothered by the absence of statistical statements. The overwhelmingly favorable attitude of supervisors to the interviewing may have arisen because they were "pretty well sold" on the program, and not because of the program itself. By stressing the anonymity of the interview, the researchers had so depersonalized it that employees could be excused for thinking that their comments were not much valued, and that as individuals they would never be recognized as the source of change in the organization of work. To remedy this, Kornhauser suggested that the interviews should be continuing and frequent rather than annual. Also, being interviewed once a year might help a person get complaints about the working environment off his chest, but the feeling of relief would last only a day or so and do little to help him resolve deep psychological problems.

Kornhauser suspected the highly positive character of the findings. He wondered about completeness of the report because no negative attitudes toward the Works were stated. And because the interviews were anonymous and confidential, he was surprised no one was reported to have mentioned trade unionism, or to have advanced a way to improve conditions through rewards to employees for suggestions adopted by the firm. He concluded that, as a rule, at work men rarely mention what is important to them, and usually say what is easily verbalized and largely superficial. So he recommended that the researchers do as others had done before them: use questionnaires to elicit balanced and statistically sound information.

Practical issues also concerned Kornhauser. He was not sure that the methods of the researchers were preferable to an employee representation scheme for enhancing the workers' control of their employment conditions; he wondered if the company would really take action on employee complaints in interviews, or tend to ignore them. And, although the illustrations were vivid and had apparently made their point, using cases and the conference method for the supervisor training was not an innovation.

Putnam thought Kornhauser's comments interesting, and asked Mayo's view. Mayo said the comments were negative and therefore unhelpful, that in general the criticisms attempted to defend the author's work against an imagined attack, and that inasmuch as Kornhauser sought to "defend to the last . . . exclusive and proprietary rights" to the field of inquiry, genial collaboration with him would be difficult. Mayo wrote that Kornhauser's preference for rigorous experimental control was "poverty stricken and fruitless," as Henderson's studies had proven; in human experimentation researchers must go on a voyage of discovery for new concepts and techniques of control. Putnam was comforted by Mayo's remarks, and reported that Kornhauser's exasperating attitude as he delivered the criticism had lost him much support.[17]

In a more positive vein, Mayo told Pennock how audience response to the November 1929 presentation had pleased Stoll. A few days later Mayo wrote to Putnam, "I am still hearing reverberations of the New York meeting—some interesting, some stupid. One University professor asked me to devise a method of eliminating the need for intelligence in business management."[18] By May 1930, on the eve of his summer vacation, Mayo could report to Edmund Day that interest in the Hawthorne studies had already extended to England and Paris. He wrote to Putnam, "I shall do my best to cram the methods of the Western Electric Co. down the throats of researchers like Kornhauser and his tribe, whatever language or dialect they speak."[19] And after speaking at Balliol College to the British Association for the Advancement of Science, he wrote to Pennock that his talk had "roused in the audience great interest in and respect for your work," and the industrialists' "vote of gratitude to you and the Company was wholehearted and unanimous."[20]

Late in 1930 Mayo began to protect the Industrial Research Division from threats inside the Western Electric Company. "Definite changes in the business situation," as D.F.G. Eliot, the personnel director, put it, were being felt generally at the company.[21] The research budget for the division was to be cut, and the interviewing program curtailed. Mayo went to help Putnam plan for 1931, then to Stoll to assure him of the value of the division's work, then back to Pennock to assure him that Stoll was as interested as ever in the division's work, that he would support an extended presentation of the Hawthorne findings to the company's supervisors, and that he had consented to publication of a monograph of the research. During 1930 Mayo stressed repeatedly the "need for making an extensive claim in order that your work shall get the attention that it deserves."[22]

Early in February 1931 Pennock was anxious to have Mayo's advice on the report of the Industrial Research Division for Stoll and the senior executives of the company in New York. The report had three sections. The first outlined the test room studies, and recommended future refinement of measures of employee effectiveness and the creation of a work group for close observation. The second described the interviewing program, its aims, benefits, and findings on the deeper motives of employees. The third outlined the changes in training for supervisors.

Mayo was expected to comment generally on the research in a way neither Pennock nor Putnam felt free to do. And Mayo was asked to answer critics among Western Electric executives who thought the new interviewing program was unnecessary, that good supervisors did not need it anyway, and that the plan, if adopted, would be seen as a spy system by supervisors and undermine their morale. To refute these assertions Pennock had proposed a questionnaire to study whether or not the supervisors' morale had dropped. Putnam wanted help to clarify the stated aim of interviewing programs.[23]

In response Mayo wrote to Pennock and compared his studies with the British work of Vernon, Myers, and Lyndal Urwick, and concluded that the Hawthorne studies were unique because they began within a firm that had imposed no clear plan or system on them and had long continued subsidiary inquiries. In the test room—a scientific adventure that should be published—intelligent direction of continuous research showed the importance of freely expressed relief from ordinary supervision, detrimental effects of personal preoccupations on production, and production changes related to changes in workers' lives outside the plant.

The interviewing program was a necessary broadening of test room inquiry to find the preoccupations with private misfortune that distort the workers' perception of employment conditions. The interviewers themselves ameliorated the effect of such misfortune on morale and production. In integrating the test room and interview findings, Mayo claimed that dissipating preoccupations raised production 30 to 40 percent; and because interviews showed these preoccupations to be widespread in the plant, if a means became available to deal with them, production levels would rise 30 to 40 percent. He dismissed the criticisms Pennock had asked him to consider as absurd accusations, coming from company executives who had never visited Hawthorne, for it was his policy always to point out openings for further industrial investigation rather than defend research unnecessarily.

Finally Mayo stated a major industrial problem—an old issue for him but one calculated to attract the attention of the Western Electric executives—the inadequacy of those in authority. He used Brooks Adams's phrase "the inferiority of the administrative intelligence" to identify the insufficiency of mere specialist logic in business affairs that call for the generalist's approach. In 1932 Mayo would address British managers on this topic, and later develop it for the last of his Lowell lectures, "The Problem of the Administrator." His letter told the company executives that an effective administrator should not only concentrate on a special technical field but also attend to the complexities of the human situation for which he is responsible. "He must capitalize his ignorance" by studying gaps in his knowledge and in the relation of his task to that of his fellows. These practical consequences would follow: the Western Electric Company should permanently raise the competence of all levels of supervision according to suggestions from the Hawthorne studies; and recruit, select, and train men of exceptional and rare capacity for executive administration.[24]

With a few excisions Mayo's letter was appended to the report for Stoll, who, in discussions of the report with Mayo, made minor changes and suggested that with editorial emendations the report could be placed with the *Journal of Industrial Hygiene.*[25] Mayo pushed the idea further and recommended the report be considered an outline for a book. He also proposed that supervisors' attitudes toward the company could be studied better through interviews than questionnaires, and that Roethlisberger be freed from duties at the Harvard Business School to do those interviews. Pursuing Putnam's notion, he advised designating a department to be supervised by someone who would abandon all interest in production and attend only to the personal situations of employees. These ideas shaped his associates' work for 1931-32.[26]

In the summer of 1931, while Roethlisberger was interviewing supervisors at the Hawthorne Works, Mayo was publicizing the research and its plans. Shortly before sailing for Europe he spoke to the American Neurological Association and repeated the "mechanization" paper with additional comments on psychopathological aspects of the indirect or conversational interview technique. Mayo's theory was that because the interviews lacked a formal structure, the workers' preoccupations or reflective thinking processes came forward, and they could readily express, and thereby gain sudden insight into, distorted, exaggerated, and unduly emotional attitudes. Also the interview technique deepened the interviewers' understanding on their task.[27]

In London, Mayo joined D.G.H. Miles from the National Institute of

Industrial Psychology (NIIP), Dr. C. H. Northcott, labor manager for Rowntree & Company, and Professor P. Sargent Florence from the Commerce Faculty at Birmingham's university in speaking before the British Research and Management Association. While the others discussed efficiency of managerial incentives, research in personnel work, and management education, Mayo spoke on the Hawthorne researches and to his usual statement added four points. First he contrasted the NIIP policy of bringing into an organization for a few months an expert to solve a problem with the Western Electric Company's policy of continuing research on a problem as it changed over several years. Second, he reviewed the strengths and weaknesses of applying academic psychology and physiology to industrial problems, and suggested that in industry human rather than academic disciplinary research was more realistic. Third, he discussed the plans by Putnam and Warner to compare the social environs of the Hawthorne Works with those of Newburyport to see the extent to which rapid and complex industrialization creates social disorganization. Fourth, he outlined how social disorganization itself produces a condition such that irresponsible production becomes directed toward meeting demands of irrational consumption, and, in consequence, that economic stability is diminished and business drepression ensues.[28]

Before sailing for Boston, Mayo sent Putnam, Pennock, and Stoll each the issue of *Week End Review* in which Myers described the Hawthorne research. And on his return home, Mayo gave the three men a report on the impact in Europe of their researches. "The fame of your researches," he wrote to Putnam, "is resounding through the chancelleries of Europe . . . the impersonal eye of the European world is regarding you fixedly through a microscope. . . . Myers . . . the European leader on industrial investigation, formally presents you with his congratulations and appreciation." To Pennock, Mayo wrote that Myers found "your work rather than the English the most interesting and . . . relevant for quotation and discussion. . . . I was astonished at the number of appreciative eulogistic references to the work. . . . Interest in England, France, and Switzerland is unmistakable and profound . . . congratulations. I have written to Mr. Stoll at length."

To Stoll Mayo was less extravagant with praise but congratulatory about Stoll's policy of maintaining the continuity of the research. In a February letter Mayo had made exactly this point, and noted for Stoll that Myers had said as much in his independent and widely publicized statement in *Week End Review.* Mayo also reported his astonishment that details of the research "had been so carefully read by many distinguished economists and men of affairs."[29]

During the fall of 1931 Mayo's Industrial Research Department formally employed William Lloyd Warner, social anthropologist, and a new man, Thomas North Whitehead, the thirty-nine-year old son of the British philosopher at Harvard College.[30]

Whitehead had come to the Business School in February, and was made a member of Mayo's staff in September. He was a graduate of Trinity College who had studied engineering at the University of London, served in the British army in France and Africa during World War I, and since the war's end been a scientific officer in the British Admiralty. He would spend nearly nine years with Mayo, publish a technical report on the relay assembly test room study and a book on leadership in democracies. In November 1939, he returned to England to advise the Foreign Office on American affairs, and in 1943 came back to the Business School to plan the personnel administration course at Radcliffe College.[31]

Mayo took Whitehead on his first visit to Hawthorne in April 1931. He was pleased to have the company of an Englishman, and enjoyed Whitehead's trained mind and sense of humor in talking over the day's work. Whitehead's English reserve and reticence, and his squeamishness about off-color jokes amused the men at Hawthorne, but they were favorably impressed by the articulate banter and debate that Whitehead could draw out of conversation with Mayo. Shortly afterward Mayo sent Whitehead to discuss the Hawthorne research with Stoll.

During the latter months of 1931 the relation between the Hawthorne research and Mayo's department was formalized. Warner would advise on sociological research; Roethlisberger would continue with psychological case work at the Business School and advise Hawthorne researchers on their interviewing; Whitehead's attention would be given to the refinement of measures of output in the test room studies and related experiments; Emily Osborne, whose personal problems had prevented her effective collaboration with Warner in the Newburyport study, would begin research on physiological and emotional correlates of work and domestic life among women at Hawthorne; Lovekin, who had been helping in the Fatigue Laboratory and in Newburyport, would assist Mayo with a new project at the Norfolk Prison; and Mayo would write the book on the Hawthorne studies.[32]

Mayo had discussed the idea of a book with Stoll earlier in the year, and later with Putnam; the three had agreed Mayo should narrate the drama of the research, avoid discussing its implications, and present fully the evidence for its conclusions.[33] Mayo suggested, and the others assented, that because recognition for work done on the studies would look like a telephone listing, only Western Electric Company, MIT, and Harvard University should claim authorship. Because Mayo had undertaken this task he would not visit the Hawthorne Works as regularly as in the past, and his associates would carry the burden of advising the firm's executives.[34]

In December 1931 Mayo told the Business School faculty how his work was progressing at Hawthorne, and in January he spent ten days at the Hawthorne helping Putnam reorganize the Industrial Research Division. They decided that the interviewers, who had been taken from all over the plant, should return to their departments in keeping with the company's policy to spread evenly the burden of the depression. This gave the division a chance to begin raising the skills of its staff.[35]

Mayo's prestige in the division was at its highest now. "They are nice to me here," he wrote to Dorothea, "all spring to attention when I enter a room." He continued publicizing the research by introducing prominent international visitors to the Hawthorne Works, and collaboration between Mayo's associates and Putnam's researchers grew.[36]

By the last week in February 1932 Wright had established parallel files at Hawthorne and Harvard so that Mayo had a standard reference system to help with the correspondence and to identify details of information needed for the proposed book. The records were kept in a newly established library for use by Mayo's students and associates.[37]

Cost-reduction practices continued at Hawthorne but did not affect Putnam's division more than any other part of the firm, and it seemed to him that they were unlikely to do so. Sharing Putnam's guarded optimism, Mayo wrote that he hoped "retrenchment will not set us all in the streets to continue our researches there."[38] Ten days later the depression shattered the Hawthorne-Harvard plans.

Emily Osborne had gone to Chicago to begin her research, and Putnam had made her welcome. But Pennock was embarrassed, and would not have her at Hawthorne. Since Mayo's visit in January, when he and Pennock had quickly agreed on Osborne's work, four cuts had been made in the manufacturing schedules. As a result some employees were dismissed, most others were put on a short work week, and sections were combined to otherwise reduce costs. In Putnam's division special interviewing was curtailed to avoid criticism that interviews were superficial when jobs were threatened. Osborne was to interview women, and the cost was to be borne by Mayo's research grant, but Pennock felt he could not permit it. There was no time to make it known that her work was not funded by the company, and he did not want to face the consequences a misunderstanding might arouse. Recognizing Pennock's problem, Mayo withdrew Osborne. After clearing the request through Ruml, Mayo asked Mary Gilson—who had helped him when he worked with Arthur Young for Industrial Relations Consellors, and who was an economist at the University of Chicago—and Dean Donald Slesinger if they could find a research task for Osborne. Remaining on Mayo's payroll, Osborne later did research at an experimental nursery school.[39]

Mayo went to Chicago and learned from Pennock and Putnam that the company had never before faced such a crisis. It had devised policies to cut labor costs that were proving insufficient to the situation. In the belief that the depression had reached its final depths, Pennock and Putnam agreed the essentials of their research would be safe if they reduced the hours of work to fourteen a week. Substitutes were put into the test room, while

Dickson and his associates kept observing the bank wiring research. Soon the depression would end it all.

Mayo saw Chicago suffering. He believed the depression would deepen. Western Electric was planning to dismiss another five thousand, and International Harvester ten thousand. Only a few floors of his hotel, the Palmer House, were in use. Outside the hotel, a blinding blizzard made him grip young Putnam's arm as the wind blew them across the icy pavement to the soft snow in the gutter. Mayo's "ancient enemy," ringworm, badly afflicted his hands and feet. He wrote to Dorothea, "I hope this is the black moment which marks the turn."[40] But there was worse to come.

Whitehead, who had begun to analyze the production data from the test room studies, developed a duodenal ulcer, and was unable to return to work until early in May. Mayo's difficulties compounded when glaucoma in his right eye required an operation to prevent blindness, but with good humor he wrote to Pennock, "My critics have often accused me of a certain monocular blindness. I do not wish to discover that after all they are right." He arranged for the surgery to be done in London, and adopted Whitehead's suggestion that Wright come to Boston and write the book with Roethlisberger.[41]

Before leaving for London, Mayo took two more opportunities to publicize the Hawthorne research. At the New York convention of counsulting psychologists he said the human relations aspect of the world's situation "is crying for enquiries which we psychologists have not been permitted to begin," repeated the need for long-term research rather than quick studies in the laboratory, and pointed to Hawthorne for illustrations.[42]

With Walter Bingham, Edward Thorndike, and Morris Viteles, Mayo gave one in a series of radio talks on psychology in industry. He offered a changed interpretation of the Hawthorne studies, traces of which had first appeared in a London paper, October 1931. He began to draw again on *Democracy and Freedom,* blending it with observations from Colorado and the delinquency studies in Chicago, and showed the influence of Warner's dictum that human relations as well as widely held attitudes were the elements of social structure. He called the talk "The Problem of Working Together," and said that fifty years ago men had lived in communities where their work was a part of communal life and their morale and amusements derived from a sense of solidarity among themselves and service to the community. But today men drift with no plans, go where work takes them, and must live in a society with an unstable economy. Because communal life outside work is neglected, it becomes urgently needed within the workplace; the need raises the requisites of working together: cooperation and collaboration.

Mayo reported the Hawthorne research and its recent extension—the observations in the bank wiring room—which found that some people who are socially inept may be quite capable if their surroundings suit them;

others who are exceedingly capable may not be so in an inappropriate milieu. Results showed that abstract managerial schemes, e.g., efficiency drives, fail because relations between people and work groups are not recognized. In response workers create their own practical schemes. To recognize an abstract work regulation and to work under concrete or formal practices irks both workers and supervisors; they see the conflict and how it prevents effective collaboration. In the Hawthorne studies the test room girls overcame the conflict between what they wanted and what was possible, and, in consequence achieved a high degree of collaboration. "The reorganization of modern industry must be based on knowledge of how to achieve effective collaboration . . . the conviction to which the Hawthorne experiments led." The knowledge applies to the problem of working together whether in factories, societies, or an international conference.[43]

Notes

1. Willard to Pennock, 28 February 1929, Mf 160.
2. Mayo to Putnam, 21 March 1930, Mayo to Stoll, 26 March 1930, Stoll to Mayo, 28 March 1930, Putnam to Mayo, 6 May 1930, MM 1.089.
3. Roethlisberger to Mayo, 16 October 1929, MM 3.090.
4. Osborne Reports, p. 49. Fritz J. Roethlisberger, *The Elusive Phenomena* (Boston: Harvard University, Graduate School of Business Administration, Division of Research, 1977), pp. 48-51.
5. Osborne Reports, pp. 51, 59; Roethlisberger to Wright, 11 September 1930, MM 1.089.
6. Roethlisberger to Mayo, 27 May 1931, MM 1.090; Osborne Reports, pp. 74, 76-77.
7. Roethlisberger's Reports to Putnam, 1 June 1931-1 June 1932, MM 3.090; Osborne Reports, pp. 80, 82, 87, 92, 98.
8. Meriam to Mayo, 12 November 1930, MM 1.089.
9. Mayo to Pennock, Mayo to Putnam, 12 May 1930, MM 1.089.
10. Warner to Putnam, 30 July 1930, Mf 159.
11. Warner to Putnam, 26 November 1930, Mf 159; conversation with Mildred Warner, 30 March 1975.
12. Warner to Dickson, 27 February 1931, Mf 157; 2 December 1931, MM 5.015.
13. Putnam to Mayo, 5 March 1931, MM 1.090.
14. Pennock to Mayo, 16 January 1930, Mayo to Pennock, 2 March, 1930, Mayo to Pennock, 18 December 1930, MM 1.089; Mayo to Young, 12 March 1930, MM 1.104.
15. Kornhauser's report accompanies Putnam to Mayo, 10 March 1930, Mf 162.
16. Jeff Sonnenfeld, "Clarifying Critical Confusion in the Hawthorne Hysteria," *American Psycologist* (December 1982): 1397-99.
17. Mayo to Putnam, 21 May 1930, Putnam to Mayo, 28 May 1930, MM 1.089.
18. Mayo to Pennock, 26 November 1929, Mayo to Putnam, 2 December 1929, MM 1.088.
19. Mayo to Day, 31 May 1930, RF; Mayo to Putnam, 31 May 1930, MM 1.089.
20. Mayo to Pennock, 10 September 1930, Mf 159.
21. Eliot to Mayo, 4 October 1930, MM 1.089.
22. Mayo to Putnam, 16 December 1930, Mayo to Pennock, 18 December 1930, MM 1.089.

23. Pennock to Mayo, 2 February 1931, Putnam to Mayo, 5 December 1931, MM 1.090.
24. Mayo to Putnam, 16 February 1930, MM 1.090; Mayo to Pennock, GB 2.563, BLA.
25. Mayo to Pennock, 9 February 1931, Putnam to Mayo, 28 February 1931, Mayo to Putnam, 3 March 1931, MM 1.090.
26. Mayo to Pennock, 24 March 1931, Mayo to Putnam, 25 March, 3 April 1931, MM 1.090; Elton to Dorothea, 23 March, 2 April 1931.
27. Elton Mayo, "Psychopathologic Aspects of Industry," *American Neurological Association Transactions* 57 (1931):468-75.
28. *Manchester Guardian,* 1 October 1930; Elton Mayo, "Industrial Research" (memorandum), 6 October 1930, MM 2.034.
29. Mayo to Pennock, Putnam, Stoll, 20 October 1931, MM 1.090.
30. Osborne Reports, p. 76; Dean's report of Harvard Business School, AB4, BLA.
31. Osborne Reports, p. 73; T. North Whitehead, "Now I Am an American" (unpublished memoirs), 1964, BLA.
32. Elton to Dorothea, 18 April 1931, Roethlisberger to Mayo, 20 July 1931, MM 1.090.
33. Mayo to Stoll, 11 May 1931, MM 1.090.
34. Mayo to Stoll, 15 November 1931, Mayo to Putnam, 27 November, 23 December, 1931, Mayo to Pennock, 7, 23 December 1931, MM 1.090; Osborne Reports, pp. 73-97.
35. Osborne Reports, pp. 82-83, 86.
36. Elton to Dorothea, 22 January 1932.
37. Wright to Mayo, 22 February 1932, MM 1.091.
38. Mayo to Putnam, 4 March 1932, MM 1.091.
39. Letter and cables between Mayo and Osborne, Putnam, Pennock, Gilson, Ruml, Slesinger, 11-17 March 1932, MM 1.091.
40. Elton to Dorothea, 20 March 1932; Wright to Mayo, 25 April 1932, MM 1.091.
41. Mayo to Wright, 14 April 1932, Mayo to Putnam, 27 April 1932, Mayo to Pennock, 10 May 1932, MM 1.091.
42. *New York Herald Tribune,* 8 May 1932.
43. Elton Mayo, "The Problem of Working Together," in *Psychology Today: Lectures and Study Manual,* ed. W. V. Bingham (Chicago: University of Chicago Press, 1932).

16

Hawthorne Reported and Early Criticism: 1932-1942

Mayo's activities at the Hawthorne Works diminished during the 1930s. Nevertheless, he encouraged the firm to use the research results, reviewed the studies in his lectures on human problems in industry, and helped his associates to publish details of the work and to tolerate its critics.

Mayo's operation for glaucoma was successful. He needed new glasses and to avoid irritation from the smoke of his cigarettes he bought a long holder of interlocking goose quills. Colleagues and associates never learned why Mayo used such a holder, and over the years alleged it was a stylish affectation—functionless, except to dramatize a well-turned phrase—merely an addition to the catalogue of eccentricities an aging academic might be allowed.[1]

While convalescing in London, Mayo learned from Whitehead how seriously the depression imperiled research at Hawthorne, and was asked to support a scheme to protect the researchers from retrenchment. Since May a third of the work force had gone, and the girls in the test room had been replaced; Wright and Dickson, being short-service men, were threatened with early retirement, but their superiors agreed that the two would not go until Mayo could be consulted. Suddenly, senior executives at Hawthorne who feared for the security of their own positions, announced Dickson would be dismissed before Mayo's return. Wright, certain he would be next to go, recommended to Putnam that the test room studies be discontinued, the bank wiring room observations be written up, all other data be analyzed, and the book be finished. Dickson and he would do all this under Mayo's direction at Harvard.[2] Pennock liked the notion, and Wright believed Stoll would accept it if it were put to him by Mayo personally. So, in October after an anxious briefing by Whitehead, Roethlisberger, and Warner in New York, Mayo talked to Stoll. At the same time he gave up his usual $2,500 retainer that Western Electric had planned to pay him. Stoll accepted both proposals. Although this much reduced Mayo's income, he rejoiced that for at least a year he was obliged to make no more "dreadful excursions to Chicago"[3] and that he would be free to write his

Lowell lectures, which he had been invited to deliver in December.[4] Meanwhile Roethlisberger planned the account of the Hawthorne research with help from Wright and Dickson, and Whitehead began to analyze the output records of the girls in the test room.[5]

The girls who had been replaced in the test room and later let go from the Hawthorne Works held Mayo's attention for several years afterward through the efforts of Emily Osborne. In January 1933 while beginning her new research in Chicago she arranged a meeting of the girls. Mary Volango had a job in a rubber factory at half her former pay. Jenny Sirchio had walked the streets before finding a poorly paid job weighing macaroni in a firm where her father was the night watchman. Theresa Layman was out of work but hoped to marry her boyfriend when the economy improved. Lottie Blazijak, unemployed, lived with a family most of whose members were also out of work. Anna Hegland, married, lived in De Kalb close to poverty. The five girls met infrequently and shared memories of the years at Hawthorne. Jenny thought there was always a strong bond between them and believed that Western Electric Company had done more than other Chicago firms for workers during the depression. Eventually Jenny got a job at thirteen dollars a week. For all the girls work was difficult to find, and keep, and pay was no more than twenty cents an hour.[6]

Mayo's Lowell lectures were published as *The Human Problems of Industrial Civilization* in 1933. In the first chapter he reviewed industrial studies of fatigue and concluded that it comprises a complex set of variables, and that further experiments should control the variables through measurement and observation rather than direct manipulation. He summarized research from the Fatigue Laboratory, compared organic imbalance in the laboratory with fatigue at work, and stated the limits of the comparison. As a rule, at work interference leads to organic imbalance among biological variables, thus affecting the individual's steady state, as measured by pulse product. Mayo's view of fatigue as a state of organic imbalance contrasted with the economist's view of fatigue as the result of taking work out of people and depleting their reserves. The second chapter reviewed studies of monotony, and showed that it varies among individuals, their social situation, and work conditions. Mayo described his study in Philadelphia, and concluded that after rest pauses monotony declined, production rose, labor turnover fell, and the mental health and general welfare of workers improved.

Chapter 3 summarized Western Electric reports of the Hawthorne studies. They showed that when rest pauses are introduced to overcome fatigue and monotony they have a secondary effect insofar as they give workers increased autonomy in decisions that affect their work. Such autonomy strengthens the workers' inner emotional equilibrium, helps them achieve a steady state so they can deal with the many experimental changes at work, and determines how well they use their skills each day. Chapter 4 reported the mica room study and the interviewing program. As interviews were changed from interrogations to personal conversations they gave case material for supervisor training, and showed that supervision, like fatigue and monotony, was a complex pattern of many variables. Chapter 5 centered on psychological and social experiences at work that help define morale. Combining data from the Hawthorne studies and British research with ideas from Janet and Freud, Mayo depicted the obsessional character: he feels incomplete, inferior to others, unreal, besieged, driven to certain thoughts against his will and to fight stressfully against them; he thinks with difficulty, cannot attend easily to his situation or ideas about it, prefers abstract intellectualization to concrete ideas and conducts long discussions with little purpose, rethinks what is obvious, and finds decisions burdensome; agonizing indecisiveness inhibits his ability to act, he exaggerates small points, substituting the literal use of language for dealing maturely with larger matters. But his behavior is not unusual, for he can be found in high offices working compulsively, checking his already corrected work, and claiming a strong belief in self-control. He venerates hard work, which he knows is right, and lives a life devoid of emotional satisfaction.

If a person works under conditions that cause him organic imbalance, feelings of diminished self-worth, and a sense that his social life is futile, then he would entertain reveries like those of obsessive characters. In a plant, Mayo stated, work organization often leads to fatigue and a sense of diminished self-worth; and he argued that outside the plant modern city life can lead workers to a sense of social futility. To study the role of social factors, Mayo outlined the observations from the bank wiring room, where formal social rules were poorly integrated with informal rules, led to output restrictions and a sense of personal futility, and showed the nonlogical bases of collaboration.

Chapter 6 considered the broad effect of industrialization on the social order and asked if modern industry creates obsessive behavior among its employees. Mayo examined the work of Park and associates (University of Chicago) and concluded that the disintegration of the traditions that a community needs for ordered living, progress, and the granting of freedom to act and think easily leads to the breakdown of socially accepted feelings and ideas, and results in crime and suicide. Further support for this comes from Durkheim, Freud, Halbwachs, and J.S. Plant. That modern industrialization leads to obsessive behavior has important implications for studies of delinquency, crime, industrial relations, psychoneurosis, suicide, education, and unstable economic consumption. Such social studies have not kept pace with the technical studies on which rapid industrialization was based.

In chapter 7 Mayo considered the role of government in the social order. He began with an attack on politicians in the United States, Europe, and Russia, pointing to their ignorance and manipulative modes of control, and to how they created an anomic society and promoted acquisitiveness to treat its ills rather than studying the conditions that led to the anomie. He outlined his functionalist theory of society, the purpose of education, the importance of traditional codes for training people in social skills for sane rather than obsessive thinking. Mayo argued that rapid technical change destroys traditions at work and requires new work organization. For workers who stay at a plant under such conditions, this leads to a decline in self-worth and a failure to adjust socially to new work schemes. To protect themselves they create an illogical social organization, which is often led by an obsessive character. Workers who leave plants continually face new living environments where their culture clashes with that of others and their routines of regular and intimate family life are destroyed. The comfort of nonlogical traditions is gone. They become exasperated because they have no social function and feel no sense of solidarity with a continuing group. While their lack of function leads to feelings of insecurity and the making of exaggerated demands on life, their lack of solidarity prevents their acquiring basic skills. Like the workers who stay on, they turn for help to illogical social organization, led by an obsessive character who, by his very personality, must promise a political salvation that never can make up for the original loss.

The final chapter reiterated the results from Hawthorne and the thesis that fatigue and monotony result from interference to the physiological and psychological equilibrium of the organism. He outlined ideas of Pareto and Brooks Adams. If the necessary movement of capable people and families—the elite—from lower to the higher class is interrupted, then the circulation of the elites will fail and society's equilibrium will be disturbed. Mayo thought this circulation had been disturbed, and society's leaders did not know it. For this reason, during the present social changes brought on by the too-rapid industrialization of work, society must produce administrators of a high "order of generalizing mind." Such a capable elite is available, but is untrained in human understanding and control, and lacks knowledge of biological and social facts to advance collaboration. These people must be found and trained in understanding nonlogical social codes as well as the logic of economics and physical science, so that in their administrative positions they can improve methods of maintaining morale at work rather than taking sides in employer-employee conflict. The problem is not who should control society, unions or management, but what research is needed for intelligent control? To this end socialism, Marxism, and communism are irrelevant; instead, we must banish ignorance and illiteracy and bring about human collaboration.

If the new administrators are to facilitate human collaboration they should be skilled in listening, know the limits of their understanding of what they hear, and see the logical, nonlogical, and irrational elements in individual and group attitudes. Such administrators need university training in how to handle concrete difficulties between people, in both national and international relations.[7]

Most reviews of the book were favorable, and many reported accurately what Mayo had written. He was described as brilliant, highly suggestive, courageous, and as an expert diagnostician and integrator of knowledge from diverse fields. One reviewer placed him in the company of A.N. Whitehead, Spengler, Stuart Chase, and Lewis Mumford. His ideas were invaluable, careful, illuminating, thorough, clear and critical; and the book was recommended to social scientists, medical people, administrators of industry and politics, and labor and trainee managers.[8]

Criticism came from the *New York Sun,* which condemned him for being out of date and recommending anthropological studies for the nation's economic problems.[9] The reviewer for the *New Republic,* who found Mayo's noneconomic explanation of society's distress distasteful, thought he was a floundering scientist who had strayed from his laboratory and, with only abracadabra to guide him, proved insensitive to hard facts.[10]

The favorable reviews were an unexpected pleasure for Mayo. After reading comments in *Mental Hygiene,*[11] which he thought showed the reviewer knew that he was talking about, Mayo wrote to Dorothea, "The high approval has surprised me—rather used to the other or being ignored."[12] A note from Bingham said the book showed how fruitful had been the studies at Hawthorne; and from the NIIP in London, Charles S. Myers sent:

> I have evidently underrated your ability to deep thought and good writings! For I had no idea that you could turn out anything so *really* first rate . . . I never expected that you had it in you to produce such a thoroughly successful book . . . somebody had to do it . . . I wish it had been in my power to do it. . . . I shall urge everyone I can to read it.[13]

Kornhauser, an early critic of the Hawthorne research, described the work as "richly suggestive . . . with more questions than it answers . . . cuts deep into modern life . . . delightfully ignores the fences separating academic fields of knowledge."[14] But in the *American Journal of Public Health,* Hayhurst complained that the book had lengthy quotations and unsummarized chapters, omitted references to some workers in the field, failed to see the economic significance of abandoning the gold standard, and was repetitious and verbose. He was prepared to admit, however, that the "concluding dogma" on collaboration was masterfully handled and the practical applications of the Hawthorne research were "instructive."[15]

The most laudatory academic praise appeared in the *American Journal of Sociology,* not in the book section but in the body of the issue. Robert E. Park reviewed the book fully and concluded that it was "lucid, illuminating . . . showing . . . an extraordinarily precise knowledge of a wide range of scientific theory," that it gave the concept of equilibrium "a new, wider . . .

more precise significance," and that it illustrated collaboration between experts on complex problems from diverse disciplines "with the best possible results."[16]

Between 1932 and 1935 Mayo had little to do with the Western Electic Company. In November 1933 he visited the Hawthorne Works to discuss problems that might arise with the introduction of an employee representation plan.[17] A year later he wrote the foreword to Roethlisberger and Dickson's report on observations of the bank wiring room; he emphasized that excellent results are produced when there exists a "comfortable equilibrium" between the authority in a workplace and the workers' spontaneous social organization.[18] In the fall of 1935 he suggested company officials use professional advice for a case of classical paranoia; and earlier that year at a London congress on scietific management he had presented his paper "The Blind Spot in Scientific Management."[19]

The paper reviewed all the Hawthorne research, and with emphasis again on observations from the bank wirers, argued that the hypothesis of necessary or inevitable hostility between management and workers is untenable. Why? The thesis is based on Marx's defective economic theory of class warfare and not on facts learned in actual organizations. Mayo warned that when scientific management presents logical, technical innovations to workers, they will resist with their established nonlogical work routines. Why? Because for too long workers have had to accommodate to changes that they had not initiated, and that robbed them of meaning, significance, and traditions. It is not surprising, then, that they take revenge for the changes imposed on them.

At the end of 1935 Mayo, Whitehead, and Roethlisberger were asked to visit the Hawthorne Works to discuss the reintroduction of interviewing as part of a plan to train supervisors in dealing with problems that could arise with the introduction of the employee representation plan. Mayo was convinced that although not many Western Electric officers were sympathetic to his approach, Rice, Pennock, Putnam, and Wright still supported his views on the need for interview training. And Mayo was heartened to hear from Putnam that Western Electric "had employed many advisors . . . on human relations and that in every instance—except Mayo—the results have been 'silly.'" "May it continue to be so," was Mayo's unspoken reply.[20]

At that time the research group at Hawthorne had moved beyond an interest in informal spontaneous groupings of workers and their relation to official management positions. Now the researchers believed that when they were observing informal groups they saw "an attitude of resistance to change." Mayo showed them that the non-European civilization deliberately imposes change on itself, and refuses to accept the idea of stabilization in social relationships or achieved economic standards. Before an achievement is complete "we nowadays break it off in order to reach out again." Mayo thought interviewing now had a new function: "a continuous operation disguised to help the individual to grow and develop—to 'complicate', make more complex, his situation continuously—and it is designed also to keep social organization *fluid,* to prevent crystallization at a given point." As Mayo understood it, the interviewer or counselor related himself to everyone at the plant, did not seek interviewees, and at the beginning of the interview did not ask questions. The tactic was to develop the interview as far as may be, and at the end leave it to another occasion to complete the pattern. This was not a clinical relationship because no diagnosis, prognosis, treatment, or catharsis was involved. "But it is as effective as ever," wrote Mayo, "indeed more so . . . because the individual is more than ever conducting his own interview." The counselor functioned thus: when the individual's "mental growth or capacity to complicate his situation is being 'held up', the interview enables him to work this out for himself, to pass the barriers and go on, and [because] it is *his own* achievement . . . he comes back for aid if further difficulties arise—the interviewer is not associated in his mind with some particular suggestion."[21]

In the early months of 1936 Mayo was busy at the Hawthorne Works consulting on management problems with large meetings and small groups of managers; and in 1937 he visited the Works twice to learn about Hosford's staff training program that had been based on results from the Hawthorne studies.[22] Nevertheless, Mayo's relations with the Hawthorne researchers was becoming more distant, leaving him with one last major task, the publication of Roethlisberger and Dickson's full account of the research studies.

At the end of 1935 Mayo was reading what had been written and was battling with what he saw at the time as Roethlisberger's slipshod and colloquial prose.[23] But by February 1936 a copy was before Stoll, who read it chapter by chapter and passed each one to Hosford.[24] At the beginning of April Mayo talked with Macmillan but then began arrangements instead with Harvard University Press.[25]

Without warning Whitehead announced that he had turned his lectures into a book on industrial society. "He is ambitious," thought Mayo, when he was given a copy to read, and noted that the preface included a paragraph eulogizing him. Mayo thought it "popular in a dignified" way, and when he suggested some minor alterations, Whitehead showed him the proposed dedication: "'To Elton Mayo. Everything he took up thereby became important'. . . . As something to live up to it scares me stiff! . . . The book is an exposition of our attitude for the general public." At the time the book had no title, and Whitehead immediately adopted Mayo's suggestion that it be called "Leadership in a Free Society."[26]

With a subsidy of $3,800 from the Business School Mayo arranged with the press to publish Roethlisberger's book, and expected that his and Whitehead's would be on sale late in 1936. Stoll and Hosford were pleased with what they were reading, and made some minor suggestions to which

Mayo agreed.[27] He sailed for Europe that summer, having given Roethlisberger the task of completing the minor revisions to the manuscript before putting it in the hands of the press. But the book did not appear for three years.

At first Hosford had minor criticisms of errors in the description of labor grades, pay rates, and operating procedures, all of which he thought reflected badly on Hawthorne's managers. Stoll's concerns centered on the title and acknowledgments of authorship. But when Hosford had finished reading the whole book, he made general comments that held up publication.

Hosford thought the book showed that the interests of the researchers not Western Electric management had controlled the direction of the studies; and that the book did not indicate what use the research was to the company. He believed that a firm simply could not justify such expensive research solely to increase knowledge, nor could it allow readers to imagine that the direction, cost, and benefit of the research was out of management's full control. He suggested, first, that in a foreword Stoll disabuse readers of such impressions. Second, because the book quoted supervisors' unfavorable comments about their superiors the readers would gather that the rule governing confidentiality of interview data had been disregarded and, worse still, that the managers were incompetent. The same applied to quotations from operators about their supervisors. Because many of the statements were derogatory, the character and the ability of these people and the morale at the company might suffer. Third, the researchers' alleged discovery of output restriction in the bank wiring room had been always known to managers. Output restriction was common in industry, but the book suggested that it was unique to the Hawthorne Works. Finally, the book should be carefully reviewed by workers and managers at the Hawthorne Works, and, in light of their comments, it should be amended "to ensure that nothing is said that is unfair to . . . employees . . . supervisors, or . . . the organization."[28]

Hosford's reactions contributed to at least a year's delay in publishing the book. Also, at the time AT&T was subject to the uncertainties of a legal inquiry, and the firm's lawyers advised that its public image could be tarnished if a federal commission were to grant a rate increase to a company that had spent large sums on research with no clear direction or immediate financial benefit,[29]

Stoll released the book for publication in May 1939.[30] *Management and the Worker* appeared in October, and no one expected it would become a classic in the social sciences, feted for the lead it would give to American industrial psychology and sociology. It also became a center of contention and the object of polemics among social scientists for over forty years.[31]

By April 1940, 874 copies had been sold, and the net investment by the Business School stood at $3,116. Between May and December, in response to some academic and industrial writers' reviews, people were buying between 27 and 68 copies a month. But in January 1941, 174 copies were sold; in February, 952. The net investment fell to $803, and the total sales were 2,348. The explanation lay in the February issue of *Reader's Digest*. Stuart Chase's article about the book had occasioned an enormous flood of mail, and he was commissioned by his editor to write another piece on similar research. By July 1942, 4,000 copies had been sold, and the book started to consolidate its reputation as a report on outstanding research in the human and social problems of industry.[32]

With one exception the early reviews of the book were favorable, and only three minor criticisms were raised; it did not mention organized labor; its style was not popular; and it contained no practical advice that a manager could use immediately.[33] Two academic reviews set the tone of the controversy over the research, Mayo, Roethlisberger, and the role of human relations for industry. In the *Psychological Bulletin* the reviewer, a man well known for his vitriolic critiques, sang the book's praises. His adjectives were: honest, precise, clear-headed, capable, serious-minded, coherent, consistent, and frank; his phrases were: excites marginal notations, transcends the limits of the field, a landmark of real importance in dynamic social psychology, avoids evangelism and dull pedantry. The authors' only fault was that they had not integrated their findings with those of other researchers, thus giving the reader the false impression that the topics were being considered for the first time.[34]

The same fault was used in excoriating the work by Mary B. Gilson. Mayo had known her well in the days when they were associated with Arthur H. Young and Industrial Relations Counselors. She wrote to Mayo how amused she was by the authors' naive remark that men commented more than did women on advancement at work; she knew from her experience at the Hawthorne Works that women were banned from promotion and for reasons that she, as a feminist, thought were contemptible. Also she said that the results of the research were painfully obvious, and that the researchers were "clever in interviewing the controllers of funds"; furthermore, she could not understand why the interviewees had not mentioned organized labor because in her research with women workers it had often appeared. Last, she told Mayo that in her interviews at Western Electric, the authority in the firm had appeared little short of military; this fact, rather than what Roethlisberger had written, was the central problem in the firm. With a note of resentment, she recalled for Mayo the early days of her career and reminded him, "You have never cared to tap my knowledge since the severance of my relations with the Rockefeller group." These personal remarks were gentle pricks compared with the vitriol-tipped barbs in her review of the book in the *American Journal of Sociology*.[35]

In view of her letters to Mayo, Gilson's printed criticism reads like a bitter, uncompromising, and personal attack on the authors and, because she assumed wrongly that he had originated the Western Electric studies, on Mayo himself. Her catalogue of faults: had the authors read anything of earlier research, they would have known what to expect; they were naive to imagine it possible to control variables in the study of human groups, and to inquire about promotion among women in a firm that bans their advancement as a matter of policy; with their charts, mathematical tables, formulas, and jargon, the authors impressed only ignorant readers; they had discovered the obvious about unpleasant work, and offered no advice on the restoration of spontaneous cooperation at work. Gilson then cited a book that would do that job. She was surprised to find no adequate mention of organized labor among the twenty thousand interviews, and said she suspected the counseling program to be a management spy system aimed at countering the organization of workers. Finally, she asserted the book raised only one important question: Why does big business finance social research? Although her remarks have been largely ignored, they are the springboard of much present-day criticism of the Hawthorne studies.

Roethlisberger was hurt by the Gilson review, and Mayo offered a comforting explanation:

> Don't let Mary Gilson worry you—everyone knows that she is crazy as hell. . . . She sent me successive and silly letters—which I answered courteously—while she was writing it. She hates all men—thinks women are badly "put upon"—and nothing of discussion can shake this compulsion. After attacking me for not employing, promoting, advocating the cause of women she suddenly changed her tune and said she had told me everything in *Management and the Worker* long ago. Then she went off on the tack that she had really done the work and that I like the usual man, had taken *her* work without acknowledgment. . . . The poor lady should really be put away somewhere. . . . Tell Srole to hit as hard as he likes—not so much at Mary G. but at the editors for printing fantastic misstatements . . . and forget it. The more successful you are the more you will be misrepresented.[36]

Mayo, who had not seen Gilson's review, sent Roethlisberger a well-intentioned comment on the book by Srole. But he was not keen to see it published as a rejoiner to Gilson's review.

> The best thing that can happen is no correspondence, no further notice, and the whole affair dying down. Gilson is obsessive, paranoid, and a "destroyer." She will make short work of Srole because no sense of validity will restrain her vicious return to the attack. One might as well reason with Hitler about Srole's race. On the other hand, if she does not get the supreme satisfaction of other statements to distort and abuse, she might (if really obsessive) begin to be uneasy herself. These things are soon forgotten, if neglected. Of course if there is really libel it is another matter. If a letter must be sent . . . [it should simply list the untrue statements in the review, because such a letter offers] little to be seized for distortion and abuse.[37]

Mayo, *Management and the Worker,* and the Hawthorne studies have been praised and denigrated since 1940. Many articles and monographs have weighed the arguments and concluded that Mayo and his associates were great or minor contributors to the social science of industry. Most of the evaluation appeared after World War II, and little of it before Mayo's death. He knew of some criticism but was neither able nor interested in answering it. Roethlisberger carried its burden at the same time as he enjoyed a career following Mayo's ideas in teaching and research at the Harvard Business School. Ten years after Gilson's review Roethlisberger analyzed the criticisms and found five major classes of objections.

First, Mayo and associates never stated their ideology, thus showing they were insensitive to and obtuse about problems of value and interest. They considered skills of cooperation without referring to the aims of cooperative action; they failed to see problems in agreeing on what were the ends of industrial organization. They assumed between managers and workers lay a fundamental identity of interest, that workers were a means to be manipulated to impersonal ends, and that cooperation was healthy while conflict was a social disease. They romanticized anthropology, and overvalued the Middle Ages, small groups, communities, and established societies. Overall their values were those espoused by managers. They held that the future of industry depends on managers, sought new symbols for them, stole liberal ideas to support sophisticated conservatism, and by "cooperation" Mayo and associates thought workers should do what managers say.

Second, they failed to acknowledge unions as a real unit in industrial relations, i.e., nowhere did they treat workers' loyalty to class, unions, and shop stewards, or mention unions in class conflict or fulfilling non-economic needs. Some reasons for this were: unionism was not important during the studies; unionists do not use counseling; and Harvard men do not want to see workers off the job.

Third, they were insensitive to and feared problems of power and authority in industry, organizing production, and the administration of political processes. Their study blurred the facts of power, minimized the evidence on class (income and property), and emphasized status and prestige. Thus, they did not see that interviewing, counseling, social-skill training, and equilibrium in social relations were all concepts for justifying manipulation of workers toward a belief that they were members of a work community best managed by the authoritarian framework of modern industry.

Fourth, the studies were neither scientific nor useful. To depict social relations they used diagrams that were complicated and undifferentiated, and that overemphasized spatial relationships; they studied small groups as if no one had ever done so before; they used techniques of analysis that were too involved for extension to large complex organizations; and they assumed that supervision in small groups was no different from that required in large factories.

Finally, the researchers used crudely defined methods, ideas, and hypotheses. They confused analytic research with problem solving and clinical diagnosis, technology with science, psychiatry with social science, social skill with tact and forbearance, spontaneous cooperation with voluntary cooperation, managers' goals with workers' interests, communication with indoctrination, and executives' responsibilities for managers' aims. Their hypotheses were never tested, and their ideas owed too much to Freud, Pareto, and the values of managers, and too little to general conceptions of social behavior. In consequence their theories were weak, ad hoc, and could not be generalized to other situations, occasions, or occupations.[38]

Much of this criticism as it applies to industrial relations would be examined closely in 1958 by Landsberger.[39] He found most criticisms were either false or overstated, and the scientific status of the inquiries was sound.

Notes

1. Conversation with Joe Bailey, 14 April 1975.
2. Wright to Reothlisberger, 25 August 1932, MM 1.091; Whitehead to Mayo, 6 September 1932, MM 1.097.
3. Elton to Dorothea, 2, 3, 8 October 1932; Mayo to Osborne, 10 October 1932, MM 1.067.
4. Stoll to Mayo, 11 May 1933, MM 1.092; memorandum to Roethlisberger, 30 March 1934, MM 1.092.
5. Elton to Dorothea, 10 November 1932; Mayo to Pennock, 13 December 1932, Pennock to Mayo, 21 December 1932, MM 1.091.
6. Osborne to Mayo, 28 January, 11 April 1933, 19 February 1935, 25 May 1936, MM 1.067.
7. Elton Mayo, *The Human Problems of an Industrial Civilization* (New York: Macmillan, 1933).
8. *American Economic Review* 24 (June 1934): 322; *Booklist* 30 (February 1934): 173; *New York Times,* 3 December 1933, 18 February 1934, p. 18; *Management Review* 23 (March 1934): 23; *Syracuse Post Standard* 26 September 1934; *Labour Management* (London), April 1934; *School and Society* 39 (7 April 1934); *Harvard Business School Alumni Bulletin* 10 (February 1934): 91; *Transcript* (Boston), 6 January 1934; *Human Factor,* March 1933.
9. *New York Sun,* 18 November 1933.
10. *New Republic,* 28 March 1934, p. 192.
11. *Mental Hygiene,* 28 (October 1934):4.
12. Elton to Dorothea, 28 October 1934.
13. Elton to Dorothea, 8 February, 26 September 1934.
14. *Annals of the American Academy of Political Science* 172 (March 1934):171.
15. *American Journal of Public Health* 24 (March 1934):291.
16. Robert E. Park, "Industrial Fatigue and Group Morale," *American Journal of Sociology* 40, no. 3 (November 1934):349-56; Elton to Dorothea, 9 November 1934.
17. Mayo to Stoll, 20 November 1933, MM 1.092.
18. Fritz J. Roethlisberger and William J. Dickson, *"Management and the Worker: Technical versus Social Organization in an Industrial Plant,"* Business Research

Studies (Harvard University, Graduate School of Business Administration, Division of Research) 9, no. 21 (October 1934).

19. Elton Mayo, "The Blind Spot in Scientific Management," *Proceedings, Sixth International Congress for Scientific Management, London, July 15-20,* vol. 3, pp. 214-18, MM 2.004; *Christian Science Monitor,* 18 July 1935.

20. Elton to Dorothea, 10, 20, 27, 28 October, 3 November, 11 December 1935.

21. Elton to Toni, 21 September 1941. These are Mayo's impressions of counseling at the Hawthorne Works. The mental process, complication, he discussed early in the 1930s and used the idea to relate his equilibrium hypothesis to Janet's theory of mental life in lectures at the New School for Social Research, 1940-41. A history of counseling at Hawthorne is William J. Dickson and Fritz A. Roethlisberger, *Counseling in an Organization: A Sequel to the Hawthorne Researchers* (Boston: Harvard University, Graduate School of Business Administration, Division of Research, 1966); Mayo's lectures are in Elton Mayo, *Some Notes on the Psychology of Pierre Janet* (Cambridge: Harvard University Press, 1948).

22. Elton to Dorothea, 22 January, 1, 9, 21, 30 March 1936; Pennock to Mayo, 2 April 1937, Mayo to Pennock, 5 April 1937, Mayo to Rice, 30 October 1937, Rice to Mayo, 20 December 1937, MM 1.092.

23. Elton to Dorothea, 24 November 1935.

24. Mayo to Stoll, 21 February 1936, Mayo to Westburgh, 29 February, 1936, Mayo to Stoll, 4 March 1936, MM 1.091.

25. Elton to Dorothea, 29 April 1936.

26. Elton to Dorothea, 27 February, 4, 6 April 1936.

27. Mayo to Stoll, 18 May 1936, Stoll to Mayo, 20 May 1936, Mayo to Stoll, 21 May 1936, MM 1.091 Roethlisberger to Mayo, 24 June 1936, FJR.

28. Hosford to Stoll, April 29, June 2, 1936, and undated (approximately July 1936) comments by Hosford, FJR.

29. Report of the Industrial Research Department, January 1937, MM 1.034; conversation with Lombard, 5 May 1975; Fritz J. Roethlisberger, *The Elusive Phenomena* (Boston: Harvard University, Graduate School of Business Administration, Division of Research, 1977), p. 53.

30. Stoll to Roethlisberger, 10 May 1936, Roethlisberger papers; see note 28 above.

31. Henry A. Landsberger, *Hawthorne Revisited* (Ithaca, N.Y.: Cornell University Press, 1958); Dana Bramel and Ronald Friend, "Hawthorne, the Myth of the Docile Worker, and Class Bias in Psychology," *American Psychologist* 36, no. 8, pp. 867-78. Landsberger gives a balanced view of the criticisms; the other authors offer a recent radical interpretation.

32. Mayo to Mitchell, 25 July 1942; Read to Trahair, 15 December 1980; Elton to Toni, 15 April 1941; Stuart Chase, "What Makes the Worker Like Work?" *Reader's Digest,* February 1942, pp. 15-20; Chase to Mayo, 8 April 1941, MM 1.026; proceeds from sales of *Management and the Worker,* MM 1.095.

33. *Business Week,* 21 October 1939; *Millers Chicago Letter,* 31 January 1940, *Harvard Business School Alumni Bulletin,* February 1940; *Management Review,* April 1940; *Advanced Management,* April-June 1940.

34. *Psychological Bulletin,* May 1940, pp. 319-21; Jenkins to Mayo, 25 January, 8 May 1940, MM. 1.051.

35. *American Journal of Sociology* 46 (1940): 98-101 Gilson to Mayo, 8, 12, 14 March 1940, MM 1.040.

36. Mayo to Roethlisberger, 24 July 1940, FJR.

37. Mayo to Roethlisberger, approximately 12-19 September 1940, FJR.

38. Fritz J. Roethlisberger, "Criticisms of Mayo and the 'Harvard Group,' Classified into Five Categories for Purposes of Discussion" (mimeographed), 21 February 1950, FJR.

39. See note 31 above.

17

Family and the Clinic: 1932–1942

During five years separation from his family Mayo wrote regularly to Dorothea and the girls, shared their interests and anxieties, and in the advice he often gave for dealing with their problems he indicated the personal experiences that gave rise to his clinical ideas at work.

From 1934 to 1939 Mayo lived in Cambridge, Massachusetts, while Dorothea lived in England, for she wanted to be near their daughters who were at Bedales school. Because her blood pressure was too high for her to manage domestic duties, Mayo wanted her to find a sanatorium where she could rest and enjoy sufficient peace to write long, descriptive letters.[1] To both of them the separation seemed preposterous and unreasonable. And although his eccentricities sometimes irritated her—he pawed his balding head, and too often would repeat his favorite jokes—she felt lonely and wanted him with her and the girls.[2] He missed her, too, and after each New Year's Eve would count the months, then the weeks and finally the days that he had to wait before sailing the Atlantic to be with her and the girls in summer.[3]

Money was a constant worry. Dorothea was not able to manage their expenses easily, and, although Mayo had a good salary, he felt that he never provided adequate funds for his family's standard of living.

Mayo's affection for his wife was strong, sentimental, and romantic. Evelyn Laye in the movie The Night Is Young reminded him of Dorothea as a young woman at their marriage in 1913. He remembered her when he heard the song "When I Grow Too Old to Dream." In Coward's "Private Lives," which he saw at least five times, he felt the separation and reconciliation of loving couples, heard the brittle dialogue that he had attempted in his story "Ring Down the Curtain," and in one letter noted, "How potent cheap music is."[4]

To help Dorothea manage their separation Mayo recommended strongly that she read Ann Bridges's *Illyrian Spring,* a popular novel in which a middle-aged English woman suddenly leaves her family, takes a long vacation in Europe to follow her interests in art, almost falls in love, returns to her family, and is loved, respected, and appreciated more than ever before. Through the novel Mayo idealized his own marriage, its changes, and his view of marriage as an adventure of independent, loving, like-minded, and mature adults.[5]

Patricia presented her father with one particularly familiar problem of adolescence: she did not know who she was or what she wanted to be. She changed her name from Patricia to Toni or Tony—a variation of Elton—and raised him to a state of high anxiety by announcing that while at university she would become an actress.[6] He was hoping she would follow seriously academic studies at Newnham College before rushing into life; he believed that a university could mature young adults by helping them to "complicate," i.e., show them how to see the meaning in events, to find a purpose, cause, or quest, and to view life as an adventure for independence.[7] He had followed something of a quest himself, and had valued the Christian moral "Our hearts shall surely there be fixed where true joys are to be found." Acting held no true joy and was far too artificial and egocentric. Mayo felt that Patricia's protests cast him in the role of the oppressive father.[8]

He gave her little advice, suggested she get an opinion from an intelligent man in a drama academy, and, since she seemed to enjoy a few stage successes in the course of attempting a "brilliant career," he let her run free, hoping she would learn that she had misperceived the world and would not drive herself into a neurotic state of ambivalence.[9]

Patricia seemed to lead a hectic life with her theatrical friends and their fast cars. Mayo hoped her university acquaintances might balance her theatrical associates. He refused to perform the role of a heavy stage father, so he anxiously sat by, watching her blaze into the world of the theater, repress her good intellect, and conceal from herself a deep sadness against which her hectic behavior was a strong reaction.[10] In the summer of 1935 he tried to retrieve Patricia from the theater. He wanted her to see that a career has a "cause," and recommended that in her maturity a trained intellect would be necessary for a happy social life. Intelligent individuals stand apart from the rest of the world, lead more interesting lives, count for more; all this can be seen from the inside looking out. He wished that he could walk the hospital wards with her and show that his clinical observations and insight—the Mayo "old fashioned magic"—provided a detailed knowledge of how to handle people. At the time he was doing exactly that with Graham Eyres-Monsell at Joseph Pratt's clinic.

A year later his wish was granted, and she came to live and work with him in Boston. She attended his seminars and went to Pratt's clinic, and in the evening after dinner they would discuss the day's events and ideas that had come to her. Mayo did not believe that he could help Patricia, so he did not tell her anything but simply listened to her comments and questions. In return he offered explanations, largely psychoanalytic, and observed the "flood of illumination."[11] At the hospital her intelligence, practicality, quickness, and unconventional approach led to her being given responsibilities that exceeded her experience. Nevertheless, Mayo saw her over-come that difficulty, adopt his work style, dissipate many of the active fears she had acquired about herself in England, and recover her vigor and youthful attitude toward life. She seemed to her loving, adoring father to have become happy.[12]

When Patricia returned to Britain and began a career in personnel and labor relations, Mayo encouraged her to see a career in front of her and to value her intellectual, cultural, and social skills. He advised her to develop her capacity to move easily between groups at different social levels and allow no group to oppress her spirit. On this he wrote: "Be kind—kind . . . but sensible. Remember often the greatest ass is telling us the most important thing. . . . If you follow the [interviewing] rules . . . you cannot fail. . . . Best wishes for the great adventure. . . . I'm very proud of my dear Poppet."[13]

For years afterward Mayo wrote Patricia telling her how daily he was reminded of their year together by small objects, occasional conversations with colleagues, comments from taxi drivers, waitresses, and doctors. She loved him and respected his judgments and opinions on seeking a career, making friends, and the personal difficulties that she was having with the possessiveness that had become Dorothea's burden. Mayo advised Patricia not to allow her energy to be sapped too much by associating closely with Dorothea at the expense of work and friendships. He wanted Patricia to realize that her mother's possessiveness and melancholia would grow as her children exercised their independence. This was because Dorothea, like all women of her time, had not been well treated in the "Victorian world," and they had learned to respond "naturally enough by becoming a deuce of a problem." A few months later Dorothea's sadness passed and, like the heroine in *Illyrian Spring,* she followed her interest in art for a time in Vienna.[14]

Patricia planned to work for two years, then marry. So the question of the right kind of man arose. When Mayo learned that she had a special interest in one of her admirers he cast himself in the role of an "old badger with a long history," and counseled patience and caution so that the "unwanted streaks" that must appear in the character of a special admirer would not hit her so hard when they become obvious. Caution would protect her against the pitfalls of early marriage and allow her to live her life at a high level of human responsibility and scientific insight, and to shape a long, continuously fascinating career by ensuring that new interests displaced early desires. "Anything else is boring!" He recalled that when he was about thirty he had undergone a "psychopathological redemption," a new start that helped him to look at people all over again, to see their struggles and "the spark concealed . . . ready to be fanned, to burn more brightly."[15]

Patricia's social life was vigorous and she pushed herself to attend many bright parties. Mayo warned her against fatigue that arises in the social whirl: "Don't go out until the limits of phantasmagoria . . . begin to appear."[16] And because she had a good intellect, he warned her against the enemy of all intelligent people, the "conviction of sin."[17] When she needed attention in the hospital he sympathized with her distress, reminded her that she was valuable and eminent, and recommended, from Bunyan's *Pilgrim's Progress,* that after lapsing toward Miss Much-Afraid and Mrs. Ready-to-Halt, she laugh into the Valley of Humiliation and model herself on Messrs. Goodheart and Valiant-for-Truth. And he rejoiced to hear that her tough heredity and sulfanilamide had cooperated to lift her out of trouble.

Her health was always his concern. He worried about her being disfigured in a car crash, asked her to be especially careful when she decided to take flying lessons, hoped she would get the best medical opinion on her suspected anemia, and gave much thought to her welfare at the hands of a psychoanalyst.[18]

Psychoanalysis had always raised issues for Mayo. He had accepted the technique but rejected the people who used it; and he was both ambivalent and eclectic in his attitude toward the ideas of Freud. He much preferred Janet's ideas. Nevertheless he agreed with Freud that obsessional compulsion was a repetitive symptom that inhibited growth, and he admired Freud's insights in individual cases. But Mayo was astounded by Freud's blindness to the importance of the group for individuals; although it is sound to seek out a childhood trauma, once the individual relives that, the therapist must press the patient wisely for identification with his own generation to discover love, satisfying friendships, and how to associate routinely in social tasks. To Mayo, the individual's strongest passion was to stand well with his fellows in an active relation; if the passion is frustrated then sexual and parental themes become elaborately overembroidered. To gratify strong passion, each individual needs an ordered community of happy families in which children can readily learn the difference between individuals and roles that they are expected to play.[19]

To help Patricia's psychoanalysis, especially the issues in sex-role identification, Mayo described his part in her childhood. When she had fallen asleep in his arms, her head on his shoulder, she had experienced the feminine protected attitude. But in discussions he had always assumed her intelligence equal to his, and that she knew the masculine intelligent attitude. In maturity her task, he advised, was to unify the masculine and feminine attitudes and retain them without inconsistencies.

Following the interviewing rules, he used to give her his full, uncritical attention and help her to expression. She felt uncertain of his open acceptance, but that would not occur with people of her own generation for they cannot, in an ordinary sense, provoke the feelings of "royal certainty" that come from the individualized attention of one's parents or elders. Mayo felt that if Patricia knew this about her past, then she could all the more easily overcome problems of positive transference with the analyst. He thought that during her stay in Boston this early relationship with him had revived, following her adolescence, during which he might well have provided a clash between the masculine and feminine attitudes in her.[20]

Religion and work were also important topics discussed in his letters to Patricia.[21] She married a Jew, Walter Goetz, and the question arose as to the value of one religion over another. Mayo wrote that in Christianity stately diction and profound human truths are mixed with pagan myths, distressing self-importance, and mental confusion. The problem for the newcomer to Christianity was to grasp the truth and the stately diction and to laugh at the pomp, circumstance, and imbecility. For some Christians, religiosity is a mask that shows they are apparently reconciled with God but conceals in their mental hinterland a confused and raging hatred.

Christianity is compounded of so many things; it is said to have come from the Jews, wrote Mayo, and they "have a most extraordinary capacity for getting themselves persecuted—from Pharaoh to Hitler—read this to Walter." To that, St. Paul contributed much from his Greek education in the dialectic. But Christianity lost more when the bitter northerners took it up, people who suffer from a deadly conviction of sin, drunkenness, suicide, irregular living, and Presbyterianism. Catholic traditions were not much better. Although Catholicism offered active social cooperation and solemn ritual unity, it combined this with a God who revenged himself on miserable sinners. In Mayo's puckish view, the best critic of what he called "Crosstianity" was Shaw, and the best place to turn was *Major Barbara.*

Mayo's personal religion, his ideology for mastering the problems of modern working life, recommended turning to the Upanishads and studies in social science that revived the value of spontaneous cooperation over aggressive, self-centered competition. From the Upanishads he took the rule that before an individual can know about humans, their passion and suffering, and escape the inevitable forces of determinism and become a detached, independent adult with a stable, coherent view of his world, he should "run the gamut of human experience." To do this he must identify himself clearly at each stage of his emotional development and know "the love of mother, children . . . home, avocation. . . ." A poem, *Song of Kabir* by Rudyard Kipling, captured the mature religious mood for Mayo:

> *He has looked upon Man and his eyeballs are clear*
> *(There was One; there is One and but One, saith Kabir)*
> *The Red Mist of Doing has thinned to a cloud*
> *He has taken the Path for bairagi avowed!*
> *To learn and discern of his brother the God,*
> *He has gone from the council and put on the shroud*
> *(Can ye hear? saith Kabir), a bairgari avowed!*

For spontaneous cooperation Mayo recommended the work of his associates. If neither the Upanishads nor social science research was acceptable to a particular individual, then Mayo recommended the slightly confused early work of Evelyn Underhill, *Mysticism*.

He warned Patricia that careerism, i.e., the belief that one's working life should be devoted to shuffling about for advantages of position, was an "unfortunate European degradation," and that it ought to be ignored. If an individual ignored careerism then he would become independent of it and, "indeed, amused by it."

When Patricia found herself attempting to introduce her father's methods into a firm dominated by men who had made their careers by avoiding Mayo's radical approach to organization life, she asked for his advice. It seemed to him that she was surrounded by self-satisfied and incompetent colleagues who were unlikely to concede her any authority to do the work she thought was worthwhile. He advised her not to worry about her superiors' stupidity, but to know the facts, state them temperately, and define clearly what she thought should be done. Eventually a clear-headed superior would see her purpose.

Finally he advised her that if she shared his wholehearted interest in humanity, then she should be guided by the principle that "without participation there can be no spontaneity of cooperation." To learn this both workers and managers need much education. Workers, particularly, need to blow off steam about personal difficulties before they can objectively see the economic problems of the organization. So, in the first stages of this education, interviewing was an important preliminary. "If we need the intelligent judgment of a man who suffers a crashing headache, we know that we must relieve the headache before we can get his cooperation."

Mayo did not have the same deep, close relationship with Ruth. As a teenager she was bored and pressured her overworked teachers, and thereby created problems for Dorothea. Mayo assured his wife that Ruth's problems had their origin in her restless imagination, which, he believed, needed a teacher with the skill to capture the restlessness and put it to work.[22] He hoped that because he was not there to help Dorothea, perhaps Patricia might guide the youngster. But Ruth was very much her own mistress. She would not attend Oxford, which disappointed him because, recalling his own adolescence, "doing nothing means degeneration to a scrap of protoplasmic flapdoodle. . . . Freedom is there for the taking . . . and [Ruth] is the only person who can choose the path. . . . The devil of it is with the immature. . . . Whatever one says is interpreted as an active shove—until they learn that no one can shove them unless they themselves translate what is said into a push (when it is not)."[23]

In the summer of 1939 Ruth married Vsevelod Gebrovosky. They were caught behind German lines when Ruth was hospitalized for the birth of their child in 1940. Mayo sent them money by way of Whitehead, the Rockefeller Foundation offices, and the Jewish underground to fund their escape via Portugal and South America to Boston. The cost severely eroded Mayo's savings, and during the period of Vsevelod's unemployment Ruth's emergencies made Mayo's income "effervesce like soda water" and severely reduce the amount normally available.[24] He loved her, admired her character, but believed that in her use of money she was like her mother, a poor manager. After four years Ruth and her husband were divorced and she married again.[25]

During the late 1930s, when Mayo's concern for his wife and daughters heightened his interest in family life and its effects on social relations outside the family, he became interested again in the psychological origins of the problems people had in collaborating with each other. This return to clinical psychology began from discussions with Dr. Joseph Pratt at Boston City Hospital.[26]

Pratt was interested in Mayo's use of Janet's theory in teaching his associates to note human problems of administration, and asked him to demonstrate Janet's techniques for handling working-class patients to Pratt's young medical associates.[27] Early in 1935 Mayo held two seminars for about thirty doctors—black and white, men and women. He described Janet's theory and practices as they related to obsessional neurosis, and, particularly to the case of a mother who had become too much involved with her daughter.[28] Although Pratt was much interested in Janet's approach, it required giving much time to individual cases; Pratt had too many patients and too few assistants to do that.

When Mayo returned from his summer in Europe, he went back to Pratt's clinic regularly. Graham Eyres-Monsell had come to Mayo to overcome the deep depression that had brought him close to wishing for the end of his life. Mayo took the young Englishman to the clinic, where he was shown how Pratt taught his patients to manage pain that had no organic origin by using self-help techniques for relaxation, and how Mayo handled recalcitrant obsessives.[29]

After discussing Pratt's clinic with Henderson, Mayo agreed to have Henderson's son Larry, a recent law graduate, attend the clinic to learn from Mayo how better to handle people who would come to him with problems. This led to Mayo's plan for about five graduates from various disciplines to use the clinic as an observation post from which to see common human problems.[30]

The first case was a tense and overactive woman, fifty-three, who was obsessed about her role in the death of her two stillborn children. Mayo established the origin of the symptoms at ten years rather than the dates of the tragic births. The second case Mrs. Malatesta, had long resisted treatment of her worries and headaches; suddenly, under Mayo's questioning, she presented clear and treatable symptoms of anxiety neurosis. A third puzzling case appeared to be mild hebephrenia. A week later Mrs. Malatesta was given to Eyres-Monsell, while Larry Henderson took down a case history of a woman who had mastered her pain. And after talking with Mayo, the apparent hebephrenic seemed better. Mayo was amused because he had neither diagnosed her problem nor begun any treatment.[31]

"Back to the army again," thought Mayo when Pratt and Mayo's colleagues commissioned him to lead the larger group into the clinic. He called his therapy "words of power." One case, Connie Faletra, twenty-five, had given up factory work for six years because she continually saw lights that frightened her. She was inarticulate and lacked both education and insight; she was not hypnotizable so hysteria was contraindicated; nor was there clear evidence of dementia or obsessional neurosis. She simply hallucinated frightening lights. In the presence of five observers, Mayo coached her in physical relaxation and in taking notice of her preoccupations.[32] Within ten days Connie said the lights had gone, and she decided to return to work. Mrs. Malatesta so improved under Eyres-Monsell's care that she left the hospital to go home and cook Thanksgiving dinner. And after therapy with Mayo, a man who had been unable to eat began enjoying his meals. These cases pleased Mayo because no one had been able to diagnose the symptoms properly, and each person had improved despite this. They all illustrated his view that psychotherapy centered on "words of power," which meant simply spending time in getting detailed knowledge of the patients and handling them by following the rules of interviewing.[33]

His quick successes at Pratt's clinic helped to prevent any serious consideration of Mayo's retiring from Harvard. He felt needed again, and that his work, training young men to help people in distress, was worthwhile again. And he liked the praise that medical men gave him. For example, the clinic staff had failed to get a history from a bedridden, sensitive, and intelligent forty-year-old man, who was so inhibited that he was unable to act. Mayo approached him and quickly found his interest in fly fishing—Mayo's vacation hobby—and within an hour the man had given a history of his suffering and agreed to see Mayo again. The case showed the doctors who were observing Mayo that clinical work should begin not with what the doctor wanted to know but with the patients' interests. Mayo's technique was to follow their interests, close out areas of no interest, and avoid having patients form worrisome opinions of their conditions. The therapist's aim, he thought, should be to observe the drama in the patients' lives, and then the salient events, the plot, would begin to emerge.[34]

Mayo's success was so dramatic that he was invited to give the annual "Care of the Patient" lecture at the Harvard Medical School in January 1938. Mayo stated the patient is both a case of disease and a human being; he requires medical attention for his disease, and for himself he needs assurance—not heartiness, breezy self-confidence, or dogma. Two diagnoses are required: the first for the organic need, the second to meet the need for assurance. To illustrate this point, Mayo recounted the experience of a Queensland doctor who had learned how to reassure his anxious patients or "frightened people."

People seek a physician for three situations. (1) In a small community, because the physician's work is embedded in accepted social routines, frightened patients are few; the need for assurance and medical treatment are well integrated. (2) The more common situation is where the patient and doctor are unknown to one another. Because they do not share a background, no help for meeting the need for reassurance can come from their social ties. Three problems emerge: first, when the patient's disorder is directly related to his anxious overthinking about it; second, when the disorder masks an apparently unrelated personal difficulty; and third, when the disorder reflects a problem in the relationship the patient has with a person who does not attend the doctor. Two points are important: in treating the disorder, assurance must be given to the patient as an individual and be relevant to the patient's social context outside the clinic. Also, in the well-integrated community, the organized family can support the doctor in his assuring of the patient, but in a complex society, where intimate social relations are weak, such a family can reinforce the patient's fears and exaggerate his disorder. (3) In the third situation, the patient's organic disorder is relatively minor but his terror is exacerbated and need for assurance heightened by a social system that seems to conspire to produce loneliness and insecurity. Mayo described cases of anomie, i.e., social outcasts who could not discern their disorders clearly—nor could the physician. Neurotic and normal anxiety ensued in the form of overreactions to the lack of assurance from the doctor.

Psychiatrists are unable to accept many such problems that call for assurance because change in the patients' social lives is often indicated. Further, society has changed from the close-knit community to a great mass that has created social dislocations and diminished human association. The need for assurance grows from this kind of change, and no effective economic or political panacea presents itself. Doctors must understand and accept this.

Finally the doctor must see that although he might have given his patient sound treatment for the medical disorder, his health will not be restored unless that treatment is accompanied by a careful and reassuring study of the patient's personal and social history.[35]

The lecture seemed successful to Mayo. A few months later he repeated it to a meeting of Boston's social workers, and twelve months later it was published.[36] At the Harvard Medical School plans were made to have doctors learn from Eyres-Monsell how to interview patients along Mayo's lines. Mayo's standing at the hospital was much enhanced. He was given his own clinic, where he saw patients for two hours on Wednesday mornings, had the services of a secretary and a social worker, and doctors in training had the opportunity to observe him in action. With each patient he built

up a case history and, for the young doctors' sake, pointed to the significance of the interview for the patient. He then added a final touch by
showing the patient and the doctors the unmistakable meaning of the
social structure they had just seen unveiled.[37]

A year after "Frightened People" was published, Mayo was invited to
give fifteen lectures at the New School for Social Research in New York.
The lectures were planned to introduce the general problem of mental
hygiene and its consequences for both medicine and politics, and to describe the radical "destroyers" from Queensland, about whom he had been
lecturing and writing for almost two years. He wanted to begin with the
subject of his 1922 Boston address, i.e., the history of theory and practice
in mental health from Braid to Janet, to outline the discoveries on hysteria,
and to state the value of hypnosis and clinical methods for science. Then he
would outline ideas from Janet, Freud, and Piaget, give special attention to
the antecedents of social maladjustment, and follow that with the work of
the French sociologists and his friend Malinowski to stress the primacy of
social over economic determinants of societal control. Finally he would
blend the sociology of the intimate with gestalt psychology and show how
clinical interviews relate to the social study of work.[38] He was spurred to
the task by memories of July 1939, when he met Pierre Janet, whom he
called "a friend and collaborator of long standing . . . I am bringing (a
much belated) understanding of Janet's importance as an observer to this
country."[39] But as Mayo's ideas developed he decided to impose the equilibrium hypothesis on Janet's theory and "watch . . . him struggle under
it."[40] The scheme so engrossed Mayo that he planned the lectures as a
book.[41]

The lectures synthesize Mayo's application of social and clinical psychology to political, industrial, and interpersonal relations. The material
was used for teaching at the Harvard Business School during the war, and
published a year after he retired.[42]

The book was intended to fill the requests of a few colleagues concerned
with difficult social, personal, and administrative tasks. The first chapter
sketches problems of mental hygiene and outlines the psychopathology of
the political agitator or destroyer in order to introduce obsession and the
rules of the clinical interview. Chapter 2 traces the history of hysteria and
hypnosis to the 1880s, when Janet learned that hypnotizability was a symptom of hysteria. To explain this he suggested that the proper study of the
malady as both a neurological and mental disorder requires close observation and description. Mayo outlined Janet's main ideas, and using the case
of Lucie, the double personality, gave illustrations of Janet's method of
distraction and the differences between hypnosis and suggestion. He used
industrial cases to show how often people are active and productive while
in a hypnoid state. In Janet's theory hysteria involves retraction of the field
of consciousness, and dissociation of the primary and secondary selves.

The two function independently, which explains why hysterics typically show alternative personalities and are more hypnotizable and suggestible than normal people.

In chapter 3 Mayo explained that a mental state comprises many elements in balanced relations: conditioned reflexes under subcortical control and primary reflexes acquired during growth; cortically controlled, acquired skills; and habitual skills that attribute meaning to a situation and change according to the active response to that situation, i.e., the point of adaptation or learning. These elements are in an ordered equilibrium; disequilibrium appears in diminished capacity for action and alert attention to surroundings, and is caused by injury, illness, personal disappointments, and grief. To the extent that the elements are well developed in a balanced relation to each other, and the act of attention is adequate to the situation, the individual is at a high point of psychological tension. Like a trained athlete the individual's metabolism is high as a result of a well-integrated and coordinated system of physiological functions.

The next two chapters concentrate on obsessive thinking and the equilibrium hypothesis. Mayo contrasted the hysteric with the obsessive, and described the latter's social origins and the major characteristics of his feelings, thoughts, and behavior. Unlike hysterics, obsessives are unhypnotizable, and to help themselves maintain their pointless reasoning and argument, they do not accept suggestions. They make difficult patients, and therapists resent them. Obsessives tend to be between twenty and forty years of age; they are intellectual, seek private rather than public medical support, and appear well educated. Usually their obsessiveness originates from a major defect in their education. And their numbers are increasing.

Obsessives appear awkward, uncomfortable, embarrassed, and inarticulate. This apparent difficulty in expressing themselves belies their capacity to spell out, with tormenting details, their symptoms and why the symptoms arose. They fear the topic of their obsession and know it is unrealistic. They have two feelings: first, a conviction of sin, i.e., self-disgust and contempt for themselves and their disorder; second, a strong compulsion to act as if they were unbalanced or even insane. To ward off accidents and misfortunes, which they know originate within themselves, they take excessive precautions; in turn they are supported by an elaborate and contrived argument, i.e., their obsession. Each day they bolster the obsession's rationalizations. And when reality contradicts them, obsessives become extremely anxious, exaggerate crises by rejecting objective evidence, and fall back even more on their elaborate arguments and preoccupations.

An obsessive's thinking has three main features. First, his arguments are inconclusive and rest on false dichotomies or alternatives. And the arguments never end because he feels compelled on one hand to generalize and on the other to make absurdly fine logical distinctions. The obsessive often sees and feels driven to consider and decide on minor points as if they were great moral issues, and yet ridicules his overthinking of problems. Second, he loses the feeling that he is part of the present world, experiences incompleteness, and senses that he is an automaton in a dream. He knows he cannot actively and adequately respond to the real world and is anxious and even phobic about this. Third, he is so scrupulous that he takes personal responsibility for all he thinks and does. An intelligent obsessive manages these responsibilities by elaborately articulating their implications, while a less intelligent obsessive attempts to do the same, usually fails, becomes swamped by misery, feels he is in a crisis, and experiences pain or some physical disorder. Actions are caught in unhappy, compulsive, and endless rituals that prevent the obsessive from developing normal routines, produce misery for others, and protect him from an emotional understanding of his preoccupations and from developing complex, mature relations with others.

In applying the equilibrium hypothesis to obsessions, Mayo emphasized "the loss of the function of the real," and the "lowering of psychological tension," i.e., the imbalance among the psychological elements in adapting to variations in the total situation. Then Mayo restated the "destroyers" characteristics and showed they too were obsessive. He asserted that fewer than one-third of the obsessives are destroyers; the remainder do not destroy others but, instead, attack themselves and in extreme cases attempt suicide.

In discussing lowered psychological tension Janet had noted that obsessives lack education in the habitual skills essential to living; consequently, they are withdrawn, impractical, and clumsy, and fail at most things they try. To Mayo this explained the behavior of the "destroyers," and gave good reason as to why intellectuals failed to relate ideas to performance and conducted endless debates. He noted that obsessives assume action may not be taken unless its logic has been predetermined, thus banishing experiment, adventurous investigation, and normal learning and growth. In his social life the obsessive often attempts to dominate conversation, believing that when he can silence others he is more successful than they; should he fail, then he withdraws with damaged self-esteem to a position he believes is superior to that occupied by individuals who do not gratify his need to dominate them.

The last chapter summarizes earlier points and extends the commentary on the social significance of obsession. Janet had noted that the obsessive was unable to attend to topics offered for consideration because too often he undergoes a crisis of revery, i.e., he becomes preoccupied with unsolvable personal problems. This lack of ability originates from a failure in infancy and adolescence to develop the social skills necessary to ordinary communication between normal people.

Normal people are always discovering that their ideas are often inadequate to a changing situation. As Janet said, they reflect on their knowledge and skills to give unity to their experience. Reflection is an act of inner attention, and helps rearrange knowledge in the light of new information. The obsessive can never complete the rearrangement because his incessant concern with verbal topics and their mere logic prevents his attending easily to anything new and systemizing his knowledge through trial and error. Poor schooling is responsible.

Mayo told his associates how obsessive behavior among the universities' intellectuals could be traced to defects in early childhood—defects that he himself had endured. In childhood obsessive academics had been isolated from their peers and dominated by parental values and standards. Thereafter in interaction with others they had acquired little social skill and had learned to solve problems by imposing solutions on others. As academics they fixed their attention on special formulae or abstract theory, which tended to oversimplify any problem. Then, because they were socially unskilled in refining ideas through group discussion, they would overthink them endlessly. Thus social scientists would produce consistent but otherwise untestable ideologies, which gave the individual a crutch for an emergency or grounds from which to deliver intellectualized criticism rather than a secure base for cooperative research.[43]

And Mayo showed that these points from Janet are relevant to industry too. Obsessives cannot easily decide or use reflective thinking. At work indecisiveness and nonreflective thinking can be caused by social constraints or fatiguing tasks that prevent a person from pursuing his line of interests and acquiring the complexity (i.e., maturity) of normal adult thought. Among normal people such constraints produce irritability, indecision, and loss of interest.

Mayo recommended that students of society learn Janet's three points: complexity of attention, interrelation of active and reflective thought, and how constraints and a sense of insecurity cause obsessive thinking to emerge. Training in psychology is needed to grasp the first two, else the student will never see the origins of feelings of insecurity and constraint, and never understand the social situation he is studying.

Mayo's book was published by Harvard University Press in 1948, and sold only thirteen hundred copies in almost twenty years. During the 1960s fewer than a hundred copies were sold. In April 1963, the book went out of print, but in 1969 it was republished by Greenwood Press.[44]

Reviews of the work were mixed. In the *American Sociological Review* an anonymous note suggested the book was a "curious book by any standards" because it recommended Janet's ideas on individual adjustment "without more than a passing reference to Freud . . . or any later developments in the field."[45] Gordon Allport, the Harvard psychologist for whom Mayo had never showed much respect, was not convinced of Mayo's view that in modern times obsessive behavior was becoming more prevalent than hysteria, and asserted that Mayo's ideas on hysteria were out of date.

However, Allport, like Mayo, commended Janet's theory of obsession and favored Mayo's first chapter over the book as a whole, which he wrote was an incomplete study of Janet.[46] In the *New York Times,* Frederick Wertheim, a personal student of Freud and Ernest Jones's, critized the work as dated and not doing justice to the clinical theory and methods associated with Janet's ideas. And he attacked Mayo for simplifying Janet's concept of obsession and not seeing how different it is from various psychoses and defective intellect. The sociological interview seemed naive and the use of Janet's ideas was unscientific, particularly when Mayo asserted, wrongly so Wertheim maintained, that individuals who commit suicide are obsessive. According to Wertheim, neither Janet nor Freud would have agreed with Mayo on that point.[47]

Mayo dismissed Wertheim as "very much a Freudian, but as usual ignorant of Freud," because he had overlooked the two main points of the book: habit is not repetition but a skilled response to a situation; and attention is also a complex act.[48]

The Janet book marked the end of Mayo's psychological writings, and his clinical work was terminated when the loss of his close associates and exigencies of war turned his attention to teaching and research during his last five years at Harvard.

Notes

1. Elton to Dorothea, 10 November 1932, 16 October 1933.
2. Elton to Dorothea, 8 February, 27 September 1934; Elton to Toni, 5 March 1934.
3. Elton to Dorothea, 13 March 1935.
4. Elton to Dorothea, 15 March 1935.
5. Elton to Dorothea, 3 November 1935; Elton to Toni, 10 November 1935.
6. Elton to Toni, 5 March 1934.
7. Elton to Dorothea, 8, 10, October, 10 November 1932; Elton to Toni, 19 October 1932.
8. Elton to Dorothea, 16, 18, October 1934.
9. Elton to Dorothea, 18 October, 8 December 1934.
10. Elton to Dorothea, 26 March 1935.
11. Elton to Dorothea, 29 March 1935.
12. Elton to Dorothea, February 1937.
13. Elton to Dorothea, 30 April, 11 May 1937.
14. Elton to Toni, 15 (?) September 1937.
15. Elton to Toni, 28 December 1937, 7 February 1938.
16. Elton to Toni, 7 January 1938.
17. Elton to Toni, 20 February 1938.
18. Elton to Toni, 27 October 1938.
19. Elton to Toni, 5 July 1939.
20. Elton to Toni, 1 February 1940.
21. Elton to Toni, 10 February 1940.
22. Elton to Toni, 5 January, 5 May 1942.
23. Elton to Dorothea, 9 January, 6 February, 10 April 1936, 30 April 1937.
24. Elton to Toni, 12 October 1938.

25. Correspondence between Elton and Toni, Christmas 1939 to January 1941.
26. Elton to Toni, 8 August 1941, 21 March, 10 June 1942.
27. Elton to Dorothea, 20 November, 16 December 1934.
28. Elton to Dorothea, 9, 11 January, 8, 17 February 1935.
29. Elton to Dorothea, 23, 31 October 1935.
30. Elton to Dorothea, 27, 31 October 1935.
31. Elton to Dorothea, 31 October 1935.
32. Elton to Dorothea, 10 November 1935.
33. Elton to Dorothea, 20, 21 November 1935.
34. Elton to Dorothea, 16, 22, 26 February 1936, 11 May 1937.
35. Elton Mayo "Frightened People," *Harvard Medical School Alumni Bulletin* 13, no. 2 (January 1939): 1-7.
36. Elton to Dorothea, 2 February 1938.
37. Elton to Toni, 26 January 1938.
38. MM 3.070.
39. Elton to Toni, 22 September 1940.
40. Mayo to Roethlisberger, 22 August 1940, FJR.
41. Elton to Toni, 10 September 1940.
42. Elton Mayo, *Some Notes on the Psychology of Pierre Janet* (Cambridge: Harvard University Press, 1948).
43. Conversation with Lombard, 2 June 1982.
44. Mayo correspondence, Harvard University Press.
45. *American Sociological Review* 13 (1948): 247.
46. *Survey Graphic,* May 1948, p. 267.
47. *New York Times Book Review,* 15 August 1948, p. 13.
48. Mayo to Lombard, 19 November 1948, MM 1.012.

18

Collaboration: 1932-1942

The chapter traces the role of collaboration at work, its origins in Mayo's theory of child rearing, his teaching, and his personal relations with his associates.

Mayo believed that in an effective democracy authority must freely move from central to peripheral organizations in response to critical changes in the society's political environment. In modern democracies centralized authority was far too common; this had arisen because people lacked the social skills needed to accept centralized control during crises and, in normal times, to adopt easily and spontaneously the cooperative relations needed for their work. As a rule individuals learn the skills of accepting either centralized or collaborative authority as children in a stable family, but the modern family lacks order and stability. In a lecture, "The Job and Mental Health," Mayo noted Brooks Adams's observation that society could no longer rely on cohesive families, and said that the consequences—"volatilized individuals"—were often found among the unemployed and raised problems for both industrialists and experts in mental health. He thought that the two groups should promote social and personal research, drop the false belief that economic factors determine work organization and control, and discover, through research, the lost characteristics of the human desire for cooperation and the ability of people to work together harmoniously.[1]

Mayo illustrated collaboration at work when his associates, Whitehead, Dickson, and Roethlisberger, presented papers on the Hawthorne research to the New York conference of the Personnel Research Federation in January 1935. Mayo joined the three for the discussion period. When a question was asked, he indicated who could best give the answer, and *sotto voce* prompted any of the three who seemed to hesitate. The audience seemed impressed by the display of researchers working so cooperatively.[2]

Later Mayo told a group of Boston businessmen that problems of working together had been ignored in government, and that administrators of Roosevelt's New Deal were like the fascists of Europe and inflexible industrialists and union officials in Britain in the way they tried to impose collaboration on their subordinates. To understand how to collaborate at work, Mayo asked for more research on human relations in industry.[3]

Research in administration and the role of human relations at work depended greatly on the social skills of researchers or administrators, and specifically relied on the technique of interviewing to establish the facts in any particular case. To Mayo this technique was central to the clinical investigation of human and social action. In November 1935 at the National Academy of Science conference on scientific problems of industrial and labor conditions, Mayo again outlined the rules of interviewing, their underlying theory, and the effect of their use on individuals and social relations at work.[4] And early in 1936 he accepted J. Edgar Hoover's invitation to talk on interviewing to instructors at the Federal Bureau of Investigation training school.[5]

To industrialists and administrators Mayo's general point was that social relations determine the course of economic activities, not vice versa. This was illustrated in his foreword to Whitehead's "The Industrial Worker" and the paper Mayo presented with Henderson at Harvard's Tercentenary.[6] From New York to Ohio and Tennessee newspapers reported their ideas.[7] Much the same argument appeared in Mayo's radio address, "Security, Personal and Social," in which he accused industrialization of creating loneliness, isolation, and insecurity, and asserted that economic remedies for insecurity are valueless. Pointing to Europe, he argued that as a rule isolated groups become hostile to each other.[8]

Not far behind the problem of collaboration at work lay an explanation: the family could no longer teach the skill of cooperation, for its members were desperately unhappy. Because the reason for human unhappiness had always concerned him, Mayo accepted an invitation to give his views to the Cincinnati chapter of the American Association of Social Workers. Mayo proposed that modern studies showed that in time of chaos people should have a view of the world based on optimism rather than the materialism of economic and political thinkers or the misrepresentations of Freud. An optimistic view, so Mayo believed, would emerge from the systematic study of conditions that promote human happiness, i.e., in a community of stable families that encourage social as well as cognitive experiences so children can develop nonlogical and logical skills. Mayo warned that because poor social discipline allowed free play to irrational sentiments and weak control of pessimistic preoccupations, many youngsters would become neurotic adults. Comparison of modern and primitive societies illustrated the thesis that if families are isolated from the community, then social routines of cooperation are destroyed and individuals who have no stable kinship affiliation become hostile to outsiders and uncooperative with one another. But if families are well integrated into a community, then its groups hold together and material needs are satisfied. In political terms the question is not who should be the sovereign to bring unity to diverse groups but what is the nature of sovereignty? The answer lies in that theory of authority that assumes humans will be happy when they feel a sense of responsible control that allows, on one hand, multiple relations with others and, on the other, a direct relation to the central authority.[9]

These ideas extend later parts of Mayo's Lowell lectures and talks he had given in Australia; they were published in two articles to which Mayo attached high value: "What Every Village Knows" and "Frightened People." Both rely on his memories of his childhood. The first article concentrated on community life and the second on relations between doctor and patient.

In "What Every Village Knows" Mayo gave a brief, colorful account of the difference between life in a small Victorian village, no doubt it was Adelaide, and a complex industrial city. In the introduction he appears as a child dominated by his Aunt Jane or his mother, watching a circle of ladies while they sew. He recalls that their work seemed integrated with their social routines. He applied this image to Continental Mills, the Hawthorne Works, and the work of other researchers. All the results showed Mayo that social relations determine economic activities. Without recognition of this—which is what every village knows—rapid industrialization will bring social chaos in a community and, in turn, that chaos will worsen economic distress. Mayo concluded, "The restoration of human collaboration, in work and out of it, is the urgent problem of our time."[10]

In reply to a telegram from Dr. Watson Davis, director of science services in Washington, Mayo described the problems of executive authority and unemployment, and the growing use of the human relations approach in American industry. The answer was needed immediately for presentation to the Temporary National Economic Committee of Congress. Mayo's letter was the core of his thinking on authority in industry, and during the next three years would be revised before becoming the first two chapters of *The Social Problems of an Industrial Civilization.* For a general discussion of human relations in industry Mayo recommended *Management and the Worker,* outlined its findings, and noted its unusually high sales due to recognition from intelligent managers and union organizers. Next he criticized the view that society is merely a horde of individuals driven by self-interest in the logical pursuit of nothing but material gain. On the contrary, asserted Mayo, research shows society is an organization of traditions, and individuals are motivated by a strong desire to share and enjoy routine associations with one another and to put aside the logical pursuit of self-interest to gratify that desire. In vocational selection and placement and in studies of the mental health of workers, psychologists and psychiatrists ignore both the informal relations among people on the job and how the social background of employees contributes to their individual behavior at work.

To understand the social bases of authority at work Mayo recommended

Chester Barnard's *Functions of the Executive*. It supported Mayo's biphasic theory of authority that he believed was appropriate in a democracy: first, authority originates from spontaneous informal groupings and receives formal and logical direction from an executive head; second, in normal times orderly change comes from below, but in crises peripheral authority is centralized. The theory Mayo wrote, is widely followed in democracies, but little or no critical study has been made of it.

Finally, Mayo criticized approaches to unemployment that begin with statistical descriptions of those out of work, propose new housing, and state the conditions for relocation and training. Such an approach treated the symptoms without diagnosing the illness. First, study the people, as Durkheim did, and note that during periods of industrial prosperity community life is seriously altered because of rapid labor mobility and changes in the social structure of neighborhoods and the personal lives of families. Thus, while industrial prosperity raises material standards, social standards of living deteriorate. Then material goods are used and displayed to compensate for and symbolize the lost social standards. As the disintegration of community life continues, demand for material display fluctuates and with it demand for labor. In short, because American capitalism has quickly raised material standards of living and unwittingly destroyed social living standards, demand for goods and services has become unstable and unemployment has risen. Again, Mayo wrote, no adequate study of this process has been made.

In support of his views, and as a source of additional advice, Mayo recommended that Davis see Henderson; Barnard; Harold Ruttenberg, researcher for the Congress of Industrial Organizations; and social psychologist John G. Jenkins. In Mayo's opinion the issues of unemployment, authority, and social relations at work included problems requiring research for which no financial outlay would be too great. All that was needed was money to pay able young people to do the research.[11]

A year later, in February 1941, Mayo would use these ideas in an address to the American Management Association (AMA) that, with minor revisions, would be published as "Research in Human Relations."[12] At this point Mayo had his recommendations for solving both the political and social issues of industrial civilization, and it remained for him to set down the ideas in the first two chapters of his book.

After the AMA conference Mayo accepted an invitation from his friend Arthur H. Young, now a vice-president of U.S. Steel, to visit Los Angeles and speak on human relations to help justify a scheme for enlarging the academic study of industrial relations in California.[13] He gave two talks—in Los Angeles, "The Feeling of Economic Helplessness"; at Stanford, "Economic Confusion and Its Diagnosis"[14]—that were a pastiche of the Davis letter and the AMA conference paper.[15] This material appeared again in April as "Descent into Chaos," given with Roethlisberger at Phillip

Cabot's New England Conference on National Defense. At the conference Mayo's statement on the origins of modern industrial problems would appear as "The Road Back to Sanity" and be delivered by Roethlisberger. And "Descent into Chaos" would appear yet again as the foreword to a manager's text by Roethlisberger, "Management and Morale."[16]

In October 1941 Mayo wrote "Industrial Morale," a chapter for a handbook in applied psychology, but the war prevented its publication; later Mayo decided to use it in *The Social Problems. . . .*[17] The book would begin with a summary of two major themes in his later work: first, modern society's failure to teach social skills to balance the rapid growth of technical skills; second, criticism of the thesis that society is a horde of individuals, motivated by self-interest in the logical pursuit of material gain, and that a central authority is only means to control such a horde. The first theme was called "Why Doth the Heathen Rage?" (Psalms 2:1) but was later changed to "The Seamy Side of Progress." The second became "The Rabble Hypothesis." The remainder of the book outlines inquiries at Continental Mills, and adds to a summary of his work at Hawthorne two wartime studies on absenteeism and labor turnover.

As well as recommending that the conditions of effective collaboration be researched in organizations, Mayo proposed that the origins of the skills for collaboration be recognized in the raising of children.

In October 1932 he addressed members of the Child Study Association, and although his views met resistance, he believed that the ideas were accepted by Dr. Marion Kenworthy, one of New York's hard-headed psychoanalysts, and the author and novelist, Dorothy Canfield Fisher.[18] Over a year later an audience questioned Mayo's views in a lecture, "Mature Responsibility in the Family," to psychologists and educators at a women's hospital in Boston. Mayo's thesis directly opposed the then popular principles of progressive education that advocated for children Freudian freedom at all stages of their growth. Mayo preferred Piaget's principle that in their first eight years children needed a regular routine in a structured family to ensure an orderly view of the world, and the opportunity to develop a well-rounded intellect.[19]

At the end of 1934 Mayo lectured at the Judge Baker Guidance Center on training children to responsibility in the modern world.[20] He summarized his approach to child psychology, and showed how problems in this field are related to general social issues in a changing industrial civilization. He reviewed the history of ideas on unconscious motivation, and used the distinction between hysteria and obsession to show the role of repression and either reaction formation or sublimation in the developing personality. He asserted then, as he had been doing for fifteen years, that civilization and organic endowment join to arouse feelings that in children suppress normal activities. He argued that Freud did not recommend abandoning repression to allow undisciplined expression of infantile impulses, and warned that if necessary repression were not established before puberty, attempts thereafter to discipline the individual would give rise to psychoneuroses. Freud was a stern disciplinarian, so Mayo said, not a radical exponent of self-expression. All social maladjustments, suicide, murder, and delinquency were the products of social changes far too rapid for most individuals to manage.

The relation between social adjustment and psychological growth uses Piaget's theory that distinguishes early egocentric from later socialized aspects of the child's life, and the primitive from the autonomous sense of responsibility. Because logical thinking and social growth advance together step by step, every child must live by the codes of social life until he has fully mastered logical thinking; to do this society must be ordered and stable, the child should be surrounded by age peers from outside the family, and in his immediate background should have available the moral support and guidance of parents and teachers. Under these conditions the child's social powers grow out of constraint into cooperation. Ideally the constraint is maintained by moral support, sympathy, and understanding from parents, while the cooperation, the goal of mature development, is learned according to the "rules of the game" as children discipline and thereby socialize themselves. If children enter adolescence with impaired logical and social thinking, then they are committed to inferior logical techniques and social skills. They become obsessive, quite unlike the well-adapted member of a cooperative group who can think independently and act autonomously.

Anthropological research distinguishes logical, nonlogical, and irrational behavior. Logical behavior shows the individual is capable of independent discriminations; nonlogical behavior reflects the social order, its discipline and rules for effective collaboration within restricted ranges of action, and leads to a sense of security and happiness; irrational, often obsessional, behavior occurs in the face of unmanageable tasks in which the individuals are unable to collaborate, social relations disintegrate, and group life disappears.

Mayo saw the remedy in a balanced education that promoted reason and independent thinking and showed how cultures confer powers of discipline, cooperation, and responsibility on its members. But why had education failed so far in providing this balance? The too rapid application of technical knowledge derived from excellent research in the physical sciences has given society its experts in logic, but these people are bereft of nonlogic and thus find cooperation alien to themselves.

So what is a responsible adult? A person who is willing to participate in group activities, to find his chief interest in a life of cooperative work, to amend the social codes with improved knowledge, and thus to substitute logic for routine. Mayo presented these ideas again a few months later at a luncheon with Eleanor Roosevelt, and a year later at a conference in Langhorne, Pennsylvania, on problems of educating the exceptional child.[21]

In his insistence that children grow socially with their age peers or else fall victim to an obsessive life style, Mayo was outlining his own childhood and describing the child-rearing practices that he and Dorothea had adopted for Patricia and Ruth. In his youth peers had been lacking, and he thought this was one primary cause of his own melancholic, self-doubting, and obsessional approach to life. He illustrated this by describing the case of an after-dinner speaker—obviously himself—who once worried so much about what he was going to say and the impression he might leave that he felt joyless rather than grateful for the chance to speak, and thus he put in jeopardy the effectiveness of his address.[22]

At the Langhorne conference Mayo introduced the Cohn Theorem when answering a question on the role of psychiatry in work among young children. He quickly rejected the cause-and-effect hypothesis for explaining human behavior, and emphasized what Henderson had put to him a year before: for an explanation of change look for conditions under which balanced relations between interrelated variables alter and then return to a more complex and harmonious state. To illustrate his point Mayo described a professor who thought logically and was eminent in his field; his wife supported him well and relieved him from worry by keeping the house in excellent order. Because the home was run so sensibly, he believed it was just another tribute to his intelligent approach to problems. One day, thinking that he had not given sufficient attention to the running of the household, he looked around the kitchen and made a great number of suggestions, most of them valid and exceedingly valuable. But the cook gave notice. Mayo then said:

> Now what has he done? He has disrupted the routine performance; you can only perform a complex task by reducing a great deal of it to something within the nature of routine so that the moment I put this [a chair] here, a collaborator whom perhaps I don't know intimately, will pick it up and do something else with it. That, you see, is a breach of the routine, against the whole of the social conception of what is right and proper. Now, I think he should first, if he wants to do that sort of thing, discuss it with the wife and allow her to give her version of the suggestion to the cook and . . . make it the consequence of something not imposed upon the cook, but a developed spontaneity of interest in a suggestion which seems to come from the cook herself.[23]

Early in 1937 Mayo published ideas from his talks on the importance of a stable family life for training children in the skills of collaboration.[24]

Problems of collaboration often faced Mayo's associates at work: Roethlisberger, Whitehead, Warner, and later Eyres-Monsell. In each of these men Mayo saw changes that he thought had their origin in the relationship between the images they held of their family members and the personal regard they held for him. In many cases their problems of collaboration involved difficulties in gaining from Mayo paternal assurance that he valued their achievements.[25] The most outstanding instance was Fritz Roethlisberger. Between the fall of 1932 and the winter of 1942 Mayo saw many changes in Roethlisberger. To Mayo he seemed a small, quiet man, unassertive, oversensitive to problems beyond his control and anxious about those he could master, intelligent, and prone to think himself into a fog. Life seemed to hold few rewards for Roethlisberger, and the most steadying influence at work was his mentor "Dr. Mayo." The young man was not confident to speak in public, inept as a teacher, and quite unable to summarize clearly ideas arising from group discussion. But all this would change.

Roethlisberger undertook to write the book on the Hawthorne research. Before it was published he had success with a paper on technical versus social factors in organizations. He enjoyed the recognition it brought but was terrified by what he imagined the recognition might imply. It led him away from his psychoanalytic orientation to a sociological view of industry. Second, when Mayo saw Roethlisberger blundering in seminars on material he once had mastered, he took him aside and taught him quickly the skills of communication needed for good teaching. In a short time Roethlisberger became a wise and competent discussant, a person who could deliver witty and well-balanced lectures, and face any audience, from eager students to skeptical businessmen. Third, he was "transformed," as Mayo put it, when given the task of representing Mayo's ideas in the counseling program at Hawthorne and, later, leading a group of researchers in Macy's and other large organizations.

Roethlisberger's growth in personal confidence, teaching ability, and social skills helped him master fretful and irritating relations with his rival for Mayo's attention, T. North Whitehead. Like Roethlisberger, Whitehead needed Mayo's continuous reassurance; whenever it seemed unavailable he used his superior influence with Dean Donham to downplay Roethlisberger's work by attributing it to Mayo, or gave Roethlisberger tasks he knew would be daunting. The behavior presented Mayo with the problem of placating the two rivals, dispersing the hostility that gave rise to their rivalry, and helping them to work amicably. In Roethlisberger's case this was made difficult by his growing ambivalence toward Mayo; one moment he was deferential and the next he would try—and always fail—to score intellectually off Mayo. One day he stormed at Mayo and shattered their old, tried friendship. Roethlisberger's wife intervened, and Mayo was amused to be told that his protégé had a "one track mind." He assured her that he understood the outburst, valued it as a sign of maturity, and that in spite of their differences Roethlisberger, not Whitehead, would be taking over the industrial side of Mayo's work.

That was February 1942. In response Roethlisberger "crashed," so Mayo wrote. The depressing impact of war and the loss of close associates combined with the fear of being responsible for Mayo's work to revive the young man's misery of those months in 1926 before he went to see Mayo. Mayo thought that Roethlisberger had been overprotected as a child, and that he made Mayo his "father" and leaned heavily on him because he feared that failure would attend everything he attempted. When it did not, the fear of being responsible for important supervised work overwhelmed him. If Roethlisberger was ever to stand up and face the world, Mayo thought, now was the time to do it. And he did.

At first Mayo was delighted to have among his associates the son of retired British philosopher Alfred N. Whitehead. And in Mayo's plans for early retirement, the younger Whitehead's engineering and industrial background held much value. But soon Mayo looked upon him as a difficult, amusing, pathetic person, ignorant of the social methods of research, and obsessed by becoming associated with influential academics at Harvard. Whitehead thought Dean Donham a "perverted genius" and maintained a supercilious attitude toward Henderson, Homans, and Warner. He combined his general air of disapproval with a habit of incessantly talking "shop." With every boring dinner party for the wrong groupings of the "right" people—he could not see the difference between individuals of senior and junior status at Harvard—Whitehead and his wife became more and more unaccepted.

Whitehead's outward show of confidence masked a core of insecurity. Whenever he wanted to make up his mind about his work he had to rehearse all the possible decisions before Mayo. Mayo listened patiently, acknowledged him as an excellent worker and as a loyal and enthusiastic follower, and, whenever possible, combined an energetic push to his career with approval for his efforts. Whitehead idealized Mayo, and in 1935, because of this relation with Mayo, Whitehead's behavior and attitude to his work began to change.

Early in 1935 Whitehead told Mayo that whenever Mayo was away collaboration among his associates diminished, but upon his return it revived. Mayo thought team collaboration depended on each individual's believing firmly that his own work was important, and that as their leader, his own task was to reassure each man as to the value of his contribution. In one instance Mayo helped Henderson and Whitehead to see clearly the meaning and importance of their opposed interests rather than simply disapproving of each other's attitudes. Eventually the two began to respect each other, and Henderson even invited Whitehead to organize and contribute to Henderson's sociology seminars. In turn, Whitehead learned to put aside his superior and critical attitude, to wait and see how events turned out rather than judging them quickly, and to admire the ways Mayo promoted collaboration rather than competition among the younger men who worked with him.

Finally Whitehead began to observe Mayo's clinical skills. He saw Mayo hypnotize his son Eric and thus help eradicate an hysterical tic from which the boy had long suffered. Later Whitehead followed Mayo's advice to send Eric to Bedales school, where he would acquire the skills of cooperation by interacting with his age peers rather than develop a neurotic lifestyle through overexposure to his parents.

Mayo observed the slow change in Whitehead as he became more tolerant of his American colleagues, and they in turn, were less offended by his manner. Early in 1938 Mayo thought that Whitehead had become an accepted member of the group; he was relaxed, independent, and able to accept criticism easily. Whitehead himself said that he felt he had changed, and that Mayo had been his therapist and helped him to escape the prejudiced thinking that he had learned in childhood. Then Mayo introduced Whitehead to clinical interviewing and put a patient in his charge; in that patient Whitehead saw a reflection of his own obsessional lifestyle. The insight was sudden and exciting for Whitehead, but he would not grow in clinical skills until he returned to Harvard after serving his country in the war.

W. Lloyd Warner, unlike Whitehead, understood Mayo's methods of clinical and social investigation. He was loyal to Mayo, became a good teacher, and made excellent progress in organizing the Newburyport study. To Mayo Warner's only fault was an inability to manage his domestic finances, and in one emergency Mayo acted quickly to help Warner with a loan from the Business School. But, when in trouble he began to idealize Mayo with most unhappy results.

Trouble began in the fall of 1934 when the head of the Department of Anthropology did not want to continue Warner on the faculty. Warner's teaching load was severely cut, and it seemed to him he was being treated in a less friendly manner. Behind the scenes Mayo worked to forestall any attempt to have Warner moved, and to give him a good chance to be offered a new position in the department. Warner showed all the symptoms of a man under great stress. His behavior changed dramatically. He began to lose trust in his colleagues and suspect them of not giving him the general support that he thought he deserved. He announced that he was far more competent than most of those with whom he worked. His teaching deteriorated, and he deluded himself into believing that, like Mayo, he could easily take a class without any preparation. What Warner did not know was that Mayo had always prepared thoroughly before entering the classroom; his lectures and discussions were only apparently extemporaneous.

At the time the new dean of social sciences at the University of Chicago, Robert Redfield, offered Warner a position, mentioning how impressed he was with the research that Mayo had undertaken and the methods he had employed. Mayo advised Warner to accept the offer. But Warner had grown even more suspicious of his associates, had become angry and depressed, felt badly used, and began to defend rather than develop his ideas. He thought it scandalous that Harvard would let him go to Chicago, and in a tearful outburst accused Mayo of setting up the Chicago offer. Mayo was astounded that his personal influence could be so easily overestimated, and saddened to be the object of such anger and resentment. Mayo accepted full responsibility for Warner's ill feeling, and with help from Warner's wife patched over the misunderstanding. The storm passed, and later their friendship was reestablished.

Early in the conflict Mayo had sensed that a clinical or therapeutic relationship with Warner would not be effective; rather than have the young man reappraise himself, Mayo had tried to get him support from people who had decided they would not give it. In this case Mayo unwittingly found the limits to collaboration are reached when individuals are deluded as to their abilities, hostile toward their friends and coworkers, and cannot engender spontaneous support to see them through difficult times. In the end Mayo believed that he had nursed Warner through a bout of mental illness, a period of extreme egotism, and that Warner had wisely decided to accept the Chicago offer because he had gone as far at Harvard as his ability and his colleagues would allow.

In London in the summer of 1935, after the Warner affair, Mayo met Graham Eyres-Monsell, the son of a British politician. He was pleasant and intelligent, had a sound knowledge of music and an excellent command of French, and was often among the associates of Britain's royal family. He had attended Eton, Oxford, and Sandhurst. But the demands of his own family, especially those of his father, and the expectations of the social set in which Eyres-Monsell moved led him to a low opinion of himself and convinced him he was a complete failure. The year before he had been so depressed that he no longer wished to live and he had sought psychiatric help. When he came to Mayo, he seemed shy, diffident, and obsessed by a conviction of sin. Mayo wanted to make a success of treating a cabinet minister's son, so he accepted Eyres-Monsell as a personal challenge. Treatment began in Boston in October.

Mayo treated Eyres-Monsell in the same way he had managed the illnesses of Ursula McConnel and Fritz Roethlisberger. The two men met daily for an hour or so, read and discussed physiology, Freud, and psychopathology. After a month Mayo, assuming mental patients could do more for Eyres-Monsell than anyone else, arranged for him to take on a case at an outpatient psychiatric clinic in Boston. The young man showed such sensitivity to the feelings of others and so ably led patients to control their reflective thinking and sense of social being that the director of the clinic concluded he was an expert in psychoneuroses.

Whenever Eyres-Monsell reverted to being shy, obsessive, and uncertain of himself, Mayo gave time to direct analysis of his dreams and personal history, and, in doing so, catalogued for him the advantages and shortcomings of his social, military, and county background in Britain. Soon Eyres-Monsell saw how bitterly he had hated his father and how the anger had been the basis of his depression. To the young man Mayo became a "chieftain of psychopathology" in his approach to patients and a "secret fount of wisdom." Eyres-Monsell began to change. As his clinical knowledge grew he preferred work to night clubs; he learned to relax, seemed happy with new men and women friends, lost his shyness, and cleared himself of his obsessive conviction of sin. He was most grateful to Mayo. By 1938 he had joined Whitehead's industrial work and was scheduled to teach both in Henderson's sociology class and at Radcliffe College. Plans were made for him to help medical students understand the relation between patients' illnesses and their social and personal histories, but in October 1939 he returned to Britain to join his regiment and serve in the war.

Mayo was able to accept patients like Eyres-Monsell, talk on child development, consult at psychiatric clinics, and speak at education conferences because in the Business School teaching was not his major responsibility. This was so until 1942 with the coming of the war, the death of his close associates, the loss of his assistants, and the end of the original grant from the Rockefeller Foundation. Nevertheless Mayo did teach informally in at least three ways.

In 1934 he introduced "Human Problems of Administration," one of several new courses. After two years he shared the work with Whitehead and Roethlisberger; in later years they were joined by Benjamin F. Selekman, George Lombard, and John Fox.[26] Mayo's early contributions came from his published work, public talks, and lectures; his students were the closest of his assistants, and their task was to read with him in psychopathology, physiological psychology, and anthropology. His later contributions were organized by his associates and he simply lectured to a large class and carried the discussion afterward.

Mayo and his associates taught a Department of Sociology graduate class, Sociology 23, attended twice weekly by seniors and graduates. The course began with Henderson's interest in the Italian sociologist Pareto, who would fall afoul of modern sociologists for his apparent interest in fascism and related political beliefs. Mayo contributed little to the seminars and in time found them boring, largely because Henderson's interests dictated the course.[27] Nevertheless Mayo continued to put in an appearance regularly, and to beam continuously "like a senile ray of sunshine," lest the seminar leader would take his absence as a personal reproach.[28] In 1937-38, Henderson's course used more studies on social and political aspects of business administration, and Mayo and his associates were joined by Phillip Cabot.[29]

Cabot had established a monthly weekend seminar at the Business School in the fall of 1934. The "Cabot Weekends," as they would become known, were attended by sixty or more senior executives from the largest corporations in the Northeast. They aimed to clarify social and human problems in industry, and Cabot's early interests were taken mainly from Mayo's ideas. Mayo was one of the first to speak at these meetings and would become a regular discussant.[30]

Again Mayo's contribution carried with it some regret. He always enjoyed speaking to and directing the discussion of groups of businessmen, but he did not like their company. So, if he could, he avoided lunching with them or attending meetings where neither he nor his associates had an active role. Early in the history of the "Cabot Weekends," Mayo, chairing a meeting was irritated by the poor presentation of excellent material by an industrial relations executive from Standard Oil. After the presentation Mayo dropped the traditional role of unobtrusive chairman and began a whirlwind of speedy repartee. He contrived sharp quick exchanges between the speaker and selected listeners, cut down those who uttered conventional wheezes or empty platitudes, and closed the meeting with a cogent summary of relevant statements from the speaker and discussants. All the while Mayo drew much delight from watching amusement gradually overtake the stern expressions of Cabot and Whitehead while terror froze on Roethlisberger's face. None had ever seen Mayo deal so outrageously with leading industrialists.[31]

After 1933 Mayo's teaching was directed at four main problems in administration: industrial relations, personnel issues, consumerism, and executive training for corporate life.[32] He argued that negotiating with unions was not the inevitable method of handling industrial relations; to Mayo, unions were *ad hoc* institutions used to meet historico-social problems in Britain's industrialization of work. Two conditions were relevant: first, in small industrial centers unions were an established element with a clear function in the social order; second, in large industrial regions unions were elements of social disorder. Mayo recommended that in the United States it was necessary to research unions before assuming any kind of attitude toward trade union policies. Personnel issues had been approached wrongly, in Mayo's opinion; techniques were too psychological, attuned too much to finding individuals with the capacity to adjust to working conditions. Mayo thought that the Hawthorne studies showed working conditions were what should be adjusted, and that anthropological research techniques suited to the study of group life should supplement the psychological and physiological techniques that personnel officers were using. Third, Mayo thought consumer research on individual buying habits was incidental to studying standards of living. Social conditions leading to expenditure, not material expenditure itself, were the proper subjects for study. He believed social controls held markets firmly even during a business depression; and social disintegration caused maximal fluctuations in markets. Finally, the corporation executive should be a generalist who could critically acknowledge the nature and sphere of specialists; thus, in addition to his own expertise and experience in, say, economics, he should have the social skill necessary to appreciate the attitudes, interests, and prejudices of the people with whom he worked.

All Mayo's teaching aims were on the boundary of existing knowledge, and in stating them he advocated extending that boundary to find the proper subject matter to teach. This is what he meant by calling teaching and learning an adventure. And scientific research provided the substance for that adventure.

Mayo was responsible for but not actively involved in research done by his associates during the 1930s.[33] He encouraged one man who almost secured a niche in the movie industry to apply Mayo's ideas to choosing stories to film. He backed Warner's Newburyport studies, and comparable research by Allison Davis in Natchez and by Conrad Arensberg in County Clare, Ireland. Such studies showed how anthropological research could describe and clarify problems in the relations between industry and home life in small communities. In industry, Mayo noted Pigors's case studies at the East Springfield plant of the Westinghouse Electric Manufacturing Company; he was interested in Whitehead's work with Eyres-Monsell on the personnel problems in Swift and Company; and discussed with Roethlisberger and Lombard studies at General Motors and Macy's. Also, he believed that George Homans was considering problems of centralized and peripheral authority at Western Electric,[34] and was much interested in a study with Homans and John Cooley at New Castle on how technological change affected employment and living standards.[35] Mayo took note, too, of Frederick Richardson's research on the organization of handicrafts in Essex County, as well as his study on the relation between economic stability and standards of living among resettled workers.[36]

Clinical teaching was important to Mayo during the second half of the 1930s. In 1935 he began occasional sessions for the students of Dr. Joseph Pratt at his outpatient clinic in the Boston Dispensary and gave lectures at McLean Hospital. Mayo wanted to introduce young doctors to the social factors that affected mental disorders and expose them to the methods of psychopathologists, particularly the techniques of Janet. At the same time Mayo wanted to secure for his students and associates the opportunity to learn interviewing by taking case histories at the clinic. Among the associates were Larry Henderson (law), John Cooley (philosophy), George Homans (history), William F. Whyte (economics), Arthur Colburn (theology), Eyres-Monsell, Gordon Bowden (sociology), John Fox, and George Lombard. These men would meet regularly in seminars to discuss the work of Mayo's favorite psychopathologists, sociologists, psychologists, and anthropologists.

Notes

1. Elton to Dorothea, 13 March 1933; MM 3.037; Elton Mayo, "Human Relations in Industry," *Mental Health Observer* 2 (April 1934):6-8.
2. Elton to Dorothea, 11, 27 January 1935.
3. Mayo's lecture to Jackson and Curtis, 29 October 1935, MM. 2.079.
4. Gregg's memorandum, 13 November 1935, RF; MM 3.064.
5. Elton to Dorothea, 12 February 1936.
6. Elton Mayo, Foreword to *The Industrial Worker: A Statistical Study of Human Relations in a Group of Manual Workers,* by T. North Whitehead (Cambridge: Harvard University Press, 1938); Lawrence J. Henderson and Elton Mayo, "The Effects of Social Environment," *Journal of Industrial Hygiene and Toxicology* 18, no. 36 (1936):401-16.
7. *New York Times,* 25 August 1936; *News Sentinel* (Knoxville, Tenn.), 30 August 1936; *World Telegram,* 24 August 1936; *Times Press* (Akron), 27 August 1936.
8. Elton Mayo, "Security, Personal and Social," *New England Journal of Medicine* 217 (1936):38-39.
9. Elton to Dorothea, 28 March 1936; Elton Mayo, "The Movement Towards Human Happiness," April 8, 1936, MM 2.044a; Elton Mayo, "The Ancient Magic Runs" (undated), MM 2.075.
10. Elton Mayo, "What Every Village Knows," *Survey Graphic,* December 1937, pp. 695-98.
11. Mayo to Davis, 28 March 1940, MM 2.032.
12. Elton Mayo, "Research in Human Relations," *Personnel* 17, no. 4 (1941):264-69; Rice to Mayo, 15 March 1941, Mayo to Rice, 18 March 1941, MM 2.032.
13. Elton to Toni, 30 January 1941, Elton to Dorothea, 25 February 1941.
14. *Times* (Palo Alto), 4 March 1941.
15. *Harvard Business School Alumni Bulletin* 17, no. 3 (1941):270; Elton to Toni, 9 March 1941.
16. Elton to Toni, 4 May 1941; *Bulletin of Harvard Business School Alumni Association* 17, no. 3 (1941):263; Elton Mayo, *The Descent Into Chaos,* and Fritz J. Roethlisberger, *The Road Back to Sanity,* New England Conference on National Defense, 5, 6 April 1941 (privately printed); Elton Mayo, Foreword to *Management and Morale,* by Fritz J. Roethlisberger (Cambridge: Harvard University Press, 1941).
17. Mayo to Fryer, 21 October 1941, Mayo to Van Toor, 20 January 1947, MM 2.009.
18. Elton to Dorothea, 16, 17 October 1932; Elton to Toni, 19 October 1932.
19. Elton to Dorothea, 27 January 1934; *Boston Globe,* 31 January 1934.
20. Elton Mayo, "Training the Child for Responsibility to His World," 23 November 1934, MM 2.061.
21. *Transcript* (Boston), 16 February 1934; *Washington Post,* 17 February 1934; *Herald* (Boston), 18 February 1934; Elton to Dorothea, 18 March 1934.
22. Elton Mayo, "Social Change and Its Effect Upon the Training of the Child," *Proceedings of the Child Research Clinic Conference in Education* (Woods School, Langhorne, Penna.) 2 (1936):11-16.
23. MM 2.024.
24. Elton Mayo, "Psychiatry and Sociology in Relation to Social Disorganization," *American Journal of Sociology* 42, no. 6 (May 1937): 825-31.

25. What follows is a reconstruction from Mayo's letters to his family of the character, changing behavior, and personal relations between his four young associates, 1932-42.
26. Dean's reports, 1929-44, BLA; AB 4:2, 9, MM 2.031; Elton to Dorothea, 29 December 1939; Fritz Roethlisberger, *The Elusive Phenomena* (Boston: Harvard University, Graduate School of Business Administration, Division of Research, 1977), p. 107.
27. Elton to Dorothea, 12, 19, 28 April, 5 May 1935.
28. Elton to Dorothea, 10 November 1935.
29. Reports to Dean, 1924-44, MM 1.034.
30. Elton to Dorothea, 20 February 1935.
31. Elton to Dorothea, 12, 14, April 1935.
32. MM. 1.034.
33. Ibid.
34. Elton to Toni, 2 February, 24 March 1940.
35. MM 1.071, 3.069.
36. Elton to Toni, 18 February 1940; MM 1.034.

19

Personal and Political Problems: 1932–1942

Mayo's family problems affected plans for his career in the 1930s. He attempted to influence the movie industry in the United States and reorganize the National Institute of Industrial Psychology in Britain. During this period he developed his political ideas on international relations, centralized authority for the state, the role of personality in political leadership, and the differences between totalitarian and democratic forms of domination.

During the five years of separation Mayo lived with his family only in summer, and often he and Dorothea thought of how he might retire from Harvard to live and work in Britain. He was bored by his work at the Business School; he had tired of repeating lectures and talks about his research, and of being simply a "little ray of sunlight that [kept] the group at work."[1]

The decision to retire was difficult to come to. Dorothea did not manage domestic expenses competently, and Mayo always felt he should supply a high income for her "emergencies," as he called them. In Britain academic salaries were low, and most other sources of income were unacceptable to him. He considered that a position at Oxford University on one thousand pounds a year could not meet his family's expenses; he did not want to work in association with Lyndall Urwick, one of England's leading management consultants; he believed that reorganizing the ailing National Institute of Industrial Psychology (NIIP) was not worthwhile; and, although he would have liked to direct the amalgamation of Britain's diverse management associations and groups, he knew that English industrialists wanted a Briton rather than an Australian with American experience.[2]

Also, his American colleagues seemed to need him, and Harvard would not allow him to retire early without good reason. He had to support his young associates in their careers; Donham and Henderson wanted Mayo's advice and help in the squabbles each was having over the role at Harvard of public and business administration and the integration of social sciences generally. And as his interests in clinical psychology and politics returned, Mayo could see much to keep him where he was.[3]

Mayo's activities centered on four main topics: movies and society; politics, psychology, authority, and propaganda; a general theory of industry and mental health in society; and family and clinical psychology. In 1938 he sought an opinion on his career from Beardsley Ruml, who advised him to keep his professorship, give up industrial research, turn more to clinical psychology, and, from that viewpoint, extend the final chapters of *The Human Problems . . .* into a theory concerning psycho-political-social problems of government and administration.[4] Ruml's advice was supportive because it reflected Mayo's ideas and efforts since 1934, and directed him in two ways; first, he looked back to 1904 and thought he would propose a study of international relations to Britain's colonial secretary; second, he looked forward to joining the NIIP when asked to reorganize it in the spring of 1939. The latter alternative might have given him the chance to live and work in England, but the Second World War intervened. When the war began Dorothea joined Mayo, Ruth married and remained in Europe, and Patricia started to follow her father's work in England.

Mayo's chance to advise producers in the movie industry during 1935 and the possibility of working for the NIIP in 1940 were the only real opportunities he had to quit academic life. Each case illustrates his capacity to make from his ideas practical and useful plans.

Mayo was a moviegoer and recognized how movies could broaden and enrich life, and make it less brutish and nasty.[5] He enjoyed some movies but many displeased him. He concluded that in Hollywood there was a systematic attempt to destroy the social order. He likened the producers to a communist he had known in Queensland, who by day worked as a journalist on a conservative newspaper and by night followed a plan to use unions for radical social change. Mayo had exposed him, and he left for the United States.[6]

So Mayo began writing articles that he hoped would redirect the influence of the movies, divert him away from the pettiness and boredom of university life, and add to his income.[7] A colleague, Georges F. Doriot, followed Mayo's approach; he had been able to predict which movies would and would not be box office successes.[8]

From movies he had seen and discussions in New York with Sam Goldwyn and in London with Alexander Korda, Mayo concluded that moviemakers were not learning from their experiences. The industry simply imitated a "sure fire" success until the copies began to show deficient technical intelligence and impoverished imagination. The scriptwriters contributed to failures by putting best-selling novels on the screen without following explicit, carefully tested procedures. When scientists and doctors replaced novelists as society's effective critical thinkers, novelists became obsessed with crime, revolution, and psychoneurosis, topics that attracted smaller audiences. Thus the movie industry paid heavily for learning what it should film. Mayo pointed to the summer of 1934, when a boycott forced Hollywood to extirpate sin, sex, and heroic lawbreaking from the movies and to close many theaters in Philadelphia. "Sure-fire" themes backfired, so Mayo wrote, and he advised Hollywood to think before choosing stories.[9]

In his second article, "Choice of a Story", Mayo used Pareto's theory to give authority to suggestions for selecting film stories. First, the story must relate to contemporary circumstances. Second, intellectual versus nonintellectual considerations must be ignored because even though movies appeal more to sentiment than to logic their plots should not be too sentimental or nonsensical nor abandon their social function. Third, the plot must never take second place to an actor because human feelings, not one person's attributes, make films successful. Fourth, the story should not be secondary to sex—love, yes, but not mere sex—because it cannot sustain interest for two hours.

Pareto's residues should guide the choice of a story, i.e., the urge to social combination, aggregation, and routine; the need to show sentiments; sociability; integrity of the self; and sex. And, despite claims to the contrary from Goldwyn and Korda, Mayo asserted that the content of stories—what the public wants—can be systematically known before a film is made. Celtic, Anglo-Saxon, and Teutonic folklore was the best source of film stories because these were the major racial strains represented in the audiences; intellectuals, pessimists, and psycho-neurotics were not the best sources. To Mayo this explained the success of *Possessed, The Barretts of Wimpole Street,* and *Cavalcade.*

Finally, Mayo argued that, using Pareto's theory, scriptwriters can find in folklore clear, persistent themes for film stories. By substituting modern derivatives of city life and industry for those of the village and forest and by turning old fairy tales into modern romances, the writers would become broadly educated and no longer need to go outside the industry for most of their material.[10]

Mayo did not allow Doriot to give the second article to a publicist in the movie industry because he suspected the man would use the ideas without acknowledgment, and that most filmmakers preferred Hebrew folklore to any other and would not in any case give his proposals a second thought.[11]

A student of Mayo's tried to introduce Mayo's ideas into the film industry, and for a brief period met with success. He was employed by the Columbia Pictures Corporation, and promised a high salary for commenting on scripts that were troublesome. To get the job, the student had used Mayo's rules for interviewing, but he met resistance to Mayo's ideas on dramatic unity and the use of Pareto's theory. In two months the student faced a problem more suited to Mayo's ideas on the exercise of authority at work than the task of choosing a film story. The president of Columbia Pictures, Harry Cohn, thrived on crises and assumed maximum efficiency came only when subordinates reported directly to him and never communicated among themselves. Because he had to work through Cohn, the student was perceived as the prime source of Cohn's criticism and dissatisfaction with the employees. The student became unpopular with his co-workers, and left the firm in November 1936.[12]

Another opportunity to join his family offered itself to Mayo in September 1938 at the International Congress on Scientific Management in Washington, D.C. He learned that his friend Dr. Charles S. Myers, director of the NIIP in London, had lost the support of its executive committee. E. S. Byng, executive vice-chairman, suggested Mayo might like the directorship. Mayo considered the suggestion an impertinence, but did offer to study the institute and think about its aims. In October Myers was retired; in November Byng put Mayo's offer to the committee and it was accepted. Mayo had support for leaving Harvard to join the NIIP from both Henderson and Donham, and he knew he had the interest and backing of some young British scholars in his field as well as two large industries and the people who no longer stood behind Myers.[13]

Mayo approached the task with two ideas in mind. He wanted a position in England, and the directorship of the NIIP seemed appropriate. Also, he wrote: "What I really hope is that there may be one or two really intelligent young men in NIIP—more or less unattached. My general idea . . . is to leave the present work more or less alone and push off with a new lead."[14]

When he got to London Mayo was told of the problems that Myers had left behind. Myers had refused to permit his staff to study industrial relations, had encouraged the use of what Mayo thought were the trivial techniques of vocational testing, and had allowed scholarship and scientific research to drop away from psychological studies of industry. Myers had contributed little to Britain's industrial rehabilitation and nothing to solving problems of unemployment; instead, the institute's work had been determined by industry. Myers had accepted this because the institute needed industry money to survive.[15]

Mayo's impression was that the institute staff members were busy at work that neither paid well nor added anything to their effective knowledge. They formed two distinct groups: one dealt with vocational guidance; the other did field work in industry. The first group tested clients and, because the staff had no experience of industry and little knowledge of psychology, the work was not successful. Members of the second group went alone to firms and recommended efficient work practices and organization. To Mayo they appeared pleased with themselves, showed they had read little psychology, and behaved like professionally irresponsible, hopeless amateurs. Whenever their work was not a success they became angry and claimed their critics were unfair.

In particular Mayo singled out the inept interview method used by a woman whose paper at the Washington meeting had gracefully acknowledged Mayo's technique and then claimed a superior procedure that used "advice-given and action after the interview which," Mayo wrote, "shows whoever is responsible doesn't even begin to understand."[16] When he discussed the procedure with her, he was riled by the extravagant claims she made for it. After satisfying himself that she was complacent, ignorant of the psychologists and psychopathologists Mayo knew, and read only her own reports, he cautiously indicated a vital flaw in her method. She bristled and immediately claimed that with her method she could give workers more than the Hawthorne employees had ever received. Mayo believed she was an incompetent who passed for a qualified psychologist.[17]

Other young members of the staff appeared to be more capable than she, but they were unsophisticated in either psychology or scientific research. It seemed to Mayo that they were searching for a simple prepotent factor that would answer all their clients' problems. In this regard the pressure that industry had put on them was not unlike that Mayo had endured in his early work in Philadelphia and Massachusetts.

Mayo's private views were omitted from his formal report. In a courteous analysis of the problem, he recommended that new leadership would help the staff in both divisions to raise their technical competence and skills in collaborative rather than separate work, and suggested a change from episodic to continuous interviewing in industry, as had been done at the Hawthorne Works. Mayo wanted two of the young staff to come to Boston with him to learn his approach and techniques. In this way he hoped to stem their irresponsible claims to scientific rigor, to instill a sense of serious purpose and a professional attitude, and, perhaps, thereby to demonstrate his fitness to direct the institute. He further suggested the necessity for a large endowment, so the institute could escape the planlessness of studies made at the request of troubled firms, train its investigators better, conduct long-term experimental studies in industry, and learn how to collaborate in the field. The alternative to accepting the recommendations was simply to abolish the NIIP.[18]

[The war put an end to Mayo's relationship with the institute, but, ironically, he became associated with its work briefly in 1947 during his retirement.[19] He gave an opening lecture for its winter program that year and promised his general support. That was a mistake. The British Institute of Management (BIM), unlike the NIIP, had acquired government support after the war and Mayo hoped that it would invite him to join, and then he would not have to stay with the NIIP.[20] The BIM employed Mayo's daughter Patricia to do the kind of research that he had followed in the United States. In the last week of November, the NIIP withdrew its offer to Mayo, but he nevertheless kept his promise to speak on its behalf in Birmingham, Manchester, and Liverpool.[21] The strain of appearing at three universities on consecutive nights was too much. On December 19 Mayo suffered a paralyzing stroke that would end his working life.]

The exercise of authority in organizations attracted Mayo's interest when Dean Donham asked him to plan a course for possible third-year students that would include problems of government as well as business administration. Mayo assented because he had never seen any reason to separate training for the public and private sectors. He also agreed to review general problems of administration as they arose in political democracies. His ideas had appeared in *Democracy and Freedom;* to illustrate them in the 1930s he noted discussions of political problems in Europe and became an active member of the Foreign Policy Association, which had been founded to awaken Americans' interest in European politics.[22]

Mayo's first contact with the association came when he heard President James G. McDonald's address "The Serious Situation in Europe." McDonald proposed that Germany follow the United States and Britain in international trade policies, and that the League of Nations should probably be abandoned. Mayo rejected the proposals because he had always believed that each nation should retain its own identity, and that only through an organization like the League could international collaboration grow. From this point on he took an active interest in the training of administrators for both business and international politics.

In the summer of 1933 Mayo accepted appointment as an American delegate from The Council on Foreign Relations to a London conference, at Chatham House, "The State and Economic Life." The League of Nations International Institute of Intellectual Cooperation had asked him to speak on the use of scientific methods of research in international relations. Mayo criticized the widely touted view that state intervention was the proper means to treat the social ills of Germany and Italy; he proposed that social ills be diagnosed before treatment is prescribed. His observations in Colorado, the Hawthorne studies, social research in Chicago, and work by Durkheim all showed that social ills, or "cultural decay" as he called it then, always appear when people fail to collaborate. Traditions that discipline individuals to spontaneous collaboration break down in the course of too-rapid industrialization. The best treatment is a liberal education; this requires, first, scientific research into society's ills and, second, training in scientific facts for the society's administrators. Mayo's views ran counter to the prevailing attitudes of the time, and his talk was not published. He noted that his views were, in fact, suppressed.[23]

Mayo's thoughts on the League of Nations suffered the same fate. In his paper "The Problem of the League," Mayo reviewed the ideas of William Rappard, F.H. Simmond, James Powers, Norman Angell, Walter Lippmann, and William McDougall. He noted that international problems were exacerbated by increasing economic and political nationalism and the diminishing influence of the League. Why? In discussions on international problems each member nation of the League dwelled on its own problems; they were largely economic and related to the balance of trade and the industrialization of work. The world seemed to comprise a chaos of con-flicting interests. Following McDougall's proposal to reduce the chaos and Brooks Adams's advice on how better to manage conflict, Mayo recom-mended that the methods of anthropology be used to study international problems, and that administrators be trained in the appreciation of such studies.

Mayo recapitulated from the early chapters of his *Democracy and Free-dom* what he thought were the mistakes of political science, and argued that modern democracy had become as tyrannical as the political system it was supposed to replace, and that the League of Nations was as guilty of tyranny as any all-powerful state authority. Why? Rather than leading the way with studies of problems that arise within and between nations and thereby aiming for spontaneous collaboration, the League dominated its members, as do fascist and communist organizations, with leadership that was ignorant of the proper relation between authority and spontaneity. It aimed for control by "seizing power and authority, supressing criticism and opposition [and] seeking to develop pseudo-spontaneity with the use of active, reiterative propaganda."

In place of propaganda, constructive questions are: What is the social order in a community? How does it relate to current political theories? What changes are occurring at present? But Mayo's questions were accom-panied by further attacks on the League. He ridiculed its research, accusing the committee that had sponsored the conference and especially the bu-reacracy of the League of being "too much a civil service and not [having] a scientific research conception." He had no time for the elegant forbearance and tact among diplomats; such was not the proper basis for authority and effective negotiation of international problems. "The only authority at Geneva that will ever serve the cause of peace and civilization is the au-thority of superior knowledge of fact and logic . . . new knowledge and especially a new kind of knowledge—this and this alone will make the League supreme."[24]

Mayo's ideas were not accepted at the time but he did not change them, and whenever opportunity arose he stated them vigorously. He saw that in 1935, as in 1915, they were anathema to people who had acquired authority and who were following what he called "parish pump reasoning" and the political administrative theories of the nineteenth century. By this he meant the ideologies that were used to justify the policies and practices of those in power. To Mayo, ideologies were, using Pareto's terms, nonlogical and irrational; in the psychoanalytic sense, they were "rationalizations" used to uphold both customary social routines and the delusion that peo-ple can deal with feelings by treating them as if they were logical axioms. A politician of such persuasion, thought Mayo, was "a museum piece—nine-teenth century enlightenment at its most fatal."[25] And when Mayo's "an-cient contexts [were] shattered" by the war, he wrote to Patricia that he hoped that her generation would take over and administer nations and their economies with an intelligence based on facts, and would stun into silence "liberal verbalizers . . . they must be quieted, put to sleep . . . the idea that endless talk can settle anything must be disposed of."[26] That was the main problem of the League.

While his ideas on the League were developments of *Democracy and Freedom* and the final chapters of *The Human Problems . . .* , Mayo's second entry into political theorizing began in a discussion with Edwin Cohn, an associate of Henderson's and one of Harvard's medical researchers whom Mayo respected immensely. The "Cohn Theorem," as Mayo would call it, was a proposition taken from biochemical theory and applied to relations among European nations in 1934. At the time Mayo was following Donham's proposals for a course of study for public administrators[27] and helping Henderson plot to control developments in the social sciences at Harvard so that the university would undertake only scientific work in its studies of society.

In this academic squabble Mayo's task was to chair the symposium "Changes in the European Equilibrium in 1934" in January 1935 at the meeting of the Foreign Affairs School of Radcliffe College.[28] The League of Women Voters of Massachusetts sponsored the meeting and the Foreign Policy Association chose the seven speakers. Mayo was selected to be chairman because on one hand he had no aspirations at Harvard and could not be aligned with empiricists like the physical scientists, and on the other he could control the political scientists and their supporters easily, amuse an intelligent audience, and leave it unruffled by a clear and articulate statement of the "Cohn Theorem."

The theorem contradicted the prevailing assumption that the attributes of one nation, its leaders or its people were the logical cause of that nation's impact on others. In the social sciences the theorem is known today as the principle of equipotentiality; it assumes that changes in relations among nations are due to no one nation's . . . goodness, stupidity, or intelligence but that relations alter in a nonlogical and mutually dependent pattern.

Mayo was flattered to be designated chairman. He believed the theorem pushed "all the 'isms' out of court (fascism, communism, and even the current attitudes held by most people at the League of Nations)" and gave a real lead to political science; it brought sudden clarity to his thoughts on Pareto and extended sensibly the ideas he had used in his Lowell lectures.[29] Also, he was amused to be asked by Mrs. Cohn to thank Count von Tippelkirsch, the German consul, for agreeing to speak at the meeting: "She musn't because she's a Jew. Apparently I am the Nordic-in-chief."[30]

Mayo opened the discussion by reminding the audience that too often international crises resemble nursery quarrels between good and naughty nations. The speakers' difficult task, he said, would be to show something of the balanced relationships that exist between European countries, to show that a change occurring anywhere immediately results in changes of attitude and relationships throughout the whole European system . . . the audience will realize that ordinary discussion reads far too much intention, will, intelligence into political crises. The problem is better stated as an almost mathematical problem of equilibrium between different national routines and national sentiments. It is a problem of non-logic; and logical descriptions involve misstatement.[31]

Mayo's contribution to the symposium and ensuing discussion were received well, and, as a result he was invited to speak on current political problems at various dinners and to the Foreign Policy Association. In these talks he began two new themes regarding political and social problems that would be published after the war.

In February 1936 he addressed the Harvard Club in New York; Phillip Cabot, an admirer of Mayo's work and founder of the "Cabot Weekends" at the Business School, had planned the meeting. Mayo's presentation was unusual. He carefully avoided rhetoric by sitting down, speaking quietly, and sacrificing everything to his main idea on the function of the sovereign state. He was hostile to both fascism and recent changes in modern democracies that he thought led to fascism and communism. The latter he dubbed the "suburban pessimism of disappointed intellectuals" and "a saintly variety of fascism." He repeated the paper at his oldest dinner club, the William James Institution. Both audiences seemed engrossed by his criticism of apparently opposed political systems, and he thought they were satisfied and amused when he left their "political thinking in ruins." Cohn's impression upon reading a copy of Mayo's paper was that he was offering "quite a new political doctrine."[32]

Mayo's theme was the precursor of "The Rabble Hypothesis," which he would publish in 1945. The idea was that society comprises not a horde of individuals fighting to survive but a set of functionally related groups that, rather that being dominated by a central state authority, would each contribute harmoniously to the society's well-being if allowed to cooperate spontaneously. Modern society has been shattered by too rapid technological changes in the major functions of its members. Proof comes from noting the preoccupations of Roosevelt in the United States, problems of cooperation in Britain and France, cruelty to Jews in Germany, eradication of intellectuals in the USSR, and a general state of anomie in many industrialized democracies. Fascist characteristics appear: isolationism, self-sufficiency, nationalism, and calls by radicals, revolutionaries, and communists for strong central authority. For his warning Mayo turned to Jenks's *Law and Politics in the Middle Ages.*

In political organization, Jenks showed the state and clan differed in kind, not in degree. The clan, based on kinship and the worship of ancestors, was replaced by the state, which organized military violence against the clan, its external enemies, and internecine conflicts. Power had been given to the state, not as a result of intelligent understanding and deliberate planning, but to resolve vexatious problems that could not otherwise be handled. In Jenks's theory the state is replaced by a partnership of interest groups in the formation of a well-integrated society.

Mayo criticized Jenks for legalistic overstatements, especially the destructive principles of political organization and the assumptions that all facets of group activity are logically related to a single principle of change. For Mayo, simple cultures like the clan reorganize into new complex social orders illogically, without deliberate planning, and not in accord with known principles. Therefore a changing society is always in danger of being controlled in the interests of logic by a centralized dictatorship. This is a form of authority that follows a single principle, a false dichotomy, one that asserts all forms of human association are either hostile or friendly. To illustrate, Mayo used the Nazi attitude toward the Lutheran Church.[33]

The next stage in Mayo's political thinking centered on the personalities of the world's political figures late in 1938, and involved the combination of his ideas about men he had seen at union meetings in Queensland and the curious behavior of Adolf Hitler.

Mayo accepted an invitation to join William Y. Elliot, Harvard's professor of government, and Mary Agnes Hamilton, from the BBC, to discuss "The Prestige of England—Up or Down?" at a luncheon of the Foreign Policy Association.[34] Elliot and Hamilton asserted that Britain's prestige would rise if it armed to safeguard peace, and that the United States would soon follow such a policy. Mayo had agreed to play the Tory, so he supported the policy of the British government, denounced Elliot and Hamilton as "bloodthirsty pacifists," and declared that Britain's prestige rested far more on the decency of the British worker than on the ideas of those who stood to gain by a policy of militarism.

Personal gain and public policy were also at the root of Mayo's criticism of the "tendency of political and social scientists to rationalize their own obsessive attitudes—and to call it political science or sociology. There is no experiment, not even close observation to check the procedure." What was "biting" him was hearing colleagues expound some highly elaborate theory of politics.[35] And Mayo raised this question again, months later, in a letter to Neville Chamberlain.

Chamberlain, condemned for not having dealt firmly with Hitler, had pursued a policy with which Mayo agreed. In the United States, many loudly disparaged Chamberlain, but his supporters were silent. William A. Grant, chairman of Grant's department stores, asked Mayo to write to Chamberlain saying that his methods of appeasement were sound. Mayo did not tell the prime minister that the methods were eventually adequate to the crises they were intended to divert, but that they seemed successful in managing at least one European crisis.

In his letter to Chamberlain Mayo applied his ideas about the personality of "destroyers," whom he had known in Queensland, to American businessmen and to Hitler. Mayo noted that at the head of U.S. industry were men whose personal history and administrative behavior were like Hitler's. They were intelligent people who in childhood had been isolated from their age peers and, consequently, as adults were unable to relate easily to others although they had extensive technical skills. For them, business organization was a strain; useful as managers, they created problems because their personal relations were a string of acute emergencies. Mayo claimed that industrial research shows how to use the capabilities of such people and, at the same time, diminish their "nuisance function." How? Be open to them, listen endlessly to their terrors, ambitions, and life stories. Two results follow: the solitary person feels friendship for the first time, and "in some fashion we cannot explain, tends to develop a greater capacity for teamwork and for ordinary human association."

Hitler, "a not-very-happy personality," had been without friends as a child, became devoted to his resentful, critical mother, and idealized Germany. As a soldier he had made no friends and earned military distinctions only in emergencies. He developed no talent for conversation, only oration. For him, human relations were something that he, as a leader, was driven to dominate; otherwise he would feel he had no function. He had few intimates and retired to solitude when no situation commanded his attention. Hitler's leadership turned Germany's national and international problems into crises to be approached with oratory rather than careful thought. The pattern was "Emergency—crisis—drive—drive—Sieg Heil!" Further, according to the "Cohn Theorem," "the fiction of an emergency in one nation strongly held tends to provoke actual emergency everywhere." Thus Hitler's personality, his leadership style, and the systemic relations among nations created a world crisis.

Mayo thought that Chamberlain's methods—at the time they were being used in the Hawthorne counseling program—"of careful listening, friendship at the ordinary level, no criticism until the individual himself becomes critical of what he says . . . [were] the pathway to appeasement." Mayo hoped that foolish critics would not divert Chamberlain from that path.[36]

A few days later in class with Roethlisberger's students Mayo extended the Chamberlain letter by stating six points about the radical communists he had known in Queensland, and discussed in his articles on the mind of the agitator in 1922.[37] First, they had no friends except at the propaganda level, and were not very friendly even there because every relation was an emergency or crisis. Second, they had no power of conversation and kept silent, orated, or gave their life histories. Third, all action was based on emergencies, not routine. Fourth, to them the world seemed hostile; they could not cooperate on equal terms with others but had to challenge, defeat, and then lead them. Fifth, they were victims of an unreasoned drive for success, such that the harder they drove the more certain they privately became of failure, because they lacked the self-confidence that grows from continued association with others. Sixth, in society they functioned as intellectual destroyers who could succeed only if supported by good organizers. In their early personal lives they had strived to stand well not with their age peers, for none were at hand, but with an older generation, i.e., their parents. Now, because they have no group of their own they try to make one. The only treatment for them is to break up their attitudes and preoccupations through the transference in an interview and to encourage them to experience something approaching a normal social relation with another person. Logical studies of problems are not effective as a cure or treatment; only reexperiencing old feelings and discovering new meanings will help.

Mayo used the first chapter of Stephen Robert's *The House That Hitler Built* to illustrate his thesis that Hitler was a potential "destroyer," and argue that if the development of routine relations with members of one's own generation is omitted from one's life, then the growth of intelligent understanding "runs off the rails." He used this material in an address to the annual meeting of Massachusetts psychiatrists three days later, and again at one of Cabot's weekend meetings.[38]

These ideas were to form the material for a small book, "The Hitler Complex," and Mayo hoped that in time he would find someone who would take up the question of the relation between psychopathology and politics. Mayo did not know that, shortly after leaving him, Harold Lasswell had done just that in *Psychopathology and Politics* (1930). At the time Mayo was developing "The Hitler Complex," an Australian friend, Duncan Hall, from the League of Nations, visited him at the Business School. Hall had been psychoanalyzed, and suggested that he and two others should apply psychoanalytic ideas to national and international problems. Mayo favored the suggestion and for two days discussed Hall's plans, but they did not suit Mayo. Mayo believed Hall was the victim of an "unreasoned drive" or obsession that centered on establishing an institute at Harvard in which two analysts would write, lecture, and propagandize through radio and films. Hall would have no other suggestions, plans, tasks, or associates. Although Mayo strongly favored the general application of psychology to politics, he had to pour cold water on Hall's proposal because its base was too narrow and it did not include plans for the training of administrators.[39]

When war was declared in August 1939 Mayo reflected on the politics and politicians in the world that had shaped his central beliefs. The world had been one of old pomposities, he thought, due for the waste bin, a dead aristocracy of wealthy individuals with functionless titles. He believed that he had been a good Victorian, a nineteenth-century relic who still believed in civilization, decency, and a sense of social order as stated by Durkheim, Pareto, LePlay, and Brooks Adams. The enemies of civilization were Germany and the USSR. Mayo could not see how anything good could emerge from the cynical, merciless regimentation of people in a Russia that had deprived itself of a highly skilled middle class, and whose leaders maintained a continuous policy of intrigue and murder. And "Germany has been the big black bogey man all our lives," he wrote to Patricia, "because of nasty little blood-thirsty, Hitler, his mob of bullies, who with his horse-trading friend Mussolini emulated Frederick the Great and Caesar."[40]

The future promised little unless those in power on both sides of the struggle were replaced when the war ended. He thought it foolish to substitute for the dead aristocracy equally dead alternatives—communism, fascism, socialism. He wanted the new leaders to be young people who could function socially, independent of material rewards, and who would have two main attributes. First, they would eschew "chop-logic . . . verbal acrobatics and . . . isms," and beside technical expertise would develop a superior administrative intelligence based on a knowledge of how to promote and achieve spontaneous cooperation. Second, they would put aside all thought of a single complex theory of authority; they would learn that in a crisis centralized authority is effective, while in quiet times authority must return to peripheral organizations. Unless such a two-phase theory of authority obtains, spontaneous cooperation will never develop and democracy will remain a muddled political system.[41]

These ideas were in Mayo's mind after the First World War; during the Second World War they reemerged, supported by Roethlisberger's ideas on informal and formal features of organizations and a book recommended to Mayo by Patricia, *Church and the Modern State* by John Figgis.

Mayo's ideas failed of publication. In July 1940 Oxford University Press invited him to write on world affairs for a series of pamphlets describing the Nazi dictatorship of labor and industry in Germany. The series would be read widely and serve as anti-Nazi propaganda. Mayo's paper, "The Last Ditch," was a summary statement of the political problems of industrial civilization. It was not published, so wrote the manager of the press, because it was so brilliant and scholarly that it would go over the heads of most readers. Mayo was unwell at the time, and no suggestion was made to revise. In a terse note to Donham, Mayo's view was that "I have said in 29 pages what should have taken 290."

The "ditch" is the English Channel, and Mayo's paper warned Americans that if the Nazis were to cross the ditch, then the Atlantic Ocean would become the "last ditch." By this Mayo meant that the war was being fought to protect democracy from annihilation by Hitler and Mussolini, not, as the dictators had claimed, from capitalism, Jews, and other alleged manipulators of international finance. To support this argument Mayo came to the aid of capitalism. He pointed to the material gains that flowed from industrialization, and said that the social ills that accompanied it were due to the rapidity of the change, not to the change itself. Next he stated that in democracies where capitalism flourished material standards were high, social improvements were great, and research into change was freely pursued; in totalitarian states inhabitants were bound to their leaders' personal limitations.

Democracy brings changes but at the same time preserves social and economic equilibrium. Other political states keep stable by discouraging change and promoting a closed economy, like that found among Australian aborigines. Unlike totalitarian states, democracies uphold a complex balance of power among diverse interests within their boundaries; they manage centralized authority during emergencies and return authority to peripheral organizations during normal times. In democracies this bi-phasic system of authority ensures widespread participation in material welfare. But in Nazi Germany material welfare is directed from a central authority, which inspires people to believe they are in a crisis. Consequently, initiative is nowhere allowed; education is linked with war, and welfare with hate; and some groups—Jews and intellectuals—never participate in decisions affecting them.

In democracies change at one point affects activities at other points, i.e., when interference to the whole system is removed it returns to its former balanced state at a higher level of adaptation. To this extent it is like a living organism. But on the question of control, a democracy is quite different from an organism. In a state under siege all authority is centralized until the emergency passes and autonomy is returned to the peripheral groups; in an organism the passage of central control is not nearly as marked. And in dictatorships the emergency is assumed to be ever present by an authoritarian regime.

Mayo summarized these theses and turned to Jenks for authoritative support on how the clan was superseded by the state. From this two points emerge: it is false to assume the state is hostile to groups within it, and to assume that the state is nothing but a collection of individuals. In democracies the state encourages initiative among local groups, and maintains itself as a series of functional groups in social contexts, each one with its own routine of interaction. And the state cannot exist if it requires from its members direct and absolute obedience; to live, the state needs to stimulate initiative, adventure, and autonomy in its constituent parts. If it does not, when it demands obedience it will meet restrictions of effort and output and go into a decline.

Following Lippmann's distinction between routineers and inventors, Mayo stated that democracy emphasizes the latter more than the former; if changes are too great, then routines of effective collaboration can be shattered. The same results follow when an authoritarian government destroys a society's functional groups and in their place attempts to rule over a "disordered dust of individuals."

To prevent the ruinous effects of sudden changes, individuals require education designed to help them adapt to the new, and education in personal and social responsibility as well as in the new technical and logical methods.

Finally, Mayo argued that the war was not about ideologies. While democracy is committed to an endless adventure of civilization, Hitler and Mussolini sought to end that adventure. So it is not in Britain, the empire, or the United States that one finds the last ditch—it is in civilization.[42]

Part of "The Last Ditch" appeared in Mayo's article "The Fifth Columnists of Business," which briefly and dogmatically stated the conflict between Hitler's allegedly new social order and the American political and business tradition. The article condemned the thesis that the chaos of class conflict in Europe would reappear in the United States and fall under the kind of control that Hitler was using. Why? The American approach to administration is experimental and innovative; American industry is open and willing to accept young, unprejudiced, promising, intelligent men from diverse backgrounds who are trained to observe the human scene. Although much needs to be done to train such people in the human problems of administration, they are superior to their counterparts in Germany because there aspirations are killed by a "dull deadening central authority."[43]

Although he was willing to write anti-Nazi propaganda—albeit abstract and unpublishable—on the differences between totalitarian and democratic nations, Mayo refused to write the case against Hitler's anti-Semitism. Carl F. Friedrich asked for an article based on forty questions about Jews. Mayo declined, and would do the same after the war. His reason for not wanting to enter discussions of Judaism and Jews arose from an incident following an informal talk initiated by the secretary of the Jewish Defense Council in London shortly after Hitler's rise to power. The secretary had approached Mayo, and the conversation ended with "the tentative conclusion that too energetic a defense often provoked criticism where before there had been no thought of it." When the secretary returned with this conclusion to the council he was asked to resign. Mayo believed the resignation had been engineered by the left-wing political scientists. Since then he had refused to write about Jews and their religion. To him the exacerbation of a conflict was not the hallmark of true democracy but the symptom of a disorder from which modern democracy now suffered; the solution lay in restating personal and social issues and not in pursuing "problems as stated by journalists and the vulgar."[44]

Ironically, Hitler's war touched Mayo's family as closely as it did some of Europe's Jews. To help his daughter Ruth bring her baby and husband to safety from occupied France, Mayo had to send money to them through the Jewish underground.[45]

Notes

1. Elton to Dorothea, 20 October 1934, 3 January 1935.
2. Elton to Dorothea, 3 January, 1, 8 February 1935; 31 October, 7 November, 25 December 1937; Elton to Toni, 26 March 1938.
3. Elton to Dorothea, 6, 20 March 1935.
4. Elton to Dorothea, 8 March 1938.
5. Conversation with Gael (Ruth) Elton Mayo, 14 February 1975.
6. Elton to Toni, 19 October 1932.
7. Elton to Dorothea, 2 February 1935.
8. Elton to Dorothea, 13 February 1935.
9. Elton Mayo, "Despair in Hollywood," MM 2.044.
10. Elton Mayo, "Choice of a Story," MM 2.014.
11. Elton to Dorothea, 30 March, 2, 6 April 1935.
12. Elton to Dorothea, 30 September 1935, 26 April 1936; Elton to Toni, 29 April 1936; MM 1.080.
13. Mayo to Donham, 9 January 1939, GC 563. BLA.
14. Elton to Toni, 6 February 1939.
15. MM 2.076.
16. Elton to Toni, 12 September 1938.
17. Mayo to Henderson, 27 May 1939.
18. Mayo to Keane, 1939-40, MM 1.022.
19. Mayo to Lombard, 15 October 1947, MM 1.012.
20. Dorothea Mayo to Donham, 11 December 1947, GC 563.BLA.
21. Mayo to Lombard, 14 November 1947, MM 1.012; Morrison to Trahair, 26 October 1981.
22. Elton to Dorothea, 8 October 1932.
23. MM 2.039.
24. Elton Mayo, "The Problem of the League," MM 2.039.
25. Elton to Dorothea, 22 December 1935.
26. Elton to Toni, 21 October 1940.
27. Elton to Toni, 2 October 1934.
28. White to Mayo, 26 December 1934, MM 1.079.
29. Elton to Dorothea, 2 October, 9, 14, 15, 25, 26 November, 16 December 1934.
30. Elton to Dorothea, 23 December 1934.
31. Elton Mayo, notes beginning "Actually . . .," 23 January 1935, MM 2.078.
32. Willcox, Jr., to Mayo, 10 February 1936, MM 1.079; Fascism notes, MM 2.008; Elton to Dorothea, 12, 13, 16 February, 14 March 1936.
33. MM 2.008.
34. Elton to Toni, 16 December 1937; *Advertiser* (Boston), 9 January 1938.
35. Elton to Toni, 28 December 1937.
36. Mayo to Chamberlain, 13 October 1938, MM 1.031.
37. Elton to Toni, 18 October 1938.
38. Elton to Toni, 30 October, 23 November 1938; Elton Mayo, "Routine Interaction and the Problem of Collaboration," *American Sociological Review* 4, no. 3 (1939): 335-40.
39. Elton to Toni, 23 November 1939.
40. Elton to Toni, undated 1939.
41. Elton to Toni, 14 October, 7 December 1939.

42. Elton Mayo, "The Last Ditch," MM 2.038.
43. Elton Mayo, "The Fifth Columnist of Business," *Harvard Business School Alumni Bulletin,* August 1941:33-34.
44. Fredrich to Mayo, 14 August 1941, Mayo to Fredrich, 21 August 1941, MM 1.037; Mayo to Finkelstein, 5 April 1946, MM 1.038.
45. Elton to Toni, 12 March, 16 April 1940, 30 January 1941.

20

Last Years at Harvard: 1942–1947

When his associates went to war and close friends at the Business School died, Mayo's working life changed. With help from Alan Gregg, Mayo began research into absenteeism, team work, and labor turnover, and wrote a book that summarized the research. He studied soldiers' rehabilitation problems, taught, and planned for retirement. In May 1947 he retired to live in England, leaving Roethlisberger and associates to carry on the work started twenty years before.

The Second World War made a sudden, immense impact on Mayo's image of himself, his work, and civilization. He was a good Victorian who, despite his experience of the Great War, was optimistic about civilization and believed that if it were orderly then mankind would always return quickly to sane, decent activities.[1] But this view was difficult to maintain when the conflict in Europe destroyed his "deep-seated conviction that the ungodly cannot prosper . . . all the ancient contexts [are] shattered."[2]

Many changes close to him altered his daily life. Whitehead and Eyres-Monsell had gone to England; letters to Patricia were sometimes lost at sea and were always written under the imagined scrutiny of a censor; early attempts to free Ruth and her family had failed.[3] His first response to these changes was "a hinterland of nightmare," and the second was work.[4]

At work he lectured in Sociology 23, taught a seminar of twelve selected students, spoke at the "Cabot Weekends," joined the group at Radcliffe to discuss personnel issues, and, at Patricia's suggestion, acquainted himself with the work of John Figgis.[5]

To help him train replacements for his associates the Rockefeller Foundation granted him $15,000 a year for two years.[6] He funded two instructors, George Lombard and John Cooley, and took George Homans and Betty Boyle, a research secretary, to begin the New Castle study, which Mayo hoped would match the researches at Hawthorne and Newburyport.[7]

On vacation he found that his nightmare of pessimistic obsessions prevented him from fishing in peace, so he began planning a book on obsession using his Janet lectures. "The need to work . . . has been a disguised blessing;" in fact, as he wrote to Patricia, he had been "frantically busy."[8]

As the war began to threaten all of European civilization Mayo felt uncommonly fortunate that his interesting work prevented the nights from being too long and dark. Good fortune had appeared in what he thought was the fair success of his Janet lectures,[9] the extraordinary sales of *Management and the Worker,* and a call from Washington for Roethlisberger's services. Also he thought that Patricia and Ruth had seen a high standard of civilization during their years in Europe, a standard that he hoped they could use to judge future efforts. His great joy was the arrival in Boston of Ruth and her family in the summer of 1941. But great losses quickly followed.

In December 1941 Phillip Cabot died, the United States went to war, and Mayo's nephew Eric was killed when HMAS *Sydney* was sunk in the Indian Ocean. Mayo broke his custom and attended the memorial service for Cabot.[10] He began to feel the heavy expense of supporting Ruth and her family and the sudden increase in income taxes.[11]

In February 1942 Mayo's close friend Henderson died. Mayo felt things were out of control: "Events have crowded in on me recently so fast."[12] Henderson's death was an unexpected shock, the heaviest blow his work had suffered. Their association had been a vital element in Mayo's daily life; together they had always been able to laugh at their disagreements and, with sympathy and consideration, to communicate clearly with each other. They were "used" to each other, which was to Mayo "the most important element in intimacy."[13]

Mayo responded to the loss of Henderson by taking up new work and putting aside his usual tasks. He decided to hand over the industrial work to Roethlisberger, and follow Henderson's advice to prod, push, and hound political scientists into studying political problems rather than merely speculating about them.[14] Roethlisberger worried that Mayo was giving him a task but not allowing him the full responsibility to perform it; he protested to Donham that he could not do Mayo's work unless he were independent of Mayo.[15] But when given that responsibility, Roethlisberger "crashed . . . felt inadequate to this quaint world," and left Mayo with an enormous teaching load and no one his own age to listen to him "batter out a scheme" for it.[16]

Mayo began what he considered at the time was a complete revision of his whole approach by studying writers whose work would add authority to his two essays "Why Doth the Heathen Rage?" and "The Rabble Hypothesis."[17] But the "complete revision" owed its origin to the last years in Queensland when he had also felt anger at problems colleagues raised, and had accepted heavy responsibilities for new work. In fact, the revision was a recall of early political writings he had summarized in *Democracy and Freedom;* and the methods he used to control his anger were not new. Following the techniques he had used in Queensland, Mayo stifled his obsessional thinking, curbed his conviction of sin, dispersed "the red mist of doing," decreased active participation with colleagues whose views he did not respect, and detached himself from academic careerists.

Among his colleagues at the university he saw a special breed of ass: they were the forerunners of the "two cultures" whom C.P. Snow would identify, i.e., technicians and liberal abstract system makers. And between them, Mayo saw a third kind of ass, i.e., lawyers with views on the political problems of postwar reconstruction that were as modern as those of Pope Innocent IV (1243 A.D.). At the same time as he sought to withdraw from the world, Mayo wished Patricia would come to Boston to help "talk myself into clarity."[18]

Problems in the summer of 1942 were eased when Mayo learned that Roethlisberger's health was improving and that one of his students had introduced employee interviewing into a management training program in a large San Francisco firm.[19] But then more problems arose. Donham retired that summer, and immediately the new dean discussed with Mayo how he saw his role in the Business School, pointing to the differences between his work and that of others in the school. The next day Mayo welcomed the opportunity to write of past achievements and the origin of his new administrative problems.

Mayo described how he, personally, had influenced Henderson and earned his respect and that of Donham by having the Rockefeller grant raised. He had guided the Hawthorne researchers and gained access to the plant for his associates. Now between him and others in the school was a wide gap. Why? He had planned that Whitehead would take his place when he retired, but the war had intervened. At the time Roethlisberger was unfit. Mayo had encouraged Homans to take responsibility for the industrial work with support from Lombard and Fox, but Homans had been called to naval duties. Mayo was left with no trained collaborators and this widened the gap. He was trying to fill it quickly by turning for support to Lombard and Fox,[20] and he hoped Roethlisberger's health would improve.

When Roethlisberger resumed work, he demanded that he and Mayo's associates Bowden, Fox, and Lombard be moved from their quarters near Mayo to another part of the school. Also, Dean David intimated that he would be glad if another institution would take Mayo for the last few years of his working life.[21] So, by the end of 1942 Mayo had accumulated heavy losses: some associates off at war; older colleagues dead; younger housed elsewhere; support from the Rockefeller Foundation eroded; contacts in the Business School weakened. In his mental hinterland all the ancient contexts had been shattered, he had lost a relative in naval action, and there was little hope that he would see Patricia soon.

Mayo needed someone about his own age with whom he could discuss his troubles. He turned to Alan Gregg, a Harvard-trained physician who had served with Britain's Royal Army Medical Corps during the Great War. Gregg was ten years younger than Mayo, and, like Beardsley Ruml, admired Mayo's charm, intellect, and sensitivity. Between 1922 and 1930 Gregg had become familiar with Mayo's work while serving as associate director of medical education and, later, medical sciences for the Rockefeller Foundation. Mayo's research had always been funded by the medical rather than the social sciences directorate of the foundation; and after 1931, when Gregg became director of medical sciences, he was in frequent contact with Mayo and had a clear understanding of how he and Henderson collaborated.[22]

In the summer of 1942 Mayo had written two chapters of a "popular book" that would become *The Social Problems of an Industrial Civilization,* and was planning another book based on Janet's studies of obsession. But Mayo had needed someone with Henderson's "pungent criticisms of lax thinking," and Gregg had been the only person to offer constructive criticism of the chapters. He had listed twenty-three points and suggested revising the chapters to improve their clarity because the "The Rabble Hypothesis" seemed too isolated from "Why Doth the Heathen Rage?" A possible link: now that the reader can understand society needs socially skilled leaders, let him see the great emphasis usually given instead to dogma and erudition by the disciplines of politics, law, and economics. Mayo was grateful to Gregg, and remarked that two deans had made useless comments, thereby proving the need to rearrange the ideas for more lucid presentation.[23]

For comment, Mayo also sent Gregg a copy of the letter to Dean David that explained the origins of the gap between his work and that of other faculty in the Business School. Gregg replied that Mayo had been both the initiator and the catalyst for the best part of the Fatigue Laboratory studies, and that his connection to the Business School had been through Henderson to Donham, and his task had always been to train men to replace them, too.[24]

When Donham retired he did not leave the Business School but, with Dean David's support, took an active interest in the field which Mayo had developed. To Mayo this was a "damned nuisance," and Gregg was not pleased by Donham's decision.[25] It threw a long shadow over Donham's own accomplishments, and put him in a position where he could, unwittingly, interfere and consequently lose the dignity of leaving office. And Mayo felt that his relation with Gregg had been put in hazard when Donham and Dean David, without consulting Mayo, approached the Rockefeller Foundation for further assistance after the Mayo-Henderson grant had terminated. Noting this development, Gregg advised Mayo to watch carefully the "flavors of the regrouping in the Business School," assured Mayo of their unbroken friendship, stating that he would offer no opinion on the Donham-David request.[26]

Early in 1943 Mayo was still depressed and detached from activities in the Business School.[27] He needed to talk with Gregg about "'developments' no longer, alas, to be discussed with L.J." He was uncertain about how to use his time.[28] As a direct consequence of his talk with Gregg, Mayo was approached by George B. Holderer, chief of the Resources Section in the War Production Board's Copper Division,[29] to study causes of absenteeism in mines, smelters, refineries, and brass mills. Such a study, Holderer thought, "would be of value to all the nation," and he chose the copper industry in Waterbury, Connecticut: Chase Brass and Copper Company, American Brass, and Scoville Brass.[30]

The absenteeism studies show how Mayo conducted his field work. First, he used the formal chain of command in the company he planned to study to secure consent for his work. He wrote to the general manager of Chase Brass and Copper for an appointment, and, at the same time, informed the company's president, asking for his views on the firm's problems. Also, he wrote to the local union official, telling him of the War Production Board's intentions and saying that Harold Ruttenburg, who had left his union post to assist the board, was looking forward to the union's collaboration in the work.[31] Having established his position and its status in the field, Mayo then answered questions as to his particular task. To the general manager he wrote that he intended to make no survey of employees because that was too ambitious, would get out of hand, and become "addicted to publicity"; instead, he would get the facts of the situation from senior managers, advise on appropriate action, but take no action himself without the management's consent. All conversations would be held in confidence, attention would be given to facts rather than opinions, and those facts would not be made public. To the union official Mayo gave an assurance that rather than conduct a survey "that might interfere with your activities or others of the company," he would consult with company officers and the union, and that no inquiry would be started unless it were appropriate to everyone concerned.[32]

Mayo took Lombard on the first field trip. They conferred with managers of the three companies, and learned the managers were unclear as to the purpose of the study because, contrary to Holderer's view, none saw absenteeism as a problem. The causes of absenteeism, however, were clear enough: too much pay; too much interest in weekend excursions; excessive alcohol consumption; and overactive unions. The union official, on the other hand, was concerned about absenteeism; he predicted that it would rise during summer due to poor ventilation and poor air conditioning at the plants.[33]

The list of reasons for absences was of no use to Mayo, so in talks with the company executives he persuaded them that they should work together on the problem, and that he was not selling a special quick system of reorganization to stop absenteeism altogether. Instead, he proposed that after careful research in each plant, the companies themselves would decide if they wanted to alter their organizations. Mayo repeated that without effective diagnosis there could be no sure remedies for absenteeism short of quackery.[34]

Because Lombard was called to other duties, John Fox joined Mayo at the next conference with managers in Waterbury. Fox toured the plants and got the general support needed for the study from the middle and first-line supervisors.[35] As the work began Mayo saw the practical problem in the field was "to make [managers, union officials, and workers] stop abusing each other and get them to look at the facts. These same facts have proved immensely surprising to all of them, and, at the moment, they are finding each other much better fellows than they had supposed."[36]

Mayo took the research findings as they emerged and introduced them to the relevant individuals. In each plant the casting shop was chosen to begin the study because Chase's vice-president Richard D. Ely thought the casting shop had been the bottleneck in the flow of operations and the origin of most absenteeism. The sheet mill was chosen as well because competent observers said that it was the most appropriate basis for comparison with the casting shop. The researchers went for their preliminary analysis to the attendance records of each firm.

Mayo was not interested in showing that sickness accounts for most absences, so he proposed that absence be defined by as being away from work without permission for so many consecutive days. Within a short time Mayo had results that showed most employees were rarely absent, and that what absences there were could readily be attributed to the work situation rather than simply to employee malingering.[37] In a preliminary report to Holderer, Mayo suggested that absence rates reflected a broad social problem.[38]

Because of labor shortages in Waterbury, employees worked long and hard; some volunteered to work as much as twelve to sixteen hours a day. Mayo warned, "This policy . . . will lead to disaster." He advised that the draft boards, the armed services, and industry must cooperate more in their moving of men from industry to the military. The research continued for a short period after Mayo's letter, and eventually Fox reported additional observations that showed that reasons for differences in the absence rates for workplaces lay in the extent to which management understood the human and social, as well as the technical, problems of industrial organization.[39]

Mayo had not wanted the work to be written up, so he and Fox reported the results to Dean David, a representative of the three firms, and Holderer. Mayo believed that a written report could get into the wrong hands and be misunderstood in Washington. Eventually Dean David was required to persuade Mayo to produce four reports: one for each firm and one for the firm's representative. The identity of the firms had to be a secret because of the war. But, as Mayo wrote, in human organizations there are no trade secrets, and if it appears that there are, then spontaneous cooperation at work will give way to mistrust and suspicion.

The reports were sent to senior executives in the plants, and responses were generally favorable, except that the president of Scoville wanted to know the secret of one company's superiority over the other, and the president of Chase thought Mayo had failed to show how absences had affected operations or to appreciate the effect of pressure from government and unions on the showing of his organization. Mayo could only repeat his earlier statement that research in human organization does not reveal secrets or formulae for success. He emphasized that the measure used for absenteeism was unique and that another measure be used to assess absence among employees with high attendance records. It would indicate differences in morale. Also, he recommended that management not use the same penalties for different forms of absence, so as to avoid arousing resentment and indignation among employees. He reminded his readers that the research did not show that one management was superior to another.[40]

Mayo kept Gregg informed of the Waterbury research, and Gregg admired Mayo's capacity to "reexamine facts and squeeze new juice out of old fruit."[41] He suggested "Waterbury [is] a paradigm for your group" because the approach was unique and promoted the value of the direct relation between research in industry and the Business School. And when he read Mayo's "Report on Absenteeism in Three Metal Companies" he recommended that it be edited to be a practical guide for a company's reorganization rather than a research report.[42] The final report was published late in 1943, with Fox and Jerome Scott as authors.[43]

For two months Jerome Scott extended the observations made at Waterbury in a study of labor turnover in the Southern California aircraft industry. Mayo had been to several plants and had had to leave the West Coast unexpectedly.[44] Scott reported his work to Mayo in April 1944, and by the end of May a report, "Plant Teamwork and Labor Turnover," was delivered to the assistant secretary of commerce for air, for whom the work had been done.[45] When Scott was called into military service, Lombard volunteered to revise the report for publication.[46]

The study shows that in 1942, due to population drift to the West Coast, the cumulative rate of labor turnover in the Southern California aircraft industry was 69 percent. The results indicated that absenteeism was a social phenomenon attributable to supervisors' methods of control. Those whose subordinates had good attendance records defined their tasks as helping individual workers perform technical activities and handling plans for work group members to contact people outside the group. And as the work groups formed and became teams, intragroup communication developed and the group disciplined its members into regular attendance. The report states that when managers are introducing technological change into worker tasks, or moving a man from one position to another, they can unwittingly defeat the natural process of grouping, and the strong desire for human association can take the form of excessive absenteeism and high labor turnover. Workers cannot sensibly be blamed for management's failure to observe the human factors in organization. As a rule, when technical and human considerations are balanced in industrial organization, relations between supervisors and workers, and among workers, become mutually supportive and contribute to overall efficiency. Without that balanced approach, discord and inefficiency ensue.

In July 1944 Mayo was invited to undertake what would be his last research inquiry. The National Research Council asked him to chair a three-man subcommittee of the Committee on Work and Industry that would study problems of rehabilitating soldiers and displaced industrial workers. Mayo's colleagues would be Dr. Clarence D. Selby from General Motors and Dr. J.G. Townsend from the U.S. Public Health Service. The invitation fed an old obsession. As John Fox noted, Mayo seemed "very excited . . . due a little bit to his being chairman over two medical people. . . . He certainly wanted the Dean to hear about it."[47] The committee first met in September and sought information from many companies and communities on their schemes for vocational rehabilitation.

The committee report commended large firms for attention to the problems of rehabilitation, and recommended that such attention be extended to small and medium-sized firms that lacked specialist help in medical counseling and engineering. Also, special research was needed on the structure and needs of the labor market. It was found that little attention had been given to securing the veteran's cooperation in making use of his skills in peacetime. Research was needed to provide courses for training in personal and social rehabilitation at work. Plans must follow a policy of "balanced attention" to the total needs of the veterans by training supervisors in how to welcome veterans to an organization, counsel them, and place them and their work in context. Since readjustment to work would determine the extent of the veteran's cooperation, special interest must be taken in his social skills, thinking, and physical health. Research and training in personal counseling was needed to make veterans able to handle problems at work and to grow personally. For this purpose, special notice should be given to Carl Rogers's counseling methods, which had been used with the United Services Organization (USO) as well as those developed at the Hawthorne Works. Finally, the report found that the nation needed research on the determinants of cooperation at work and a scheme whereby such research could be turned into action for veterans.

Mayo had had Lombard as the committee's secretary, and it was he who prepared the report. Mayo's task as chairman had been extended to include company visits to discuss rehabilitation programs, and to address a Business School conference on the problems of the returning veterans, recalling his Australian experiences with shell-shocked soldiers in "The Discharged Veteran as a Member of an Organization."[48]

In June 1944, at the suggestion of Dr. Joseph Willits, Mayo was invited to submit a paper for the September Conference on Science, Philosophy and Religion. He agreed, but when the time came he could not attend because of his commitment to the rehabilitation inquiry, so he sent for discussion a copy of "Group Tensions in Industry." It blended the two essays he had written in 1942 with the two absenteeism studies. In November 1944 he was invited to open the McGill University lecture series on supervision sponsored by National Breweries. His talk, "Supervision and What it Means," included the same ideas as "Group Tension in Industry" but discussed work groups controlled by supervisors.[49]

In his last major publication, *The Social Problems of an Industrial Civilization,* Mayo presented once again ideas from recent lectures and papers published between 1917 and 1945. Ideas on the need for cooperation and the ill effects of industrialization had appeared in *Democracy and Freedom,* the Australian papers, and two forceful essays, modifications of the unpublished "The Last Ditch."[50]

In the first essay, "Why Do the Heathen Rage?" later given the title "The Seamy Side of Progress," Mayo stated LePlay's contrast between simple and modern industrial communities. In the simple community, the economy comprises rural occupations and the social order is well founded because each person understands the economic activities and social functions he is expected to perform. Kinship ties relate him to social events, and from them he learns how to cooperate with others. Social codes and individual desires are congruent, and, as a result, individuals are content and the society remains stable. In the modern community, rapid technological changes make occupational careers uncertain, so the social order based on them becomes unstable. Communication and cooperation among individuals is no longer spontaneous or effective, they feel insecure and miserable, and turn for compensation and happiness to an endless chain of novelties. Durkheim had noted that whereas in the simpler communities the children and adolescents learned willingly to subjugate infantile desires to the purposes of their groups, in the more complex societies the unity of individuals and group interests diminishes and with it goes collaboration among people. Work satisfaction declines, and social disunity and individual unhappiness follow.

Mayo noted that the state is unable to organize the intimate social life of its citizens, and no scientific studies have been made to indicate how to compensate for the social and personal unhappiness that followed rapid industrialization. He asked that collaboration among people and groups should no longer be left to chance but administered competently so as to give each person and group gratifying material and economic goals, and to maintain spontaneous cooperation among people in organizations. A return to the primitive, simple community is not realistic.

The prime fact in cooperative relations is communication: "the capacity of an individual to communicate feelings and ideas to another . . . of groups to communicate effectively and intimately with each other." Communication is a simple social skill that if not learned tends to bring about psychoneurosis in individuals and intellectualized formulae finding in international relations, which, in turn, prevents parties from understanding one another. This led Mayo to assert that if social skills had advanced with technical skills a second European war would not have occurred.

People who lack social skills—and their numbers are increasing—think like Janet's obsessives. They can be found among scholars in universities as well as political agitators in unions. Mayo listed their attributes—no friends, no conversation, anxious in a hostile world—and traced the origins of the pathology to a childhood that had either limited the variety of personal relations outside the family or encouraged the development of social skills irrelevant to urban industrial organizations. This personal problem could be resolved for many people through skilled interviewing at work.

Also, because technical changes in industry radically alter occupations and the social life associated with them, and, consequently, individuals suffer deep depression and lose their confidence in democratic leadership, there come into being political conditions that provide domination like Hitler's. Mayo recommended that along with technical changes "intelligent attention at the top" of industrial organization must introduce retraining into industry. He assumed that workers would respond loyally, capably, and willingly if their needs were understood by socially skillful administrators.

"The Rabble Hypothesis" condemns economic theory for assuming that society comprises rabble rather than organizations of individuals, and that individuals act logically to serve only their self-interest. Mayo admitted this may be so in a crisis when routines for cooperation disintegrate and no leaders emerge to organize individual activity; however social research in industry showed workers organize themselves and will pursue, nonlogically, their social interests even when they have the opportunity to maximize gains logically. As a rule human desires for association are stronger than individual desires or the logical pursuit of self-interest.

Powerful centralized states were once assumed to be the organizing agents of the alleged rabble. But the historian John Figgis and the administrator Chester Barnard argued otherwise. In a democracy, organizations, not the absolute state, have authority over and plan people's tasks according to the cooperative attitudes they hold toward one another. Those in authority need the skill and understanding of human collaboration that only a close and thorough study of human interaction can provide. For this reason administrators of organizations need to augment their technical education with training in social skills if they wish to exercise authority effectively and efficiently.

State domination of individuals is hostile to the view that organizational authority can integrate social groups. To illustrate this point Mayo used

Jenks's theory of differences between the state and the clan to uphold Barnard's assertion that organizations can meet their goals and those of their members only when individuals in the organization cooperate. The alternative, a powerful centralized state, produces the tyranny of Hitler and Mussolini. So, for democracy to flourish, active social skills and insights are mandatory.

The other chapters of *The Social Problems . . .* outline Mayo's inquiries at Continental Mills, the Hawthorne studies, the wartime research on absenteeism and labor turnover, and there is a summary.

The 150-page book was well publicized. Most reviews summarized it without evaluation, and many quoted Mayo's provocative speculation: "If our social skills had advanced step by step with our technical skills there would not have been another war." One journalist did not agree that Mayo had stated the most important problems of industrial civilization, and wondered what had happened to issues of unemployment and maldistribution of wealth; he characterized the Hawthorne studies as solely intended to raise productivity, and complained that the book was pretentious, apocalyptic, and too broadly motivated.[51] The industrial correspondent for the *Times* (London), in light of the industrial strife facing Chancellor of the Exchequer Hugh Dalton on the eve of his budget speech, recommended that Mayo's ideas on group psychology at work might give direction to attempts at reviving the economy.[52] In "Calling All Social Scientists," Stuart Chase described fully all Mayo had written, warmly praised it, and concluded that "we need about a thousand more Professor Mayos."[53]

Early reviews in industrial magazines said the book was thoughtful, practical, and, perhaps at first too serious for the average manager, it was a simple plea for cooperation at work in the interests of production.[54] Two Catholic reviewers were not so impressed: one objected to the positivism of Mayo's approach to the scientific study of mankind's problems, the other, without stating a reason, found that he could not accept the book's arguments and conclusions even though they were stimulating and challenging.[55] Two British reviews were highly favorable.[56] Although Mayo's views were not new, according to *Scope*'s reviewer, their scientific basis was vital and practical, and he congratulated Mayo for devising instruments to uncover the resentment among workers and to reveal the false economic theories. But the British review that most pleased Mayo came from Urwick and Brech. Long quotations interlarded high praise, and the final tribute said of the book: "*nunc dimittis* of a great man, the harbinger of his [retirement] . . . it is beyond our power to pay fitting tribute to one of the great figures of the time . . . grand leadership in the blazing of a pioneer trail."

Much praise came from academic colleagues. Harvard's President Conant liked the book but could not see how evidence could be adduced to support the generalization that the number of unhappy people was growing. Mayo assured Conant the facts were soundly based on forty years of clinical experience.[57] A leading psychiatrist and anthropologist, Alexander H. Leighton, said the book illuminated and integrated his own half-formed notions, touched on vital problems of the times, and helped him in planning his teaching.[58] Similarly affected were Cyril James and Ewen Cameron from McGill; Lord Marley at the British House of Lords; Dawson, whose ideas Mayo had used extensively; William O. Douglas of the Supreme Court; and the senior staff of BOAC.[59] From U.S. industrialists Mayo heard that his findings were valued in their relation to productivity and warranted extended distribution among personnel executives.[60] Jenkins, the psychologist with a reputation for sharp criticism of social science, thought the "The Seamy Side of Progress" should be required reading for all graduate students.[61] Meanwhile, Lloyd Warner enjoyed "The Rabble Hypothesis" for the influence it might have on the thinking of economists and political scientists.[62] And Howard Mumford Jones, president of the American Academy of Arts and Sciences, saw more educational wisdom in the two early chapters than the Harvard University Report, and ranked Mayo's work with Erich Fromm's *Escape from Freedom.*[63]

Nature reviewed Mayo's ideas in the context of Britain's postwar industrial strife, and recognized that new incentives were needed to improve industrial relations by pointing to the practical possibilities of group cooperation and its relation to a renewed form of democracy. The reviewer did note, however, that perhaps economists would find Mayo's "rabble hypothesis" irritating.[64] And they did. John W. Harriman of Dartmouth College and D.N. Chester of Oxford University wrote that, contrary to Mayo's assumption, economists had long realized the importance of nonmonetary compensation, and that Mayo had confused scarcity in the economic sense with scarcity during a famine. Further, they could not agree with Mayo that all social malaise was due to industrialization or that mere social skills could have been used effectively to combat Hitler; and they asserted that it was a myth that everyone had been happy in the established society of long ago.[65]

Other reviewers shared the opinion that conflict had been commonplace among established societies where, so they assumed Mayo had argued, social skills had always been highly developed.[66] One reviewer ventured that political scientists would find Mayo had offered nothing new; after all, Aristotle had observed that man was a political animal. And, ignoring Mayo's obvious humanism, the reviewer wrote that to advocate the extension of social skills without giving direction as to its use could justify the spirit of cooperation behind Hitler's social groupings that had gained their "strength through joy."[67] Mayo's theory of cooperation was too simplistic because it lacked normative considerations, he had pushed too far the analogy between methods of the social and physical sciences, and he had ignored too much of the traditional research in politics and economics, as well as social inquiries that were in line with his own.[68]

Sociologists were critical of the book, especially when they saw that Mayo had disowned them, and, at the same time, had done sociological research himself.[69] Although the book was praised by many social scientists for its humane, useful, and hopeful tone, they took Mayo to task for not dealing with how unions could win security and self-respect for their members through cooperative action.

The most disparaging review came from Wilbert E. Moore, the industrial sociologist at Princeton. Between *The Human Problems . . .* and *The Social Problems . . .* Mayo's "voice [had] merely become shrill." Mayo was now a radical empiricist, ignorant of theory in social research and differences between science and technology, insensitive to problems of value, and an advocate of random observation in place of purposeful research. Of cooperation, Moore asked, "towards what goals, with what inducements, under whose direction, with what safeguards for, participants?" And for what Moore alleged to be Mayo's pontificating generalizations and misinformed condemnation of sociology as well as all the universities that had taught discipline, he recommended that Harvard take Mayo to court for libel.[70]

James S. Plant, whose work on the sociological determinants of mental health Mayo had often quoted, was not so prone to overlook Mayo's democratic and humane values, and described the book as "one of the brilliant and penetrating pieces of work of our time . . . [with] insights of unmatched importance in the field of mental hygiene." He hoped that "the way Mayo [looked] at data . . . will be some day the way that all science will view its material." Apart from Mayo's overenthusiastic approach, Plant found two flaws in the work: the distinction between knowledge-about and knowledge-of-acquaintance was not fully discussed; and there was mental illness, i.e., obsessive traits, among capitalists as well as their political opponents.[71]

Mayo irritated many psychologists too. His book was seen by them as provocative and interesting, but it did not provide enough evidence for dismissing the value of psychological tests in selecting supervisors. And they questioned the validity of his ideas on authority.[72]

Despite the criticisms from the professions that had come under Mayo's sharp and brief attack—economics, political science, sociology, and psychology—Mayo's book was reviewed often and fully, and won many adherents. Nevertheless it did not sell as well as projected. To boost sales of *The Social Problems . . .* the Business School's Division of Research arranged to have *The Human Problems . . .* republished, and for Mayo to be the subject of an article in the November 1946 issue of *Fortune*. The first draft of the article opened an old wound when it referred to him as "Doctor Mayo." Rather than tell the writer that he had never qualified as as a medical doctor, Mayo wrote, "It is easy to confuse what I am now doing with my original medical studies; and when I took my degree, a very long time ago, the Ph.D. degree was only German, [and] . . . regarded by us with a species of unmerited contempt as a Germanic overstatement."[73] The appropriate alterations were made. In a year sales of *The Social Problems* . . . stood at thirteen thousand.

Mayo's books were translated into German, Japanese, Spanish, Italian, and Arabic; the British edition of *The Social Problems* . . . went through five printings to 1966 and was republished in 1975.

While revising the two essays on the ill effects of industrialization, Mayo was asked for advice on how to guide academic retirees, who, for lack of preparation for a new role, had become discouraged and resentful at being pushed aside. The problem seemed apposite to Mayo, because he was hoping to retire too. Mayo answered with a letter—which he distributed widely among colleagues and family—in which he applied his ideas to the changing role and circumstances of academics over the last eighty years, i.e., academics tend to have highly developed technical skills and poor social skills. Mayo said that pamphlets on how to think about retiring painlessly would have little effect on those who, as a matter of course, overthink their situations, and suggested establishing settlements where retirees could join their peers, continue their major activities, and be useful to the local community.[74] At the time Mayo was hoping that he might do just that: retire into the Community of the Resurrection. Dorothea had other plans.

Mayo delayed retirement until 1947 because he was needed to teach the staff who would carry forward his work. Also he continued to give occasional talks. In January 1946 he prepared a lecture for the Boston Institute for Religion and Social Studies, "Economic Threats to American Unity."[75] First, he drew upon letters from Patricia to illustrate the plight of Europeans,[76] and argued that Americans cannot isolate themselves from Europe as they had done after the Great War. He believed that the United States would be affected by the "material insufficiency of the European economy . . . and . . . European despair, the lack of capacity for spontaneous cooperative effort." Second, he pointed to the current industrial conflicts, asserting that the quarrel was not between management and workers but, "rather, between management and union organizers, on one side, and rank and file workers on the other." Third, after summarizing his views on the "seamy side of progress" and the "rabble hypothesis," he advocated augmenting technical studies in science and economics "with a sociology, developed far beyond anything . . . in any university." Endowments and "gifted . . . well-trained men and women" were needed to develop a sociology that would show how to replace suspicion and hostility with effective collaboration.

Later that year Mayo informally aired his views on coal strikes in Britain, the United States, and Australia to the Visiting Committee at the Business School. He was asked to repeat them at a conference in New York in December.[77]

Mayo's last talk to the officials at the Western Electric Company was in

January 1947. He reminded them that modern education taught clear articulate expression and logical analysis but neglected careful listening to the nonlogical through rational attitudes that directed behavior. This showed that widely accepted beliefs in a long-established culture are at sword's point with views and techniques in counseling. This talk was to have been followed by an address at the University of California, Berkeley—the institution where he had been scheduled, unsuccessfully, to give a course on his ideas about the social and psychological factors affecting industrial conflict when he first arrived in the United States—but he refused to go when he found that the conference's director of industrial relations had cut out part of the address without having seen more than its subheadings. To Mayo, this was an infringement of academic freedom, and would have left nothing for him to follow but "mangled . . . unrelated fragments," too disjointed for the listener to understand.[78]

Mayo's last address was at "The Mayo Weekend," a conference on human relations and administration at the Business School on May 10 and 11.[79] Among the sixty-odd discussants were Alan Gregg and Joseph Willits from the Rockefeller Foundation; executives from Western Electric, AT&T, Ford Motor Company, General Motors, and Standard Oil; Stuart Chase, whose article had drawn so much attention to the Hawthorne studies; and academics from Colgate, Yale, and the University of Maryland. From Bennington College came a special guest, Peter F. Drucker, who had made himself known to Mayo a year earlier by sending him a copy of *Concept of Corporation*.

Donham, Roethlisberger, and Lombard traced the origin and development of Mayo's work at the Business School; Benjamin Selekman and Edmund Learned applied Mayo's work to industrial relations and the human aspects of administration; William Dickson spoke of Mayo's influence on the counseling program in the Western Electric Company; and John Jenkins told of the value of Mayo's ideas for integrating formal and informal organization, for morale, efficiency, and the resistance to fatigue in military exercises.

Mayo began his address by saying that conflict between nations was a problem in unity and cooperation that arises in disagreements between conceptions of society and methods of social control. Although all people desire to be free of dictatorship, Green's liberal principle—"Will, not force is the basis of the State"—had been ignored, consequently allowing powerful, centralized control to become established. Mayo preferred phasic alternation of control. Continued central control promoted militarism and heroic domination like that of Hitler, Mussolini, Hollywood stars, and the desk-thumping business executive. Popular opinion is then misled into the belief that equates such domination with success. Phasic alternation is found in organizations where administrators understand the relation among parts of the organization and support a general policy of control by cooperation rather than tyranny. The USSR illustrates the thesis well. Aiming to become a modern civilization it adopted heroic methods of control to unify society. Such methods once had the benefit of overcoming hostility among its minorities, but the leaders, because they were enmeshed in crises, failed to see the peacetime reactions against heroic leadership, and did not appreciate that organization for spontaneous cooperation was better than organization for emergencies. Second, the early Russian revolutionary leaders had dictated to the proletariat and avenged themselves on the bourgeoisie, which they thought comprised nothing but exploiters of labor and greedy profiteers, and which a classless society could well do without. But today, recognizing that the bourgoisie knows principles of industrial organization and can act responsibily, Russian leaders reward educated citizens even more than workers. Nevertheless, the centralized controls remain, hostile relations with neighbors grow, and internal crises are probable.

From his industrial studies Mayo asserted that a group of cooperative workers with high morale often were suspicious of and felt threatened by outsiders. Similarly, primitive societies protect and benefit their members and also are hostile toward outsiders. So, personal security varies directly with the area of active cooperation. In a primitive society that area is limited geographically, and eventually the society collapses. Although the USSR had overcome this problem, it needed to relate its development more to lands beyond its frontiers and use freely the recent developments in communications or else it too would collapse.

In the Middle Ages the rise and collapse of European nations ended with the growth of Christianity and the creation of Western civilization. The Christian felt he was part of all Europe, a participant in the church's work, and that he had a duty to cooperate with everyone. Thus human cooperation guided civilization. But inasmuch as science continuously opened new areas for study, the view of man's Christian duty became unacceptable, the authority of the clergy was questioned, and faith in universal human cooperation weakened. Western civilization broke into separate nations or cultures. Instead of the belief that when individuals work together mutual benefits follow and self-interest becomes secondary, the claim was made that self-interest must be primary, and if it is pursued vigorously, general social benefits ensue. Mayo declared that recent research contradicted the claim; at work, individuals subordinate self-interest to group goals, and the solitary who pursues self-interest is unhappy. So as the high purpose of Christianity disappeared, the value put on purely economic theories of man rose and rivalries grew among different cultures. To control the conflict participatory democracy gave over to militaristic, centralized control. And with the decline in cooperative social relations, individuals felt insecure and lost their sense of personal well-being.

Industrial studies were showing that where cooperation is maintained personal security grows and discontent diminishes, so Mayo recommended that managers deal honestly with employees and take a genuine interest in them in order to win their trust and confidence; and that union officers not organize members with militant and heroic methods. Joint work is the best means for mutual cooperation. For organizations, Mayo recommended scientific studies of the systematic ordering of operations, economic needs, and the conditions of effective communication and cooperation. Without such studies, political leaders would remain ignorant of the basis for effective control in civilized life and continue with old techniques of centralized control that would never provide spontaneous cooperation. Such cooperation originates in the will of individuals and groups and cannot be effectively imposed on them from outside.

Mayo's address was given in two parts.[80] At the end of the first, in informal discussion, Peter Drucker took the opportunity to show how he, a political scientist with an interest in the social responsibility of businessmen, looked at politics in industry. Some members of the audience knew that Drucker's work at Bennington had begun to turn to human and social problems of management, and that because of this Drucker was being considered for a faculty position at the Harvard Business School.[81] Drucker had failed to appreciate Mayo's main point, taken from Green's maxim and Chester Barnard's administration theory, i.e., in an organization spontaneous cooperation requires the willing consent of subordinates and cannot be effectively imposed on them by a domineering executive. Drucker left the impression that political ideas derived from studies in human relations at work could be used by managers as tools to manipulate subordinates. The impression was given largely through Drucker's illustrations drawn from his European experience, and from his attitude toward supervisors and workers, which he conveyed in answers to questions and other remarks in the discussion. Mayo was upset by hearing the conclusion he had reached in his study of situations in industry distorted in these ways, and took the floor to poke fun at Drucker's ideas. To show what a subordinate thinks about a manipulative boss, Mayo put his thumb to his nose and, looking at Drucker, asked: "You know what this means?" Drucker did not. "Then you should," replied Mayo. The audience could see that Mayo's gesture signified not only the attitude of a subordinate who was unwilling to consent to directives from a domineering boss but also Mayo's view of the ideas that Drucker had expressed.[82]

Drucker subsequently wrote to Mayo and apologized that, in the rush of departure at the end of the meeting, he had not had the opportunity to take proper leave, and, as he had done frequently, highly praised Mayo's work. In reply Mayo alluded to his remarks following Drucker's commentary, and asked that Drucker forgive him; they had been intended to "lighten the whole atmosphere and to reassure those who might have succumbed" to a misunderstanding of Drucker's ideas. And, Mayo added, "One must be intelligent to the maximum in work, but one must also be exceedingly careful in the display of intelligent capacity before Anglo-Saxon audiences. I am sure that your Continental training will enable you to understand what I am talking about."[83] From that point Drucker's negotiations for a position at the Business School ceased, and Mayo's work was carried forward by Roethlisberger and Lombard with support from Edmund Learned and their students.

A few days later Mayo and Dorothea flew to England.

Notes

1. Elton to Toni, 31 December 1939.
2. Elton to Toni, 17 June, 19 August 1940.
3. Elton to Toni, 12 January, 3, 12 March 1940
4. Elton to Toni, 17 June 1940.
5. Elton to Toni, 12 January, 3, 12 March 1940.
6. Elton to Toni, 17 June 1940.
7. Elton to Toni, 14 October 1940.
8. Elton to Toni, 10 September, 14 October 1940.
9. Elton to Toni, 30 January 1941. Lombard recalled that the series was not well attended and Mayo did not finish the course. Later lectures were used in Harvard Business School courses to train teachers and administrators.
10. Elton to Toni, 25 January 1942.
11. Elton to Toni, 11 December 1941.
12. Elton to Jordan, 14 February 1942, MM 1.048.
13. Elton to Goetz, 24 February 1942; Elton to Willard, 13 April 1942; Elton to Hanson, 21 April 1942, MM 1.063.
14. Elton to Toni, 21 March, 3 May 1942.
15. Gregg's diary, 16 April 1942, RF.
16. Elton to Toni, 21 March, 3 May 1942.
17. Elton to Toni, 3 May, 10 June 1942.
18. Elton to Toni, 3 May, 14 June 1942.
19. Lombard to Mayo, 10 July 1942, MM 1.012.
20. Mayo to David, 1 August 1942, MM 1.033.
21. Gregg's diary, 16 November 1942, RF.
22. *Who Was Who in America: Vol. 3, 1951-60* (Chicago: Marquis, 1960), p. 346. Because the Rockefeller philanthropies did not fund the social sciences before 1928, Mayo's work was supported by the Division of Medical Education. The practice continued under the Directorate for Medical Sciences when the divisional arrangements were dropped in 1929. Because Mayo's work was closely linked with Henderson's research on industrial physiology and industrial hazards, his relations with the Rockefeller Foundation continued to be handled by medical rather than the social sciences officials. Hess to Trahair, 25 October 1982.
23. Gregg to Mayo, 13 November, 1942; Mayo to Gregg, 16 November 1942, MM 1.072; Mayo to Gregg, 6 December 1942, RF.
24. Gregg to Mayo, 10 December 1942, MM 1.072.
25. Mayo to Gregg, 6 December 1942, RF.
26. Gregg to Mayo, 30 December 1942, 30 April, 19 June 1943; Mayo to Gregg, 24 April 1943, MM 1.072.
27. Donham to Gregg, 10 March 1943, RF.

28. Mayo to Gregg, 20 February 1943; Gregg's diary, 26 February 1943, RF.
29. Mayo to Gregg, 14 March 1943, RF.
30. Holderer to Mayo, 12 March 1943; Mayo to Holderer, 15 March 1943, MM 1.084.
31. Mayo to Jackie, Mayo to Cashin, 15 March 1943, MM 1.084.
32. Mayo to Cashin, 18 March 1943, MM 1.084.
33. Mayo to Holderer, 24 March 1943, MM 1.086.
34. Mayo to Lombard, 3 April 1943, MM 1.013.
35. Jerome F. Scott, "Notes on Waterbury Conference," 6-9 April 1943, MM 1.086.
36. Elton to Toni, 17 April 1943.
37. Mayo to Gregg, 18 April 1943, RF.
38. Mayo to Holderer, 19 May 1943, MM 1.086.
39. John B. Fox and Jerome F. Scott, *Absenteeism: Management's Problem* (Boston: Harvard University, Graduate School of Business Administration, Division of Research, 1943).
40. Mayo to Gross, 19 August 1943; Hart to Fox, 31 August 1943, MM 1.086.
41. Gregg to Mayo, 19 June 1943, MM 1.072.
42. Gregg to Mayo, 2 September 1943, MM 1.072.
43. Fox and Scott, *Absenteeism*.
44. Scott to Fox, 7 January 1944, MM 1.073.
45. Mayo to Burden, 25 May 1944, MM 1.030.
46. Elton Mayo and George F. F. Lombard, *Teamwork and Labor Turnover in the Aircraft Industry of California* (Boston: Harvard University, Graduate School of Business Administration, Division of Research, 1944).
47. Fox to Lombard, 31 July 1944, MM 1.012.
48. Committee on Work in Industry, Subcommittee on Rehabilitation, *Rehabilitation: The Man and the Job*, reprint and circular series, 121 (Washington, D.C.: National Research Council, March 1945).
49. Elton Mayo, "Group Tension in Industry," in *Approaches to National Unity*, ed. L. Bryson, L. Finkelstein, and R. M. McIver (New York: Harper, 1945), pp. 46-60; Elton Mayo, "Supervisor and What It Means," in *Studies and Supervision*, ed. D. E. Cameron (Montreal: McGill University, 1945), pp. 5-27.
50. Elton Mayo, *The Social Problems of an Industrial Civilization* (Boston: Harvard University, Graduate School of Business Administration. Division of Research, 1945).
51. *Commonweal* (New York), 5 April 1946, pp. 625-26.
52. *The Times* (London), 9 April 1946.
53. *Nation*, 4 May 1946.
54. *Tracks* (New York), June 1946; *Railway Age*, 30 March 1946, p. 682.
55. *American Catholic Sociological Review*, June 1947; *Bulletin of the Institute of Social Order* (Jesuit), February 1947.
56. *Scope: Magazine for Industry* (London), April 1947, p. 100; *Industry Illustrated*, July 1946, pp. 11-17.
57. Conant to Mayo, 5 February, 1946; Mayo to Conant, 12 February 1946, MM 1.028.
58. Leighton to Mayo, 30 January 1946, MM 1.059.
59. MM 1.057.
60. Wolf to Mayo, 9 April 1946, MM 1.057.
61. Jenkins to Mayo, 18 October 1946, MM 1.057.
62. Warner to Mayo, 16 May 1946, MM 1.057.
63. Jones to Mayo, 25 May 1946, MM 1.057.
64. *Nature* 159, no. 4036 (8 March 1947):313-15.

65. *American Economic Review* 36 (June 1946):394-96; *Economic Journal,* June 1946.
66. *Accounting Review*, 3 (July 1946):359-60.
67. *American Academy of Political and Social Science Review* 145 (May 1946): 206-7.
68. *University of Chicago Law Review,* April 1946, pp. 393-95; *United States Quarterly Book List,* June 1946, p. 130.
69. *Sociology and Social Research,* March-April 1946.
70. *American Sociological Review* 12 (February 1947):123-24.
71. *Mental Hygiene* 36 (1946):659-62.
72. *Journal of Abnormal and Social Psychology* 42 (1947):375-77; *Journal of Applied Psychology* 31, no. 3 (June 1947).
73. Mayo to McDonald, 4 October 1939, MM 1.039.
74. Correspondence with James, July-September 1943, MM 2.012.
75. MM 2.006.
76. Elton to Toni, 21 January 1946.
77. Elton to Toni, 28 November 1946.
78. Elton to Toni, 20 February 1947; Mayo to Sproul, 17 February 1947, MM 1.029.
79. MM 2.095.
80. Elton Mayo, *The Political Problem of Industrial Civilization* (Boston: Harvard University, Graduate School of Business Administration. Division of Research, 1947).
81. Correspondence between Mayo, Dean David, and Drucker, 1946-47, MM 1.035.
82. Conversations with Lombard and Bailey, 14 April 1975.
83. Correspondence between Mayo, Dean David, and Drucker, 1946-47, MM 1.035.

21

Retirement and Death in England: 1947–1949

Six months after Mayo landed in England his plans for retirement went awry; he worked too hard, suffered a stroke, and had to rest. When he recovered he began to write, consult with colleagues on Britain's industrial problems, and plan another book. His income was low, and he was often tired. Dorothea was tired and ill, too. In the summer of 1949 Mayo's health, which had been improving, took a turn for the worse and he died in September.

"I have not celebrated my last morning here," wrote Mayo to Dean David, "by trailing drearily about to every member of the Faculty inter-rupting his work to say 'good-bye'. . . . It is part of my own defective disposition to feel that an old fellow, when the time comes, should merely fade out with as little fuss as possible."[1] He walked out of his office, leaving his papers for the archives in the Baker Library and many of his books to be shipped to England.

But he could not leave Harvard without some new mission. He had declined Cyril James's offer to spend a year or two at McGill; he did not accept an invitation to Australia to give radio talks and address business groups. Instead he decided, so he wrote to Beardsley Ruml, to "turn the English from their conventional ways and from the barbaric economic theory to which they are so devotedly attached."[2] By this Mayo meant he would accept the offer from the National Institute of Industrial Psychology (NIIP) of a thousand pounds a year to chair its Technical Advisory Board.[3] If this plan fell through he could rely on his daughter Patricia to introduce him to Britain's top industrialists, who were beginning to see the value of his work. They would be able to help him supplement his monthly pension of two hundred dollars that Harvard would begin in August.[4]

After Mayo retired no one was chosen to fill his place. Roethlisberger had been promoted to a professorship in human relations in January, and in July Lombard would be made associate professor. They would have most of the responsibility for carrying forward the work Mayo had initiated.

Roethlisberger began teaching what he called the "Mayo Syndrome."[5]

341

He showed students that fatigue and monotony do not adequately express the many aspects of an individual's total situation; that skill is developed gradually; and that learning advances such that an attentive act must be seen as a highly complex experience. Obsessions are excellent examples to illustrate the complexity of the attentive act because their content and form are important for an understanding of how individuals interact. And the way adult behavior is affected by preoccupations in obsessive characters can be understood best by reading Freud and others on family life and early childhood training.

Using a more sociological perspective, Roethlisberger and associates followed Mayo's notions by thinking of business as a social system that requires exploratory research to answer specific managerial questions. They assumed that the elements of business, as a social system, are interdependent—not randomly occurring—and tend toward equilibrium, a balanced state. The main object of study in a social system is interaction among people. That interaction reveals nonlogical as well as logical forms of behavior, and experiences variously categorized as meanings, intentions, residues, derivations, and sentiments. Some of these behaviors and experiences are latent, others are overt; some are functional for the balanced state of the system, others are dysfunctional. Human experiences contribute to, and are affected by, the equilibrium of the system, depending upon the individual's state of physiological equilibrium or homeostasis, and his degree of psychological tension, i.e., obsessional versus syncretic thinking, conviction of sin, skills, sense of adaptive growth or complication of thinking and experience, and ego versus sociocentricity. The interaction may seem purposeless and disordered for the individual, and when it does, can give rise to feelings of anomie and actions intended to reduce this feeling.

The context of business is also a social system; that context is changing from a primitive, traditional, or established state to a complex, adaptive state.

The most appropriate methods for the scientific study of society, social systems, interactions, and individuals are controlled observation and clinical interviewing. Research studies following this principle had been done on adjustment to problems by students, in the Hawthorne researches, and in Newburyport. Within industry Mayo's associates had studied absenteeism, labor turnover, the training of foremen, problems of middle managers in a growing organization, and the relations between office and production plants. Teaching had been informal, no classes were held, no regular courses were given; training had been through apprenticeship, reading, discussion, and the use of clinical interviewing.

On the basis of these assumptions and experience, Mayo's followers began to state more clearly the elements of business-as-a-social-system and to study industrial groups and human interaction at work. The terms they used to extend their thinking were: the logic of management, formal versus informal organization, effectiveness and efficiency, group norms as expressions of output restriction, and resistance to technological change; authority and control in relation to employee participation, teamwork, and cooperation; two-way communication, nondirective counseling, intensional and extensional orientations, maps, and territories at work. Major problems facing foremen centered on relations between them and their subordinates, workers, and management, self-awareness of both, and how to diagnose and take action on problems at work. Research emerging from this approach included clinical cases in cooperation, control, communication, and changes in small work groups and large organizations. Cases were described and academic theses were written. Teaching was done in a second-year course on the study of human problems of administration, and was offered as lectures and case material from the viewpoint of the expert in personnel; later these ideas were extended to teaching a more practical, action-oriented, and generalist position. At the same time studies were published, executive weekend courses were established, and books were published to inform the business community.

The conceptual framework turned more to testing hypotheses on the determinants of behavior in work groups, and to changes in organizations using the ideas drawn from special fields in the social sciences. Administrative practices and human relations were first- and second-year courses and advanced training was offered in teaching and in clinical and doctoral-level research. There were also upper-level courses in the recent developments of organizational behavior for senior executives.[6]

Mayo and his wife flew to Britain, a new experience for both. "Dorothea was at first interested in going up and coming down, but finally somewhat bored" by the fourteen-hour journey.[7] They stayed in a London hotel for a few days, and Patricia arranged meetings for her father with senior industrialists. Then Mayo and Dorothea moved to a hotel on the Thames in Berkshire, and began to search for a place to live in London. But the city was overcrowded, and they thought that rents were exorbitant. Through a friend of Patricia's husband they learned that the National Trust had available private apartments in Polsden Lacey, a manor house about two and a half miles from a small town in Surrey. The Mayos were deemed suitable tenants.[8] Dorothea, exhausted by moving, was instructed to rest under medical care.

Mayo's first task was to make himself known to businessmen and industrial psychologists, and he started by giving a lecture in London.[9] At home he was correcting the proofs for the book on Janet. Two matters disturbed him: about 45 percent of his income went for taxes, so he could not afford the services of an intelligent secretary, and he missed discussions with colleagues. But Jerome Scott, who was studying at Oxford, visited Mayo, and British colleagues began to entertain him at dinner. Also, the arrangements for work with the NIIP were in order, so financial problems would soon be solved.[10]

In the NIIP's winter program Mayo gave the opening lecture, "An Industrial Civilization," which paid tribute to C.S. Myers, briefly reviewed the Hawthorne studies, and considered Britain's industrial strife.[11] Conflict in industry was a "silent revolution," Mayo said, against a management that ignored the human element for the sake of technical and financial rewards. If a manager wants employees to cooperate with him, he must come to the shop floor and see for himself work from a worker's viewpoint. If he does this, then workers give their wholehearted cooperation, and output and morale rise. Industrial psychologists could help in solving the problems of Britain's industrial conflicts.

Ten days later Mayo delivered "Problems of an Industrial Civilization" in Blackpool at the annual conference of the Institute of Personnel Management. The lecture outlined the social relation between groups of managers and workers, the uneven progress in the growth of technical and social skills, the Hawthorne studies, the absenteeism research, and concluded with a strong plea for scientific research in industry as a basis for training administrators.[12]

By mid-October 1947 Mayo knew his work for the NIIP would not be as he had been led to expect.[13] Rowntree had written to Joseph Willits at the Rockefeller Foundation that Mayo would be supervising an NIIP study of incentives in industry and that the institute was hoping for government funds. Would the foundation also fund the institute, especially because it had Mayo's services?[14] "There is no getting away from the fact," wrote Rowntree, "workers are not working well. That is why I feel an investigation . . . is important." The British government did not support the NIIP but gave funds to the newly constituted British Institute of Management (BIM), where Patricia held a research position. Mayo hoped that the BIM would offer him a position, too, because the NIIP plans were far too ambitious, and he did not want to lecture any more.[15] Nevertheless, he agreed to keep his promise to the NIIP to go "barnstorming . . . to Birmingham, Manchester, Liverpool—three days—after which, when convalescent, I'll write again."[16]

Mayo overstepped the limits of his health; lecturing on three successive nights was far too strenuous. On December 1 he had a stroke that paralyzed his left arm and affected his speech. In a few days his speech improved, and his face became less twisted, but little hope was held out for his left side. After a week at a London hospital, room was found for him in the hospital at Guilford, a few miles from home. Dorothea could visit him, but she herself was ill and her doctor insisted she rest. Mayo's mind was clear, but he was restless and made a nuisance of himself trying to leave his bed and ringing the night bell. A special nurse had to be hired to attend to him.

Daily massages were beneficial, and his doctor gave Dorothea hope that he would survive.[17]

By the end of February Mayo had convalesced sufficiently to write again in a shaky, almost indecipherable hand. He advised Roethlisberger on how to bring forward their work, and corresponded regularly with Lombard, who was shepherding the Janet book through difficulties in publication and handling tax problems that were unexpectedly eroding Mayo's income.[18] He enjoyed visits from Alan Gregg, Jerome Scott, and Ruth and Patricia. Recovery was slow, but by April he was able to walk a half-mile, and his mental vigor was returning to normal.[19] Food was short, so he and Dorothea were pleased by parcels from relatives in Australia. The cost of living was so high that expenses had begun to exceed their income, and travel was out of the question.[20]

In the middle of the summer of 1948, Mayo was well enough to write a paper for the August meeting of the International Congress of Industrial Medicine, and to begin plans for a book on politics. And although he could walk outside with little trace of his paralysis, to Dorothea he seemed to toddle and shuffle for no good reason. She was annoyed that he would not follow the doctor's advice to exercise more. But his blood pressure had remained high, which meant that he would have to lead a much quieter life than before.[21]

In August he wrote to the London *Times* recommending the development of free communication at all levels between the United States and Britain because Britain was facing a problem that had already been partly answered by Mayo's work.[22] "Why, in countries where industries have been nationalized, is it so difficult to induce workers to cooperate with managers in peacetime?" Free communication and collaboration at work affects the efforts and activities of workers; in fortunate conditions their behavior is fully cooperative, in less fortunate conditions workers are doubtful and suspicious to the extent that they withhold their best efforts. Knowledge of these conditions would clarify the problem. Mayo cited experience at Harvard where union officials had been encouraged to study administrative problems, especially those centering on communication between different levels of authority, and he reported the growth of research and teaching in the social sciences to help understand general human and social problems that accompany industrialization. To add support to his recommendation Mayo suggested to Stuart Chase that he send his recent work, *The Proper Study of Mankind,* to Sir Stafford Cripps because Mayo's letter and Chase's book made much the same point.[23]

By September 1948 Mayo was even better, but he was troubled by having to pay taxes in two countries and annoyed that when Harvard University Press had taken over the publication of *The Human Problems . . .* he had not been allowed royalties on its sales.[24] And he was feeling remote from

the Business School in what he called "this Socialist-ridden country."[25]
Gloomy weather, Patricia's impending divorce, his inability to write easily,
the absence of secretarial assistance, and the hesitancy of English publishers to print *The Social Problems* . . . all together led Mayo to write to
Dean David, "We may be nearly, but not quite, done."[26]

In a letter to the *Times* his main point concerned "remote control," to
which he had alluded in his valedictory lecture.[27] He cited research in
Pennsylvania and Newburyport that found that "a central policy forming
body must learn to leave decisions to management and men in the locality.
Otherwise adaptability and spontaneity of cooperation will be lacking."
This led Mayo to consider adaptability as the most important issue in
industrial growth. In a modern, adaptable society rapid technical developments occur at work; such techniques and processes require adaptable
people to manage them. People learn to become adaptable only when they
are trained well in the profession of management. If people are untrained
in both human and technical aspects of change, then spontaneous cooperation among people will not be forthcoming and the rapidity of development cannot be maintained. Such people need to be vigorous and have
initiative; they do not need what Mayo believed impeded change: "the
ancient political parrot cries [i.e., conservative or radical ideologies] of a
century ago."

A few days after the letter appeared Mayo was well enough to go to
London to advise colleagues, and to begin work on his next book, tentatively titled "Political Opportunism and Industrial Method."[28] Shortly after
the visit he was tired and felt wearied of being disabled, "crippled in walking and writing," and disinclined to accept four hundred dollars from the
Business School to pay for a part-time secreatry. Nevertheless, he wanted to
say something "before the gates shut."[29]

He made a pastiche of his two letters and main points from *The Social
Problems* . . . and sent it for publication to the *World Review*.[30] Now his
main interest was in "political drift." The drift was to large-scale organization of work in both the private and public sectors. With the drift came
remote control and its ills, disloyalty and lack of discipline among employees. The reason for the ills was, again, poor communications between
remote executives and their workers, who feel they do not participate in
decisions affecting their work. "Where this feeling is present, there will be
no spontaneity of collaboration between management and workers. The
. . . problem demands attention and remedy." These were Mayo's last published words.

Mayo's health was becoming uncertain. Patricia thought that because he
was having frequent discussions with people of different political parties
that his mind was as alert and active as ever, and that he would have no
trouble writing another book if he had secretarial help. But Dorothea

thought he would never produce enough material to warrant a part-time secretary at regular hours. Dorothea was right.[31]

Mayo knew he was too old and ill to travel far, but he did accept invitations to advise the Director General of UNESCO in Paris and to visit Kings College, Cambridge, to meet Professors Kilcaldy (industrial relations) and Macgregor (economics). He found the younger university men were following his ideas, but in Paris his main interest seemed to be the excellent food.[32]

On his return from Paris he had a visit from Chester Barnard, now president of the Rockefeller Foundation, and took the opportunity to support Lombard and Roethlisberger's application for funds for advanced research in industrial training. Mayo thought of what he had recommended in 1919: if industrial democracy were to be effective and employees were to join managers in deciding the course for business to take, then all members of an organization must be well trained in economics, accounting, and other relevant topics.[33]

By the summer of 1949, when the *Times* industrial correspondent was arguing the relevance of *The Social Problems . . .* to Britain's industrial problems, Mayo's health was in decline. Dorothea saw that he was quite unable to consult, as he had planned, with United Nations officials on the appointment of a director to their employee training program. Late in August he was returned to the nursing hospital in Guilford because Dorothea was too ill to continue nursing him. A few days later, early on Thursday morning, September 1, Mayo died peacefully and without pain.[34]

Notes

1. Mayo to David, 24 May 1947, MM 1.044.
2. Mayo to Ruml, 7 May 1947, MM 1.071.
3. Rowntree to Mayo, 8 February 1947, RF; Elton to Herbert, 6 May, 4 June 1947; Elton to Helen, 7 May 1947, SAA.
4. Elton to Herbert, 4 June 1947, SAA.
5. Roethlisberger to Mayo, 12 December 1947, FJR.
6. George F. F. Lombard, "The Developing Field of Organizational Behavior at the Harvard Business School" (mimeographed), 1960, BLA.
7. Mayo to Lombard, 2, 7 June 1947, MM 1.012.
8. Dorothea to Gardner, 13 June 1947, MM 1.012.
9. Lawton to Norton, 7 December 1947, MM 1.012.
10. Mayo to Lombard, 24 June, 24 July, 9 September 1947, MM 1.012.
11. *News* (National Institute of Industrial Psychology, London), 3 November 1947.
12. Elton Mayo, "Problems of an Industrial Civilization," *Journal of the Institute of Personnel Management,* November-December 1947, pp. 264-69.
13. Morrison to Trahair, 26 October 1981.
14. Rowntree to Willits, 7 July 1947, RF (NIIP files).
15. Dorothea to Donham, 11 December 1947, AFFD 1, BLA.
16. Mayo to Lombard, 15 October, 14 November 1947, MM 1.012.

17. Dorothea to Donham, 11 December 1947, AFFD 2, BLA; Dorothea to Herbert, 11 December 1947, SAA; Dorothea to Lombard, 12 December 1947, MM 1.012.
18. MM 1.012.
19. Dorothea to Lombard, 25 April 1948, MM 1.014.
20. Elton to Helen, 30 April 1948; Elton to Herbert, 30 April, 26 May 1948, SAA.
21. Mayo to Lombard, 6, 31 May 1948, MM 1.014; Elton to Herbert, 11 July 1948, SAA.
22. *The Times* (London), 11 August 1948.
23. Mayo to Chase, 27 September 1948, MM 1.012.
24. Delaney to Lombard, 18 October 1948, MM 1.012.
25. Mayo to Wilson, 2 December 1948, MM 1.012.
26. Mayo to David, 8 November 1948, AFFD 2, BLA.
27. *The Times* (London), 2 December 1948.
28. Mayo to Lombard, 28 December 1948, MM 1.012.
29. Mayo to David, 19 January 1949, AFFD 2, BLA.
30. Elton Mayo, "Human Problems in Industry," *World Review,* new series, 3 (May 1949):5-8.
31. Mayo to David, 19 January 1949, AFFD 2, BLA; Patricia Mayo to Lombard, 20 January 1949, MM 1.015.
32. Elton to Herbert, 20 January 1949, SAA; Mayo to Lombard, 8 February, 19 April 1949, MM 1.012.
33. Mayo to Lombard, 19 April, 26 May 1949, MM 1.012.
34. Scott to Lombard, 5 September 1949, MM 1.012; Dorothea to Herbert, 9 September 1949, BLA.

22

The Character and Contributions of Elton Mayo

The character and contributions of Elton Mayo are reconstructed from the impressions he left with the people who were closest to him at work and in family life.[1] His appearance and manner, his style of family and social life depict his general role. His institutional role—teaching and research—precedes an account of his interpersonal style and the four major roles that he played so uniquely. Finally, these are augmented and partly explained by the way that Mayo thought and how he came to value what he thought about.

Mayo stood a bit over five feet, seven inches, and weighed about 125 pounds. He had little hair, freckled fair skin, deep blue eyes, and a wide smile that showed perfect teeth. He dressed neatly and to advantage; when he entered a room he gave the impression that an important person had arrived. On the street in good weather he wore a brimmed hat with a colorful band, carried a cane, sported a handkerchief up his sleeve, and walked with a jaunty swagger that used the full length of his slim body. Mayo was always in good health and anxious to stay that way. His great fear was appendicitis. He exercised regularly, sometimes played tennis, was a good swimmer, and danced. He enjoyed watching cricket and horseracing. He understood the value of proper relaxation, and to this purpose would sometimes fall into long periods of silence, or would fish, read detective stories, play patience occasionally, or solve a crossword puzzle. He loved jazz and went to musical comedies. Although he was deeply moved by the paintings of Antoine Wiertz, where fine arts were concerned Mayo was a philistine. He asserted that, with the exception of Prokofiev, all Russian musicians were mad. His favorite play in later life—he saw it at least five times—was Noel Coward's *Private Lives*. Its witty dialogue depicts a romantic pattern of seduction, marriage, divorce, reconciliation, and marital discord. The dramatic strain in relations among the four characters echoed the quality of love between Mayo and his wife.

Difficulties in the Mayos' marriage were obvious, but the ways in which they were managed were hidden. During the last few years they were together in Cambridge, Dorothea enjoyed holding social gatherings, particularly tea parties. The occasions bored Mayo unless they had something intellectual to offer. In conversations Dorothea would interrupt his story-telling, and his retorts were in tones too sharp and rude to be missed. Mayo's young associates thought that such behavior between mature married adults was improper, especially for a clinical psychologist and senior professor at Harvard. At home the children heard their parents bicker, but the arguments were not destructive. Mayo could be irritating when he fussed about punctuality, but in most things he was the easier of the two to live with because he was more considerate of others. He disliked heated arguments and petty contention, so whenever he went on a trip he would leave home saying, "Be kind to each other, ladies." And when Dorothea insisted that their daughters be educated in England, where they could enjoy access to valuable social connections, Mayo did not object. He himself put a similar value on England; and he knew she needed relief from the daily burden of rearing children and immediate access to them. When he and the girls were reunited every summer, they knew from his reassuring voice that his affection for them was always warmly loving, while Dorothea's tended to be expressed in a possessive manner.

Alone in Cambridge, Mayo gave his colleagues the impression that he was a man of the world or, as Henderson put it, "a man of affairs." He used England, or "home" as Australians had called it for generations, as his criterion of excellence. Mayo's young asssociates were often impressed by his stories of how he moved among the British aristocracy and dined at exclusive London clubs. Mayo's speech was "very British": clipped, staccato, like that of a sophisticated Noel Coward character, and quite unlike what Americans expected of an Australian. For his academic colleagues Mayo gave excellent dinner parties; the menus were well chosen and the French wines were superb. He had "god-given style."

But Mayo's style could turn into arrogance and embarrass his guests in a restaurant when he sent back to the kitchen food and wine that had fallen short of his standards. And sometimes in dinner conversation he would offend his listeners when he used a thrusting manner to overstate a position and drive home a point they seemed to have missed but in fact had no wish to acknowledge. Nevertheless, his persuasive charm could usually carry his arguments and allow him to move easily between levels in the social hierarchy so as to exercise his worldliness on people of influence.

Mayo's national allegiance was divided. He did not make a home in the United States. It had been his mother's wish that, if he chose to live abroad, it would be in England. He saw himself as a colonial gentleman, and revered Britain for its influence in the world that had raised him. Yet, when he retired to England, he loathed its vulgarities. Away from Australia, he yearned often for its long, clear moonlight nights.

His associates in the Business School deemed Mayo an influential adviser to both Henderson and Donham. Faculty could not see Donham except by appointment, but to Mayo he was always available because he valued Mayo's unique advice, based as it was on unusual clinical insight. Henderson used Mayo as a sounding board for political problems within the university and the personal problems raised by the young men selected for Henderson's Society of Fellows.

In the Business School Mayo's formal position was professor and head of the Department of Industrial Research. It was the only department in the School, and Mayo's connection with it was through Henderson and Donham. Among the faculty Mayo's status was high, not so much for the value placed on his work as for the privileged access he had to Donham and the location his office—last on the right, first floor, Morgan Hall. Mayo did little teaching and, because he did not involve himself in the affairs of the school, rarely attended faculty meetings. Thus his function in the School was not well understood.

To the faculty, Mayo's associates—Henderson, Donham. Roethlisberger, and Whitehead—were a clique dominated by Henderson. Their apparently closed ranks and well-known grant from the Rockefeller Foundation made them the object of envy and resentment and earned them the title "Donham's Million Dollar Folly."

Research was the leading task in Mayo's department. In the field he applied the principle of functional penetration by level. He alone persuaded the senior management of a firm to allow him to study their organization; his assistants met with employees and staff at lower levels. Often Mayo's assistants were apprehensive because they were unsure of what he had claimed he could do or had promised to senior managers so they would follow his ideas.

His technique was to approach a company, or be asked to consult with it on a labor problem. He would see senior executives first and later persuade foremen and employees of the need to study the "human factor" at work, i.e., fatigue. That meant blood pressure readings to assess the physiological factors, and interviews to establish psychological reveries. Most subjects were women; they giggled at the suggestion of an interview with a man, and could not see the relevance of the blood pressure readings. Such resistance was easily overcome when Mayo gave a medical tone to the expectations that he wanted met. Because the purpose of Mayo's research was exploratory, and therefore ambiguous, data collection was not as systematic as would often be required in present times. The value of the research was always in doubt and rested on finding some order in the data rather than in testing specific hypotheses. When found, that order would be used to recommend whatever changes seemed necessary to promote individual welfare and cooperation at work. Full reports of research were not important to Mayo.

In the Hawthorne research Mayo did not state systematically all findings; instead he gave speeches about them, and frequently spoke in an uplifting and revolutionary style. His associates were anxious lest inaccuracies creep in and his speeches claim more than the research had achieved. For this reason Roethlisberger believed strongly that he should write an accurate and full report of the Hawthorne research. Mayo was not interested in the niceties of research design or the techniques and procedures of data collection or analysis that nowadays social scientists value so highly. Nor was he interested in writing research reports. He preferred to let his associates do these tasks. Consequently, the data collected on New Castle—a planned extension of the Hawthorne and Newburyport studies—were not analyzed or written up after Homans went to war, and they remain untouched in Mayo's files.

Action based on results of scientific research was Mayo's strong interest, and the counseling program at Western Electric was a good example of this interest. But Mayo was shocked when he learned what had happened to the counseling program. On his last visit to the Western Electric plant, he commented warmly on how valuable personal counseling was to administrators; when he was told that counselors saw only workers, Mayo stopped in his tracks, amazed that counseling had ceased at the supervisory level.[2]

At the Business School Mayo did little teaching. In his own way he followed the school's tradition of teaching by the case method. But to Mayo a case was a clinical history taken from a person or situation, and useful to illustrate points in a lecture. His teaching method was always informal in lectures, seminars, and with individuals.

In lectures Mayo would walk around the table between the class and himself, put a leg over the table corner, and speak in a relaxed way, pausing skillfully and using his long cigarette holder to dramatic advantage. His stories were amusing, well constructed, and placed carefully but not obviously to hold the listeners' attention. He had a fine sense of humor, would chuckle and laugh in many different ways, but never before his story had made its point.

Lectures ran for one hour and were followed by a half-hour of good discussion. Mayo used notes only when the material for the lecture had not been well prepared beforehand. His delivery was clear, and he was careful not to speak over the students' heads. It was important to him that lectures finish well, not with a thud; he would close with encouragement to discussion by drawing out individuals to whom his material was both familiar and important. So each one felt Mayo had spoken directly to him, that he had been selected for special notice, and, as a rule, each one responded loyally.

Most of Mayo's teaching was done in seminars to which members were admitted by invitation only. Meetings were held on Tuesday or Thursday at his office or his rooms in the Brattle Inn.

In his rooms or office or sometimes over lunch Mayo would see individual students. While the young man outlined his research Mayo would listen attentively, ask questions to clarify the purpose of the study, make some subtle or otherwise valuable distinction, and close the discussion with commendation of the student's choice of research plan. The student would leave, buoyed that Mayo had appreciated the research proposal, had thought it worthy of his attention, and had given it wise, purposive guidance. Mayo himself would seem gratified, even flattered, to have an intelligent young man seek advice and follow the idea that research was a long scientific adventure that would eventually win worthy rewards.

Mayo's unusual methods of teaching extended to his workday routine, and sometimes led to envy among his associates who found that they could not admire Mayo's attitude toward work. In the Business School the faculty and staff kept the regular working hours, and they made the practice obvious to one another. Such a ritual was not for Mayo. After his arrival at his office, by taxi, no later than 9:45 A.M., he became available to others at 11:00 A.M. He would hold court, talk a while with Henderson or Donham, then lunch at St. Clair's. After a walk he would spend the afternoon at the Brattle Inn. Such was the observer's impression; in fact, Mayo was at work all day, talking and listening. Mayo shied from heavy effort or busy work and the appearance of both. To this extent he seemed eccentric, to violate tradition at the Business School. But this was how he defined his own work style; and central to it was helping others to clarify problems and to enjoy emotional well-being and a full career, and especially encouraging his younger associates to be noticed as much as possible for work well done.

After Henderson's death and Donham's retirement Mayo seemed withdrawn and isolated, and to have no friends. The few people who knew him well saw the condition as a legacy of his and Dorothea's initial unwillingness to put any effort into sustaining friendships in the United States. In 1927, when settled in Cambridge, they seldom entertained; and after Dorothea took their girls to England, Mayo would accept invitations to lunch on Sundays with two friends. They soon realized that they bored him because he often said how much he enjoyed the company of notable people in Britain, and preferred the summers in Europe to those in Maine or Vermont. Thus, Mayo and Dorothea appeared to collide with the United States, leaving the impression that Cambridge was merely a stopover on the way to somewhere else. In turn, Mayo felt that he enjoyed little respect from his Harvard peers and could probably earn little more no matter what he did.

People admired Mayo for his skill in conversation. Wherever he sat was the head of the table. He loved the challenge of intelligent conversation, talked rapidly as ideas came into his head, twisted the meanings of words, and, with puns, jokes, and allusions, created brilliant flashes of humor. He had a remarkable capacity to show that a current issue with which every one of his listeners was familiar illustrated an abstract generalization. In this way he could turn dry, intellectual conversation into a vivid exchange.

The slightest trace of stupidity bored him, no matter whether in family, colleagues, or people he knew less well. He could hurt those whose views did not command his respect. So Mayo had few friends and many acquaintances, largely because he was quick to dismiss people whose conversation fell short of his standards and because he did not have the patience or skill needed to maintain lasting friendships.

However unable or uninterested he might have been in initiating or maintaining friendships, Mayo was highly competent at sustaining social relations that centered on care and consideration for the feelings that others found hard to manage. He was noted for his kindness, tolerance, thoughtfulness, and charm, which were what made it possible for him to move so easily up and down the social hierachy. But his considerate manner was limited to people who he felt needed help. The exception was Henderson, who was probably Mayo's only close and lasting friend in the United States. Their relationship was based on at least two important factors: Henderson was the only peer to whom Mayo could defer with respect, and Mayo was the only peer who could offer Henderson the deep compassion needed to understand his wife's mental illness.

So Mayo's interpersonal relations were the product of his intolerance for foolishness, especially among the intelligent, and his openheartedness toward those whom he felt he could help. These are the major elements of a therapeutic style of friendship. And even when he spoke in public these two elements dictated his relation with the audience. Each listener felt that when Mayo used personal, intimate cases to illustrate his points, he was speaking to that individual. In this way the whole audience could be seduced. When Mayo finished the talk each listener, realizing suddenly that he was not really alone with Mayo, joined with his fellows in applause to reduce the inner tension to which the sudden awareness had given rise. Applause was the personal praise that Mayo needed. In the discussion afterward Mayo would concentrate intently on particular persons, showing compassion for those who needed his wisdom and, with good humor, dismissing those whose ideas seemed to him foolish. Mayo loved the discussion periods because they brought him close to the social relation he enjoyed and could control best. With the exception of Henderson, whom Mayo revered, all Mayo's close associates were in a therapeutic relation with him. In this relation lay the tragedy of Mayo. Whitehead and Eyres-Monsell left Mayo to go to war; Roethlisberger escaped into his (probably) creative illness; Homans and Warner had avoided the therapeutic relation with Mayo as had the young anthropologists who worked with Warner; and Mayo's later associates were not working for him because of the heavy duties imposed by the role of the Business School in training wartime administrators. Without associates in a therapeutic relation with him at work, Mayo lacked his most important source of self-esteem. But after the summer of 1942 this need was not so potent for Mayo, because retirement to England was imminent and with it a new adventure. Fortunately, he had the personal support of Alan Gregg to help mourn the many losses in life that affected him so deeply before the summer of 1942.

Difficuties emerge in defining Mayo's major roles and contribution to social sciences in industry. Charles Merriam, an admirer of his work, wrote that he was a "rare bird . . . I should like to be with [him], and if we had a few more like . . . Mayo, something might be started in the good old social sciences."[3]

A "rare bird" is difficult to identify because its characteristics are elusive. To identify the characteristics of Mayo by reference only to the positions he held in organizations and the tasks allocated thereto misses the unique, personal quality of his role performance. Usually roles are defined as expectations held for a person's behavior by those with whom he interacts. As a "rare bird" Mayo was elusive because he himself defined the roles he was going to play. As one colleague noted, Mayo would study the mores and expectations governing the behavior of others but would respond to none himself. This observation caricatures Mayo's style but at the same time points to a way that Mayo's self-defined role can be understood, and directs attention to his unique contribution to the application of social and psychological ideas to work.

From the reconstruction of impressions Mayo made on his colleagues, four roles emerge: healer, doctor, catalyst, magician. Mayo was a "healer" of disease in industrial society. His main task was to help people to cooperate and collaborate, i.e., to bring unity to conditions that aroused conflict. To this end he helped to spread ideas from the Western Electric research and to dissipate the sadistic criticism that it attracted; he helped people to meet others who could be useful; he helped many people to see the value of their work and where it fitted well with that of others; he helped people who were angry at one another to develop productive relations at work; he ministered to those who came to him with family, financial, emotional, intellectual, and career problems; he showed people how to find work that best suited their talents.

At home this healing was evident too. It dominates the tone of letters to the family, especially to Dorothea. He wrote to assure her that every day that they were apart his spirit was beside her. He cared for the experiences she had with others, her well-being and harmonious social relations, the unity of her conscious and unconscious thinking, and the wholeness and unity of life around her. He showed great concern that his family and friends like one another, and for the times when they were separated.

Second, Mayo played the role of doctor. In the United States he was always known as "Dr. Mayo." Associates thought that he had acquired his knowledge of shellshock from experience in the trenches in France during the Great War. Mayo did not avoid using the title "doctor," and when he came to Harvard he brought as his research assistant a registered nurse, who often was seen taking blood pressure readings for Mayo. In his office he had a set of scales for weighing patients and measuring height. As the years passed, the scales were moved out of the way but they were never out of sight. Mayo did not keep company with medical doctors nor have them among his few friends. He did not refer to himself as a doctor nor claim the rights and privileges of that profession. To those close to him he said that he felt uneasy about being addressed as "doctor," but that to explain that he was not a doctor disturbed the flow of discussion and good conversation.

Mayo's third role was that of catalyst for others rather than as a worker who followed through on his ideas and wrote up research based on them. To the work of others he brought challenges and innovation, a fresh twist to an old problem, and the encouragement needed to study it.

Finally Mayo was a magician, not a trickster but a man whose sense of mystery and preference for the unexpected could produce surprising ideas, propositions, explanations, and predictions. This was partly because he had developed fine clinical skills and could observe important items that others would miss. He could hypnotize people and once predicted the whereabouts of a missing person by reconstructing his character from sketchy police information. Mayo's magic came from the unusual insight and confidence of one who could persuade others to reexamine closely their own thinking.

Mayo's four roles and the relation between them can be illustrated by the research with which his name is so closely associated, the Hawthorne studies.[4] At Hawthorne, Mayo did not, as many textbooks assert, initiate, direct, or control research. He played four distinct roles, all of which were unique to him at Hawthorne, and stemmed from his personal style. For the first eighteen months he was an "appreciative helper." He visited Hawthorne to study the physiology of the women at work in the relay assembly test room, but beyond that he advised on the health of a woman no longer in the study, suggested possible changes in interviewing methods and purposes, praised the researchers and encouraged them to follow new, uncharted courses of action. During the next fifteen months he was a "counselor-cum-publicist." He counseled executives on family and work problems, praised the study, thereby helping its status within the Western Electric Company, and publicized the results so that the research gained prestige in the United States and Europe. Third, for almost thirty months he was a "cooperative collaborator." He encouraged the exchange of personnel between Harvard and Hawthorne and laid the social basis for specific, defined joint activities. Finally, during the four years of close association with the Hawthorne Works, Mayo was a "protective supporter." He helped the researchers to endure destructive criticism of their work from inside the company and out, and to tolerate their own doubts about the value of their work.

In these roles, specific to Mayo at Hawthorne, he was applying, more or less consciously, his general healer-doctor-catalyst-magician roles. As healer, he aimed to unite and integrate divisive elements within the firm and protect the researchers from outside attack; as doctor, he diagnosed and offered treatment for administrative ills that others could not discern; as catalyst, he encouraged the researchers to be fearlessly curious in their scientific study of human experience at work and taught them an uncommon interviewing technique for this purpose; and as magician he showed them the value of surprise, challenges, anxiety about one's goals, and the unexpected rewarding turn events could take.

Mayo's contribution appears in his attitude toward universities and administration. Mayo was not a psychologist, sociologist, or anthropologist, although sometimes he was cast as such. These are academic, professional roles acquired after training within disciplines that separate and divide the study of the problems of mankind. Mayo would not take a disciplinary role, preferring to integrate the study of human experience and behavior, not pursue a separate discipline. The same applies to Mayo's approach to administration, the point on which he and Donham were in such close agreement. Both men believed that administration was the means of integrating special functions into a well-formed and cohesive organization.

The four roles that were unique to Mayo's character originate in the values he was taught, the conditions of his childhood, and the sentiments and impulses that gave so much energy to his life. The role of healer is a mystic's role because it upholds the value of unity, especially between opposites and among incongruent elements. To accept this value requires a sense of high purpose, and this was instilled into the Mayo children by their parents and reinforced by their Christian education, academic studies, and personal reading. The role helped Mayo compensate for disappointing the family by not continuing his medical studies, and, at the same time, allowed him to follow the adventures of his mind—not discipline his mind to one academic course—and match them with the mental adventures of others in the psychiatrist's clinic. In Mayo's mental hinterland strong anxieties were aroused originally by opposing views of life held by his parents, the absence of playmates to help him become used to life with peers, a strong need to be regarded well by others and to be rebellious toward them. To bring unity into his emotional life and the residue of his family experiences, and to heal the world about him Mayo used reflective thinking and concentrated thought. In his own mental life the task for him was to integrate the two and learn to move easily from the highest to the lowest levels of mental consciousness.

Mayo behaved like a doctor, the accepted role of healers. By taking rather than denying the role, Mayo could realize the values of the healer,

especially those no doctor could pursue and still keep the respect of colleagues, i.e., the importance of sexuality in the origins of psychoneuroses.
In Australia there had been no opportunity to heal unless he did so under
the supervision of a medical practitioner; only in the United States could
he be known as a doctor, behave like one, be respected as if he were one, yet
not have to possess the technical qualifications that the law demanded. In
his role Mayo's need to integrate conflicting impulses joined with the wish
to identify and treat the imagined ills in his body. His sense of self-worth
and identity was enhanced by this role: in it he was what he felt he ought to
be, and eventually believed he had good reason to be known as—a doctor.

The roles of catalyst and magician uphold the values of unexpected
change, challenge, and innovation. For Mayo, these values lay along the
highly valued path of science. They are the obverse of healer and doctor,
but they were well-chosen roles for Mayo because they also helped compensate for having failed to meet family expectations and at the same time they
set limits within which rebellious, hostile clashes could be promoted. From
the conflict of opposites come new ideas, and their origins are always a
mystery. Mayo's skill as a catalyst was developed through the use of words
and the way his magical thinking could make them run.

Mayo's thinking can be compared with that of his close friend Henderson. Henderson used his intellect as Mayo's destroyers used their obsessions. For Henderson three questions could destroy another intellect: Why?
What do you mean by . . . ? And, Can you give an example of that . . . ?

"Why?" exposes the underlying assumptions of an argument or the
unconscious direction given to an observation. Mayo's thinking was allusive, innovative, intuitive, and insightful; in conversation it seemed brilliant and often profound. Those who could not match his thinking, or
otherwise lost his respect, were either dismissed or dealt with brutally. So,
in different ways, but to the same purpose, Mayo and Henderson would
find the weaknesses in the thinking of others. And if Henderson put
"Why?" to Mayo, not only did one answer appear, there being no end to
allusive thought, but other answers tumbled forth aimed at reversing conventional assumptions and exposing or concealing unconscious wishes.
"Why?" became "Why am I the way I am?" That question was important
to Henderson because its answer helped him understand the impoversh-
ment of feeling that family tragedy had introduced to his life.

Henderson's "What do you mean by . . . ?" shows the speaker's ambiguous and irrational thinking. Mayo thrived on ambiguity and irrationality;
it was the raw material of his career and had provided him with criteria for
accepting or rejecting others, sharpening his wit, displaying his humor, and
for winning recognition and praise from individuals who thought him
brilliant and from groups who were entertained by his speeches and discussion. The "twisteroo," "The problem is not the . . . sickness of the acquisitive society . . . [but] the acquisitiveness of the sick society," illustrates how

Mayo could produce entirely fresh questions by making his terms unclear and using irrational reversals of meaning.

Henderson's third question, "Can you give me an example of that . . . ?" attacks the academic intellectuals. In Mayo's terms such individuals take a too-simple theory or formula and overthink it into a fog of elaborate distinctions. They are unable to connect their ideas with their observations of the world and turn away from it. While Henderson would make any person who could not answer the question feel foolish, Mayo would take a more constructive approach and invite the individual to attend the psychology clinic with him to see others whose mental processes had become far too elaborate for normal dealings with reality. Larry Henderson was one such observer. Mayo was fond of examples, illustrations, and anecdotes and had cases for all occasions. In principle, Henderson would rub the intellectual's nose in his own futile abstractions, while Mayo would lead him to test the abstractions against reality; Henderson had no time for fools, but Mayo thought that even the greatest fool had something of value to say if one had the patience to hear him out.

Both men valued Henderson's questions. If Henderson put them to Mayo he would not only answer them but also turn them to his own advantage in relations with Henderson. While Henderson occasionally used his questions sadistically, Mayo was far more humane. To this extent Mayo's thinking was more open, thus allowing him to move easily from theories of the central nervous system to those of the economy in a primitive tribe. He seemed to be able to integrate ideas from diverse fields without many restrictions. But two restrictions on his thinking stand out. Mayo took the ideas and findings of others and regularly imposed on them his own theses about the origin and dynamics of human social and political problems of an industrial civilization. Second, he saw obsessive characters everywhere. "Normal" obsessives in everyday life he liked; intellectual obsessives in academia he helped; the destructive obsessives in power he feared; and the remaining obsessives he dismissed.

The feelings that determine the intensity of human attitudes, beliefs, and behavior are laid down at an unexpectedly early age; therefore, important experiences shape the expression of those feelings but they cannot eradicate them. Fragments from Mayo's early life help reconstruct a pattern for his important feelings and beliefs.

Mayo saw at first hand the consequences of the industrialization of work in South Australia. Movement to the towns and the social ills accompanying economic depression were familiar to him, although it was not true that he suffered directly. Also he saw that unionization of the work force and charity failed to meet these problems. Ignorant part-time politicians and crowd-stirring demogogues were no solution either. Mayo was taught that science would establish the facts and proper public education could disseminate them; social problems could not be solved other than by careful and dispassionate study—raging ideologies and revolutionary politics were nothing but dangerous.

Mayo's patients had helped him to see these features of his social world from the standpoint of a highly respected medical family, one that had served the community as a matter of duty, had enjoyed the studied leisure available to the well-off, and had made England its cultured center. A measure of conflict that was evident in the society that reared Mayo was found in his family also. His mother was unmotherly to the extent that she presented herself as a strong, cool, and distant figure; but his father seemed a warm, amiable protector. The older Mayo preferred to view life as an adventure shaped by fortune rather than as a career achieved through heavy effort; yet he insisted that the son take the arduous path of medicine. His mother preferred to assert herself in public speaking and uphold hard work and ambition, yet she did not like to see thrusting assertiveness in the behavior of her elder son. His father wanted his children to have access to parents and grownups at all times; thus they would always feel cared for, be given direction when lost, be helped in solving family squabbles, and have a place to come home to. He wanted his children to get on well with one another and he promoted a democratic atmosphere in family life; his elder son made participation and cooperative social relations at work a leading goal for modern industrial society. His mother wanted her children to be spared the presence of adults and to have playmates to help them learn the social skills needed to stand well with their age peers; her elder son made this recommendation the center of his theory about the socialization of children and a vital condition for the establishment of a personality free from disabling obsessions. Both parents taught Mayo to value science and education, not only to provide him with technical skills but also to impart a high moral purpose and the social skills to achieve it that would aid him in efforts to make the world a better place than it had been when he entered it. To Mayo's father, this was a dream, like shooting for the moon; to Mayo's mother, it was realistic goal, especially if one could become accepted in England and serve or influence important people. And medicine was the proper path.

School introduced Mayo to more of life's inconsistencies. At home he had become well read by learning simply to follow his own interests, and he did not welcome being pushed along a specific course of learning, but in the classroom he saw that others were achieving better results than he. He responded by becoming an eccentric among his fellow pupils and chose independent rather than team games. He seemed to have no school friends. And school conflicted with family life on many points: authority, hard work, daydreaming, talking, leisure. So it was at school Mayo began on his collision course with society; when he was hurt he felt himself unworthy and this lack of self-esteem was exacerbated by the religious instruction that placed so much emphasis on the conviction of sin that young people were obliged to suffer.

Olive's death at the hands of an incompetent doctor put a question mark over the high value placed by the family on medicine as a career, but Mayo accepted his parents' demands that he, like his respected grandfather, enter medicine. It was to be a matter of how he did so. His failure to prepare successfully for a medical career after a good beginning showed he was caught between his mother's insistance on achievement through hard work and his father's view of great effort as comical. Also university life allowed him freedom with companionship, but he had not acquired the skills for disciplined social relations. As an act of adolescent defiance, Mayo's failure dealt a heavy blow to his parents' respectability and to his own self-esteem. To mature, he was sent away to endure a depressing series of failures and a listless period of adolescent melancholy in England.

In England he was drawn out of melancholy and dark obsessions about his worthlessness when his sister patiently applied her newfound clinical skills to his unmerited view of personal inadequacy. From the emotional life of a young patient emerged the skill and knowledge of clinical observation. Mayo began to take an interest in the outside world. Briefly he entered the Working Men's College to teach and join in the social life of working men; there he learned that he could interest a group, conduct a lively discussion, and combine the technique of teaching with the social life of pupil and teacher. Also, in the paintings of Antoine Wiertz he saw vividly how universal were the miserable consequences of rapid industrialization of society and work. These feelings of anger at an unfair world were clarified, refined, and given communicable form when Mayo returned home and found a consistently admirable model for his intellectual life in Professor William Mitchell at the University of Adelaide. Mitchell, more than anyone else, helped Mayo to master his inner conflict, to integrate his ideas and, as Mayo himself once put it, "to answer my questions."

Not until he met Henderson did Mayo again find such a stabilizing figure to help him make his ideas and feelings cohere.

Notes

1. The people who provided information for this chapter were: Arlie V. Bock; Eliot D. Chapple; Hilda Carter Fletcher; John H. Findley; George Homans; Frances and "Kitch" Jordan; Harold D. Lasswell; George F.F. Lombard; Osgood S. Lovekin; Edmund P. Learned; Patricia and Ruth Elton Mayo; Henry A. Murray; Ruth Norton; Andrew Towl; and Lord Monsell.
2. The training of supervisors and managers had been separated formally from the activities of counselors; consequently, their expert knowledge of human problems was not directly communicated to those who planned the training programs. Also, the counselors did not fully understand how to contribute what they had discovered to the training staff because they did not appreciate how the therapeutic role that they filled could best be related to formal authority structure that usually directs behavior at work.
3. Merriam to Ruml, 24 April 1926, Merriam Papers, University of Chicago Library.

Elton Mayo, 1892

Elton Mayo at St. Peter (1896?)

Elton Mayo as a university student, 1906-1910

George Gibbs Mayo, Elton's father

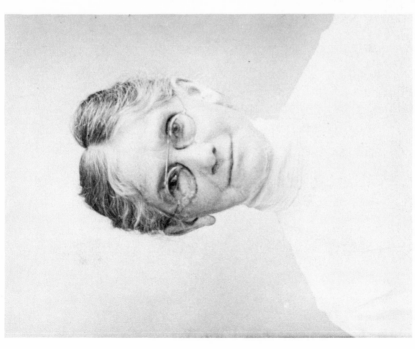

Henrietta Mayo, Elton's mother

Writings of Elton Mayo

1904

"The Australian Crisis." *Pall Mall Gazette* 78, 12 May, pp. 1-2.

1911

Official Report of the Inaugural Ceremony, ed. Brisbane; University of Queensland.
"The Inadequacy of Pragmatism." Address to Students' Christian Union, University of Queensland.
"Criticism." Address to Students' Christian Union, University of Queensland.

1912

"The Function of Religious Services." Special lecture to Presbyterian Men's Society, Brisbane, Queensland.
"Religion and Psychology." Special lecture to Theological College, Nundah, Queensland.
"Religion and Religious Services." Address to Students' Christian Union, University of Queensland.

1913

"The University and the State." *Queensland University Magazine* 1,5: 148-49.
"School." *Queensland University Magazine* 2, 1: 9.
"Professional Ethics." *Australian Journal of Dentistry* 17: 264-67.
"The Philosophical Attitude to Religion." *Official Report of the Australian Church Congress* 8: 69, 74.
"The Modern Development of Banking." Inaugural address to Queensland Bankers Association, Brisbane.
"The Divinity of Christ." Address to Students' Christian Union, University of Queensland.
"Sub-consciousness." Special lecture to Theological College, Nundah, Queensland.

1915

"The Limits of Logical Validity." *Mind,* New Series, 24: 70-74.
The University War Committee, ed. Brisbane: McGregor.

Some Considerations Affecting Organisation for the Production of Munitions of War, ed. Pamphlet No. 1. Brisbane: University War Commitee (McGregor).
Industrial Organisation and the Cost of War, ed. Pamphlet No. 2. Brisbane: University War Committee (McGregor).

1916

"National Organization: The Referendum and After." Unidentified newspaper clipping, October 29. State Library of South Australia.
"Ring Down the Curtain," with Anna F. Booth. In *Lady Galway's Belgium Book,* ed. M. C. Galway. Adelaide: Hussey & Gillingham. Pp. 40-48.

1919

"Industrial Autonomy." *Magazine of the University of Queensland,* pp. 5, 6, 8.
Democracy and Freedom: An Essay in Social Logic. Workers' Educational Series, No. 1. Melbourne: Macmillan.
"Notes on Consciousness and Attention." In *Human Relations: Concepts and Cases in Concrete Social Issues, vol. 1,* ed. H. Cabot and J. A. Kahl. Cambridge: Harvard University Press, 1953. Excerpts from Mayo's psychology lectures at the University of Queensland.

1920

"Australian Political Consciousness." In *Australia: Economic and Political Studies,* ed. M. Atkinson. Melbourne: Macmillan. Pp. 127-44.

1921

Discussant, G.E. Rennie, "Psychoanalysis in the Treatment of Mental and Moral Deficiency." In *Transactions of the Australian Medical Congress, 11th Session, Brisbane, Queensland, August 21-28, 1920.* Brisbane: Government Printer.

1922

Psychology and Religion. Melbourne: Macmillan.
"Civilisation and Morale"; "Industrial Unrest and 'Nervous Breakdown'"; "The Mind of the Agitator"; "The Will of the People"; "Revolution." *Industrial Australian Mining Standard* 67, January-February: 16, 63, 111, 159-60, 263.
"Psychology in Relation to Psychoanalysis and Applied Psychology." Address to Victorian Branch of the British Medical Association, 24 February 1922. Published in *Medical Journal of Australia,* April, p. 365.

1923

"The Irrational Factor in Society." *Journal of Personnel Research* 1: 419-26.
"Irrationality and Revery." *Journal of Personnel Research* 1: 477-83.

"The Irrational Factor in Human Behaviour: The 'Night-Mind' in Industry." *Annals of the Academy of Political and Social Science* 110: 117-30.
"Superstitions." *Continental Pathfinder* (Continental Mills, Germantown, Philadelphia, Pa.) 3: 1, 5.

1924

"Revery and Industrial Fatigue." *Journal of Personnel Research* 3: 273-81.
"Mental Hygiene in Industry." *Transactions of the College of Physicians* (Philadelphia), Third Series, 46: 736-48.
"Civilized Unreason." *Harper's* 148: 527-35.
"Civilization—The Perilous Adventure." *Harper's* 149: 590-97.
"The Basis of Industrial Psychology: The Psychology of the Total Situation Is Basic to a Psychology of Management." *Bulletin of the Taylor Society* (New York) 9: 249-59.

1925

"Daydreaming and Output in a Spinning Mill: An Investigation in a Pennsylvania Mill." *National Institute of Industrial Psychology Journal* 2: 203-9.
"The Great Stupidity." *Harper's* 151: 225-33.
"Open Letter to Robert W. Bruere." *Survey* (East Stroudsburg, Pa.) 54: 644-45. Reprinted with R.W. Bruere," "The Great Obsession," in *Bulletin of the Taylor Society,* October, pp. 220-25.
"Should Marriage Be Monotonous?" *Harper's* 151: 420-27. Reprinted in *Journal of Social Hygiene* 11: 521-35.

1926

"Psychiatry in Industry." *Bulletin of Massachusetts Society for Mental Hygiene* 5: 2, 4.
"The Approach to Psychological Investigation." *Proceedings of the Social Science Research Council Conference, Hanover, NH, August 27, 1926.*

1927

"Sin with a Capital 'S.'" *Harper's* 154: 537-45.
"The Dynamics of Family Relationships." *Child Study,* May, pp. 6-7.
"The Scientific Approach to Industrial Relations." *Proceedings of Y.M.C.A. Conference on Human Relations in Industry, September, 19-23, 1927.*
"Surrey Textile Company." *Harvard Business Reports* 4: 100-115.
"Orientation and Attention: Mental Hygiene in Industry." In *The Psychological Foundations of Management,* ed. H.C. Metcalfe. New York: Shaw. Pp. 261-90.

1929

"The Maladjustment of the Industrial Worker." In *Wertheim Lectures in Industrial Relations, 1928.* ed. O.S. Berger et al. Cambridge: Harvard University Press. Pp. 165-96.
"What Is Monotony?" *Human Factor* 5: 3-4.

1930

"Changes in Industry: The Broad Significance of the Western Electric Investigations." In *Research Studies in Employee Effectiveness and Industrial Relations.* New York. Western Electric Co. Paper presented at the annual autumn conference of the Personnel Research Federation at New York, November 15, 1929.

"The Western Electric Company Experiment." *Human Factor* 6, 1: 1-2.

'Changing Methods in Industry." *Personnel Journal* 8: 326-32.

"The Human Effect of Mechanization." *American Economic Review* 20, supp: 156-76.

A New Approach to Industrial Relations. Boston: Graduate School of Business Administration, Harvard University.

An Experiment in Industry. Proceedings of the First Annual Meeting of the Two Hundred and Fifty Associates of the Harvard Business School. Boston: Graduate School of Business Administration, Harvard University.

"Psychology in Industry." *Ohio State University Bulletin* 35, 3: 83-92.

"The Work of Jean Piaget." *Ohio State University Bulletin* 35, 3: 140-46.

"Recent Industrial Researches of the Western Electric Company in Chicago." *Proceedings of the Balliol College Conference, September, 1930.* Pp. 38-55.

1931

"Psychopathologic Aspects of Industry." *Transactions of the American Neurological Association* 57: 468-75.

"Economic Stability and the Standard of Living." *Harvard Business School Alumni Bulletin* 7, 6: 290-94. French translation in *Le Travail Humain* (Paris, 1933) 1, 1: 49-55.

"Supervision and Morale." *National Institute of Industrial Psychology Journal* 5: 248-60.

1932

"The Problem of Working Together" (broadcast). In *Psychology Today: Lectures and Study Manual,* ed. W.V. Bingham. Chicago: University of Chicago Press.

"The Study of Consumption and Markets." Paper delivered before a meeting of the Management Library, London, July. Reviewed, *Bulletin of the International Management Institute* (Geneva) 6, 11 (November).

1933

"The Dynamic Pose." *Harvard Business School Alumni Bulletin* 9, 3: 95-97.

The Human Problems of an Industrial Civilization. New York: Macmillan.

1934

"Human Relations in Industry." *Mental Health Observer* 2, 4: 1, 8.

Foreword to *Management and the Worker: Technical versus Social Organization in an Industrial Plant,* by F.J. Roethlisberger and W.J. Dickson. Boston: Division of Research, Graduate School of Business Administration, Harvard University.

1935

"The Blind Spot in Scientific Management." *Proceedings of the Development Section, Sixth Annual Congress for Scientific Management* 3: 214-18.

1936

"Social Change and Its Effect on the Training of the Child." *Proceedings of a Conference on Education and the Exceptional Child, Woods Schools, Langhorne, Pennsylvania* 2: 11-16.
"The Effects of Social Environment," with L.J. Henderson. *Journal of Industrial Hygiene and Toxicology* 18: 401-16.

1937

"What Every Village Knows." *Survey Graphic* 26 (13 November): 695-98.
"Security, Personal and Social." *New England Journal of Medicine* 217: 38-39.
"Psychiatry and Sociology in Relation to Social Disorganization." *American Journal of Sociology* 42: 825-31.

1938

"Significant Conclusions of Personnel." *Proceedings of the Seventh International Congress, Washington, D.C.* Baltimore: Waverley Press. Pp. 198-99.
Foreword to *The Industrial Worker: A Statistical Study of Human Relations in a Group of Manual Workers,* by T.N. Whitehead. Cambridge: Harvard University Press. Pp. vii-viii.

1939

"Frightened People." *Harvard Medical Alumni Bulletin* 13, 2: 2-7.
"Routine Interaction and the Problem of Collaboration." *American Sociological Review* 4: 335-40.
"Homo Mensura." *Journal of Comité National de l'Organisation Française.*
Preface to *Management and the Worker,* by F.J. Roethlisberger and W.J. Dickson. Cambridge: Harvard University Press.

1940

"Industrial Research." *Harvard Business School Alunmi Bulletin* 16, 2: 3-8.

1941

"Research in Human Relations." *Personnel* 17, 4: 264-69.
Descent into Chaos. New England Conference on National Defense, April 5. Boston: Graduate School of Business Administration, Harvard University.
"The Fifth Columnists of Business: Opportunities in Management for Men Who Can Grasp Handling of Human Affairs." *Harvard Business School Alumni Bulletin* 18, 1: 33-34.
Foreword to *Management and Morale,* by F.J. Roethlisberger. Cambridge: Harvard University Press. Pp. xv-xxii.

1942

"The Study of Human Problems of Administration." *Harvard Business School Alumni Bulletin* 18, 1: 231-32.

1943

Foreword to *Absenteeism: Management's Problem,* by John B. Fox and Jerome F. Scott. Boston: Division of Research, Graduate School of Business Administration, Harvard University.

1944

Teamwork and Labor Turnover in the Aircraft Industry of Southern California, with G.F.F. Lombard. Boston: Division of Research, Graduate School of Business Administration, Harvard University.

1945

"Group Tensions in Industry." In *Approaches to National Unity,* ed. L. Bryson, L. Finkelstein, and R.M. MacIver. New York: Harper. Pp. 46-60.
"Supervision and What It Means." In *Studies in Supervision,* ed. D.E. Cameron. Montreal: McGill University. Pp. 5-27.
The Social Problems of an Industrial Civilization. Boston: Division of Research, Graduate School of Business Administration, Harvard University.

1946

"What Do Workers Want?" *Reviewing Stand* 8, 1: 3-10.
"Letter to the Editor." *Harvard Law School Record,* August 21.

1947

The Political Problem of Industrial Civilization. Boston: Division of Research, Graduate School of Business Administration, Harvard University.
"Problems of an Industrial Civilization." *Journal of the Institute of Personnel Management,* November: 264-69.
"An Industrial Ciivilization" (review of lecture). *News* (National Institute of Industrial Psychology), November.

1948

Some Notes on the Psychology of Pierre Janet. Cambridge: Harvard University Press.
"Britain and America: Industrial Studies: Development of Free Communication." Letter to *Times* (London), August 11.
"Remote Control in Industry: An Organizational Difficulty." Letter to *Times* (London), December 2.

1949

"Human Problems in Industry." *World Review,* New Series, 3 (May): 5-8.

References

Anon. *South Australian Directory, 1883-1915.* Adelaide: Sands & McDougall.

Anon. *The University of Queensland, 1919-1922: A History.* Brisbane: University of Queensland, 1923.

Anon. *Industrial Relations Counselors, Inc.* New York: Industrial Relations Counselors, 1951.

Baker, Elizabeth F. "Economic and Social Consequences of Mechanization in Agriculture and Industry—Discussion." *American Economic Review* 20, 1 (1930): 177-80.

Banks, Mary M. *Memories of Pioneer Days in Queensland.* London: Heath, Cranton, 1930.

Barnes, John A. Introduction to *The Family Among the Australian Aborigines,* by B. Malinowski. New York: Schocken, 1962; originally published in 1913.

Berger, O.S., et al., eds. *Wertheim Lectures in Industrial Relations.* Cambridge: Harvard University Press, 1928.

Bingham, W.V., ed. *Psychology Today: Lectures and Study Manual.* Chicago: University of Chicago Press, 1932.

Bramel, Dana, and Friend, Ronald. "Hawthorne, the Myth of the Docile Worker, and Class Bias in Psychology." *American Psychologist* 36, 8: 867-78.

British Association for the Advancement of Science. *Report of Eighty-Fourth Meeting.* London, 1915.

Bruere, Robert W. "The Great Obsession." *Bulletin of the Taylor Society,* October 1925: 220-25.

Cameron, D.E., ed. *Studies in Supervision.* Montreal: McGill University, 1945.

Cannon, Walter B. *Biographical Memoir of Lawrence J. Henderson.* Washington, DC: National Academy of Sciences, 1943.

Castlehow, S. *The Thirty Club.* Mimeographed. Robinson MSS, Fryer Library, University of Queensland, 1956.

Chase, Stuart. "What Makes the Worker Like Work?" *Reader's Digest,* February 1942: 15-20.

Chinner, C. "Earthly Paradise: A Social History of Adelaide in the Early 1890s." Honors thesis in history, University of Adelaide, 1960.

Collier, Peter, and Horowitz, D. *The Rockefellers: An American Dynasty.* New York: Holt, Rinehart & Winston, 1976.

Committee on Work and Industry of the National Research Council. *Fatigue of Workers with Relation to Industrial Production.* New York: Reinhold Publishing Co., 1941.

Conway, J.J. "The Round Table: A Study of Liberal Imperialism." Ph.D. thesis, Harvard University, 1951.

Copeland, Melvin T. *And Mark an Era.* Boston: Little, Brown & Co., 1958.

Crawford, D. *Thinking Black: Twenty Two Years Without a Break in the Long Grass of Central Africa.* London: Morgan Scott, 1913.

Dickson, William J., and Roethlisberger, Fritz J. *Counseling in an Organization: A Sequel to the Hawthorne Researches.* Boston: Division of Research, Graduate School of Business Administration, Harvard University, 1966.

Duncan W.G.K., and Leonard, R.A. *The University of Adelaide, 1874-1974.* Adelaide: Rigby, 1974.

Ellenberger, Henri F. *The Discovery of the Unconscious: The History of the Evolution of Dynamic Psychiatry.* New York: Basic Books, 1971.

Frosch, John, and Ross, Nathaniel, eds. *The Annual Survey of Psychoanalysis* London: Hogarth, 1956.

Fox, John B., and Scott, Jerome F. *Absenteeism: Management's Problem.* Boston: Division of Research, Graduate School of Business Administration, Harvard University, 1943.

Hall, Richard. *The Secret State: Australian Spy Industry.* Melbourne: Cassell, 1978.

Harrison, J.F.C. *A History of the Working Men's College, 1854-1954.* London: Routledge & Kegan Paul, 1954.

Hersey, Rexford B. "Rests Authorized and Unauthorized." *Journal of Personnel Research* 4 (1924): 39-45.

Hirst, John B. *Adelaide and the Country: 1870-1917, Their Social and Political Relationship.* Melbourne: Melbourne University Press, 1973.

Horan, Margaret B. "A Goodly Heritage; An Appreciation of the Life and Work of the late Dr. Helen Mayo." *Medical Journal of Australia,* 20 February 1971: 419-24.

Jones E. "On the Necessity for the Establishment of Psychiatric Clinics." *Transactions of the Austalian Medical Congress,* 21-28 August 1920:410.

Karl, Barry D. *Charles Merriam and the Study of Politics.* Chicago: University of Chicago Press, 1974.

Kipling, Rudyard. *Verse.* New York: Space, 1939.

Kyle, William M. "Elton Mayo." Australian and New Zealand Association for the Advancement of Science Conference, 29 May 1951.

_____. *The Psychologist in Industry.* Mimeographed. St. Lucia: University of Queensland, n.d.

Landauer, A.A., and Cross, M.J. "A Forgotten Man: Muscio's Contribution to Industrial Psychology." *Australian Journal of Psychology* 23, 1 (1971): 235-40.

Landsberger, Henry A. *Hawthorne Revisited.* Ithaca, NY: Cornell University Press, 1958.

Lucas, Sir Charles. *Notes on a Visit to Australia, New Zealand and Fiji in 1909.* London: H.M.S.O., 1910.

Ludlum, Stanley D., and McDonald, Ellice E. "The Mechanism of Disease." *Medical Journal and Record.* 20 May 1925: 1-14.

McConnel, E.W.J. *James McConnel of Carsiggan, His Forebears and Descendants.* Privately printed, 1931.

McConnel, Mary. *Queensland Reminiscences and Memories of Days Long Gone By.* Privately printed, n.d.

Malinowski, Bronislaw. *A Diary in the Strict Sense of the Term: 1914-1915 and 1917-1918.* London: Routledge & Kegan Paul, 1967.

Matthewson, T.H.R. "The Psychic Factor in Medical Practice." *Medical Journal of Australia.* 24 July 1920: 73-77, 86.

Mayo, Charles H. *A Geneological Account of the Mayo and Elton Families of Wilts and Herefordshire and Some Other Adjoining Counties, Together with Numerous Biographical Sketches.* London: privately printed, Chiswick Press, Whiltingham & Co.; 2d ed., 1908.

National Bureau of Economic Research, Inc. *National Bureau Report,* No. 14, February 1975: 12-13.

Nicholas, R.J. "Private and Denominational Secondary Schools of South Australia." Education thesis, University of Melbourne, 1951.

Park, Robert E. "Industrial Fatigue and Group Morale." *American Journal of Sociology* 40, 3 (November 1934): 349-56.

Pennock, George A. "Test Studies in Industrial Research at Hawthorne." In *Research Studies in Employee Effectiveness in Industrial Relations: Papers Presented at the Annual Autumn Conference of the Personnel Research Federation at New York, November 15, 1929.* New York: Western Electric Co., 1930.

Pike, Douglas. *The Paradise of Dissent.* Melbourne: Melbourne University Press, 1957.

Potvin, Jules. *Antoine Wiertz* (1806-1865). Brussels: Weissenbruch, 1913. English translation by the author, 1924.

Putnam, Mark. "A Plan for Improving Employee Relations on the Basis of Data Obtained for Employees. In *Research Studies in Employee Effectiveness in Industrial Relations. Papers Presented at the Annual Autumn Conference of the Personnel Research Federation at New York, November 15, 1929.*New York: Western Electric Co., 1930.

Ralstan, A. "Biographical Sketch" (of Douglas Price). In *The Place of Ethics in Religion and Education,* ed. Meredith Atkinson. Douglas Price Memorial Lecture, No. 1. Brisbane: Cumming, 1920.

Roberts, Stephen H. *The House That Hitler Built.* London: Methuen, 1937.

Robinson, Kenneth A. *Essays Toward Truth.* New York: Holt, Rinehart, & Winston, 1924.

Roethlisberger, Fritz J. *The Elusive Phenomena.* Boston: Division of Research, Graduate School of Business Administration, Harvard University, 1977.

_____. *The Road Back to Sanity.* Privately printed; New England Conference on National Defense, 5 April 1941.

Roethlisberger, Fritz J., and Dickson, William J. *Management and the Worker: Technical versus Social Organization in an Industrial Plant.* Boston: Division of Research, Graduate School of Business Administration, Harvard University, October 1934.

_____. *Management and the Worker.* Cambridge: Harvard University Press, 1939.

_____. Introduction to *The Human Problems of Industrial Civilization,* by Elton Mayo. New York: Viking, 1960.

Sonnenfeld, Jeff. "Clarifying Critical Confusion in the Hawthorne Hysteria." *American Psychologist,* December 1982: 1397-99.

_____. "Commentary: Academic Learning, Worker Learning, and the Hawthorne Studies." *Social Forces* 61, 3: 904-9.

Stocking, G.W., Jr. "Clio's Fancy: Documents to Pique the Historical Imagination." *History of Anthropology Newsletter* 2 (1978): 10.

Subcommittee on Rehabilitation of the Committee on Work and Industry, National Research Council. *Rehabilitation: The Man and the Job.* Reprint and circular series, 121. Washington, DC: National Research Council, March 1945.

Trahair, Richard C.S. "Elton Mayo and the Early Political Psychology of Harold D. Lasswell." *Political Psychology* 3 (1982): 171-88.

Trahair, Richard C.S., and Marshall, Julie G. *Australian Psychoanalytic and Related Writings, 1884-1939: An Annotated Bibliography.* Library Publication No. 16. Bundoora, Victoria: La Trobe University, 1979.

University of Adelaide. *The Calendar.* Adelaide: University of Adelaide, 1898-1911.

University of Queensland. *Manual of Public Examination.* Brisbane: University of Queensland, 1910-12.

_____. *The Calendar.* Brisbane: University of Queensland, 1914-22.

University War Committee. *The University War Committee,* vol. 1. Brisbane: McGregor, 1915.

_____. *Industrial Organization and the Cost of War,* vol. 2. Brisbane: McGregor, 1915.

Whitehead, T. North. *Leadership in a Free Society: A Study in Human Relations Based on an Analysis of Present-Day Industrial Civilization.* Cambridge: Harvard University Press, 1936.

_____. *The Industrial Worker: A Statistical Study of Human Relations in a group of Manual Workers,* 2 vols. Cambridge: Harvard University Press, 1938.

_____. *Now I Am an American.* Mimeographed. Boston: Baker Library, Graduate School of Business Administration, Harvard University, 1964.

Young, I. Theodore. *His Life and Times.* Sydney: Alfa, 1971.

General Index

Aberfoyle Textile Company, 178-80
Adams, Brooks, 177, 219, 231, 250, 315
Addis Index, 205, 206, 216, 229
Addison, Stanley S., 144, 145, 148, 165
Adelaide University Arts Association, 54, 56
Adelaide University Union, 38
Adler, Alfred, 103
Advertiser (Adelaide), 98
Advertising Men's Institute, 120
Allport, Gordon, 216, 283
ALP (Australian Labour Party), 42-43, 45, 56, 57, 89, 90, 91, 94, 95, 123, 135
AMA (American Management Asssociation), 290
American, The, 152
American Academy of Political and Social Science, 187
American Association of Social Workers, 288
American Brass Company, 325
American Journal of Public Health, 261
American Journal of Social Hygiene, 193
American Journal of Sociology, 261-62, 265
American Psychological Association, 156, 159
American Sociological Review, 283
Amulree, (Lord), 241
Anderson, Francis, 130
Angell, James R., 153, 190, 308
Archibald Prize (University of Queensland), 78
Arensberg, Conrad, 300
Argus, The (Melbourne), 98, 145
Atkinson, Meredith, 95, 96, 114, 122, 130
Australia Club, 103
Australian Christian Commonwealth, 98
Australian Education Fraternity, 121

Baker, Elizabeth F., 239-40
Barker, Ernest, 91, 214
Barnard, Chester, 290, 330-31, 337, 341
"Barnstorming" in England, 344
Barton, Sir Edmund, 103
Bernheim, H., 121
Beveridge, Sir William, 221
Bezanson, Anne, 154
Biggs, Aubrey W., 80
BIM (British Institute of Management), 307, 344
Binet, Alfred, 117
Bingham, Walter V., 151, 187, 190, 230, 237, 240, 254, 261
Bjerre, Andreas, 214, 235
Bjerre, Paul, 177
Blazijak, Ladislas, 229, 258
Boer War, 87
Bogotowicz, Adeline, 229, 230
Bohemian Club (San Francisco), 148
Booth, Anna, 89
Bosanquet, Sir Day, 54
Boston Chamber of Commerce, 197
Boston Manufacturing Company, 206
Boston Psychopathic Clinic, 160
Boston Psychopathic Hospital, 197, 200
Bott, E.A., 184, 190
Bowral (New South Wales), 103
Boyle, Betty, 321
Braid, James, 121
Bramwell, Milne, 214
Bridges, Ann, 271
Brill, Alexander A., 105, 153
Brisbane Courier, 95
British Association for the Advancement of Science, 83, 192, 241, 248
British Industrial Fatigue Board, 221

British Medical Association, 143
British Red Cross Society, 89, 129, 143
British Research and Management Association, 251
Brown, Colonel, 176, 177
Brownell, (Mr.), 207
Bruce, H. Addington, 159
Bruere, Robert W., 192
Bryn Mawr, 160, 181, 197
Bulwurradah, 79
Burr, Charles W., 191
Byng, E.S., 306

Cabot, Phillip, 291, 298-99, 311, 322
"Cabot Weekends," 298-99, 311, 321
Cambridge Chamber of Commerce, 215
Cameron, Ewen, 332
Campbell, McFie, 190, 197, 200, 238, 240
Canada, 47-48
Cattell, James McKeen, 150, 160, 187
Cavan, Ruth, 210
Chamberlain, Neville, 312-13
Charcot, Jean-Martin 117, 121, 216
Chase Brass and Copper Company, 325, 326, 327
Chase, Stuart, 265, 331, 335, 345
Chester, D.N., 332
Child's Conception of the World, The, (Piaget), 235
Ching, C.S., 204-5, 240
Clark, Marcella, 61
Clark, Pierce, 156
Clay, Henry, 240
Cleland, John, 39, 40, 41, 44, 47
Cobb, Stanley, 145
Cohn, Edwin, 310, 311
Cohn, Harry, 305-6
Colbert, Jessica, 146, 147, 148, 149, 152
Colbourne, Frances, 181, 187
Colburn, Arthur, 300
Collins and Aikman Company, 173, 174
Colonial Inn (Bryn Mawr), 188
Colorado Fuel and Iron Company, 208-10
Columbia Pictures Corporation, 305
Columbia University, 152
Commonwealth Arbitration Court, 94, 120
Commonwealth Bank, 96
Commonwealth Department of Health, 145
Commonwealth Institute of Science and Industry, 131
Community of the Resurrection, 334
Conant, James B., 331

Conklen, E.G., 184
Continental Mills, 174, 175, 176, 178, 179, 191, 199, 207, 215, 216, 289, 331, 346
Cooley, John, 300, 321
Corey, Raymond E., 13
Council on Foreign Relations, 308
Coward, Noel, 349, 350
Crawford, Donald, 116
Cressbrook, 65, 66, 79-80
Cripps, Sir Stafford, 345
Culpin, Millais, 221
Curtis, Lionel, 87-88
Curtis, Melville, G., 173, 174

Daily Mail (Brisbane), 98
Daily Standard (Brisbane), 98, 115
Dana, Charles L., 155
Dartmouth College, 151, 216, 332
Dartmouth conferences on social sciences, 181, 190-91, 193, 216,
Davis, Allison, 300
David, Donald K., 323, 324, 326, 341, 346
Davis, Watson, 289, 290
Dawson, Christopher L., 332
Day, Edmund E., 240, 248
Delboeuf, J., 117, 121
Dennison, Henry, 246
Department of Correspondence Studies, 119
Dewey, John 155, 156, 162
Dicey, Albert V., 45, 138
Dickson, William J., 6, 7, 243, 244, 246, 254, 257, 258, 287, 335
Dodge, Raymond, 150, 156, 190
Dods, Espie J., 132
Dods, Mary, 160
Donaldson, H.H., 181
Donaldson, May Henrietta. *See* Mayo, Henrietta (Hetty)
Donaldson, St. Clair, 70, 155
Donham, Wallace Brett, 4, 5, 6, 10, 197, 198, 199, 213, 249, 294, 295, 303, 308, 310, 315, 322, 323, 324, 335, 351, 353, 357
Doriot, George F., 240, 304-5
Dorset (England), 218
Douglas, William O., 332
Drake, Barbara, 139
Drucker, Peter F., 335, 337, 338
Duggan, Stephen P., 143
Dunlop, Knight, 146, 187
Durkheim, Emile, 214, 259, 290, 308, 315, 329
Dyason, C.E., 145

Malinowski, Bronislaw, 4, 17, 83-85, 97, 133, 184, 191, 199, 201, 210, 213, 214, 221, 222, 240

Management and the Worker (Roethlisberger and Dickson), 7, 201, 264-66, 289, 322

Mansbridge, Albert, 62, 221

Markovitch, Eloinia, 229

Marley, (Lord), 332

Martin, Everett D., 155

Masland & Sons, 172-73, 182

Masson, Elsie, 85, 222

Matthewson, Thomas R.H., 104-13, 125, 126, 131, 149

Maurice, C.E., 45

Maurice, F.D., 44

Mauss, Marcel, 221

Mayo, Charles (Colonel), 39, 40

Mayo (neé McConnel), Dorothea (wife), 46, 65, 66, 67-70, 79-82, 84, 85, 95, 96, 103, 104, 108, 111, 112, 113, 123, 131-32, 136-38, 139, 144, 145, 148, 149, 155, 156, 157, 158, 160, 161, 162, 163, 164, 165, 188, 201, 203, 218, 222-23, 232, 233, 234, 253, 254, 271, 273, 276, 293, 304, 334, 338, 341, 343, 344, 345, 347, 349-50, 353, 355

Mayo, Eric, 322

Mayo family, 25-32

Mayo, George ("Old Doctor Mayo" [grandfather]), 25-26, 30, 31, 32, 39, 137

Mayo, George Elton. *See* Elton Mayo Index, 385-92

Mayo, George Gibbes (father), 26, 29, 30, 31, 36, 38, 39, 46, 47, 51, 79, 136-37, 360

Mayo, Helen (sister), 26, 27, 28, 29, 30, 31, 32, 36, 37, 38, 40, 41-42, 43, 44, 46, 47, 48, 51, 53, 58, 145, 217, 361

Mayo, Herbert (later Sir Herbert [brother]), 25, 26, 30, 31, 32, 36, 37, 51, 52, 61, 145, 149, 152

Mayo (neé Donaldson), Henrietta (Hetty [mother]), 26, 29, 30, 38, 39, 43, 51, 152, 221, 289, 360

Mayo, John Christian (brother), 26, 32, 51, 145

Mayo, Mary Penelope (sister), 26, 32, 36, 51, 54

Mayo, Maria (grandmother), 26

Mayo, Gael Elton (Ruth [daughter]), 81, 188, 223, 271, 276-77, 293, 304, 317, 321, 322, 345

Mayo, Olive (brother), 26, 30, 31, 36, 137, 361

Mayo, Patricia Elton (Patty, Toni [daughter]), 79, 80, 81, 103, 184, 187, 188, 223, 271, 272-76, 293, 304, 309, 315, 321, 322, 334, 341, 343, 345, 346

"Mayo Syndrome," 341

"Mayo Weekend, The," 335-38

Mayo, William Godfrey (brother), 26

Medical Diseases of the War (Hurst), 118

Meehan, 132

Melbourne (Australia), 84, 143-45

Melbourne University Association, 144

Mental Hygiene, 261

Meriam, Richard, 243, 245

Merriam, Charles E., 150, 185, 190, 355

Mesmer, Franz A., 121

Michie, John, 66, 69, 70, 77, 83, 129, 149

Miles, D.G.H., 221, 251

Miller Lock Company, 174, 175, 178

Mitchell, Wesley, 240

Mitchell, Sir William, 52-54, 56, 57, 59, 70, 75, 98, 144, 145, 165, 199, 361

Montpelier Private Hotel, 61, 70, 79, 82, 105, 109, 112

Moore, Wilbert E., 333

Mumme, Horace G., 52

Murray, Charles, 197

Murray, Henry A., 197, 214

Muscio, Bernard, 130

Musgrove, 147-48, 149

Mussolini, Benito, 99, 315, 331, 335

Muzzey, David S., 191

Myers, Charles S., 129, 184, 221, 249, 261, 306, 344

Myerson, Abraham, 197

Nathan, Sir Matthew, 139, 221, 222

National Council for Mental Hygiene, 153, 156, 159

National Council of Women, 95

National Research Council (Washington), 93, 148, 149, 150, 156, 162, 190, 225, 329

Nature, 332

Nellie the maid, 79

Neuroses, Les (Janet), 189

Newburyport ("Yankee City") studies, 200, 201, 202, 246, 251, 252, 296, 300, 321, 342, 346, 352

New Castle study, 300, 321, 352

New Republic, 261

Elton Mayo Index

This index is divided into the following categories: Life: Personal; Life: Work and Career; Major Topics of Interest; On Himself; On Other People; Other People on; Published/Unpublished Addresses and Other Writings; Published Books

Life: Personal

Life: Work and Career

Major Topics of Interest

On Himself

Achievements and abilities: ambivalence toward, 104, 147, 149, 155, 158, 160, 164, 165, 166, 182, 187, 303, 322; confidence in, 149, 166; pessimism and low self-esteem toward, 35, 39, 67-68, 80, 82, 91, 95, 99, 137, 146-47, 152, 155, 156, 160, 161 164-65, 166, 218, 232-33, 273, 321, 322; pleased with, 104, 132-33, 144, 149, 156-57, 162, 182, 191, 278, 310, 323

Aging, image of himself, 298, 315, 321, 341, 346

British subject, as a, 164, 188, 350

Childhood and mental health, 218, 293
Conflict, 135-38, 156, 164, 166
Conviction of sin, 136, 155, 160, 322

Death, impact of, 136-37, 322, 324
Doctors, feelings about, 132-33, 182, 278
Dream of social revolution, 136

Father, as a, 95-96, 272, 273, 274-75
Father, impact of his, 79, 136-37

Malinowski, impact of, 84
Money worries, 146, 147, 148, 149, 152, 153, 156, 157, 159, 160, 166, 173, 303, 322, 343

Needs: chair of philosophy (University of Sydney), 130; overseas experience, 144; regular work, 160, 321

"Ostracized Agnostic," as an, 51-52

Status, sensitivity toward, 131-32, 152, 153

On Other People

Allport, Gordon, 283
American psychologists, 146

Businessmen, 90, 207, 299

Cattell, James McKeen, 150
Colleagues, 83, 88, 104, 113, 129-30, 140, 153, 155, 160, 322-23, 324, 353
Communist agitator, 133-34
Curtis, Lionel, 88

Doctors, 63, 103, 104, 108, 132, 137, 328, 356, 361
Drucker, Peter F., 337-38

Eyres-Monsell, Graham, 297-98

Gilson, Mary, 266

Heaton, Herbert, 98
Henderson, Lawrence J., 203, 298, 322

Jews, 83, 275, 317-18

Knibbs, George, 131

Lawyers, 323

McConnel, Barbara, 112-14
McConnel, Ursula, 80-81, 111-12
Malinowski, Bronislaw, 84
Marx, Karl, 89-90
Matthewson, Thomas H.R., 107-8, 129
Mayo, Dorothea (wife), 81-82, 136, 303
Muscio, Bernard, 130

Pitt-Rivers, George H.L.F., 133
Priestley, Henry James, 83
Psychical researchers, 129

Roethlisberger, Fritz J., 200, 263, 294-95

Theodore, Edward G., 91-92

Warner, W. Lloyd, 296-97
Whitehead, T. North, 263, 295, 296

Yerkes, Robert M., 150

Other People on

Brill, Alexander A., 153
Bruere, Robert W., 192
Burr, Charles W., 191
Businessmen, 90, 148, 157, 172, 178, 208

Cabot, Phillip, 311
Chase, Stuart, 331
Cohn, Edwin, 311
Colleagues and associates, 77, 88, 93, 104, 150, 204, 222, 261, 332, 350-51, 355

Published and Unpublished Addresses and Other Writings

Published Books